WEBSTER'S FAMILY ENCYCLOPEDIA

WEBSTER'S FAMILY ENCYCLOPEDIA

VOLUME 9

1995 Edition

Exclusively distributed by
Archer Worldwide, Inc.
Great Neck, New York, USA

Worldwide distribution rights assigned to Archer Worldwide, Inc.
Great Neck, New York 11021

Printed in the United States of America.

Abbreviations Used in Webster's Family Encyclopedia

AD	After Christ
Adm.	Admiral
Ala.	Alabama
Apr	April
AR	Autonomous Republic
at no	atomic number
at wt	atomic weight
Aug	August
b.	born
BC	Before Christ
bp	boiling point
C	Celsius, Centigrade
c.	circa
Calif.	California
Capt.	Captain
CIS	Commonwealth of Independent States
cm	centimeters
Co.	Company
Col.	Colonel
Conn.	Connecticut
d.	died
Dec	December
Del.	Delaware
E	east, eastern
EC	European Community
e.g.	for example
est	estimated
F	Fahrenheit
Feb	February
Fl. Lt.	Flight Lieutenant
Fla.	Florida
ft	feet
Ga.	Georgia
Gen.	General
Gov.	Governor
ht	height
i.e.	that is
in	inches
Ind.	Indiana
Ill.	Illinois
Jan	January
K	Kelvin
Kans.	Kansas
kg	kilograms
km	kilometers
kph	kilometers per hour
kW	kilowatts
lb	pounds
Lt.	Lieutenant
Lt. Gen.	Lieutenant General
m	meters
M. Sgt.	Master Sergeant
Mar	March
Mass.	Massachusetts
Md.	Maryland
mi	miles
Mich.	Michigan
Minn.	Minnesota
Miss.	Mississippi
mm	millimeters
Mo.	Missouri
MP	Member of Parliament
mp	melting point
mph	miles per hour
N	north, northern
NATO	North Atlantic Treaty Organization
NE	northeast
Neb.	Nebraska
N.H.	New Hampshire
N.J.	New Jersey
N.M.	New Mexico
NNE	north-northeast
NNW	north-northwest
Nov	November
NW	northwest
N.Y.	New York
OAS	Organization of American States
Oct	October
Okla.	Oklahoma
OPEC	Organization of Petroleum Exporting Countries
Pa.	Pennsylvania
PLO	Palestine Liberation Organization
Pres.	President
R.I.	Rhode Island
S	south, southern
S.C.	South Carolina
SE	southeast
Sen.	Senator
Sept	September
Sgt.	Sergeant
sq mi	square miles
SSE	south-southeast
SSW	south-southwest
SW	southwest
Tenn.	Tennessee
Tex.	Texas
UN	United Nations
US	United States
USSR	Union of Soviet Socialist Republics
Va.	Virginia
Vt.	Vermont
W	west, western
wt	weight

schizophrenia A severe mental disorder characterized by disintegration of the processes of thinking, contact with reality, and emotional responsiveness. Delusions and *hallucinations are common, especially those that produce the feeling of a loss of personal identity. Schizophrenics often become withdrawn and apathetic. The condition tends to get worse (in about half of all cases) unless treatment is given. Modern treatment has improved the outlook: it consists of such drugs as *phenothiazines and vigorous psychological and social rehabilitation. Schizophrenia is largely caused by genetic factors, but environmental stress can trigger an episode of illness. *See also* paranoia; psychosis.

Schlegel, August Wilhelm von (1767–1845) German critic, poet, and translator. With his brother, he exerted a powerful influence on the early romantics through critical works, such as *Über dramatische Kunst und Literatur* (3 vols, 1809–11), and translations, especially his superb rendering of Shakespeare. His brother **(Carl Wilhelm) Friedrich von Schlegel** (1772–1829) was a writer and critic. The chief influence on the romantic movement, his literary and philosophical works appeared first in *Das Athenäum*, a periodical published by him and his brother. He later studied Sanskrit in Paris and published the first study in comparative philology (1808).

Schleiden, Matthias Jakob (1804–81) German botanist, who first formulated the theory that plants are composed of *cells (this was later extended to animals by Theodor *Schwann). Schleiden also recognized the importance of the cell nucleus, although he mistakenly believed that new cells budded from its surface.

Schlesinger, Arthur M(eier), Jr. (1917–) US historian and statesman. He taught at Harvard University (1946–61) and served as a special assistant to Pres. John F. *Kennedy (1961–64). From 1967, he taught at City College of New York. His works include *The Age of Jackson* (1945; Pulitzer Prize), *The Vital Center* (1949), *The Age of Roosevelt* (3 vols., 1957–60), *A Thousand Days* (1965; Pulitzer Prize), *The Imperial Presidency* (1973), *Robert Kennedy and His Times* (1978), and *The Cycles of American History* (1986).

Schleswig A breed of draft horse originating in the Danish duchy of Schleswig. It has a long body with relatively short legs, a powerful neck and a fairly large head. The coat is usually chestnut but sometimes bay or gray. Height: $15^1/_3$ hands (about 5 ft; 1.60 m).

Schleswig-Holstein A low-lying *Land* in NE Germany bordering on the North Sea, the Baltic Sea, and Denmark. Grain and potatoes are grown and cattle reared; industries include shipbuilding and engineering. *History*: during the 19th century the **Schleswig-Holstein question** arose when Denmark and the Austrian-led German confederacy both laid claim to the two duchies of Schleswig and Holstein. War broke out in 1863 and the duchies were annexed to Prussia in 1866. In 1949 the Land of Schleswig-Holstein was formed. Area: 6059 sq mi (15,696 sq km). Population (1988): 2,613,000. Capital: Kiel.

Schlick, Moritz (1882–1936) German philosopher. Schlick was professor of philosophy of the inductive sciences at Vienna University (1922–36). The leader of the *Vienna Circle (*see also* logical positivism), he approached philosophy in a basically experimental way and concerned himself with problems of truth and verifiability. His published work includes the *General Theory of Knowledge* (1918) and *Problems of Ethics* (1930).

Schlieffen, Alfred, Graf von (1833–1913) German general, who, as chief of the general staff (1891–1905) devised the **Schlieffen Plan**, on which German strategy at the outbreak of World War I was unsuccessfully based. The plan provided for a concentration of German forces on the western front, which would rapidly defeat France in a flanking movement through the Low Countries, while a smaller army held off Russia in the east.

Schliemann, Heinrich (1822–90) German archeologist. After a successful business career, Schliemann retired (1863) to pursue his childhood ambition of discovering Homeric *Troy. Ignoring scholarly derision, he excavated Hissarlik on the Asia Minor coast of Turkey, finding ruins of nine consecutive cities. The second oldest (Troy II), which he wrongly identified with Homer's city, yielded a hoard that Schliemann romantically called "Priam's Treasure." His spectacular finds at *Mycenae (1874–76), Orchomenos in Boeotia (1880), and *Tiryns (1884–85) established him as the discoverer of *Mycenaean civilization.

Schlieren photography A method of observing differences of density in a transparent medium, such as air. Light from a spark is photographed as it passes through the medium; any differences in density present cause local variations in the refractive index, which show up as streaks (German word: *Schlieren*) in the photograph. The method is used for observing sound waves, shock waves, and flaws in glass.

HEINRICH SCHLIEMANN *A contemporary engraving showing his excavations at Hissarlik.*

Schmeling, Max (1905–) German boxer, the first European to win the world heavyweight title in the 20th century (1930). In 1936 he beat Joe *Louis but Louis took his revenge in two minutes in 1938.

Schmidt, Helmut (1918–) West German statesman; Social Democratic chancellor (1974–82). He worked in transport administration in Hamburg before entering federal politics (1953). He became minister for domestic affairs in Hamburg (1961–65) and was then federal minister of defense (1969–72) and for finance (1972–74) before becoming chancellor. He has written several books, mainly on foreign affairs. □Giscard d'Estaing, Valéry.

Schmidt telescope A *telescope developed by the Estonian instrument maker Bernard Voldemar Schmidt (1879–1935). It produces very sharp photographic images of celestial objects over a very wide angle of sky. The incoming light passes through a thin correcting plate, is reflected by a large short-focus spherical mirror, and focused on a curved photographic plate.

Schnabel, Artur (1882–1951) Austrian pianist, especially famous for his performances of Beethoven. He studied in Vienna and in Berlin, where he later taught until 1933, after which he lived mainly in Switzerland and the US. He also composed three symphonies and a piano concerto.

schnauzer A breed of dog originating in Germany and used as a guard dog. Strongly built with a docked tail, it has a characteristic square muzzle with long sidewhiskers. The wiry coat is black or light gray and brown. Two varieties have been bred from the standard schnauzer—the giant schnauzer for farm and police work and the miniature schnauzer as pet. Height: 13–14 in (33–35 cm) (miniature); 18–19 in (45–48 cm) (standard); 21–25.5 in (54–65 cm) (giant).

Schnitzler, Arthur (1862–1931) Austrian Jewish dramatist and novelist. A physician, he was especially interested in psychiatry and his works are notable for their psychological observation. They include the witty dramatic cycles *Anatol* (1893) and *Reigen* (1900; filmed as *La Ronde*, 1950) and his prose masterpiece, *Leutnant Gustl* (1901).

Schoenberg, Arnold (1874–1951) Austrian-born composer. He studied in Vienna with Alexander von Zemlinsky (1872–1942) and began his career by orchestrating theater music. In 1910 he became a teacher at the Vienna Academy; his students included Berg and Webern. Mahler became a champion of his music. In 1933 Schoenberg, as a Jew, was forced to leave Berlin; he became a US citizen in 1941 and was professor at the University of California (1936–44). His early compositions, in a late romantic style, include two string quartets, *Verklärte Nacht* (for string sextet; 1899), and the symphonic poem *Pelleas und Melisande* (1902–03). His subsequent works were characterized by *atonality; they include the melodrama *Pierrot Lunaire* (for soprano and five instruments; 1912) in which the voice part is noted in *Sprechgesang* (German: speech song). Schoenberg subsequently developed the theory and technique of *serialism (1924), which he employed in most of his later works, including a violin concerto (1936), a piano concerto (1942), and the unfinished opera *Moses und Aaron* (1932–51).

scholasticism The intellectual discipline comprising all the philosophical and theological activities pursued in the medieval universities (schools). As the international philosophy of Christendom it respected orthodoxy and was concerned with the philosophies of *Plato and *Aristotle as assimilated over centuries of Christian thought. For scholastics religion was predominant and in their method philosophy was the servant of theology. It was by theology that the selection of problems for study and the scope of scientific inquiry were to be decided. *Anselm was an early scholastic, and *Abelard perfected its method. After *Aquinas, *Aristotelianism became increasingly important until, in the Renaissance, it was virtually synonymous with scholasticism.

schooner A □sailing vessel with at least two masts, a shorter one set near the bow, a taller one at some distance behind it. Schooners, being quite fast and efficient when sailing off the wind, were widely used before the advent of steam and motor vessels in both coastal and long-distance commercial trade, especially fishing. Because they do not sail well into the wind, they are not a favored rig for racing yachts.

Schopenhauer, Arthur (1788–1860) German philosopher. Schopenhauer's main contribution to philosophy is contained in the emphasis that he placed upon the human will. The will was, he maintained, the means by which all other things were understood. *The World as Will and Idea* (1818) sets out his principal ideas and pessimistic conclusions. He was distrustful of rationalism and the scientific method and was instead concerned with intuitive cognition. He saw the ideal state of man as one of contemplative freedom, achieved through art.

Schrödinger, Erwin (1887–1961) Austrian physicist and one of the major contributors to *quantum theory. He shared the 1933 Nobel Prize with *Dirac for his development of the form of the quantum theory known as *wave mechanics. Although not Jewish, he was an ardent anti-Nazi and went to England when Hitler took Austria. He was professor at the School for Advanced Studies in Dublin, Ireland (1940–56), returning to Vienna after his retirement.

Schubert, Franz (Peter) (1797–1828) Austrian composer, who had a musical upbringing but little formal training, other than at the imperial choir school in Vienna. He made a precarious living as a composer and teacher, rarely leaving Vienna and achieving little recognition. He died from typhoid fever at the age of 31. Schubert's melodic genius is perhaps most evident in his 600 *Lieder*, which include such famous examples as "Erlkönig," "Death and the Maiden," and "The Trout." Some of his greatest songs are to be found in the song-cycles *Die Schöne Müllerin* (1823) and *Die Winterreise* (1827). His other works demonstrate his mastery of large-scale composition. They include nine symphonies (of which one is lost and the eighth, unfinished), string quartets, piano trios, an octet, two quintets, piano sonatas and pieces, and much choral music. He also wrote several operas, the only musical genre in which he had little success.

Schuman, Robert (1886–1963) French statesman. He held several ministerial posts from 1946 to 1956 and was briefly prime minister (1947–48). As foreign minister (1948–52), he proposed the **Schuman Plan** (1950) for European unity, which advocated the establishment (achieved in 1952) of the *European Coal and Steel Community. He was president of the EEC assembly (1958–60).

Schuman, William (Howard) (1910–92) US composer. He taught at Sarah Lawrence College in New York (1935–45) and was president of the Juilliard School of Music (1945–61). His compositions include *The Undertow* (1945); a ballet, choral works, nine symphonies, an opera about baseball, entitled *The Mighty Casey* (1953); *Song of Orpheus* (for cello and orchestra; 1962), and a cantata, *A Free Song* (1943) which won a Pulitzer Prize.

Schumann, Robert (Alexander) (1810–56) German composer. He played and composed music from an early age and at Leipzig University devoted more time to it than to his law studies. Almost all his musical compositions up to 1840 were for the piano; he also wrote much as a critic, editing (1835–44) the journal *Die Neue Zeitschrift für Musik*, which he had founded. Gradual insanity in later life culminated in his attempt to drown himself and he died in an asylum. His compositions include four symphonies, the opera *Genoveva* (1847–50), songs, including the cycles *Dichterliebe* (1840) and *Frauenliebe und Leben* (1840), violin, piano, and cello concertos, and piano pieces, including the *Davidsbündlertänze* (1837) and *Kreisleriana* (1838). His wife **Clara Schumann** (1819–96), whom he married in 1840, was the daughter of Friedrich Wieck (1788–1873), with whom he had studied the piano in Leipzig (1830–32). She was a famous pianist and became a great interpreter and editor of her husband's works. She was also a composer and a noted teacher.

Schuschnigg, Kurt von (1897–1977) Austrian statesman; chancellor (1934–38). He tried in vain to prevent the Nazi annexation (**Anschluss*) and was forced to resign after Hitler's invasion of the country. He was imprisoned by Hitler throughout World War II. After his release he taught in the US until 1967, when he returned to Austria.

Schütz, Heinrich (1585–1672) German composer. He sang in the choir of the royal chapel at Kassel and studied with Giovanni Gabrieli in Venice (1609–12). He was court kapellmeister in Dresden after 1615. He composed much sacred music, including Passions and *The Seven Words of Christ on the Cross* (c. 1645), as well as madrigals and the first German opera, *Dafne* (1627), which is now lost.

Schwann, Theodor (1810–82) German physiologist, who applied *Schleiden's cell theory to animals—an important conceptual advance in biology. Schwann pointed out that egg cells develop by successive divisions and he identified the Schwann cells that surround nerve fibers. He was the first person to isolate a digestive enzyme (pepsin) from animal tissue and he also coined the term metabolism for the chemical changes that take place in living tissues.

Schwarzenberg, Felix, Fürst zu (1800–52) Austrian statesman. He served in the diplomatic corps before becoming first minister during the Revolution of 1848. He restored order in the Hapsburg Empire, issuing a new constitution (1849) that strengthened the absolute power of the emperor. He also frustrated Prussia's attempts to establish a Prussian-dominated union of German states.

Schwarzenegger, Arnold (1947–) US actor and physical fitness advocate, born in Austria. He became a popular film star after making *The Terminator* in 1984. A Republican, Schwarzenegger served as chairman of the President's Council of Physical Fitness and Sports (1990–93). Long interested in body building, he won the "Mr. Universe," "Mr. World," and "Mr. Olympia" titles in 1970. His other films include *Conan the Barbarian*, *Commando*, *Predator*, *The Running Man*, *Twins*, *Kindergarten Cop*, *Total Recall*, and *Last Action Hero*.

Schwarzkopf, H. Norman (1934–) US Army officer who led the UN coalition forces in the Persian Gulf War in 1991. A graduate of West Point (1956), he served two tours in Vietnam. In 1983 he was deputy commander of the Grenada invasion, and by 1988 he had been promoted to full general and was commander of the US Central Command in Florida. In this post, he developed contingency plans for a war in the Middle East and then commanded the US elements sent to Saudi Arabia after Iraq invaded Kuwait in August 1990. He oversaw the buildup of US and UN coalition forces for the rest of 1991 (Operation Desert Shield), while also refining the strategy for the actual conflict with Iraq (Operation Desert Storm) in January–March 1991. Schwarzkopf's use of massive bombing attacks preceding the advance by ground forces was credited with keeping allied casualties at a minimum. Schwarzkopf retired from the army in 1991 and in 1993 published his memoirs, *It Doesn't Take A Hero*.

Schweitzer, Albert (1875–1965) Alsatian-born theologian, medical missionary, and organist. A theologian in the liberal Protestant tradition, Schweitzer wrote *The Quest of the Historical Jesus* (1906), emphasizing Christ's humanity. His writings on Bach and his recitals of Bach's organ music were highly acclaimed. From 1913 until his death, Schweitzer practiced as a doctor in the hospital he founded in Gabon at the jungle village of Lambaréné. His philosophy is best summarized in his ethic of "reverence for life." In 1952 he received the Nobel Peace Prize.

Schwerin 53 38N 11 25E A city in N Germany, on Lake Schwerin. Largely destroyed by fire in the 16th and 17th centuries, the city was rebuilt with squares and wide streets. Schwerin has machinery and chemical industries. Population (1990): 130,000.

Schwitters, Kurt (1887–1958) German artist and poet, born in Hanover. Associated with the *dada art movement, he became famous for his poems of meaningless sounds and his invention of elaborate structures and collages of ticket stubs, broken glass, and other trash, which he salvaged from gutters and garbage cans and labeled *Merz* (trash) constructions. He worked in Britain from 1940 until his death.

sciatica Severe pain that starts in a buttock and spreads down the back of the leg. It is caused by pressure on the roots of the sciatic nerve—the longest nerve in the body. The commonest cause is pressure from a slipped disk in the backbone. Other kinds of injury to the back may also lead to sciatica. The pain usually disappears eventually: treatment is by bed rest and painkillers.

science fiction A literary genre in which scientific knowledge is used as a basis for imaginative fiction. The chief precursors of modern science fiction were Jules *Verne, who made use of speculative developments in engineering in such works as *Twenty Thousand Leagues Under the Sea* (1869) and *Propeller Island* (1895), and H. G. Wells, who dealt with time travel, space travel, and alien invasion in *The Time Machine* (1895), *The First Men in the Moon* (1901), and *The War of the Worlds* (1898). In the 20th century such magazines as *Amazing Stories* (founded 1926) and *Astounding Science Fiction* reflected a growing popular interest in the science fiction inspired by advances in the fields of rocketry, electronics, and computers. Notable works of science fiction have been written by such scientists as Fred Hoyle and Isaac Asimov. Among writers who have written imaginative accounts of the origin, evolution, and destiny of the human race are Olaf Stapleton (1886–1950), author of *Last and First Men* (1931), and Arthur C. Clarke (1917–   ), author, with Stanley *Kubrick, of *2001: A Space Odyssey* (film, 1967; novel, 1968). Other leading writers of science fiction include Edgar Rice Burroughs, Robert Heinlein, Aldous Huxley, Brian Aldiss, Ray Bradbury, Kurt Vonnegut, Jr, and Anthony Burgess.

scientology The doctrine of the Church of Scientology, founded in 1954 in California by L(afayette) Ron(ald) Hubbard (1911–86). Originally this doctrine was presented as a method of psychotherapy in Hubbard's *Dianetics: The Modern Science of Mental Health* (1950). It was later presented as a religious philosophy by which the member passes through many rigidly structured levels, increasing his IQ, creativity, etc., until he is finally "not on the body level" at all and has realized his full spiritual potential. While claiming to achieve man's spiritual liberation, its methods, particularly its practice of counseling ("auditing") to release adherents from past emotional bonds, have been widely criticized.

Scilly, Isles of (*or* Scillies) A group of British islands, consisting of about 140 islands and islets in the Atlantic Ocean, off the extreme SW coast of England. Only five are inhabited. Their mild climate has been exploited to produce early spring flowers for the UK market, their major source of income. Area: 6 sq mi (16 sq km). Population (1981): 2628. Chief town: Hugh Town.

scintillation counter An instrument that measures the number of radioactive atoms that decay in a certain time. The emitted radiation strikes a scintillation crystal causing it to emit a flash of light. The light then activates a *photomultiplier, producing a pulse of electrons, which are counted to enable the activity of the source to be calculated. A **scintillation spectrometer** is used to show the energy distribution of a source.

Scipio Aemilianus Africanus (c. 185–129 BC) Roman general, politician, and literary patron; the grandson by adoption of Scipio Africanus. After military successes in Greece and Spain, he blockaded and destroyed Carthage in 146 (*see* Punic Wars), becoming a national hero. After subduing Spain with the destruction of Numantia in 133, he lost popular support when he attacked the reforms of his murdered brother-in-law, Tiberius *Gracchus. Scipio died during the subsequent political upheaval.

Scipio Africanus (236–183 BC) Roman general of the second *Punic War. After defeating the Carthaginians in Spain, he won permission, despite *Fabius's opposition, to invade Africa. After crushing Hannibal at the battle of Zama in 202, he became a national hero, receiving the title Africanus. Subsequent pro-

Greek policies provoked political hostility and he retired from public life. His son was the adoptive father of Scipio Aemilianus Africanus.

sclerosis Stiffening and hardening of the tissues. This is a feature of many diseases: it can affect the brain and spinal cord, causing *multiple sclerosis, and the walls of the arteries, causing *arteriosclerosis or *atherosclerosis.

Scone 56 25N 3 24W A parish in E central Scotland. It consists of the villages of New Scone and Old Scone, the Pictish and later Scottish capital where most Scottish kings were crowned. The coronation stone was taken from here by Edward I in 1296 and placed in Westminster Abbey.

Scopes Trial (1925) US court trial, also known as the "monkey trial," of John T. Scopes, a Tennessee high school teacher, who taught *Darwin's theory of evolution to his students. Testing a Tennessee law forbidding the teaching of anything but literal interpretation of the Bible, the case was prosecuted by William Jennings *Bryan and defended by Clarence *Darrow. Scopes was convicted of breaking the law, but the publicity from the case was instrumental in making it very difficult for similar laws to be passed.

scopolamine A drug with similar uses and actions to *atropine. It also has a depressant effect on the brain and is therefore used to prevent motion sickness and for sedation before surgery.

scops owl A small *owl of the mainly tropical genus *Otus*, also called screech owl because of its call. Scops owls are 8–12 in (20–30 cm) long and mostly arboreal, with camouflaging plumage resembling bark. They feed on insects, birds, and small mammals.

Scorpio (astrology). *See* zodiac.

scorpion An *arachnid of the order *Scorpionida* (about 800 species), found in warm dry regions. Scorpions are 0.51–7 in (13–175 mm) long; the second pair of appendages (pedipalps) form large pincers and the elongated abdomen curls upward and bears a poisonous sting, which can be fatal to man. They live under stones or in shallow burrows in soil during the day and prey at night, mainly on insects and spiders. Mating is preceded by a courtship dance and the female produces live young, which ride on her back for several days.

scorpion fish A carnivorous fish, often called rockfish or zebra fish, belonging to the family *Scorpaenidae*, found mainly on rocky beds of tropical and temperate coastal waters. It has a stout body, up to 40 in (1 m) long, a large spiny head, and strong fin spines, which can inflict painful wounds and may be venomous. Order: *Scorpaeniformes*.

scorpion fly An □insect of the order *Mecoptera* (400 species), so called because the males of many species curl the abdomen over the body, like a scorpion; 0.47–1 in (12–25 mm) long, scorpion flies have long legs and antennae and, typically, two similar pairs of net-veined wings. The larvae develop in soil, feeding—like the adults—on dead animals and plants.

Scorpius (Latin: Scorpion) A conspicuous constellation in the S sky, lying on the *zodiac between Sagittarius and Libra. The brightest star is *Antares. The constellation contains several notable open and globular *star clusters and the intense X-ray binary star **Scorpius X-1**.

Scotland A country occupying the N part of Great Britain and comprising a political division of the *United Kingdom. Most of the population lives in a narrow lowland belt, which runs E–W across the country and separates the lower hills of the S (including the Tweedsmuir and Cheviot Hills) from the higher mountains of the N (including the Grampian and Cairngorm Mountains). Ben Nevis in the W is the highest point in the British Isles at 4406 ft (1343 m). There are many islands off the N and W coasts, including the Hebrides and the Isle of Arran to the W and the Orkneys and Shetlands to the N. The principal rivers are the Clyde, which flows into the North Channel, and the Forth, Tay, and Spey, which flow into the North Sea. There are several lochs (lakes) in the northern mountains, including Loch Ness. *Economy*: the central belt of the country is highly industrialized, based originally on coal, still mined in the Lothian and Fife Regions. Other long-established industries include ship building (on the Clyde) and steelmaking. Whisky, for which Scotland is internationally famous, is produced in Highland and Grampian Regions. The discovery of oil in the North Sea has led to a boom on the E coast of the country. Agriculture remains important and includes sheep farming in the upland areas (especially in the border hills, where there is a famous textile industry), dairying in the SW, and beef production in the E and NE lowlands. Fishing is a major source of revenue, especially on the E coast at such ports as Aberdeen. *History*: Scotland was never completely subdued by the Romans, but the barbaric northern tribes were kept N of *Hadrian's Wall and, for some 40 years, the more northerly *Antonine Wall. The diverse peoples (Picts, Scots, Britons, and Angles) of Scotland gradually united, helped by the spread of Christianity, and Kenneth I MacAlpine (died c. 858) is regarded as their first king. During the Middle Ages there was recurrent war between England and Scotland. In 1296 Edward I of England declared himself king of Scotland but after his death Robert the Bruce reasserted Scottish independence, which was recognized by England in 1328. In 1603 James VI of Scotland succeeded as James I to the throne of England but political union between the two countries was not established until 1707 (*see* Union, Acts of). Rapid industrialization in the 19th century encouraged considerable Irish immigration. In the late 1980s, Scotland became a center of the UK computer industry. Area: 30,405 sq mi (78,769 sq km). Population (1991): 4,957,300. Capital: Edinburgh.

Scots law Originally Scots law differed little from English law, but from the beginning of the 16th century there was a tendency to introduce elements of *Roman law, especially as embodied in the *civil law of France and the Netherlands. This resulted in marked differences from English law, which were retained after Scotland's union with England in 1707.

Scott, Paul (Mark) (1920–78) British novelist. He is best known for the "Raj Quartet," a series of novels dealing with the dramatic changes and conflicts of the final period of British rule in India. They are *The Jewel in the Crown* (1966), *The Day of the Scorpion* (1968), *The Towers of Silence* (1972), and *A Division of the Spoils* (1975). His last novel, *Staying On* (1977), was awarded Britain's prestigious Booker Prize.

Scott, Robert Falcon (1868–1912) British explorer and naval officer. He led two expeditions to the Antarctic, the first in the *Discovery* (1900–04) and the second (1910–12) in the *Terra Nova*. With a party of four he reached the South Pole by sledge on Jan 17, 1912, only to find that *Amundsen had preceded them. Delayed by illness and blizzards they perished only a few miles from safety. Their bodies and Scott's diaries were found in November.

Scott, Sir Walter (1771–1832) Scottish novelist. His early works included a collection of border ballads (1802–03) and the popular narrative poem *The Lay of the Last Minstrel* (1805). *Waverley* (1814) was the first of a series of hugely successful historical novels that included *Old Mortality* (1816) and *The Heart of Midlothian* (1818). His last years were spent in frantic literary activity to pay off his creditors after his bankruptcy in 1826.

Scott, Winfield (1786–1866) US Army officer. He served in the *War of 1812 and in various campaigns from the Indian wars in Florida to the *Aroostook border dispute in Canada. He was made general in chief of the Army (1841–61) and headed US forces during the *Mexican War, leading the troops in their long victorious trek to capture Mexico City, where he governed for almost a year (1847–48). He was the Whig nominee for president in 1852, but was defeated by Democrat Franklin *Pierce. He continued as head of the Army until 1861 and helped plan strategy at the beginning of the Civil War.

Scottish literature The literature of Scotland comprises a diversity of works in Scottish Gaelic, Lowland Scots (Lallans), English, and combinations of these. Literary Gaelic as practiced by the *bards continued in use up to the 18th century and drew upon the same traditions as *Irish literature (especially the Ulster cycle and the *Fenian cycle). In the Scottish (non-Gaelic) vernacular, the first important work is John *Barbour's 14th-century epic *The Bruce*. In the 15th and 16th centuries were produced the greatest works of early Scottish literature, the poetry of the *makaris* or Scottish Chaucerians. In the 17th century, by contrast, there was little outstanding literary production. *Burns's evocative use of the Lowlands dialect in the 18th century had a lasting effect on Scottish literature and national consciousness and influenced later poets. Many Scottish writers since the 17th century have written in English: the works of *Boswell, *Smollett, Sir Walter *Scott, *Carlyle, Robert Louis *Stevenson, and many others form an essential part of the literature of English.

Scottish terrier A breed of dog, originally called Aberdeen terrier, used to chase foxes from their burrows. It is thickset with short legs, a short erect tail, and pricked ears. The long muzzle has characteristically long whiskers and the wiry coat can be black, brindle, gray, or yellow-brown. Height: 10–11.2 in (25–28 cm).

Scouting A movement founded by Britain's Robert *Baden-Powell in 1908 to encourage boys to become enterprising members of society. Baden-Powell founded the Scout Association in Britain. The Boy Scouts of America was founded two years later. The Scouts' motto is *Be Prepared*. The Boy Scouts Association classifies its members into Cub Scouts (for boys aged 8–10), Scouts (11–17), and Explorers (15–20). There are 14 million Scouts throughout the world. The Girl Scouts of America was founded in 1912 by Juliette Low, who modeled the group on the British Girl Guides Association. Girls 6–8 are Brownies, 9–11 are Junior Girl Scouts, 12–14 are Cadettes and 15–17 are Senior Girl Scouts.

Scranton 41 25N 75 40W A city in Pennsylvania. It had a thriving anthracite industry and iron and steel operations until the 1950s. Since then it has shown great initiative in attracting many light industries to the city. It is the site of the University of Scranton (1888). Population (1990): 81,805.

screamer A marsh-dwelling bird belonging to a family (*Anhimidae*; 3 species) occurring in tropical and subtropical South America; 30 in (75 cm) long, screamers have dark plumage, a short hook-tipped bill, two paired wing spurs, and either a crest or a horny protuberance on the head. They feed on water plants and the skin contains air sacs that can produce crackling noises. Order: *Anseriformes* (ducks, geese, etc.).

scree. *See* talus.

screech owl. *See* scops owl.

screw pine A treelike plant of the genus *Pandanus* (about 150 species), native to the Old World tropics. The name derives from the spiral arrangement of the leaves, which leave scars in a corkscrew spiral when they fall. Stout aerial prop roots grow down from the stem into the ground: the part of the stem below these roots decays, so that the plant is supported entirely by the prop roots. The leaves, which are long and stiff with parallel sides, are used for matting and weaving. The flowers grow in large heads enclosed in leafy structures (spathes) and the fruits of some species are edible. Several species are grown as house plants. Family: *Pandanaceae*.

screwworm. *See* blowfly.

Scriabin, Alexander (1872–1915) Russian composer and pianist. His mature compositions were characterized by chords built on the interval of the fourth. His works include three symphonies—the third entitled *The Divine Poem* (1903)—a piano concerto (1894), 10 piano sonatas, and *Prometheus* or *The Poem of Fire* (1909–10), intended to be accompanied by a sequence of colored lights projected onto a screen.

scribes (Hebrew: *sofrim*) Ancient Jewish biblical scholars. They preserved the textual tradition of the *Torah and cultivated its study and interpretation. In the Gospels they are frequently linked with the *Pharisees. In later Jewish usage the term applies to copyists of the Torah and other sacred texts.

Scriblerus club An English literary club founded in about 1713. Its members included *Pope, *Swift, *Gay, and John *Arbuthnot. In their collaborative *Memoirs of Martinus Scriblerus* (1741) they ridiculed literary pretentiousness.

scrofula Ulceration of a lymph node infected with *tuberculosis, seen most commonly in the neck. This form of tuberculosis is now uncommon in developed countries but is still seen in poorer countries. Treatment is with antibiotic drugs and surgery. It was formerly known as king's evil, as it was believed that the touch of the sovereign would cure it.

scrub Vegetation consisting mainly of short, often aromatic, evergreen shrubs, typically found in coastal regions with hot dry summers; the Mediterranean maquis and the Californian chaparral are examples. This type of vegetation is transitional between grasslands and forests. The shrubs are adapted to survive dry summers and usually flower and fruit in the spring.

scrub bird A rare Australian passerine bird belonging to a primitive family (*Atrichornithidae*; 2 species). Scrub birds are brown with long pointed tails and loud voices, and are poor fliers, feeding on insects and nesting on the ground. The noisy scrub bird (*Atrichornis clamosus*) is about 9 in (22 cm) long and occurs in SW Australia, where it was thought to be extinct until 1961. The smaller rufous scrub bird (*A. rufescens*) is found only in the wet forests of New South Wales.

Scullin, James Henry (1876–1953) Australian statesman: Labor prime minister (1929–1931). The problems of the Depression plagued his administration, his deflationary measures bringing electoral defeat in 1931.

sculpin. *See* bullhead.

sculpture The art of shaping or modeling such materials as stone, wood, clay, and metal either in relief (*see* relief sculpture) or in the round. Stone, particularly marble, has been most popular with sculptors since it is the most durable material for outdoor sculptures. Wood is principally associated with *African art and medieval indoor sculptures (*see also* wood carving). Clay is most often employed in preliminary models for sculptures later cast in metal. Of all the metals, bronze has been most favored for casting, although in the 20th century aluminum, iron, and sheet metal have been increasingly used to fabricate sculptural concepts.

Most civilizations have left a legacy of sculpture, the earliest known work being Paleolithic representations of human and animal figures, believed to be of religious significance. More detailed figures, indicating the hierarchy of the social organization, appeared in Egypt in the 3rd millennium BC. The 5th and 4th centuries BC saw the rise of classical Greek sculpture with the work of *Praxiteles, *Phidias, and others. The Romans subsequently developed these classical themes, introducing more personalized portrait sculpture. In India from the 2nd century BC, Japan from the 6th century AD, and China from the 7th century AD, sculpture was devoted primarily to representations of the Buddha and his life. In medieval Europe, sculpture became largely an embellishment of architecture, until the revival of classical ideals in the Italian Renaissance with the works of such major sculptors as *Donatello and *Michelangelo. The spread of Renaissance ideas throughout the rest of Europe led to the work of Jean *Goujon in France and Grinling *Gibbons in England, while baroque sculpture attained its finest expression in the virtuosity of *Bernini. The neoclassicism of the 18th century saw a new respect for ancient Greek models. Outstanding among the sculptors of 19th-century romanticism was *Rodin. Although the figural tradition has been continued into the 20th century by such sculptors as Marino *Marini and Ernst *Barlach, semiabstract and abstract sculpture, influenced by African and other primitive carving, have become the principal forms of sculptural expression. Semiabstract sculptures include the innovative work of *Modigliani, *Epstein, and Henry *Moore, as well as the geometricized forms of Jacques *Lipchitz and the simplified shapes of Constantin *Brancusi. Abstract or nonrepresentative sculpture includes the organic forms of such sculptors as *Arp and the geometric constructions of Naum *Gabo (*see also* constructivism). Kinetic and environmental sculpture are also specifically 20th-century developments. Kinetic sculptures, i.e. sculptures that move either by motor, magnetism, or air currents, were pioneered by Gabo and Alexander *Calder (*see also* mobiles). Environmental sculpture is the recreation of an environment as in Claes *Oldenburg's work of the 1960s. The principal uses of sculpture have been architectural and commemorative, that is for memorial monuments and tombs.

scurvy A disease caused by deficiency of *vitamin C (which is present in most fresh fruits and vegetables). In the past scurvy was common among sailors on long voyages, but it is now rarely seen except in old debilitated people. The symptoms are weakness and aching joints and muscles, progressing to bleeding of the gums and—later—other organs. Scurvy can be readily treated by giving vitamin C or fresh fruit.

scurvy grass An annual, biennial, or perennial herb of the genus *Cochlearia* (about 25 species), occurring in temperate regions, especially near coasts. Up to 20 in (50 cm) tall, it has simple often heart-shaped leaves and the white or mauve flowers, each with four rounded petals, are borne in small clusters. Family: **Cruciferae*.

Scutari. *See* Shkodër (Albania); Üsküdar (Turkey).

Scylla and Charybdis In Greek mythology, two sea monsters on opposite sides of the Strait of Messina who menaced *Odysseus, the *Argonauts, and other legendary heroes. Scylla was a monster with six heads and a pack of baying hounds, while Charybdis was a raging whirlpool.

Scyphozoa. *See* jellyfish.

Scythians An Indo-European people who temporarily settled in Asia Minor before settling in what is now S Russia in the 6th century BC. The true Scythians, called Royal Scyths, established a kingdom N of the Black Sea and traded wheat for luxury goods with the Greek colonies there. Their skill as horsemen and archers halted Persian and Macedonian invasions but they remained a nomadic people until their disappearance from history during the Gothic onslaughts of the 3rd century AD. Objects recovered from their royal tombs demonstrate their metalworking skill and, especially in the animal designs that predominate as decorations, their artistry.

SCULPTURE *A cast of one of the relief sculptures of Trajan's Column, depicting Trajan speaking to his soldiers inside a fortified camp. The Column, which was erected in the Roman forum in 113 AD, is 125 ft (38 m) high. Its spiral frieze depicts the emperor's campaigns in Dacia (modern Romania). The detail and crude realism of the many panels are typical of Roman sculpture.*

sea anemone A sedentary marine invertebrate animal belonging to a worldwide order (*Actiniaria*; over 1000 species) of *coelenterates. It has a soft columnar body (*see* polyp) of a few millimeters to about 5 ft (1.5 m) in diameter, with a mouth at the top surrounded by rings of tentacles, which—when expanded—give the animal a flowerlike appearance. Sea anemones are usually blue, green, or yellow and are found attached to rocks or weeds or associated with other invertebrates. They feed mainly on fish and other animals. Class: *Anthozoa*.

sea bass A carnivorous fish, also called sea perch, of the family *Serranidae* (about 400 species), found mainly in coastal waters of tropical and temperate seas. Its elongated body ranges up to 12 ft (3.75 m) long and varies in color with the species. They may be active or sedentary and certain species are *hermaphrodite while others, such as *groupers, are able to change sex. Many are valued food and game fish. Order: *Perciformes*. *See also* bass.

Seaborg, Glenn Theodore (1912–) US physicist, who as professor at the University of California has led the search for *transuranic elements. Working with Edwin *McMillan, he produced plutonium in 1940 by bombarding neptunium and neutrons. Working with another group of researchers, Seaborg has prepared samples of all the transuranic elements with atomic numbers from 95 to 105 by similar methods. For this work he shared the Nobel Prize with McMillan in 1951.

sea bream A fish, also called porgy, belonging to a family (*Sparidae*; about 400 species) found mainly in shallow waters of tropical and subtropical seas. It has a deep laterally flattened body covered with large scales, a single long dorsal fin, and well-developed teeth. It lives in shoals and feeds by scraping algae and small animals off rocks.

sea butterfly A *gastropod mollusk belonging to the subclass *Opisthobranchia*, also called pteropod. Some sea butterflies (order *Thecosomata*) have a shell, are filter feeders, and swim by means of winglike appendages (parapodia). Others (order *Gymnosomata*) are naked, with only small parapodia, and prey on small animals.

sea cow. *See* dugong.

sea cucumber A marine invertebrate animal belonging to a worldwide class (*Holothuroidea*; 1100 species) of *echinoderms. Its cucumber-shaped body, 0.8–79 in (2–200 cm) long, is covered with leathery skin containing small calcareous plates or spicules. There is a mouth at one end surrounded by a ring of tentacles, which are used for feeding on detritus and plankton. It crawls sluggishly on the sea bottom or burrows in sand or mud. □oceans.

sea eagle An *eagle belonging to the widely distributed genus *Haliaeetus* (8 species); 28–48 in (70–120 cm) long, sea eagles have a wedge-shaped tail and are typically brown with white markings. The smaller species feed mostly on fish but the larger species eat carrion, large birds, and mammals.

sea fan A colonial *coral of the genus *Gorgonia*, in which the tiny cylindrical *polyps have a horny internal skeleton and grow upon one another to produce a fanlike structure. Sea fans are commonly yellow, pink, brown, or purple and occur mainly in shallow tropical waters.

sea-floor spreading A concept developed in the 1960s that provides a mechanism for *continental drift. Magma rises from the earth's mantle to the surface along midocean ridges (constructive plate margins; *see* plate tectonics), cools to form new oceanic crust, and displaces the older material sideways at an average rate of 1.5 in (4 cm) per year. Magnetic reversals recorded in the rocks in approximately symmetrical strips at each side of the midocean ridges provide strong evidence for sea-floor spreading.

sea gooseberry. *See* ctenophore.

seagull. *See* gull.

sea hare A marine *gastropod mollusk belonging to the family *Aplysiidae*. Growing up to 14 in (35 cm) long, sea hares are often green or yellow in color; they have a pair of tentacles (resembling a hare's ears) and a much-reduced shell. When disturbed, they eject a cloud of purple ink into the water. Subclass: *Opisthobranchia*.

sea holly **1.** A perennial herb, *Eryngium maritimum*, found on sandy and pebbly European shores. Growing to a height of 12–24 in (30–60 cm), it has spiked hollylike leaves and bears clusters of purplish-blue flowers. Family: *Umbelliferae*. **2.** *See* gulfweed.

sea horse One of several small bony-plated marine □fish of the family *Syngnathidae* (*see also* pipefish), especially the genus *Hippocampus*, that lives in shallow warm waters. They are 1.5–12 in (4–30 cm) long and the horselike head with its long tubular snout is set at an angle to the body. They use the prehensile tail to cling to seaweed and swim in a vertical position by undulating the dorsal fin. The males have a brood pouch in which the young are hatched. Order: *Gasterosteiformes*.

Sea Islands A chain of islands off the coasts of South Carolina, Georgia, and Florida. Production of long-stapled Sea Island cotton was important until infestation by the boll weevil in the 1920s. The islands are popular for vacations.

sea kale A bushy perennial herb, *Crambe maritima*, found on Atlantic coasts of Europe. Growing to a height of 16–24 in (40–60 cm), it has cabbagelike leaves and bears clusters of small white flowers. It may be cultivated for its tender young edible shoots. Family: **Cruciferae*.

seal (sigillography) A stone, metal, or wooden stamp and its impression in wax or lead used to authenticate documents. The engraved surface of a seal is usually rock crystal or other hard stone but bronze and gold are also used. The impression cut into the seal generally consists of a central device of a heraldic or personal motif, surrounded by a legend. Officials' seals are practical in design but other seals, such as desk seals and fob seals (worn as jewels), enable jewelers and goldsmiths to exhibit their skills. **Sigillography** is the study of seals.

seal (zoology) A carnivorous marine mammal belonging to the order *Pinnipedia* (32 species). Seals have a streamlined body with a smooth rounded head and an insulating layer of blubber under the sleek-coated skin. Both pairs of limbs flatten into flippers. They feed mainly on fish and breed on land or ice.

There are two main families: the *Otariidae* (eared seals; 13 species) including fur seals and *sea lions, which have external ears and can turn their hind flippers forward for walking on land; and the *Phocidae* (true seals; 18 species), which lack external ears and have trailing hind flippers. The *walrus is the only member of its family, *Odobenidae*.

sea lavender A perennial or annual herb of the genus *Limonium* (about 300 species), found on coasts and salt marshes of W Asia, Europe, and North America. The common sea lavender (*L. vulgare*) has a basal rosette of slender leaves and a branched flower stem, 3.1–12 in (8–30 cm) high, bearing clusters of purple-blue flowers. Family: *Plumbaginaceae*.

sea lettuce A green *seaweed of the genus *Ulva*, found mainly between high and low tide levels on most rocky shores. It has broad flat translucent fronds, which resemble lettuce leaves, and grows in bunches up to about 12 in (30 cm) long. It is rich in iodine and vitamins and is sometimes used in salads and soups.

sea lily. *See* crinoid.

sea lion A large *seal belonging to the family *Otariidae*. California sea lions (*Zalophus californianus*) of the Californian coast are popular circus animals. They grow to 7 ft (2 m) and live in groups with a definite social hierarchy. Steller's sea lion (*Eumetopias jubatus*) is the largest species, growing to over 10 ft (3 m).

Sealyham terrier A breed of □dog developed between 1850 and 1891 in Wales, for hunting foxes and badgers. It is sturdily built with short legs, drooping ears, and a short thin tail. White with darker markings, Sealyhams have a soft undercoat and a wiry outer coat. Height: 11–12 in (27–30 cm).

sea mouse A marine *annelid worm belonging to a family (*Aphroditidae*) found in North Atlantic coastal waters. Sea mice grow up to 7 in (18 cm) long and 3 in (7 cm) wide with 15 pairs of scales buried in a dense covering of iridescent hairs. They are foraging carnivores and are generally found buried in fine sand or mud with only the hind end protruding. Class: *Polychaeta*.

sea otter A marine *otter, *Enhydra lutris*, of the N Pacific; 4 ft (1.2 m) long and weighing 77 lb (35 kg), it floats in colonies of up to 90 individuals. The cubs, well-furred and with open eyes and sharp teeth, are born in the sea. Sea otters feed on mollusks, crustaceans, and fish and can crack open shells using a pebble balanced on the chest. Once hunted for their valuable fur, they are now a protected species.

sea pen A fleshy colonial marine invertebrate animal belonging to an order (*Pennatulacea*; 300 species) of *coelenterates, especially one forming a feather-like colony (e.g. *Leioptilus*). A central stalklike individual—the primary *polyp—is anchored into mud or sand and secondary polyps branch from it. Class: *Anthozoa*.

Sea Peoples The seafaring tribes who colonized Asia Minor, the Aegean, and N Africa in the 13th and 12th centuries BC, destroying the *Hittite empire. About 1170 they were almost annihilated by Rameses III of Egypt and those that survived scattered to Palestine, the Aegean, and perhaps to the W Mediterranean. They have been variously and uncertainly identified and may have been Achaeans, Etruscans, or Philistines.

sea perch. *See* sea bass.

Searle, Ronald William Fordham (1920–) British cartoonist. He worked for such journals as the *Sunday Express* and *Punch* but is best known for his cartoon creation of the outrageous schoolgirls of St Trinian's, who subsequently featured in four films.

sea sickness. *See* travel sickness.

sea slug A marine *gastropod mollusk of the order *Nudibranchia*. Sea slugs have exposed feathery gills, two pairs of tentacles, and no shell. They browse on sponges, sea anemones, and corals and are often brightly colored. Some sea slugs retain the stinging cells of their prey for their own defense.

sea snake A venomous fish-eating snake belonging to the family *Hydrophiidae* (50 species) occurring mainly in coastal waters of Australasia and SE Asia. Sea snakes are adapted to an underwater life by having a flattened body with an oarlike tail and valvelike closures in the nostrils. Most produce live young (rather than eggs).

sea spider A spiderlike marine arthropod of the class *Pycnogonida* (or *Pantopoda*; over 600 species). Its short thin body, 0.12–20 in (3–500 mm) long, usually bears four pairs of walking legs and a long sucking proboscis. Sea spiders occur up to depths of 11,800 ft (3600 m), feeding on soft-bodied invertebrate animals. Fertilized eggs are carried by the males and many larvae are parasitic on polyps or mollusks.

sea squirt. *See* tunicate.

SEATO. *See* South East Asia Treaty Organization.

Seattle 47 35N 122 20W A city in Washington, between Puget Sound and Lake Washington. A port of entry to the Klondike, it became a boomtown with the 1897 Alaska Gold Rush. Educational institutions include the University of Washington (1861) and Seattle University (1852). It is Alaska's main supply port. There are large timber mills and various forest-based industries. Other major industries include the manufacture of aircraft, ship building, and ship repair. Population (1990): 516,259.

sea urchin A marine invertebrate animal, belonging to the class **Echinoidea*, with a typically spherical rigid body covered by long movable spines. Sea urchins live on shores and ocean floors and use a complex feeding apparatus—Aristotle's lantern—to masticate algae and other organic material scraped off rocks. Phylum: *Echinodermata* (*see* echinoderm).

sea water The water constituting the world's oceans and seas. It is usually saline, average salinity being about 15 g per lb (35 g per kg) of sea water. The principal dissolved salts are sodium chloride (2.8%), magnesium chloride (0.4%), and magnesium sulfate (0.2%). Where evaporation is high, salinity is increased, as in the Red Sea. Sea water is desalinated (*see* desalination) in some areas, e.g. Saudi Arabia, to obtain fresh water, although the process is costly. The properties of sea water, including its chemical composition, temperature, and movements (waves and tides) are studied in *oceanography.

seaweed Large multicellular red, brown, or green marine *algae that are generally found attached to the sea bed, rocks, or other solid structures by rootlike structures called holfasts. The plants have stemlike stalks and fronds, which may be flat and undivided, threadlike, or branched, sometimes with small air bladders for buoyancy. Seaweeds often occur in dense aggregations along shores but are also found to depths of about 650 ft (200 m). Many are of commercial importance as food (e.g. *carrageen, *laver, and *sea lettuce), as fertilizers, in chemical and pharmaceutical products, etc. *See also* kelp; wrack.

sebaceous glands. *See* skin.

Sebastian, St (3rd century AD) Roman martyr. According to tradition, he was an officer of the Praetorian Guards until his Christianity was discovered by Diocletian. His martyrdom at the hands of archers is a frequent subject of painting. Feast day: Jan 20. Emblem: an arrow.

Sebastiano del Piombo (S. Luciano: c. 1485–1547) Venetian painter. Although he was a pupil of Giovanni Bellini, his early works, notably *St John Chrysostom* (c. 1509; S Giovanni Crisostomo, Venice), were influenced by Giorgione. Moving to Rome in 1511, he painted decorations in the Farnesina with *Raphael, whose *Transfiguration* he directly challenged with his *Raising of Lazarus* (1517–19; National Gallery, London). He was also known as a portraitist; his sitters included Christopher Columbus and Pope Clement VII, who appointed him keeper of the papal seals (*piombi*) in 1531—hence his nickname.

Sebastopol. *See* Sevastopol.

second **1.** (s) The *SI unit of time equal to the duration of 9,192,631,770 periods of the radiation corresponding to a specified transition of the cesium 133 atom. The unit was formerly defined by astronomical measurement. *See also* cesium clock; time measurement. **2.** A unit of angle equal to 1/60th of a minute.

secondary emission The ejection of electrons from the surface of a metal when it is bombarded with charged particles of sufficient energy. Secondary emission is best observed when the bombarding particles are themselves electrons, which are then known as primary electrons; the ejected electrons are called secondary electrons. In certain metals, as many as 10 secondary electrons can be emitted by the impact of one primary electron. The effect is used in such devices as the electron multiplier.

secretary bird A long-legged terrestrial bird of prey, *Sagittarius serpentarius*, that lives in dry uplands of Africa; 48 in (120 cm) tall with a wingspan of 80 in (200 cm), it has a hawklike face and gray plumage with a long pair of central tail feathers and a black crest of quills behind its head—hence its name. It feeds on snakes and lizards and is the only member of its family (*Sagittaridae*). Order: *Falconiformes* (falcons, hawks, etc.).

Secret Service, United States US division of the Department of the Treasury, charged with law enforcement. Established in 1865, it is responsible for protecting the president and the vice president, and also presidential candidates, the president-elect, and their families. It watches over the Treasury, detecting counterfeiting and guarding the buildings and vaults. Originally established by Pres. Abraham Lincoln to combat counterfeiting, the Secret Service's duties increased through the years.

Securities and Exchange Commission (SEC) US government agency that helps to regulate the securities and financial markets. In the interest of protecting the public and investors, it is charged with keeping the investment public informed of malpractices and irregularities. The commission, consisting of five members appointed by the president, oversees the stock exchange and investment and holding companies and also serves as adviser to district courts in connection with reorganization proceedings for debtor corporations. It was created under the authority of the Securities Exchange Act of 1934.

Sedan 49 42N 4 57E A city in NE France, in the Ardennes department on the Meuse River. It was the site of a decisive defeat (1870) for the French in the Franco-Prussian War. Its industries include textiles, metallurgy, and food processing. Population (1982): 25,400.

Sedan, Battle of (Sept 1, 1870) The battle in the *Franco-Prussian War in which German forces, invading France, surrounded the army of Napoleon III and forced him to surrender with 100,000 men. The French defeat precipitated revolution in Paris (*see* Commune of Paris) and marked the end of the Second Empire.

sedan chair An enclosed single-seater chair carried on poles by two men, one in front and one behind. Sedans probably originated in Italy.

sedatives Drugs that relieve restlessness, anxiety, and tension. Most drugs that depress the activity of the nervous system have this effect (including barbiturates and narcotics), but the most widely used sedatives are the minor tranquilizers, for example *benzodiazepines, as they relieve anxiety without causing sleep and their use carries less risk of dependence. Sedatives are also useful in the treatment of muscular aches associated with tension and stress.

Seddon, Richard John (1845–1906) New Zealand statesman, born in England; prime minister (1893–1906). His government implemented labor-protection measures and introduced old-age pensions and women's suffrage.

sedge A perennial herbaceous grasslike plant of the genus *Carex* (about 2000 species), growing throughout the world, mainly in swampy places. Sedges have solid stems, triangular in cross-section, with long narrow leaves and small male and female flowers usually grouped into separate clusters (spikes). The sand sedge (*C. arenaria*), found on the coasts of Europe and North America, has been used to bond sand dunes. Family: *Cyperaceae*.

Sedgemoor, Battle of (July 6, 1685) A battle in England SE of Bridgewater, in which the forces of James II of England defeated the rebellion of his nephew, the duke of *Monmouth.

sedimentary rock One of the three major categories into which rocks are divided (*compare* igneous rock; metamorphic rock). Sedimentary rocks are deposited mainly under water, usually in approximately horizontal layers (beds). **Clastic sedimentary rocks** are formed from the erosion and deposition of preexisting rocks and are classified according to the size of the particles. Arenaceous rocks have sand-grade particles and include the sandstones; argillaceous rocks have silt- or clay-grade particles and include siltstones and mudstones; rudaceous rocks, with gravel-grade and larger fragments, include the breccias, conglomerates, etc. Organically formed sedimentary rocks are derived from the remains of plants and animals, for example limestone and coal. Chemically formed sedimentary rocks result from natural chemical processes and include sedimentary iron ores. Many sedimentary rocks show complex internal structures, formed during or after deposition.

Sedum. *See* stonecrop.

Seebeck effect. *See* thermoelectric effects.

seed The reproductive structure formed after pollination and fertilization in higher plants. In flowering plants (angiosperms) the seed begins to develop after the *pollen nucleus has fused with the egg. In gymnosperms (conifers and related plants) the ovule begins dividing before pollination. All seeds contain an embryo and usually a food store, which is mobilized on germination. Angiosperm seeds are surrounded by a seed coat (testa) and contained within a *fruit; gymnosperm seeds are naked (*see* cone). The development of the "seed habit" has given the higher plants a marked advantage over the ferns, mosses, algae, and fungi. Water is not needed for fertilization, and therefore the plants can colonize arid habitats. In addition, seeds—unlike the spores of lower plants—can survive adverse conditions and may remain viable for many years before germinating.

seed fern A *gymnosperm plant belonging to the extinct order *Pteridospermales*, abundant during the Carboniferous and Permian periods (370–240 million years ago). Seed ferns had large fernlike fronds but—unlike ferns—produced seeds, in cuplike structures. They were probably the ancestors of plants that evolved into the angiosperms (flowering plants).

Seeger, Pete (1919–) US folksinger and songwriter, who, with Woody Guthrie, led the US folk music revival in the 1960s. He worked to collect folk songs before becoming a founder of the Weavers singing group. He wrote such songs as "Where Have All the Flowers Gone" and "Kisses Sweeter than Wine." He was also an active conservationist, particularly on the Hudson River.

Seferis, George (Georgios Seferiadis; 1900–71) Greek poet and diplomat. He was influenced by the French symbolists and by T. S. *Eliot, whose poetry he translated into Greek. His lyrical poetry was published in a number of collections, including *Strophe* (1931) and *Poiimata* (1940). He won the Nobel Prize in 1963.

Seghers, Hercules Pieterzoon (c. 1589–c. 1638) Dutch landscape painter and etcher. His desolate and dramatically lit mountain landscapes influenced Rembrandt, who owned some of Seghers's works. He is also known for his novel method of etching with colored paper and inks.

Segovia 40 57N 4 07W A city in central Spain, in Old Castile. It has a fine Roman aqueduct that still supplies the city with water, a 16th-century cathedral, and the restored alcázar (citadel). Industries include potteries and flour milling. Population (1989 est): 54,500.

Segovia, Andrés (1893–1987) Spanish guitarist. He played all over the world, reviving the popularity of the guitar as a concert instrument and inspiring composers to write new works for it.

Segrè, Emilio (1905–89) US physicist, born in Italy, who shared the 1959 Nobel Prize with Owen *Chamberlain for their discovery in 1955 of the antiproton (*see* antimatter). Segrè was also the first physicist to produce an artificial element, *technetium, by bombarding molybdenum with deuterium nuclei.

Seine River A river in N France. Rising on the Plateau de Langres, it flows mainly NW through Paris to the English Channel, S of Le Havre. It is the second longest river in France, linked by canal with the Somme, Scheldt, Meuse, Rhine, Saône, and Loire rivers. Length: 482 mi (776 km).

seismic belts (*or* seismic zones) The narrow distinct belts on the earth's surface that are subject to frequent earthquakes. They usually follow the line of plate boundaries (*see* plate tectonics), especially along midocean ridges, near young orogenic belts, along island arc systems, and along major *faults.

seismic wave An elastic shock wave emanating from the focus of an *earthquake or explosion. When seismic activity is recorded, several types of wave can be identified: longitudinal P (*primae*) waves and transverse S (*secundae*) waves are small rapid vibrations that come directly through the earth's interior. They form the first and second parts of the preliminary tremor of an earthquake. The main earthquake consists of large slow L (*longae*) waves traveling along the surface. This type of wave is limited to a narrow depth range and can also occur along deeper strata. Its components are Rayleigh waves (after R. J. S. Rayleigh), which are vertical vibrations in the plane of propagation, and Love waves (after A. E. H. Love), which are horizontal and transverse. The study of seismic waves has provided much of our knowledge of the earth's interior.

seismology The branch of geophysics concerned with the study of *earthquakes: their origin, the waves they produce (*see* seismic wave), their effects, and their distribution. The instruments used are the **seismograph**, which records the magnitude of the oscillations during an earthquake, and the **seismometer**, which detects and records the motions of the earth in a particular direction (usually used in sets of three). In recent years considerable research has gone into the prediction and modification of earthquakes. The study of nuclear explosions has also concerned seismologists, since in many respects they resemble earthquakes. Seismological data has provided the bulk of our knowledge of the earth's interior. It is estimated that an average of 14,000 lives are lost annually through earthquakes.

sei whale A widely distributed *rorqual, *Balaenopteris borealis*, also called sardine whale. Up to 60 ft (18 m) long, it has a dark back, a white belly, and a large dorsal fin.

Sekhmet An Egyptian war goddess, consort of the creator-god Ptah and destroyer of the enemies of Ra. She was usually portrayed as a lioness or with a lion's head.

Sekondi-Takoradi 4 59N 1 43W A port in Ghana, on the Gulf of Guinea. Formerly two separate towns, Sekondi and Takoradi were linked in 1946. Bauxite is exported and industries include food processing. Population (1988 est): 103,653.

Selaginella A genus of mosslike *pteridophyte plants (about 700 species), also called spike mosses, found mainly in damp tropical forests. They are similar to the related *clubmosses but differ in having scales (ligules) at the bases of the leaves and two kinds of spore capsules (male and female). The prickly clubmoss (*S. selaginoides*) occurs in arctic and N temperate regions. Family: *Selaginellaceae*; class: *Lycopsida.*

Selangor A state in W Peninsular Malaysia, on the Strait of Malacca. It became a British protectorate in 1874. It is the economic center of Malaysia with industry concentrated in the Klang Valley, mainly between Kuala Lumpur and Port Klang; the chief products are tin and rubber. Area: 3167 sq mi (8202 sq km). Population (1990): 1,978,000. Capital: Shah Alam.

Selby 53 48N 1 04W A market city in N England, in North Yorkshire on the River Ouse. It has a famous 12th-century abbey church. Industries include beet-sugar refining, ship building, paper, and chemicals, and development of the rich Selby coalfield is under way (the first mine went into production in 1983). Population (1981): 107,726.

Selective Service Acts US laws requiring military service registration. The Act of 1917 enabled the military to draft 500,000 men between 21 and 30 years old (extended in 1918 to ages 31–40) for the duration of World War I. The Act of 1940 required all men between 21 and 35 years of age to register (extended to age 45 in 1941). After World War II the draft declined and in 1948 another selective service act (later amended) was passed that required all men between 19 and 26 years, who had not previously served, to register and serve. The draft lasted until 1973. A new law in 1980 required registration of all 19- and 20-year-old males and thereafter, whenever a male reached his 18th birthday. Although no draft existed, the purpose was to facilitate mobilization of forces if necessary.

Selene The Greek moon-goddess, daughter of the Titan Hyperion and sister of Helios (the sun) and Eos (dawn). She became identified with the later Greek goddess *Artemis and with the Roman *Diana.

selenium (Se) A chemical element that is a member of the sulfur family and is obtained from sludges produced during electrolytic copper refining. It exists in several forms, including deep-red crystals, but the commonest allotrope is gray. The element has photovoltaic properties and is used in photocells, light meters, and in photocopying machines. It is a semiconductor and is widely used in rectifiers. The hydride (H_2Se) has a very noxious smell and, like other selenium compounds, is very toxic. At no 34; at wt 78.96; mp 423°F (217°C); bp 1266°F (685°C). *See also* selenium cell.

selenium cell A type of *photocell based on the *photovoltaic effect. It consists of a metal disk coated with selenium on top of which is placed a layer of gold or platinum sufficiently thin to transmit light. When light falls on the disk a small current is generated. They are used in exposure meters in cameras, etc.

Seles, Monica (1973–) Yugoslav professional tennis player. While still a teenager, she won the grand slam of tennis (Wimbledon and the Australian, French, and US opens) in 1990 and followed with many other tournament wins, rising to the number one ranking among women in 1991. She won the Australian Open to begin 1993, but at a German tournament in April was stabbed on court by a fan of Steffi Graf, her chief rival. The injury threatened Seles's future career.

Seleucids A Middle Eastern dynasty of the Hellenistic age (323–27 BC) founded by *Seleucus I Nicator, the Macedonian general who, after Alexander the Great's death, became governor and then ruler (312) of Babylonia. He extended his kingdom to the frontiers of India in the east and then into Syria in the west but his successors, in the face of Egyptian aggression and internal unrest provoked by the Seleucid promotion of Greek culture, failed to maintain his conquests. *Antiochus the Great (reigned 223–187) briefly restored Seleucid power in the east but could not prevent Rome's Mediterranean expansion. Under *Antiochus IV Epiphanes (175–163) the empire was further weakened by the revolt of the *Maccabees and although they were repressed by *Antiochus VII Sidetes (139–129) his failure to push back the Parthians anticipated the final disintegration of the Seleucid empire. In 64 BC Pompey annexed what was left of it to form the Roman province of Syria.

Seleucus I Nicator (c. 356–280 BC) Macedonian general, who founded the *Seleucid dynasty. After Alexander the Great's death (323) Seleucus became governor and then ruler (312) of Babylonia, taking the title of king in 305. He subsequently conquered Syria, which brought him into conflict with the Ptolemies of Egypt, Asia Minor, and Macedonia before being murdered by Ptolemy Ceraunus (d. 279 BC), the son of Ptolemy I Soter.

Seljuqs A Turkish dynasty that ruled in E Islam from 1055. During the 10th century the Seljuqs (descended from Seljuq, chief of the Oguz tribes) led bands of migrating Turks into the Islamic world and in 1055 their head, *Toghril Beg, captured Baghdad. The dynasty was at its peak under Toghril Beg and his successors *Alp Arslan and *Malik-Shah, under whom the great vizier *Nizam al-Mulk administered the empire. After the death of Malik-Shah the empire disintegrated into rival kingdoms. His successors in Persia maintained a nominal suzerainty over the other kingdoms until defeated by invaders from central Asia in 1153. In Anatolia the Seljuqs of Rum ruled an important independent kingdom until coming under the domination of the Mongols in 1243.

Selkirk, Alexander (1676–1721) Scottish sailor. He joined the South Sea buccaneers and in 1704, after quarreling with his captain, was voluntarily left on one of the uninhabited Juan Fernández Islands. He was discovered in 1709 by a ship piloted by *Dampier. His experience inspired Defoe's *Robinson Crusoe* (1719).

Selkirk, Thomas Douglas, 5th Earl of (1771–1820) Canadian settler; born in Scotland. He founded a settlement on Prince Edward Island in Canada in 1803 for Scottish immigrants wishing to escape poverty. By 1810 he acquired land, through part ownership by the Hudson's Bay Company, and established the *Red River Settlement (1812), now Winnipeg, Manitoba.

Sellers, Peter (1925–80) British comic actor. He made his name in the 1950s in the radio comedy series *The Goon Show*. His many films include *I'm All Right, Jack* (1959), *The Millionairess* (1961), *Dr Strangelove* (1963), *What's New, Pussycat?* (1965), *The Pink Panther* series (1963–77), and *Being There* (1980).

Selznick, David O(liver) (1902–65) US film producer. In 1936 he formed his own production company and produced *A Star Is Born* (1937) and *Gone with the Wind* (1939) among other films. Many of his later films, including *Duel in the Sun* (1946) and *A Farewell to Arms* (1957), starred Jennifer Jones (1919–), his second wife.

semantics Broadly, the branch of philology concerned with the study of the relationship between words and meanings. The study of signs and their relationships to the things or concepts that they signify is also called semiotics or semiology and has application in mathematical logic and in the philosophy of language. Semantics as the study of meaning in individual words is part of *linguistics, but there are philosophical problems involved in trying to account for the relationship between words and the objects they refer to, particularly when a theory is extended to cover words that have no concrete referent (e.g. "honesty"). A distinction is often made between literal (or cognitive) meaning and associative meaning, and many linguists believe that the meaning of words can be broken into constituents by means of analyses similar to those used by *Chomsky to derive the surface structure of sentences from their deep structure. Some linguistic philosophers, such as *Wittgenstein in his later period and J. L. *Austin, account for word meaning not in terms of logical structures but rather according to the speaker's intention in using a word or utterance. However, logical analysis is widely accepted in explaining the aspect of meaning that is a function of grammatical structure, i.e. sentence meaning is seen as a matter of internal relationships among the words, word particles, and phrases involved.

semaphore **1.** A visual method of communication between ships at sea, used mainly by warships wishing to maintain radio silence, and consisting of a pattern of signaling by the use of two flags, held by a signalman, their relative positions symbolizing an alphabetical or numerical character. **2.** A mechanical railroad signaling device, consisting of a steel arm the position of which is changed by a signalman or by the tripping of a release by a passing train.

Semarang 6 58S 110 29E A port in Indonesia, in central Java on the Java Sea. A commercial center with textile and ship building industries, it exports sugar, rubber, coffee, kapok, and copra. The port is sometimes disrupted by the monsoon. Its university was established in 1960. Population (1980): 1,026,671.

Semele In Greek mythology, the daughter of *Cadmus, king of Thebes. She was killed by lightning when her lover Zeus appeared to her in his divine form but her unborn child, the god *Dionysus, was saved.

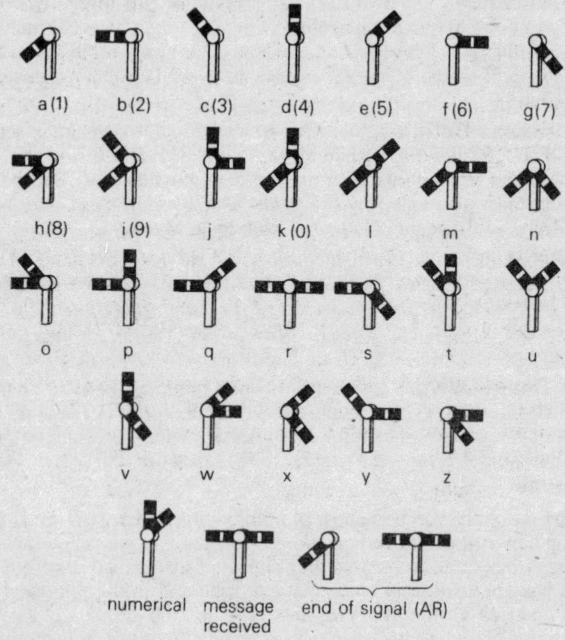

SEMAPHORE

semen. *See* sperm; testis.

semiconductor A crystalline material in which the electrical conductivity increases with temperature and is between that of a conductor and an *insulator. The conductivity is also sensitive to minute quantities of impurities in the crystal lattice (□energy band). Some (donor) impurities increase the number of negative charge carriers (electrons), creating what is known as an n-type semiconductor. Other (acceptor) impurities increase the number of positive charge carriers (holes), creating a p-type semiconductor. The introduction of these impurities is called doping. *Solid-state electronic components, such as diodes, *transistors, and *integrated circuits depend on the properties of junctions between p-type and n-type regions in the same piece of semiconductor crystal (p-n junctions). Metal oxide semiconductor (MOS) devices also use the properties of a thin layer of insulating oxide on the semiconductor surface. The element silicon is now the most widely used semiconducting material. Others are germanium, now used only for special applications, and gallium arsenide, which is used in high-speed logic circuits and microwave equipment.

semiconductor diode A *solid-state electronic device with two electrodes. It consists of a single p-n junction (*see* semiconductor). When the p-region is at a more positive voltage than the n-region (forward bias), the current flow increases exponentially as the voltage rises. In reverse bias, very little current flows until a sufficiently high reverse voltage has built up to cause breakdown; the current then increases sharply. The diode is, therefore, commonly used as a rectifier. The **Zener diode** is designed to break down at a specific reverse bias voltage, above which the voltage across it remains effectively constant. The higher the doping levels on both sides of the junction, the lower the breakdown voltage. It is used as a voltage regulator.

Semiconductor diodes, which have largely replaced thermionic diodes, are also used to generate microwaves by the *Gunn effect, to detect light in *photocells, and to emit light in low-voltage displays. The latter, called **light-emitting diodes** (LEDs), are widely used in calculators and digital watches. They emit radiation (light) when holes and electrons combine, the color of the light depending on the material of the crystal.

Seminole A group of North American Indians related to the *Creeks, who speak a Muskogean language. In the late 18th century they migrated from Georgia to Florida, where, in several wars, they resisted domination by the government. They developed a simple hunting and fishing culture suited to the conditions of the region.

Seminole War (1835–42) Second US-Seminole Indian conflict. Protesting US expansion, slave policies, and treaty injustices, the Seminoles, led by *Osceola and others, employed guerrilla-warfare tactics against the larger superior US forces. The long frustrating war ended victoriously for the government in 1842; most of the Seminole Indians were relocated to Indian Territory in the West. *See also* Seminole.

semiotics (*or* semiology) *See* semantics.

Semipalatinsk 50 26N 80 16E A city in NE Kazakhstan, on the Irtysh River. Its name means "seven palaces" and refers to the nearby remains of seven ancient stone structures. Meat packing, food processing, and metalworking are among its industrial activities, and it is an important communications center. Population (1991 est): 344,700.

semipermeable membrane A material that allows certain molecules in a fluid to pass through it but not others. It will usually permit solvent particles to pass but not the solute molecules. It thus creates *osmosis when placed in a suitable fluid. Examples of semipermeable membranes include cell walls and parchment.

Semiramis A legendary queen of Assyria, who, with her legendary husband Ninus, was the alleged builder of *Babylon and, after his death, ruler of a vast empire extending to India.

Semites A group of people, including the *Jews and *Arabs, said in the Bible to be descended from Shem, Noah's eldest son. The Babylonians, Assyrians, Canaanites, and Phoenicians were ancient Semitic peoples.

Semitic alphabets The earliest known truly alphabetic writing systems, developed among the Semitic peoples of the E Mediterranean around 2000 BC. From them all the major alphabets of today are derived: the south Semitic version gave rise to the modern Amharic script of Ethiopia; from North Semitic were derived Greek (and from Greek came the Roman, *Cyrillic, *runic, and other alphabets), Phoenician, and Aramaic (from which came the scripts of Hebrew, Arabic, and *Devanagari in India). The earliest records in North Semitic date from around 1300 BC and indicate that it was a purely consonantal system of 22 letters, generally written from left to right.

Semitic languages A subgroup of the *Hamito-Semitic language family spoken in a large area of N Africa, extending through Palestine to the SW corner of Asia. The Semitic languages originated in Mesopotamia in the 3rd millennium BC and are recorded in Sumerian *cuneiform inscriptions. There are three subgroups recognized by language scholars, although, in comparison to other language groups, these subdivisions are very similar to each other in structure and vocabulary. NW Semitic consisted of Ugaritic, Canaanite, and *Aramaic, all now extinct. From these are descended Phoenician and *Hebrew, the only living language of this subgroup. NE Semitic, the second subgroup, consisted of Assyrian and Babylonian, both now extinct. The third group, S Semitic, is that from which modern *Arabic and Maltese are descended, as well as Amharic (*see* Amhara) and Tigrinya, the language of Eritrea.

semolina Fine grains of durum wheat used in the manufacture of *pasta and also for making milk puddings.

Senanayake, D(on) S(tephen) (1884–1952) Ceylonese statesman; the first prime minister (1947–52) of Ceylon (now Sri Lanka). In 1919 he helped to found the Ceylon National Congress and campaigned for the introduction of legal and constitutional reforms by the British Government. His son **Dudley Senanayake** (1911–73) was prime minister (1952–53, 1960, 1965–70).

Senate In ancient Rome, the state council. During Republican times the Senate was largely composed of ex-magistrates and, although its role was primarily to advise the magistrates, it carried much weight, especially in foreign policy, finance, and religion. Under the Empire membership of the Senate became largely hereditary and its chief function was to ratify imperial decisions. *See also* curia.

Senate of the United States Upper chamber of the Congress. Its 100 members consist of two senators from each state who are elected by popular vote and serve six-year terms, staggered so that about one-third of the Senate is elected every two years. A candidate for the Senate must be at least 30 years old, a US citizen for nine years, and a resident of the state represented. The US vice president is president of the Senate; the *president pro tempore is chosen by his colleagues and presides in the absence of the Senate president. The majority leader, elected by majority party members and assisted by the majority whip, directs and coordinates the daily routine of the Senate. Besides approving Congressional acts, the Senate is empowered to ratify treaties (by a two-thirds vote) and to approve or reject appointments made by the US president. It also hears impeachment trials, which are initiated by the *House of Representatives.

Sendai 38 16N 140 52E A city in Japan, in NE Honshu. It is the largest city of N Japan and an important commercial center. Tohoku University was established there in 1907. Population (1991): 930,520.

Seneca North American Iroquoian-speaking Indian tribe, part of the *Five Nations, found in central New York. Hunters, traders, and warriors, the men generally left the agricultural activities to the women. They sided with the British during the American Revolution. Descendants of the Seneca live in New York and Ontario, Canada.

Seneca Falls Convention (1848) US woman suffrage meeting at Seneca Falls, N.Y. Led by Elizabeth Cady *Stanton and Lucretia Coffin *Mott, women began their movement for equal rights. Their Declaration of Sentiments, consisting of 11 resolutions, included the adoption of women's voting rights.

Seneca the Elder (Marcus Annaeus Seneca; c. 55 BC–c. 41 AD) Roman rhetorician, born at Córdoba (Spain). Parts of his work on oratory, addressed to his sons, have survived: the *Suasoriae* (a compendium of styles and themes of earlier rhetoricians) and the *Controversiae* (imaginary court cases). One of his sons, **Seneca the Younger** (Lucius Annaeus Seneca; c. 4 BC–65 AD), was an author and politician. His career at court, interrupted by exile (41–49 AD), culminated in his appointment as tutor and later chief minister to *Nero. Retiring in 64 AD as a millionaire, he was accused of treason and forced to commit suicide. Thirteen philosophical treatises and numerous essays disguised as letters advocate *Stoicism in a highly rhetorical style. His nine tragedies, which influenced the Elizabethan dramatists, also survive.

Seneca Lake A long, narrow lake in W central New York, one of the Finger Lakes. It is connected to the New York State Barge Canal system by the Seneca River on the N. Area: 67 sq mi (174 sq km).

Senegal, Republic of A country in West Africa, on the Atlantic Ocean. The Senegal River forms its N boundary and the Gambia River flows E–W through the country to the border of The Gambia, which forms an enclave within Senegalese territory. Senegal consists chiefly of level plains rising to a dissected plateau in the SE. The majority of the population are Wolof, Sere, and Tukolor. *Economy*: chiefly agricultural, the production of groundnuts being dominant. Other crops include millet, rice, and corn; livestock is important and fishing is being developed with foreign aid. Phosphates, iron ore, and offshore oil and natural gas have been found in significant quantities. Hydroelectricity is a valuable source of power. Industry, mainly concentrated on Dakar, includes cement, food processing, and textiles; tourism is expanding. The main exports are phosphates, groundnuts, and preserved fish. *History*: in the 14th and 15th centuries the area was part of the Mali empire. St Louis was founded in 1659 by the French, who extended their control in the mid-19th century over most of the region. The country achieved self-government in 1958 as a member of the French Community and in 1959–60 briefly formed the Federation of Mali with Sudan. Senegal became a separate independent republic in 1960, with Léopold Senghor as its first president. In 1966 all parties except the Senegalese Progressive Union (UPS) were made illegal but in 1976 the existence of up to three parties was permitted. In 1982 it formed the Senegambia Confederation with Gambia, with each country retaining its independence but having joint defense, foreign, and monetary policies. The confederation was dissolved in 1989. A state of emergency was declared in 1988 when Diouf's reelection triggered rioting by opposition party followers. In 1989, an incident on the Senegal-Mauritania border precipitated violence against Senegalese living in Mauritania and Mauritanians living in Senegal. Violence erupted between government forces and separatist movement forces in the Casamance region from 1991. Despite these problems, Diouf was reelected for a third term in 1993. President: Abdou Diouf. Official language: French. Official currency: CFA (Communauté financière africaine) franc of 100 centimes. Area: 76,320 sq mi (197,722 sq km). Population (1990): 7,740,000. Capital and main port: Dakar.

Senegal River A river in West Africa. Rising in the Fouta Djallon highlands in N Guinea, it flows mainly NW to the Atlantic Ocean forming part of the Mauritania-Senegal border. Length: 1050 mi (1690 km).

Senghor, Léopold Sédar (1906–) Senegalese statesman; president (1960–80). Educated in France, he was Senegalese deputy to the French National Assembly (1946–58). He formed the Senegalese Progressive Union, which took Senegal to independence in 1960. He is also a poet, the author of *Chants d'ombres* (1945), *Ethiopiques* (1956), and *Nocturnes* (1961).

senna. *See* Cassia.

Sennacherib (d. 681 BC) King of Assyria (704–681): the son and successor of *Sargon II. After 16 years of leniency toward the constantly rebellious Babylonians he sacked the city of Babylon in 689. He also crushed an Egyptian-inspired revolt of Palestine led by *Hezekiah. A patron of art and learning, he restored *Nineveh. Murdered by one of his sons, probably incited by Babylonian rebels, he was succeeded by *Esarhaddon.

Sennar 13 31N 33 38E A town in the SE Sudan, on the Blue Nile River. It is the site of the Makwar Dam (completed 1925), a part of the *Gezira irrigation system. Population: 10,000.

Sennett, Mack (Michael Sinott; 1884–1960) US film producer and director, born in Canada. In 1912 he joined the Keystone Company, for which he produced numerous short slapstick films featuring the *Keystone Kops and such comic actors as Charlie Chaplin and Harold Lloyd.

Sens 48 12N 3 18E A city in central France, in the Yonne department of the Yonne River. The site of one of the earliest gothic cathedrals in France, its manufactures include agricultural implements, leather products, and chemicals. Population (1982): 27,000.

sensitive plants. *See* Mimosa.

sentimental novel A type of fiction popular in 18th-century England and France in which scenes of emotional distress were intended to arouse the reader's pity and compassion. Examples include *Manon Lescaut* (1731) by the Abbé *Prévost and *Pamela* (1740) by Samuel *Richardson.

Seoul 37 30N 127 00E The capital of the Republic of (South) Korea, in the NW on the Han River near the coast. The capital of Korea since 1394, the city served as the center of Japanese-occupied Korea (1910–45). It suffered considerable damage in the Korean War (1950–53). It is a rapidly developing industrial as well as administrative and commercial center. Its 16 universities include the Seoul National University (1946). Seoul hosted the 1988 Summer Olympic games. Population (1990): 10,627,790.

sepak takraw A three-a-side ball game similar to *badminton and *volleyball, played in SE Asia. The ball may be played with the feet and other parts of the body but not the hands.

separation of powers The division of governmental powers between legislature, executive, and judiciary. Such separation is most clearly seen in the US *Constitution, in which separation of powers was seen as the best way to safeguard liberty. These institutions are the Congress (legislature), presidency (executive), and Supreme Court (judiciary). One branch is not permitted to encroach on the domain of another.

Sephardim (Hebrew *Sepharad*: Spain) Jews who went to Spain and Portugal in the *diaspora. When the Jews were expelled from Spain in 1492 they spread to many parts of the world, preserving their customs and their language, *Ladino. The term is now sometimes applied, especially in Israel, to all non-*Ashkenazim.

September Ninth month of the year. Derived from the Latin word *septus*, which means seven, it was the seventh month of the ancient Roman calendar. It has 30 days. The zodiac signs for September are Virgo and Libra; the flowers are morning glory and aster, and the birthstone is the sapphire. In the US, Labor Day is celebrated on the first Monday of the month.

septicemia. *See* blood poisoning.

septic tank A large tank of steel or concrete sunk in the ground to provide *sewage disposal for isolated buildings or small communities. Effluent flows into the tank, the settled sludge being decomposed to a certain extent by bacterial action.

Septuagint (Latin: seventy) A Greek translation of the *Old Testament and *Apocrypha made for the use of Greek-speaking Jews in Egypt and improved and completed in stages between the 3rd century BC and the 1st century AD. It derives its name and symbol (LXX) from the legend that 72 Jewish scholars completed the work in 72 days. Many Old Testament quotations in the New Testament are taken from it.

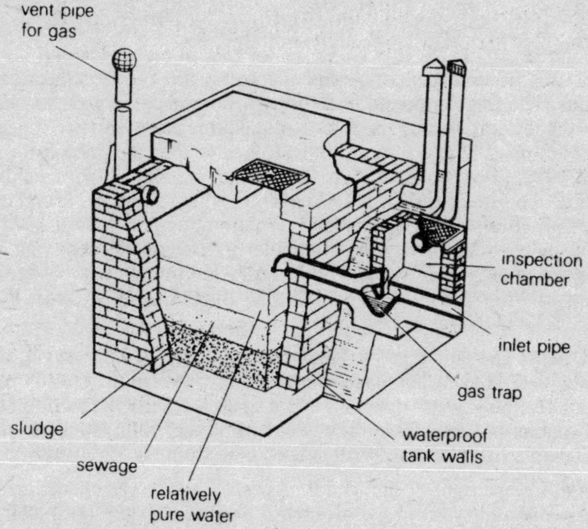

SEPTIC TANK *The sewage enters low in the tank without disturbing the contents. Purer water separates at the top and sludge forms at the bottom.*

sequence An ordered set of numbers, generally denoted by $a_1, a_2, \ldots a_r, \ldots,$ in which the *r*th term a_r can be expressed as a function of *r*. *See also* series.

sequoia Either of two Californian coniferous trees, the *redwood (*Sequoia sempervirens*), which is the world's tallest tree, or the giant sequoia, *Sequoiadendron giganteum* (formerly *Sequoia gigantea*). The giant sequoia forms natural forests in California's Sierra Nevada, where some trees are over 3000 years old, with a height of over 262 ft (80 m) and a girth of over 79 ft (24 m). In Europe it is grown as an ornamental. The red-brown bark is soft and fibrous and the shoots are densely covered with pointed scalelike leaves. The woody brown egg-shaped cones are 2–3.1 in (5–8 cm) long. Family: *Taxodiaceae*.

Sequoia National Park A national park in central California, SE of Fresno. In the Sierra Nevada, the park includes Mt Whitney (14,494 ft; 4418 m), the highest mountain in the contiguous United States. Established in 1890, the park protects the giant sequoia trees that grow on the slopes of the mountains. Area: 386,863 acres (156,563 hectares).

seraphim. *See* cherubim and seraphim.

Serapis A god combining Greek and Egyptian elements, introduced into Egypt by *Ptolemy I in order to unite the worship of the two peoples. He was the lord of the universe and was identical with *Osiris, with characteristics borrowed from *Zeus and *Asclepius. The center of his cult was Alexandria.

Serbia (Serbo-Croat name: Srbija) A constituent republic of Yugoslavia, incorporating the autonomous regions of Vojvodina and Kos ovo. It is chiefly mountainous, descending in the N to the basin of the Danube River. Agriculture is of major importance, especially stock raising and the growing of wheat, maize, and vines. It possesses important mineral deposits including copper (at Bor), antimony, coal, and chrome. *History*: first settled by the Serbs in the 7th century AD, it later came under Turkish control (1389–1804), finally regaining its independence in 1878. It played a major role in events leading up to World War I: in 1914 Austria accused Serbia of direct involvement in the assassination of Archduke Francis Ferdinand and subsequently declared war. Serbia suffered badly during the war, losing about 23% of the population. In 1918 it became part of the kingdom of Serbs, Croats, and Slovenes, later renamed Yugoslavia. In 1991 and 1992, after Slovenia, Croatia, Bosnia and Hercegovina, and Macedonia declared their independence, Serbia, along with Vojvodina, Montenegro, and Kosovo, formed a smaller Yugoslavia. Fighting continued from 1992 between the newly independent countries, particularly *Bosnia-Hercegovina, and their large Serbian populations (backed by Yugoslavian troops) who favored remaining a part of Yugoslavia. Area: 49,528 sq mi (128,278 sq km). Population (1991): 5,753,825. Capital: Belgrade.

Serbo-Croat The language of the Serbs and Croats of Yugoslavia, where it is the most widely spoken language. Serbian and Croatian differ only marginally in terms of vocabulary and not at all in grammar but Serbian is written in *Cyrillic and Croatian in Latin script. The standard literary form is based on a central dialect known as Shtokavian. Written texts date from the 12th century.

serf An unfree peasant of the Middle Ages. Serfdom was characteristic of the manorial economic system (*see* manor). A serf was bound to the soil he tilled, paying his lord a fee and providing service in return for the use of his land. Serfs had their own homes, plots, and livestock and enjoyed customary rights that distinguished them from slaves (*see* slavery). While serfdom declined in W Europe in the late Middle Ages, it was strengthened in E Europe, where it was only abolished in the 19th century.

Sergius of Radonezh, St (1314–92) Russian monk, who founded the monastery of the Holy Trinity (now called Zagorsk) in the forest of Radonezh near Moscow. It became a famous spiritual and missionary center, helping to reestablish monasticism after the disruption caused by the invading Tatars. Feast day: Sept 25.

serialism (*or* twelve-tone music) A method of composing music using all 12 notes of the chromatic scale equally, invented by Arnold Schoenberg in the 1920s. Schoenberg sought an alternative to *chromaticism and *atonality by using a fixed sequence of 12 notes (called a **series** or tone row) as a source of melody and harmony. The series could be transposed so as to begin on any degree of the scale and could also be inverted and used in a retrograde form. In strict serialism no single note of the row could be repeated until the other 11 had occurred in melody or harmony; Schoenberg himself did not always follow this rule.

In place of traditional *harmony he developed chords built on fourths. Schoenberg's pupils (Webern, Berg, and others) adopted serialism, although sometimes in a modified form.

In **total serialism** musical elements, such as rhythmical figurations, degrees of volume, and types of tone color are classified in strict serial form. Such composers as Berio and Boulez have used this technique.

seriema A bird belonging to a family (*Cariamidae*; 2 species) occurring in dry grassland regions of South America. The crested seriema (*Cariama cristata*) is 24 in (60 cm) tall and has a brown plumage with pale underparts and a red bill and legs. Seriemas feed on insects, snails, reptiles, and berries. Order: *Gruiformes* (cranes, rails, etc.).

series The sum of the terms in a *sequence written as $a_1 + a_2 + a_3 + \ldots a_r + \ldots$. The partial sum to the *n*th term is denoted by S_n. A series is convergent if S_n approaches a particular value as n increases and divergent if it increases without limit. A geometric series has the general form $a + an + an^2 + \ldots$, where a and n are constant. It is convergent if n is less than one, divergent if n is greater than or equal to one. A power series has the general form $a_0 + a_1x + a_2x^2 + a_3x^3 + \ldots$, where x is a *variable. *See also* arithmetic progression.

serin The smallest European *finch, *Serinus serinus*, closely related to the canary and having a sweet trilling song. Serins have a streaked olive-colored plumage with a bright-yellow rump and, in the male, a yellow head and breast. Although a southern species, its range extends to N Europe.

serotine bat An insect-eating *bat, *Eptesicus serotinus*, of Eurasia. It is about 5 in (12 cm) long including the tail and has a 14 in (35 cm) wingspan. Dark brown in color, it flies at early dusk and dawn. Family: *Vespertilionidae*.

serotonin (*or* 5-hydroxytryptamine) A compound, synthesized from the amino acid tryptophan, that occurs in certain nerve endings of the *hypothalamus (in the brain) and the autonomic nervous system. It is involved in the regulation of emotion; such drugs as LSD affect mood and behavior by altering serotonin levels in the brain.

serow A hoofed mammal, *Capricornis sumatraensis*, inhabiting wooded mountainous regions of S Asia. About 35 in (90 cm) high at the shoulder, serows have short wrinkled horns and a coarse black or reddish-gray coat with white patches on the face and legs. Serows and *gorals are sometimes called goat antelopes. Family: **Bovidae*.

serpentine A group of minerals consisting mainly of hydrous magnesium silicates, with a layered structure. They are usually green or white, and often streaked or mottled like a snake's skin. The two main varieties are chrysotile (fibrous, used in the manufacture of asbestos) and antigorite (platy). They occur in basic and ultrabasic igneous rocks from the breakdown of olivines and pyroxenes. **Serpentinite** is a rock consisting mainly of serpentine, formed by the hydrothermal alteration of ultramafic rocks; some are quarried for ornamental stone.

serpulid A small marine *annelid worm belonging to the family *Serpulidae*. Serpulids build limy tubes on stones and seaweed and extend a crown of tentacles to feed in the same way as the related *fanworms. Class: *Polychaeta*.

serum The fluid that remains after blood has been allowed to clot. It can be obtained by centrifuging clotted blood and is similar in composition to plasma, except that it lacks the factors, such as fibrinogen, that are involved in blood clotting.

serum sickness Illness resulting from an allergic reaction to injected serum or antiserum. It is seen most commonly following the injection of horse tetanus antitoxin; 6 to 12 days after the injection the patient develops fever, a rash, and painful joints. Treatment is with steroids.

serval A slender long-legged *cat, *Felis serval*, of the African bush. It is about 4 ft (1.25 m) long including the tail (1 ft; 30 cm) and has large ears and a spotted coat. Servals hunt birds and small mammals, such as hares and duikers, mainly at night.

Servetus, Michael (Spanish name: Miguel Serveto; 1511–53) Spanish theologian and physician, who discovered that the blood circulates to the lungs from the right chamber of the heart. Working chiefly in France, he published several treatises attacking the orthodox doctrine of the Trinity. These incurred the hostility of both Roman Catholics and Protestants and, while hiding from the Inquisition in Geneva, he was arrested by Calvin and burned as a heretic.

Service, Robert William (1874–1958) Canadian writer and poet; born in England. He emigrated to Canada in 1894 and then traveled in W Canada and the US. During World War I he worked as a correspondent and ambulance driver and was in the Canadian Army. After the war he lived in France, returning to Canada only during World War II. His poetry is collected in *Songs of a Sourdough* (also known as *The Spell of the Yukon*; 1907), *Rhymes of a Rolling Stone* (1912), and *Ballads of a Red Cross Man* (1917). His novels include *The Roughneck* (1923) and *The House of Fear* (1927). His two most popular poems are "The Shooting of Dan McGrew" and "Cremation of Sam McGee."

service tree A tree, *Sorbus domestica*, about 5 ft (15 m) high, native to S Europe, W Asia, and N Africa and commonly grown for ornament. Related to the *mountain ash, it has compound leaves of 11–21 leaflets and its small green fruits are used for making wine. The wild service tree (*S. torminalis*) has simple lobed leaves, while the bastard service tree is an ornamental hybrid between the mountain ash and the *whitebeam. Family: *Rosaceae*.

sesame An annual herb, *Sesamum indicum*, cultivated in Central and South America, the Middle East, and SE Asia. Several varieties are known, growing 20–98 in (50–250 cm) high and bearing small purplish flowers. The seeds are used in confectionery and as food flavoring. Oil extracted from the seeds is used as a cooking and salid oil and in margarines and other products; the residue (sesame cake) is used as cattle feed. Family: *Pedaliaceae*.

Sesostris I King of Egypt (c. 1971–1928 BC) of the 12th dynasty. He extended Egyptian rule into Nubia, exploiting its mineral resources. His ambitious building projects include a magnificent funerary complex at Lisht.

Sesostris II King of Egypt (c. 1897–1878 BC) of the 12th dynasty. He began the land-reclamation works in El *Faiyum continued by *Amenemhet III. Excavations at the town he founded, al-Lahun, have produced much valuable evidence about this period.

Sesostris III King of Egypt (1878–1843 BC) of the 12th dynasty. The sudden cessation of the construction of the nobles' extravagant tombs and an evident rise in middle-class prosperity indicate great changes in Egyptian society during his reign. Sesostris extended his control of Nubia as far south as Wadi Halfa.

Sesshu (Sesshu Toyo: 1420–1506) Japanese landscape painter. After a visit to China (c. 1467) he introduced to Japan the Chinese techniques of monochrome ink painting on long scrolls.

Sessions, Roger (1896–1985) US composer. A pupil of Ernest Bloch, he has held several teaching posts in the US. From 1925 to 1933 he lived mainly in Germany and Italy. His works include two operas, *The Trial of Lucullus* (1947) and *Montezuma* (1962), eight symphonies, a violin concerto, a piano concerto, and chamber music, including *When the Lilacs Last in the Dooryard Bloom'd*.

Set An Egyptian deity. Originally a sun and sky god, he was the murderer of his brother *Osiris and so came to represent all evil. He was killed by *Horus, son of Osiris. He is usually portrayed as a composite figure with various animal features.

Sète (former name: Cette) 43 25N 3 43E A major port in S France, in the Hérault department on the Gulf of Lions. Established in 1666, it developed as the terminus of the Canal du Midi and today has ship building, oil-refining, metallurgical, and fishing industries. It is the birthplace of Paul Valéry. Population (1975): 40,179.

Seton, (Saint) Elizabeth Ann (1774–1821) US religious leader and teacher. A convert to Roman Catholicism (1805) after the death of her husband, she founded a Roman Catholic girls' school in Baltimore, Md., in 1809 and is credited with starting the US parochial school system. With a group of women from the school, she organized the Sisters of Charity (1812), the first American order of nuns, whose activities were mainly teaching and performing charitable works. She was canonized in 1975.

Seto-Naikai. *See* Inland Sea.

Seton, Ernest Thompson (1860–1940) US naturalist and writer, born in England. His experiences as a hunter in Canada were the foundation for his many books about animals, notably *Wild Animals I Have Known* (1898). He was actively concerned with conservation and was a founder of the Boy Scouts of America.

setter One of three breeds of sporting □dog with a lean deep-chested body and drooping ears. Setters are named for their habit of squatting flat ("setting") after finding game. The English setter has a long white silky coat flecked with darker markings. The heavier Gordon setter is black with chestnut markings, while the Irish, or red, setter has a flat silky chestnut coat. Height: 24–27 in (61–69 cm).

set theory The study, founded by Georg *Cantor, of the logical and mathematical laws of sets. A set is a defined collection of objects or elements; for example the set of odd integers between 0 and 10 is $\{1, 3, 5, 7, 9\}$. The empty or null set, denoted by the symbol *0*, has no elements. All sets are contained in the universal set E. The relationships between sets can be illustrated in a Venn diagram, named for the British logician John Venn (1834–1923), or shown by symbols. $a \in A$ means the element a is a member of the set A. $A \subset B$ means set A is contained in set B. $A \cup B$ means the union of A and B. $A \cap B$ means the intersection of A and B, i.e. those elements in both. A^c or A' is the complement of A, all elements in E but not in A.

Settlement, Act of (1701) The act that established the Hanoverian succession to the English throne. In the absence of heirs to William III or Anne, the crown was to pass to James I's granddaughter *Sophia, Electress of Hanover, or to her Protestant descendants. The act stipulated that the monarch must be a Protestant and that foreigners must not hold public office or enter Parliament. Anne was succeeded by the first Hanoverian king, George I, in 1714.

Setúbal 38 31N 8 54W A port in SW Portugal, on the Bay of Setúbal. It is an important center for sardine fishing with associated fish-curing industries. Exports include oranges and muscatel wine and grapes. Population (1981): 77,885.

Seurat, Georges (1859–91) French painter, famous for developing neo-impressionism, popularly called *pointillism. Influenced by writings on aesthetics and the color theories of *Delacroix and the chemist Michel-Eugène Chevreul (1786–1889), he based his dots of pure color and static compositions on scientific study. Although he finished only seven paintings in this demanding style, for example the famous *Sunday Afternoon on the Island of the Grande Jatte* (1884–86; Art Institute of Chicago) and *Le Cirque* (1890–91; Louvre), his work was very influential, one disciple being Paul *Signac.

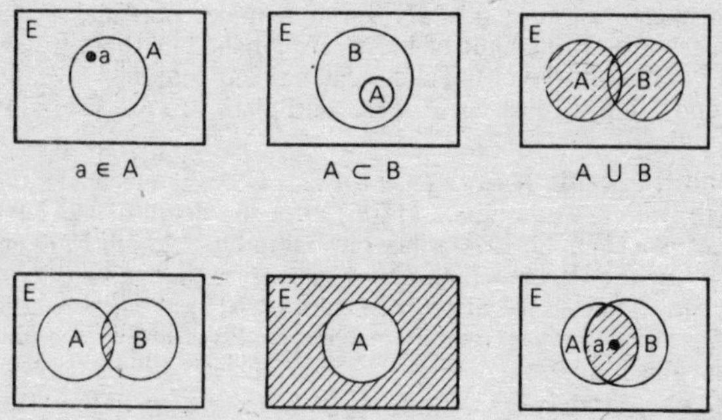

SET THEORY *Venn diagrams.*

Sevastopol (English name: Sebastopol) 44 36N 33 31E A port in the S Ukraine, on the Black Sea. It is a popular seaside resort. *History*: founded in 1783, after Russia's annexation of the Crimea it became an important naval base and, later, a commercial port. It was besieged by the British and French during the Crimean War, falling after 11 months. Population (1991 est): 366,000.

Seven against Thebes In Greek legend, seven champions who fought against Eteocles, who had gained the throne of Thebes after the death of his father Oedipus and refused to relinquish it to his brother *Polyneices when his term as ruler had ended. The seven champions, led by Polyneices, attacked the seven gates of Thebes. Eteocles and Polyneices died at each other's hand. The story is the subject of a play by *Aeschylus. *See also* Antigone.

Seven Deadly Sins Pride, covetousness, lust, envy, gluttony, anger, and sloth. The traditional Christian list was already established by the 6th century and during the Middle Ages representations of the Seven Deadly Sins were a common feature of art and literature.

Seven Sleepers of Ephesus A legend of seven Christian soldiers who were entombed in a cave while hiding to escape religious persecution under the Emperor Decius in the 3rd century. They slept until the reign of Theodosius II (408–50), who, on hearing their miraculous experience, was converted to belief in the resurrection.

seventeenth parallel The latitude of 17°N and the line of demarcation between North and South Vietnam established by the *Geneva Conference (1954).

Seventh Day Adventists. *See* Adventists.

Seven Weeks' War. *See* Austro-Prussian War.

Seven Wonders of the World The supreme man-made structures of the ancient world. They were the *Pyramids of Egypt, the *Colossus of Rhodes, the *Hanging Gardens of Babylon, the *Mausoleum of Halicarnassus, the statue of *Zeus at Olympia, the temple of *Artemis at Ephesus, and the *Pharos of Alexandria. Only the Pyramids have survived.

Seven Years' War (1756–63) The war between Prussia, Britain, and Hanover on one side and France, Austria, Russia, and Spain on the other. The war had two main aspects: the rivalry between Austria and Prussia for domination of Germany and the struggle between France and Britain for overseas supremacy. The conflict in North America, known as the *French and Indian War, effectively ended French influence. The war was precipitated by Austria's desire to regain Silesia, lost to Frederick the Great of Prussia in the War of the *Austrian Succession, and began with Frederick's invasion of Saxony. Russia's defection (1762) to Prussia enabled Frederick ultimately to emerge victorious and Prussian ascendancy was confirmed by the Peace of Hubertusberg. Overseas, the British despite initial reverses won a series of spectacular victories in India (by *Clive) and Canada (by *Wolfe). By the Treaty of *Paris (1763) Britain was confirmed as the supreme world power.

Severini, Gino (1883–1966) Italian painter, born in Cortona. After training under *Balla, he moved to Paris (1906), where he became a pointillist. In 1910 he signed the futurist manifesto and thereafter his work combined *futurism and *cubism, especially in his nightclub scenes and his few military subjects. He later returned to painting more conventional landscapes and figure studies.

Severn River (Welsh name: Hafren) The longest river in the UK, rising in central Wales and flowing NE and E into England, then S to the Bristol Channel. It is linked by canal to the Thames and Trent Rivers and is spanned near its estuary by the **Severn Bridge**. Length: 220 mi (354 km).

Severus, Lucius Septimius (c. 145–211 AD) Roman emperor (193–211). Severus was governor of Upper Pannonia (S of the Danube) before being proclaimed emperor. He defeated his rival Pescennius Niger in 194 and embarked on a punitive campaign against Pescennius's supporters. He introduced administrative and military reforms at Rome before embarking on a campaign in Britain, where he died.

Severus Alexander (?208–35 AD) Roman emperor (222–35); the adopted son of his predecessor Elagabalus. Severus's mother, Julia Mamaea, murdered Elagabalus to secure Severus's accession. Severus's rule depended upon the army, which construed his attempt to prevent warfare on the German frontier as cowardice, and murdered him and his mother.

Sevier, John (1745–1815) US pioneer and soldier; first governor of Tennessee (1796–1801; 1803–09). He fought in *Lord Dunmore's War and in the *American Revolution where he distinguished himself at the battle of King's Mountain (1780) in Tennessee. He was part of an unsuccessful plan by settlers to establish the separate state of Franklin in 1784. A member of the US House of Representatives from North Carolina (1789–91), he was elected governor of the new state of Tennessee in 1796 and later served again in the US House of Representatives (1811–15).

Sévigné, Marie de Rabutin-Chantal, Marquise de (1626–96) French letter writer. In over 1500 letters, mostly written to her two children after the death of her husband in 1651, she described the social pleasures and intellectual diversions of Parisian society—and life at her country house in Brittany—in a style that became a model for letter writing throughout Europe.

Seville (Spanish name: Sevilla) 37 24N 5 59W A city and port in SW Spain, in Andalusia on the Guadalquivir River. Important during Roman times, it also thrived under the Moors (711–1248) as a cultural center and became a major port with a monopoly of trade with the West Indies in the 16th century. The painters Velázquez and Murillo were born there. There is a university (founded 1502) and one of the world's largest cathedrals (1401–1591). The Easter festival with its procession of floats bearing religious subjects is a notable event. It is an important industrial center, with textiles and engineering; exports include wine, fruit, and olive oil. Population (1991): 659,126.

Sèvres porcelain The finest French porcelain, first produced in 1738. Originally at Vincennes, the Sèvres factory moved to near *Versailles in 1756. It always enjoyed royal patronage and by 1759 Louis XV was proprietor. The early products were soft-paste porcelain but from 1768 hard-paste was made. Products were figures, vases, ornaments, and table services with blue, rose Pompadour, yellow, or green grounds richly gilded for royal taste. Now the national porcelain factory, it continues its fine output.

sewage disposal The collection, treatment, and eventual discharge of domestic sewage and industrial waste. Sewers, systems of underground piping, channel the effluent to a sewage-treatment plant. There it is screened to remove solid objects before passing to a primary sedimentation tank, where suspended solids settle out. The liquid then passes through aeration tanks, where the oxygen content is increased by blowing air through it, and a final sedimentation tank before being discharged into rivers, etc. The solids meanwhile enter a sludge digester, a tank in which bacterial action partially eats away the organic material. Following thickening and drying the solid residue is incinerated, spread on the land, or sold as fertilizer. In some coastal areas raw sewage is pumped into the sea untreated.

Seward, William H(enry) (1801–72) US statesman; secretary of state (1861–69). He was governor of New York (1838–41) and a member of the US Senate from 1848, until chosen by Pres. Abraham *Lincoln to be his secretary of state, continuing through Andrew *Johnson's administration. He was an efficient administrator and helped to prevent European support of the Confederacy during the Civil War and to implement *Reconstruction. In 1867 he purchased Alaska from Russia; although ridiculed at the time, he was later vindicated. *See also* Alaska Purchase.

Sewell, Anna (1820–78) British children's writer. A childhood accident left her partially handicapped for life. Her only book, *Black Beauty* (1877), is a protest against the cruel treatment of horses, told from the horse's point of view.

sewing machine A device for sewing together pieces of cloth or other materials. The familiar lockstitch machine was invented in the US by Elias *Howe and patented by Isaac Merrit Singer in 1851. In this machine, a needle with a thread passing through its eye penetrates the cloth from above, a loop being formed below the cloth either by passing a separate thread from a bobbin through the loop or by a rotary hook carrying the loop around a stationary bobbin. A toothed platform moves the material forward in preparation for the next stitch. Sewing machines are powered by hand, treadle, or electric motor and modern machines have facilities for hemming, buttonholing, etc.

sex chromosome A *chromosome that carries the genes for determining the sex of an individual. In humans there are two types of sex chromosomes, called X and Y. The body cells of normal males possess one X and one Y chromosome while those of normal females have two X chromosomes. Human sperm is therefore either "male" or "female" depending on whether it carries an X or a Y chromosome. The sex of the embryo is determined by which type of sperm fertilizes the female egg (which always carries an X chromosome). Abnormal numbers of sex chromosomes cause a range of disabilities, including physical abnormalities, mental retardation, and sterility.

sex hormones Hormones that regulate the growth, development, and functioning of the reproductive organs and determine external sexual characteristics. The major female sex hormones are the *estrogens, *progesterone, and *prolactin while the *androgens are the principal male ones. Their production is regulated by *gonadotrophins from the pituitary gland.

sextant An instrument used primarily in navigation for determining latitudes by measuring the angle subtended by some celestial body to the horizon. Thomas Godfrey of Philadelphia and John Hadley of London, working independently, discovered the sextant's principle in 1730. The graduated metal strip, shaped in an arc of the sixth part of a circle, gave the instrument its name. In use the movable index arm is slid along the scale until the image of the reference star as viewed in the half-silvered index mirror is aligned with the horizon. The reading on the scale then indicates the angle subtended.

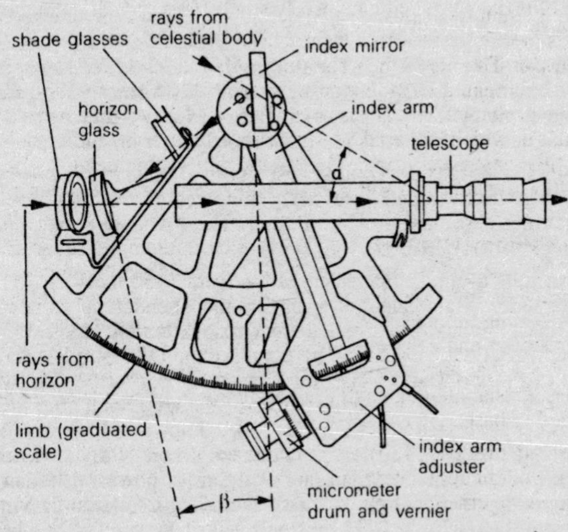

SEXTANT *Angle α measures the angle between horizon and reference arm; β is the angle between index mirror and horizon glass, marked by the angular movement of the index arm along the limb. α = 2β, therefore the graduations on the scale are marked twice the actual angular movement to give the correct altitude reading of the reference star.*

Seychelles, Republic of A country consisting of 87 widely scattered islands in the W Indian Ocean, NE of Madagascar. The main island is Mahé and others include Praslin, Silhouette, and La Digue; the islands of Aldabra, Farquhar, and Desroches were returned to the Seychelles in 1976. Most of the population is of mixed African and European descent. *Economy*: the chief products and exports are copra and cinnamon bark. Other occupations include fishing and some industry, including tobacco and brewing. Tourism is important and has expanded rapidly since the opening of a new airport (1971). *History*: the uninhabited islands became a French colony in the mid-18th century as a spice plantation. Captured by the British in 1794, they became a dependency of Mauritius from 1814 until 1903, when they became a British crown colony. In 1976 the country became an independent republic within the Commonwealth of Nations, with James Mancham as its first president. While attending the Commonwealth conference in London in 1977, he was overthrown and superseded as president by his prime minister, Albert René. An invasion by mercenaries in 1981, in which South Africa was implicated, attempted to overthrow the government. It was the third attempt by forces from outside the country to seize power. Through the 1980s there were several other coup attempts. In the early 1990s, environmental concerns caused the government to limit tourism, the mainstay of the economy. Official languages: English and French; the majority speak Creole. Official currency: Seychelles rupee of 100 cents. Area: 171 sq mi (444 sq km). Population (1990): 71,000. Capital and main port: Victoria.

Seyfert galaxy A class of galaxies with exceptionally bright central regions, the majority of which are otherwise normal spiral galaxies. Radiation is emitted from the center at radio, infrared, visible, and, especially, X-ray wavelengths, the source of this energy being relatively small. This type of galaxy was first described by the US astronomer C. K. Seyfert (1911–60).

Seymour, Jane (c. 1509–37) The third wife (1536–37) of Henry VIII of England. She had been a lady-in-waiting to both his former wives, Catherine of Aragon and Anne Boleyn, and married Henry 11 days after Anne's execution. Jane was the mother of Edward VI, dying shortly after his birth.

Sfax 34 45N 10 43E The second largest city in Tunisia and a major port on the Gulf of Gabes. It developed as an early trade center and still fulfills that role today, exporting phosphates, olive oil, cotton and woolen goods, and sponges. Population (1989 est): 222,000.

Sforza An Italian family that ruled Milan from 1450 to 1499, 1512 to 1515, and 1522 to 1535. Originating in Romagna as the Attendoli, its name was changed to Sforza (Italian: force) by the condottiere **Muzio Attendoli** (1369–1424). His son **Francesco Sforza** obtained Milan by his marriage (1441) to Bianca Maria, the only child of Filippo Maria *Visconti. Francesco was succeeded by **Galeazzo Maria Sforza** (1444–76), a notable patron of the arts. Soon after his assassination his brother **Lodovico Sforza** (1452–1508), known as Lodovico il Moro (the Moor), seized power (1480) from Galeazzo's son **Gian Galeazzo Sforza** (1469–94). Lodovico made Milan one of the most powerful Italian states and was also an outstanding patron of artists, including Leonardo da Vinci. He was expelled from the duchy in 1499 by Louis XII of France. After a brief restoration (1512–15), the Sforza were again ousted by the French but in 1522 Lodovico's son **Francesco Maria Sforza** (1495–1535) was reestablished by Emperor Charles V. With the failure of the line at Francesco's death, Milan passed to Charles.

's Gravenhage. *See* Hague, The.

Shaba (former name: Katanga) A province in SE Zaïre, bordering on Zambia. Economically and politically the most advanced of the provinces, it was directly involved in the civil war in Zaïre following decolonization by Belgium in 1960 (*see also* Zaïre). It is an extremely important mining area (especially for copper) centered on Kolwezi. Other minerals include cobalt and zinc. Area: 191,878 sq mi (496,964 sq km). Population (1991 est): 5,207,000. Capital: Lubumbashi.

Shache (So-ch'e *or* Yarkand) 38 27N 77 16E A city in NW China, in Xinjiang Uygur AR on a fertile oasis in the *Tarim Basin. It is an agricultural and trading center on the *Silk Road to Europe. Many handicrafts are produced.

Shackleton, Sir Ernest Henry (1874–1922) British explorer. He accompanied *Scott's expedition of 1901–04 and on his own expedition in 1908–09 nearly reached the South Pole. In an expedition of 1914–16 his ship, the *Endurance*, was marooned but he and his men reached Elephant Island by sledge and boats. With five others he then journeyed 800 mi (1300 km) to find relief. He died on his fourth expedition.

shad A food fish, belonging to a genus (*Alosa*) related to herrings, that occurs in the Atlantic, Mediterranean, and North Sea. It has one or a succession of black spots along each side and a notch in the upper jaw. They migrate in large shoals to spawn in fresh waters. The American shad (*A. sapidissima*) occurs from Canada to Florida and has been introduced along the Pacific coast. It reaches a length of 30 in (75 cm). The slightly smaller hickory shad (*A. mediocris*) is also found along the Atlantic coast. The allis shad (*A. alosa*), about 30 in (75 cm) long, and the smaller twaite shad (*A. fallax*) are European species.

shaddock An evergreen tree, *Citrus grandis*, also called pomelo, native to SE Asia and cultivated in tropical regions of the Old and New Worlds. Growing 20–43 ft (6–13 m) high, it bears pale-yellow oval fruits, with coarse thick skins and bitter-tasting pulp, which are sometimes eaten or used to make liqueurs. Family: *Rutaceae*. *See also* Citrus.

shadoof An ancient water-raising device still used, especially in Egypt and S India, for irrigation. It consists of a pole mounted on a pivot with a bucket at one end and a counterbalancing weight at the other.

Shadwell, Thomas (c. 1642–92) British dramatist. His varied dramatic works included the comedies *Epsom Wells* (1672) and *The Virtuoso* (1676). He sustained a lengthy political and literary feud with *Dryden, who satirized him in *Absalom and Achitophel* (1681) and *MacFlecknoe* (1682). He succeeded Dryden as poet laureate in 1688.

Shaffer, Peter (1926–) British dramatist. He established his reputation with the domestic drama *Five-Finger Exercise* (1958). His ambitious epic treatment of the Spanish conquest of Peru, *The Royal Hunt of the Sun* (1964), was later filmed and made into an opera. His later plays include *Equus* (1973) and *Amadeus* (1979).

Shaftesbury, Anthony Ashley Cooper, 1st Earl of (1621–83) English statesman. In the 1650s he sat in Oliver Cromwell's parliaments before participating in the Restoration of Charles II (1660). Becoming chancellor of the exchequer (1661–72) and lord chancellor (1672–73), he was a member of the political group called the *Cabal. Dismissed in 1673 he led the movement to exclude the Roman Catholic James, duke of York (later James II), from the succession. Charged with treason in 1681, the case was dismissed but Shaftesbury fled to Amsterdam, where he died. He was satirized as the Achitophel in Dryden's *Absalom and Achitophel* (1681). His grandson **Anthony Ashley Cooper, 3rd Earl of Shaftesbury** (1671–1713) is best known for his collection of essays, *Characteristics of Men, Manners, Opinions, Times* (1711) on a variety of philosophical and other topics.

Anthony Ashley Cooper, 7th Earl of Shaftesbury (1801–85) was a reformer and philanthropist. He became a member of Parliament from 1826 and obtained important reforms in industrial conditions and child labor laws.

shag A small *cormorant, *Phalacrocorax aristotelis*, confined to rocky coasts and offshore islands of Europe and North Africa. It is 30 in (75 cm) long and has a glossy green-black plumage with a distinct crest in the breeding season. It feeds on fish.

Shah Jahan (1592–1666) Emperor of India (1628–58) of the Mogul dynasty; the son of *Jahangir. His powerful reign was as ruthless as his means of attaining it; he put his nearest relatives to death in 1628. His passion for fine architecture produced such monuments as the *Taj Mahal and the Delhi Red Fort. He was deposed by his son *Aurangzeb.

Shahn, Ben (1898–1969) Lithuanian-born US artist, who lived in New York from 1906. He is best known for his social realist and political paintings, notably the series (1931–32) on the Italian anarchists Nicola Sacco and Bartolomeo Vanzetti.

Shah of Iran. *See* Mohammed Reza Pahlavi; Reza Shah Pahlavi.

Shaka (c. 1787–1828) Zulu chief, who made the Zulu nation the strongest in S Africa and set the period of warfare called the *Mfecane in motion. Shaka claimed the Zulu chieftainship in about 1816, introduced military reforms, and ruthlessly expanded his possessions. He was stabbed to death by his half-brothers Dingane and Mhlangana.

Shakers An austere sect originating in England as an offshoot of the *Quakers (1747). Led by Ann Lee (Mother Ann; d. 1784), in whose person they believed the Second Coming of Christ to be accomplished (*see* millenarianism), the Shakers founded a colony in New York and later other communities were established; eventually there were 18 in several states. They flourished until the 20th century. In the 1980s there was disagreement among the few remaining members concerning the disposal of the fortune amassed by the nearly extinct sect. Celibacy, faith healing, common ownership of property, prescribed modes of dress, separation from the world in self-regulating communities, and abstinence from tobacco and alcohol characterized their way of life. Known more formally as the Millennial Church, they received their popular name from their practice of violent trembling in religious ecstasies during their meetings.

Shakespeare, William (1564–1616) English dramatist, universally recognized as the greatest English writer. The son of a tradesman who became high bailiff (mayor) of Stratford-upon-Avon in 1568, he was educated at the local grammar school and in 1582 married a local girl, Anne Hathaway, by whom he had three children. Soon afterward he went to London, where he became an actor in the leading theatrical company, the Lord Chamberlain's Men (called the King's Men after 1603). The historical tetralogy comprising the three parts of *Henry VI* and *Richard III* were his first plays (1589–92). His dramatic poems *Venus and Adonis* (1593) and *The Rape of Lucrece* (1594) were dedicated to his patron Henry Wriothesley, 3rd earl of *Southampton. His *Sonnets* (1609), probably written at this time, betray nothing of his private life despite their themes of love and friendship. His early comedies (1593–95) were *Love's Labour's Lost, The Two Gentlemen of Verona*, and *The Taming of the Shrew*. These were followed (1595–1600) by *A Midsummer Night's Dream, The Merchant of Venice, Much Ado About Nothing, Twelfth Night,* and *As You Like It*. During this period he also wrote his first significant tragedy, *Romeo and Juliet*, as well as *Richard II* and *Julius Caesar*. In 1597 he bought New Place, a large house in Stratford, and later became a shareholder in the Globe Theater in London and bought other property in London and Stratford. The two parts of *Henry IV* were completed before *Hamlet, Othello, King Lear*, and *Macbeth*, his major tragedies, which were written between 1600 and 1606. His final experimental plays, including *The Winter's Tale* (c. 1610) and *The Tempest* (c. 1611), were written for the educated audience of the indoor theater at Blackfriars, which the King's Men had acquired in 1608. In about 1611 he retired to Stratford, where he died. The first collected edition of his works, known as the First Folio and containing 36 plays, was published in 1623. His other plays were: *The Comedy of Errors, Titus Andronicus, Henry V, Antony and Cleopatra, Coriolanus, Troilus and Cressida, Measure for Measure, All's Well That Ends Well, Timon of Athens, Pericles, Cymbeline*, and (in collaboration with John *Fletcher) *Henry VIII* and *The Two Noble Kinsmen.*

WILLIAM SHAKESPEARE *An engraving by Martin Droeshout, perhaps based on a portrait from life, which was printed in early editions of Shakespeare's works.*

Shakhty 47 43N 40 16E A city in S Russia. Situated in the E Donets Basin, it is a major coal-mining center. Population (1991 est): 227,700.

shale A fine-grained *sedimentary rock that splits easily along the closely spaced bedding planes as a result of the alignment of the clay mineral particles parallel to the bedding planes. Shales may disintegrate in water but do not become plastic. They are softer and lighter than *slate.

shallot A hardy perennial herbaceous plant, **Allium ascalonium*, probably of Asiatic origin. Its small hollow cylindrical leaves are often used for dressing food and in salads. Its small angular bulbs occur in garlic-like clusters and are used for flavoring and pickling. Family: *Liliaceae*.

shamanism The religious beliefs and practices common in certain tribal societies of Asia, such as the *Samoyed. The term is also applied to North American Indian practices. The shaman is a tribal priest generally felt to be possessed by a spirit or deity and hence to have supernatural powers. He is liable to trances or ecstasies, may diagnose and cure disease, find lost or stolen goods, or foretell the future. He is usually a source of beneficial (white) magic, able to counteract the effects of evil men or spirits. As the intermediary between man and the spirit world, he may also act as the tribal ruler and judge. The office may be hereditary or there may be a long training period.

Shamir, Yitzhak (1915–) Israeli statesman; prime minister (1983–84; 1986–92); born in Poland. He came to Israel in 1935 and fought for Israeli independence. He was in the secret intelligence service (Mossad) (1955–65) and was first elected to the Knesset in 1973. He became foreign minister in 1980, before succeeding Menahem *Begin as prime minister in 1983. His failure to stabilize Israel's inflationary economy led to an indecisive election in 1984, after which a coalition was formed between his Likud Party and the Labor Party, led by Shimon Peres. Peres agreed to be prime minister until September 1986, when Shamir took over. Reelected in 1989, Shamir and Peres formed a new coalition government in 1990. Shamir left office after his government fell amid charges that Likud was too conciliatory toward the Palestinians.

shamrock Any of several plants bearing leaves with three leaflets, especially various *clovers, black *medick (*Medicago lupulina*), and *wood sorrel (*Oxalis acetosella*). St Patrick is said to have adopted the shamrock as a symbol of the Holy Trinity and it is worn on St Patrick's Day.

Shandong (*or* Shantung) A province in NE China, on the Yellow Sea, with central mountains. Densely populated, its fertile farmland produces chiefly wheat and cotton. From early times it has been an important trading area. Floods and famine in the 19th and 20th centuries have led to much emigration northward. Area: 59,189 sq mi (153,300 sq km). Population (1990): 84,392,827. Capital: Jinan.

Shandong Peninsula (*or* Shantung Peninsula) A hilly peninsula in E China. Together with the *Liaodong Peninsula opposite, it forms the mouth of the Gulf of Chihli.

Shanghai 31 13N 121 25E An administratively autonomous port in E China, on the Yangtze estuary. The largest city in China, it is its chief port and industrial city. Its many educational establishments include two universities. It grew rapidly after it was opened to foreign trade in 1842, coming under British, US, and French rule until World War II. Industries include steel, textiles, chemicals, ship building, engineering, and publishing. Population (1990): 7,496,509.

Shankar, Ravi (1920–) Indian *sitar player, who has toured the US and Europe. He popularized Indian music in the West, influencing the Beatles, performing with Yehudi Menuhin, and inspiring André Previn to write a sitar concerto.

Shannon, River The longest river in the Republic of Ireland. Rising in NW Co Cavan, it flows S to Limerick and then W into an estuary 70 mi (113 km) long, before entering the Atlantic Ocean. It powers Ireland's main hydroelectric plant. Length: 161 mi (260 km).

Shansi. *See* Shanxi.

Shantou (*or* Swatow) 23 23N 116 39E A port in SE China, in Guangdong province on the South China Sea. A village until the 19th century, it has developed greatly since 1949 and its varied industries include food processing and ship building. Population (1990): 578,630.

Shantung. *See* Shandong.

Shantung Peninsula. *See* Shandong Peninsula.

Shanxi (Shan-hsi *or* Shansi) A province in NE China. It is mainly a high hilly plateau, prone to drought, although irrigation and reforestation projects are now under way. It is important for its coal and iron reserves and the industry they supply. Its relatively sparse Chinese population lives chiefly by keeping animals and growing cotton and cereals. It is famous for its traditional opera, metalwork, and pottery. *History*: a buffer zone between the settled Chinese and the nomadic tribes of the N and W in the Middle Ages, it became politically stable in about the 14th century. In the 18th and 19th centuries it was famous for its merchants and bankers. Opposition to foreigners was strong and the *Boxer rebellion broke out there (1900). Its industry was established by the warlord Yan Xi-shan (*or* Yen Hsi-shan; ruled 1911–49). Area: 60,656 sq mi (157,099 sq km). Population (1990): 28,759,014. Capital: Taiyuan.

Shapur II (309–79 AD) King of Persia (309–79) of the Sasanian dynasty; the posthumous son of his father and predecessor. During his long and successful wars to recover lost territory in Armenia and Mesopotamia from Rome, the emperor *Julian was killed and Christians, suspected as followers of Rome's offical religion, were persecuted.

Shari River. *See* Chari River.

shari'ah. *See* Islamic law.

Sharjah. *See* United Arab Emirates.

shark A *cartilaginous fish belonging to the worldwide order *Selachii* (about 250 species). Ranging in size from the smallest *dogfish to the enormous *whale shark, they have a torpedo-shaped body with a muscular tail used in swimming, five to seven pairs of gill slits on the sides of the head, and numerous sharp teeth. They are chiefly marine and carnivorous, feeding on fish and invertebrates but in some cases, plankton, carrion, and other vertebrates. They produce live young or lay eggs. Subclass: *Elasmobranchii.*

Sharon, Plain of A coastal plain in Israel, extending 50 mi (80 km) between Haifa and Tel Aviv-Yafo. It is noted for the production of citrus fruit.

Sharpeville A black African town in South Africa, in the S Transvaal near Vereeniging. It was the scene of a riot on Mar 21, 1960, in which a crowd of African demonstrators were fired on by the police. Over 60 of the demonstrators were killed and many others wounded.

Sharpsburg, Battle of (1862) Name used by the Confederates for the Battle of *Antietam because it was fought at Sharpsburg, Md.

Shastri, Shri Lal Bahadur (1904–66) Indian statesman; prime minister (1964–66). As a young man he was imprisoned by the British while a member of Gandhi's noncooperation movement. He held four ministerial positions before becoming prime minister. His greatest achievement was in negotiating the ceasefire agreement with *Ayub Khan after the India-Pakistan war. He died the following day.

Shatt al-Arab A river in SE Iraq, formed by the confluence of the Tigris and Euphrates rivers. It enters the Persian Gulf via a delta in Kuwait, Iraq, and Iran, passing Basra and Abadan along its course. Length: 118 mi (190 km).

Shaw, Artie (Arthur Arshawsky; 1910–) US jazz clarinetist and band leader, who introduced strings into his swing band in 1935. His version of Cole Porter's "Begin the Beguine," recorded in 1938, was a great success. After 1955 he gave up his band to write and compose.

Shaw, George Bernard (1856–1950) Irish dramatist, critic, and man of letters, born in Dublin. He went to London in 1876 and after writing five unsuccessful novels, he became a music and drama critic, an active socialist, and one of the founding members of the Fabian Society. He soon made a reputation with his brilliant speeches and pamphlets supporting the Fabian cause. He popularized the works of Wagner (*The Perfect Wagnerite*, 1898) and Ibsen, (*The Quintessence of Ibsenism,* 1891). Concerned with the moral and social issues of the times, he turned to writing drama. He wrote more than 40 plays, the first of which, *Widowers' Houses* (1892), an attack on slum landlords, was printed in *Plays Pleasant and Unpleasant* (1898), which included *The Philanderer, Mrs Warren's Profession* (on prostitution), and the "pleasant" comedies *Arms and the Man, You Never Can Tell, Candida*, and *The Man of Destiny*. With *Three Plays for Puritans* (published 1901), which comprised *The Devil's Disciple, Caesar and Cleopatra*, and *Captain Brassbound's Conversion*, Shaw achieved a certain popularity. The epic comedy of ideas, *Man and Superman* (1903), was based on the Don Juan legend and developed Shaw's ideas on the "life force" and social evolution; it was followed by *John Bull's Other Island* (1904) and *Major Barbara* (1905). His next plays were *The Doctor's Dilemma* (1906), *Getting Married* (1908), *Misalliance* (1910), and *Androcles and the Lion* (1913). *Pygmalion* (1913) was an outstanding commercial success and became a perennial favorite (and the basis of the musical *My Fair Lady*, 1955). It was followed by *Heartbreak House* (1917) and the series of plays entitled *Back to Methuselah* (1921). The historical drama *St Joan* (1924), on Joan of Arc, is generally regarded as his greatest work. His late plays (from 1929 onward) include *The Apple Cart, The Village Wooing*, and *In Good King Charles's Golden Days*. In 1925 he was awarded the Nobel Prize. Among many important prose works are *The Intelligent Woman's Guide to Socialism and Capitalism* (1928) and *The Black Girl in Search of God* (1932).

Shaw, (Richard) Norman (1831–1912) British architect. In partnership with W. E. Nesfield (1835–88), he broke the hold of the *gothic revival on English architecture. Using a variety of styles, including gothic, Tudor, Queen Anne, and later *classicism, Shaw produced more comfortable buildings than those of his predecessors.

Shawinigan 46 33N 72 45W A city in E Canada, in Quebec on the St Maurice River near waterfalls 150 ft (46 m) high. Developed around 1900 to utilize their hydroelectric potential, Shawinigan is a center for pulp and paper, chemicals (especially calcium carbide), and other heavy industries. Population: 24,921.

Shawnee North American Algonkian-speaking Indian tribe, found in the mid-Atlantic area, especially Pennsylvania, South Carolina, Kentucky, and Tennessee. By 1798 they had settled in Indiana and Ohio and resisted the westward advances of white settlers. Under *Tecumseh they fought and were defeated by the US forces at the Battle of *Tippecanoe (1811). Descendants of the Shawnee live on reservations in Oklahoma.

Shays' Rebellion (1786–87) Uprising in W Massachusetts by disgruntled farmers and debtors who were dispersed by federal troops. Protesting excess taxation, low farm prices, and unfair debtor laws, dissidents, organized and led by former soldier Daniel Shays, attempted to capture the arsenal at Springfield, raided border towns, and were finally dispersed at Petersham. A new state legislature, elected in 1787, brought about reform regarding taxes and the jailing of debtors; however, the matter of the issuance of paper currency and other demands of the dissidents were not met.

Shcherbakov. *See* Rybinsk.

shear stress A form of *stress in which the applied force acts tangentially to the surface of the body. Thus a shear stress applied to the top of a pack of cards would cause the cards to slide over each other.

shearwater One of a group of birds (about 15 species) of the oceanic family *Procellariidae*; 11–35 in (27–90 cm) long, shearwaters have a dark plumage (some species have white underparts), long narrow wings, and slender bills; they feed on fish from the sea surface. The great shearwater (*Puffinus gravis*) breeds in the South Atlantic, migrating to spend summer and autumn in the North Atlantic. The Manx shearwater (*P. puffinus*) breeds off British and Mediterranean coasts and winters in E South America and Australia. Order: *Procellariiformes*. *See also* petrel.

sheathbill A small compact scavenging bird belonging to a family (*Chionidae*; 2 species) occurring on coasts near Antarctica. Sheathbills are 16 in (40 cm) long and have a thick white plumage, shortish wings, and a horny sheath covering the nostrils at the base of the bill. Order: *Charadriiformes* (gulls, plovers, etc.)

Sheba In the Bible, a land corresponding to Sabaea in present-day Yemen (SW Arabia). It was known for its trade in spices and gold. Its most famous monarch was the Queen of Sheba who visited King Solomon in Jerusalem (1 Kings 10.1–13). According to Ethiopian tradition, she bore him a son, the first king of Ethiopia.

Shechem. *See* Nablus.

sheep A hoofed *ruminant mammal belonging to the genus *Ovis* (7 species), native to mountainous regions of Eurasia and North America. Related to goats, sheep are generally 30–40 in (75–100 cm) tall at the shoulder and weigh 110–330 lb (50–150 kg). They have a compact body with slender legs and a short tail and the coat ranges from white to brown in color. Males (rams) have large spiraled horns; females (ewes) have smaller less curved horns. There are over 200 breeds of domestic sheep (*O. aries*), probably descended from the Asian red sheep (*O. orientalis*), which are reared worldwide for meat, wool, and milk (*see* livestock farming). They typically have a long woolly coat, unlike the coarser coat of wild sheep. Family: **Bovidae*. *See also* aoudad; argali; bighorn; mouflon.

sheepdog A dog used for handling sheep. Many breeds are used for this purpose, including the *collie, *German shepherd, *Old English sheepdog, and *Shetland sheepdog, as well as crossbred derivatives.

sheep ked A flat wingless fly, *Melophagus ovinus*, also called sheep tick, that is parasitic upon sheep. Both sexes are bloodsuckers and attach to the fleece, often causing serious skin irritations. The larvae are retained within the body of the female until they reach maturity, when they are deposited on the ground. Family: *Hippoboscidae*.

Sheffield 52 23N 1 30W A city in N England, on the Don River. It is world famous for steel, produced here since the mid-18th century. Special and alloy steels are now more important than the traditional cutlery and tool-making trades. Sheffield also produces silverware, glass, and engineering products. There is a cathedral (partly 15th century) and a university (1905). Population (1981): 477,142.

Sheffield plate Articles that are made by fusing a silver coat onto copper. The process was discovered (c. 1742) by a Sheffield, England, cutler. Used as a substitute for solid silver, Sheffield-plated articles, usually tableware, followed contemporary silver designs and were of the highest quality. Sheffield plate became obsolete after the introduction of electroplating in the mid-19th century, but Sheffield-plated articles are now prized.

Shelburne, William Petty Fitzmaurice, 2nd Earl of (1737–1805) British statesman; prime minister (1782–83). An advocate of conciliation toward the American colonies, his ministry negotiated the Treaty of Paris (1783), which ended the American Revolution.

shelduck A large *duck, *Tadorna tadorna*, found around coasts of W and central Eurasia. It is 25.5 in (65 cm) long and has black-and-white plumage with a green head, chestnut shoulders, and a red bill, which in the male has a red knob at the base. It feeds chiefly on mollusks and nests in disused rabbit burrows.

shellac A natural thermoplastic *resin made from the secretions of the lac insect, *Laccifer lacca*, which is parasitic on certain trees in India and Thailand. It was formerly used for molding records but was replaced by vinyl resins. Its solution in alcohol is used as a varnish and in lacquers. It is also used in sealing wax, printing inks, and electrical insulation.

Shelley, Percy Bysshe (1792–1822) British poet. Expelled from Oxford University for publishing a pamphlet defending atheism in 1811, he settled briefly in the Lake District. He wrote the revolutionary poem *Queen Mab* in 1813 and soon after left for the Continent, where he met Byron. From 1818 until his death he lived in Italy, where he wrote the verse dramas *The Cenci* (1819) and *Prometheus Unbound* (1818–19), the elegy *Adonais* (1821) prompted by the death of Keats, and much lyrical poetry. He was drowned in a sailing accident off the Italian coast. His wife **Mary Wollstonecraft Shelley** (1797–1851), British novelist, was the daughter of William *Godwin and Mary *Wollstonecraft. She eloped with Shelley in 1814 and married him in 1816. In addition to her best-known book, *Frankenstein: the Modern Prometheus* (1818), she edited Shelley's *Poetical Works* (1839).

shells The hard casings secreted by some animals to protect themselves or their eggs. The term usually refers to the shells of mollusks, which consist largely of calcium carbonate and come in a wide variety of shapes and sizes. They may be spiraled or flat, with one valve (in gastropods, such as snails) or two (in bivalves, such as mussels). A single valve of a giant clam may weigh up to 200 lb (90 kg). The pearly nautilus has a many-chambered shell, which provides buoyancy, while the female paper nautilus (*Argonauta*) secretes a shell-like cradle to transport its eggs and young. The shells of marine mollusks, particularly gastropods, are prized by collectors.

Shenandoah National Park A national park in N Virginia, in the Blue Ridge Mountains. It preserves the spectacular scenery of the mountains and the valley of the Shenandoah River. Heavily forested, the park, established in 1935, includes many species of plants, wildlife, and birds. Area: 300 sq mi (777 sq km).

Shenandoah River A river in the E US, flowing mainly NE through Virginia to join the Potomac River as its main tributary. It was a major *Civil War battleground (*see also* Sheridan, Philip H.). The **Shenandoah National Park**, in the Blue Ridge section of the Appalachian Mountains, lies to the S of the river. Length: 55 mi (88 km).

Shensi. *See* Shenxi.

Shenxi (Shen-hsi *or* Shensi) A mountainous province in central China. In the Wei He (River) and Han River valleys wheat, millet, and cotton are grown. Coal, iron, and oil are also produced. *History*: the Wei He valley was the center of successive Chinese dynasties from 1122 BC. Its economy rested on an impressive irrigation system from about 300 BC until about 600 AD, when it began to deteriorate. From about 1860 until 1928 the N suffered from famines, epidemics, and civil wars. Following the *Long March, it was the communist base (1936–1949). Area: 75,598 sq mi (195, 800 sq km). Population (1990): 32,882,403. Capital: Xi An.

Shenyang (former name: Mukden) 41 50N 123 26E A city in NE China, on the Hun River, the capital of Liaoning province and the site of its university. China's fourth largest city, it is a major industrial center. The **Mukden Incident** (1931), an explosion on the Japanese-controlled South Manchurian Railroad,

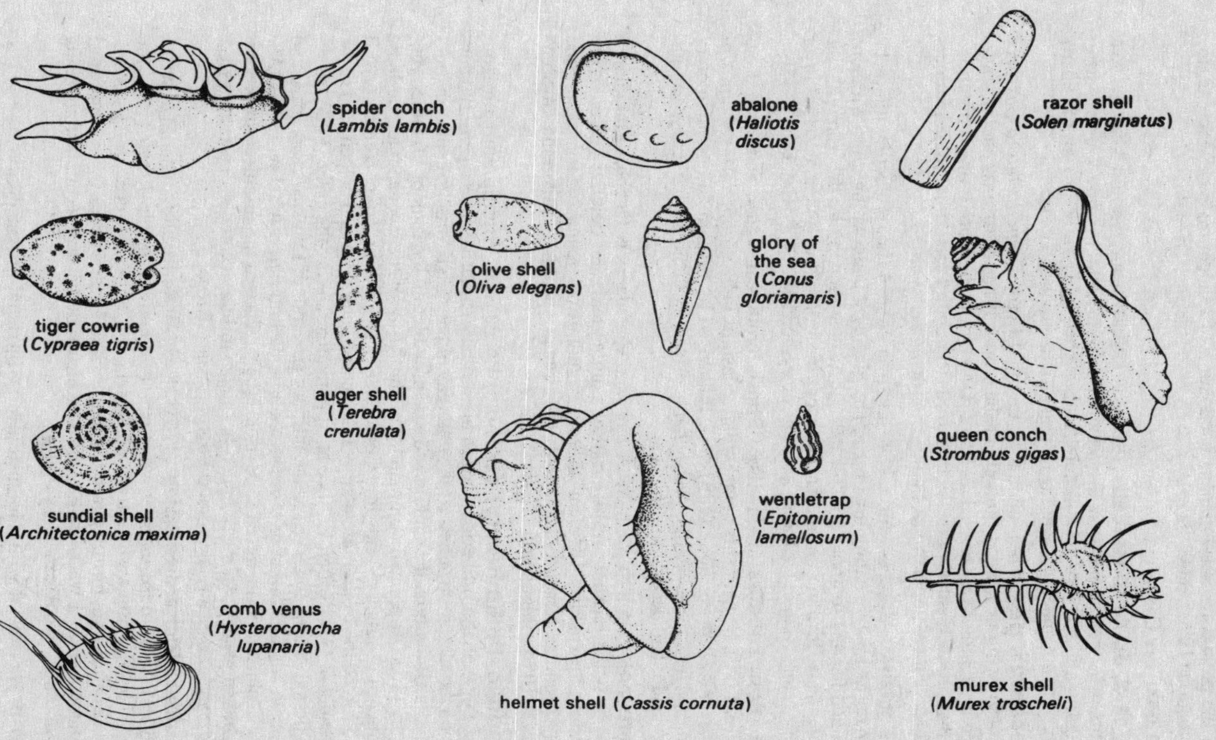

SHELLS *A selection of mollusk shells, drawn to scale (the largest, the helmet shell, is 13.5 in or 35 cm long). All these species are marine and several, including the glory of the sea, are collectors' items.*

was the pretext for the Japanese occupation of Manchuria (*see* Manchukuo). Population (1990): 3,603,712.

she oak. *See* Casuarina.

Shepard, Jr, Allan Bartlett (1923–) US astronaut, who on May 5, 1961, became the first American in space. His flight, which came 23 days after *Gagarin's flight, lasted 15 minutes and reached a height of 115 mi (185 km). He also commanded the Apollo 14 flight to the moon in 1971.

shepherd's purse An annual or biennial herb, *Caspella bursa-pastoris*, found growing as a weed throughout the world. It has a basal rosette of leaves and a branching leafy stem, 1.2–16 in (3–40 cm) high, bearing tiny white flowers that produce small purse-shaped fruits. Its ability to self-pollinate produces distinctive local populations. Family: **Cruciferae*.

sheradizing A process for galvanizing iron or steel (i.e. protecting the metal from corrosion by coating it with zinc) by placing it in a rotating drum with zinc dust and heating to about 500°F (260°C). At this temperature the iron and zinc amalgamate, forming an internal layer of zinc-iron alloys and an external layer of pure zinc. Named for the British inventor Sherard Cowper-Coles (d. 1935).

Sheraton, Thomas (1751–1806) British furniture designer. Settling in London (c. 1790), he made his name with the designs in his *Cabinet-Maker and Upholsterer's Drawing Book* (1791–94). Influenced by *Adam and contemporary French styles, these designs were characterized by elegance, delicacy, straight lines, and inlaid decoration.

Sherbrooke 45 24N 71 54W A city in E Canada, in S Quebec. Founded in 1794, it is the farming, transportation, commercial, and cultural center of the *Eastern Townships. Its manufactures include textiles, machinery, paper, and dairy produce. Sherbrooke houses the French-speaking University of Sherbrooke (1954). Population (1991): 76,429.

Sheridan, Philip H(enry) (1831–88) US general. After graduation from West Point in 1853, Sheridan began his military career with service in the cavalry on the western frontier. At the outbreak of the *Civil War, he gained distinction as a Union infantry captain and was promoted to the rank of brigadier general in 1862. Appointed commander of the Army of the Shenandoah, he led a number of destructive raids into Confererate territory. His deployments in April 1865 forced the Conferderate army to evacuate Petersburg and helped lead to the surrender of Gen. Robert E. *Lee at Appomattox. During the early *Reconstruction period, Sheridan served as the military governor of Louisiana and Texas and his harsh administration of those states brought him into conflict with Pres. Andrew *Johnson. Transferred to Missouri, he supervised the resettlement of various Indian groups. Sheridan ended his active military career with service as US military observer in the *Franco-Prussian War (1870).

Sheridan, Richard Brinsley (1751–1816) Anglo-Irish dramatist. He wrote witty comedies of manners, of which the best known are *The Rivals* (1775), in which his most famous character, Mrs. Malaprop, appears, and *School for Scandal* (1777). He was a manager of the Drury Lane Theatre and a Whig member of Parliament from 1780 to 1812, during which time he was recognized as being one of the great parliamentary orators.

sheriff An official with administrative and judicial responsibilities in the US, England, and Scotland. Originating in 10th-century England, the sheriffs' powers were reduced by Henry II (reigned 1154–89) and became little more than ceremonial in the 16th century. US Sheriffs are elected and are the principal law enforcement officers in a county.

Sherman, William Tecumseh (1820–91) US general. An 1840 graduate of West Point, Sherman served in the *Mexican War, but resigned from the Army in 1855 to pursue a career in banking. He returned to the Army as a Union officer at the beginning of the Civil War and served at the first Battle of *Bull Run (1861) and at the Battle of *Shiloh (1862), where he was promoted to the rank of major general. Replacing Gen. U. S. *Grant as commander of the West (1864), Sherman launched his invasion of Georgia, capturing and burning Atlanta and leading the famous "march to the sea." After the capture of Savannah, he continued the march northward through the Carolinas, eventually joining Grant's forces in Virginia in April 1865. In 1869 he succeeded Grant as commanding general of the US Army, a post he held until his retirement in 1884. His brother **John Sherman** (1823–1900) was a politician who began his political career as a Republican congressman from Ohio (1855–61). After serving almost three terms in the US Senate (1861–77), he resigned to become secretary of the treasury in the administration of Rutherford B. *Hayes (1877–81). Sherman returned to the Senate after Hayes's retirement and served as the chairman of the Finance Committee (1881–97). The *Sherman Anti-Trust Act was largely his work. He was later named secretary of state in the administration of Pres. William *McKinley (1897–98).

Sherman Anti-Trust Act (1890) US law that prohibited competition restraint abuses and monopolies. Named for Senator John *Sherman, the act prohibited business combinations in any way that violated fair competition practices between states and in international trade.

Sherman Silver Purchase Act (1890) US law that required the federal government to purchase a substantial amount of US-produced silver with treasury notes redeemable in either gold or silver. Enacted to increase the amount of currency in circulation, it instead drained government gold reserves and precipitated the Panic in 1893, at which time the act was repealed. *See also* Free Silver.

Sherpa A people of Nepal who speak a dialect of Tibetan. They are farmers, cattle breeders, and traders and also spin and weave woolen cloth. They often act as porters for Himalayan expeditions. With Edmund Hillary, the Sherpa *Tenzing Norgay reached the summit of Everest in 1953.

Sherrington, Sir Charles Scott (1857–1952) British physiologist, whose work provided the basis for present-day understanding of the nervous system. Sherrington demonstrated that reflex actions in higher animals and man are integrated with the rest of the nervous system and do not occur as isolated activities. He proposed the terms neuron for a nerve cell and synapse for the point at which an impulse is transmitted between nerve cells. He shared a Nobel Prize (1932) with Lord *Adrian.

sherry A fortified *wine, made around Jerez de la Frontera (whence its name) in S Spain; similar wine is now also made elsewhere. It is blended by the *solera* system: sherry is drawn off from several different casks to make a blend and those casks are then topped up with younger sherry, maintaining its future character. There are two basic types of sherry: fino is a pale dry wine on which the *flor* (flower or yeast) has developed fully; oloroso is a rich full-bodied wine on which the *flor* is little developed. Other types of sherry are related to these two, for example amontillado is a strong dark derivative of a fino and cream sherry is a heavily sweetened oloroso.

's Hertogenbosch (*or* Den Bosch) 51 41N 5 19E A city in the S central Netherlands, the capital of North Brabant province. It has a famous gothic cathedral (rebuilt 1419–1520). The painter Hieronymus Bosch was born there. Population (1981 est): 88,585.

Sherwood, Robert E(mmet) (1896–1955) US playwright and writer. Between 1919 and 1928 he was an editor or drama critic for various magazines, including *Vanity Fair, Life*, and *Scribner's*, and the New York *Herald*. He later worked in Franklin D. Roosevelt's administration, in which he was director of the overseas Office of War Information (1941–44). His plays include *The Road to Rome* (1927), *Reunion in Vienna* (1931), *The Petrified Forest* (1934), *Idiot's Delight* (Pulitzer Prize, 1936), *Abe Lincoln in Illinois* (1938; Pulitzer Prize, 1939), and *There Shall Be No Night* (1948; Pulitzer Prize, 1949). A book about the Roosevelt administration, *Roosevelt and Hopkins* (1948) brought him his fourth Pulitzer Prize in 1949, and his movie, *The Best Years of Our Lives*, received an Academy Award (1946).

Sherwood Forest An ancient forest in the Midlands of England, in Nottinghamshire. Once an extensive royal hunting ground, it is now much reduced; it is famous for its associations with Robin Hood.

Shetland Islands A group of about 100 islands in the North Sea, off the N coast of Scotland. The largest islands include Mainland, Yell, and Unst. Agriculture, based on crofting, chiefly produces wool; Shetland ponies are also bred. Herring fishing, centered on Lerwick, is important. The few industries include fish curing and knitting (especially in the Shetland and Fair Isle patterns). The islands are a base for North Sea oil exploitation. Area: 551 sq mi (1427 sq km). Administrative center: Lerwick.

Shetland pony Small British pony, native to the Shetland Islands. It has a sturdy compact body with short legs and a relatively large head. The mane and tail are profuse and the coat becomes thick in winter. Shetlands are now popular pets for children. Height: up to 10½ hands (3.4 ft; 1.05 m).

Shetland sheepdog (*or* Sheltie) A breed of dog developed in the Shetland Islands for working sheep. Related to and resembling the *collie, it has a soft undercoat and a long outer coat and may be black, brown, or blue-gray, with white and tan markings. Height: 14 in (36 cm) (dogs); 14 in (35 cm) (bitches).

shield An extensive rigid block of Precambrian rocks unaffected by later periods of mountain building. Shields are the oldest continental regions, frequently of igneous granite or metamorphic gneiss. The shields were once the site of Precambrian mountain belts, although the mountains have been completely eroded. The **Canadian** (*or* Laurentian) **Shield** is the largest, covering about 2 million sq mi (5002 million sq km) of NE North America. The **Baltic Shield** (*or* Fennoscandia), reaching the surface in Finland and Sweden, is another well-known example.

shield bug A *plant bug, also called stink bug, belonging to the families *Acanthosomidae, Cydnidae, Scutelleridae*, or *Pentatomidae*. Shield bugs have heavy shieldlike bodies, 0.20–2 in (5–50 mm) long, and are usually green or brown. They suck insect or plant juices, often becoming agricultural pests. Some species also foul plants with an evil-smelling secretion. □insect.

shield fern A tufted *fern of the widely distributed genus *Polystichum* (about 135 species). It has a scaly stem and tapering branched fronds made up of toothed pointed leaflets. Small round clusters of spore capsules (sori) occur in rows on the undersides of the leaflets. The soft shield fern (*P. setiferum*) and the hard shield fern (*P. aculeatum*) are common species. Family: *Aspidiaceae*.

Shih-chia-chuang. *See* Shijiazhuang.

Shih Huang Ti. *See* Qin.

Shih tzu A breed of small dog originating in Tibet. It has a long body with short legs, a short muzzle, and drooping ears. The long straight coat can be of various colors and the plumed tail is held over the back. Height: about 10 in (26 cm).

Shiites (*or* Shiah) The general term applied to a number of different Muslim sects, the main body of which is dominant in Iran. The distinctive belief of the Shiites, which differentiates them from the other major Muslim group, the *Sunnites, is that *Ali, the fourth caliph, is the only legitimate successor of Mohammed. The leader of Islam, the *imam, must be a descendant of Ali and has exclusive authority in secular and religious matters. The Shiites differ among themselves as to the true line of imams after a certain stage. Some, known as "the twelvers," expect the return of the 12th imam (d. 9th century AD) at the end of time, while others recognize a different line from the seventh imam onward.

Shijiazhuang (*or* Shih-chia-chuang) 38 04N 114 28E A city in NE China, the capital of Hebei Province and the site of its university. A communications center, its industries include coal mining, textiles, chemicals, and engineering. Population (1990): 1,068,439.

Shikoku The smallest of the four main islands of Japan, separated from Honshu and Kyushu by the Inland Sea. Mountainous and forested, its population is concentrated on the coastal plains, with industry mainly in the N. Copper is mined at Besshi; other products are fish, rice, grain, tobacco, mulberry, and camphor. Area: 6857 sq mi (17,759 sq km). Population (1990): 4,195,069. Chief cities: Matsuyama and Takamatsu.

Shillong 25 34N 91 53E A city in India, the capital of Meghalaya. Rebuilt following its virtual destruction by an earthquake in 1897, Shillong is an important military base and agricultural trading center and has a university (1973). Population (1991): 130,691.

Shiloh 32 03N 35 18E A city of Samaria in ancient N Palestine, now in Jordan. Hannah brought her son Samuel to this important Israelite religious center to dedicate him to God in the temple where Eli was priest of the *Ark of the Covenant. Shiloh was the traditional sanctuary of the Ark until the Philistines destroyed the city and captured the Ark in the mid-11th century BC.

Shiloh, Battle of (1862) Civil War battle in SW Tennessee; also known as the Battle of Pittsburg Landing. Having suffered extensive losses in the area, Confederate forces under Gen. Albert Sidney Johnston (1803–62) surprised Gen. Ulysses S. *Grant's troops, who were awaiting reinforcements. Although both sides claimed victory, the Union fared better, regaining all ground lost in the initial attack and forcing the retreat of the Confederates. Casualties were extremely high for both armies.

Shimonoseki 33 59N 130 58E A seaport in Japan, in SW Honshu, linked to *Kitakyushu by tunnels under the Shimonoseki Strait. The treaty ending the first Sino-Japanese War was signed there (1895). Industries include engineering, ship building, chemicals, and fishing. Population (1990): 262,635.

shingles An infection caused by the *herpes zoster virus, which lodges in nerve cells in the spinal cord. Shingles affects adults who have had chickenpox as children. It usually starts with pain along the course of a sensory nerve, followed by a band of blisters around half of the body or face. The rash usually eventually disappears but the patient may be left with severe neuralgia.

Shinto The native religion of Japan. Shinto is primarily an attitude of nationalistic and aesthetic reverence toward familiar places and traditions, rather than a set of religious beliefs. However, the central themes are the belief in numerous usually amoral *kami* or nature spirits, together with ancestor worship and an ideal of military chivalry.

The two principal *kamis* are the sun-goddess (reputedly mother of the emperor) and her brother the storm-god. The conflict between them expresses the creative and destructive forces of nature. The scriptures of Shinto, the *Ko ji ki* and the *Nihon Shoki*, are both semimythological histories of Japan, written around 720 AD. The hereditary priesthood officiates at ceremonies of birth, marriage, and death, ensuring ritual purification. After World War II, Shinto was disestablished as the state religion.

ship money A tax raised by English monarchs in times of emergency for the defense of the coast. It gained notoriety under Charles I, who levied it indiscriminately between 1634 and 1639. It was pronounced illegal by the *Long Parliament.

ships Man's earliest sea voyages were probably made on rafts and in hollowed-out tree trunks. Larger and more stable vessels were certainly known to the ancient Egyptians, whose rock carvings and paintings depict ships that were made of planks and were propelled both by oars and sails. Other early mariners included the Chinese and the Phoenicians; the short broad 13th-century Phoenician merchant ships (known as round ships) were propelled by oars and a single square sail to catch the prevailing wind (*see* sailing). The Greeks developed biremes (with two banks of oars) and triremes (with three banks) as warships, especially strengthened for ramming enemy vessels. The Romans also relied on oars, but their larger grain ships, capable of carrying up to 300 tons of cargo, had a number of square sails. In the N the longships of the Vikings were double-ended and rose high out of the water to cope with the rough and windy North Sea; they still relied on oarsmen but the holes for the oars were fitted with shutters that could be closed when the ship was under sail. Developed in the 8th century AD, ships of this kind brought William the Conqueror to England. It was not until the 12th century and the stimulus of the Crusades that the art of using sails was sufficiently developed for oars to be dispensed with. Sailing into the wind was originally pioneered by the Chinese in their junks, but it was the Arabs who perfected the lateen sail, which made it a reliable means of propulsion for large ships. By the 14th century sailing ships were commonplace. The warships of the period had "castles" built at each end to house fighting men, and guns were usually carried on the forecastle. However, muzzle-loading cannons were too heavy to be mounted on the forecastle and by the end of the 15th century they were carried in gun ports low in the hull. During this period, too, the single-master with one large heavy sail gave way to the three-master with more manageable small sails and full rigging. During the next 300 years sailing ships developed in many ways, usually with the merchantmen following the innovations in hull design and rigging made by the designers of warships. Sailing ships reached their zenith in the 19th-century clippers, which remained supreme until Newcomen's *steam engine revolutionized seafaring. The first steamer to cross the Atlantic (in April 1827) was the Dutch *Curaçao*. For the next century the N Atlantic crossing continued to be a proving ground for great ships. The propeller completely replaced the paddle and the steam *turbine largely replaced the reciprocating engine. Passenger travel across the Atlantic has now been almost entirely captured by the airlines; modern ship building concentrates on cargo vessels, especially oil *tankers.

Warships in the age of steam were largely modeled on the turbine-driven *battleship *Dreadnought* (1906), which together with the *cruiser, *destroyer, *frigate, and *submarine dominated naval warfare in World War I. By World War II the *aircraft carrier had evolved and with its long-range striking power became the supreme weapon of the war at sea. However, since the middle of the 20th century the importance of the surface warship has diminished and the

Roman merchantman (c. 100 AD) *The Romans' need to transport grain from N Africa to Europe encouraged the building of imposing ships up to 180 ft (55 m) long.*

Portuguese caravel (c. 1450) *Although it was only a little longer than a large rowing boat, the caravel took part in most of the 15th-century voyages of discovery. The lateen sail, derived from Arab examples, enabled it to sail against the prevailing winds.*

Cutty Sark (1869) *The 19th-century clippers were renowned for their speed and grace. The* Cutty Sark, *built to bring tea from China, was one of the fastest and most consistent sailing ships of its time. It is now permanently moored at Greenwich, England.*

Great Britain (1843) *The second steamship designed by I. K. Brunel, the* Great Britain *was the first all-iron propeller-driven ship to cross the Atlantic, taking 15 days between Liverpool and New York. Wrecked off the Falkland Islands in 1937, it was returned to England in 1970 for restoration.*

WARSHIPS

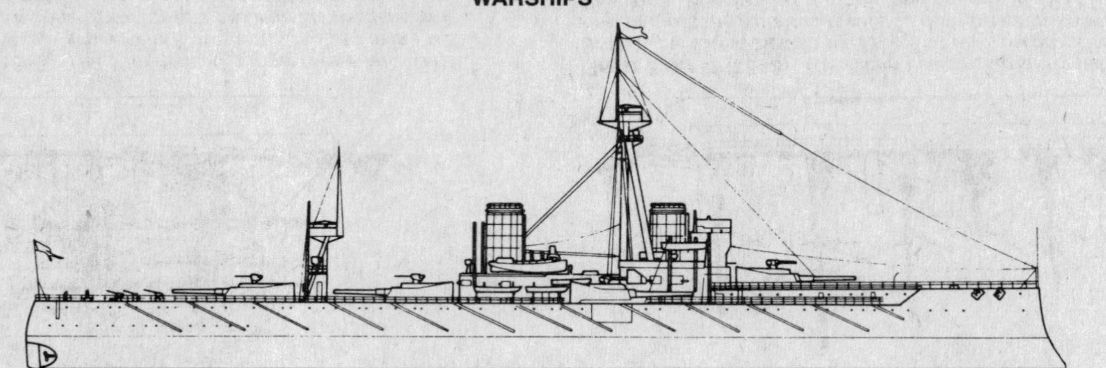

Dreadnought (1906) *The design of the British* Dreadnought *became the model for battleships in a period in which a country's naval strength was calculated in terms of how many battleships it possessed. The* Dreadnought *carried 10 12-inch guns, 27 smaller guns, and five underwater torpedo tubes.*

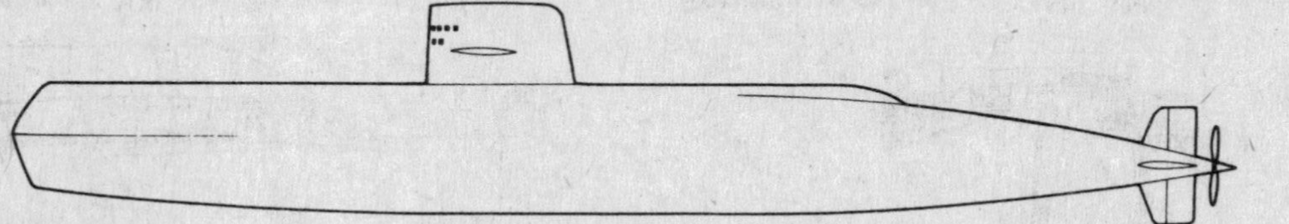

Nautilus (1954) *The first nuclear-powered warship, the US* Nautilus *heralded an era in which naval strength is calculated in terms of nuclear submarines. They are armed with torpedoes and long- and short-range missiles carrying nuclear warheads, all of which can be fired while the vessel is submerged.*

WARSHIPS

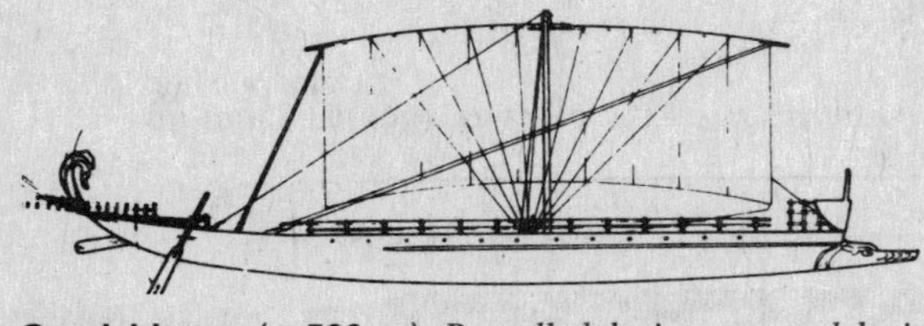

Greek bireme (c. 500 BC) *Propelled during an attack by its two ranks of oars, the bireme was strongly built around a keel to support the strain of the ram attached to its bows.*

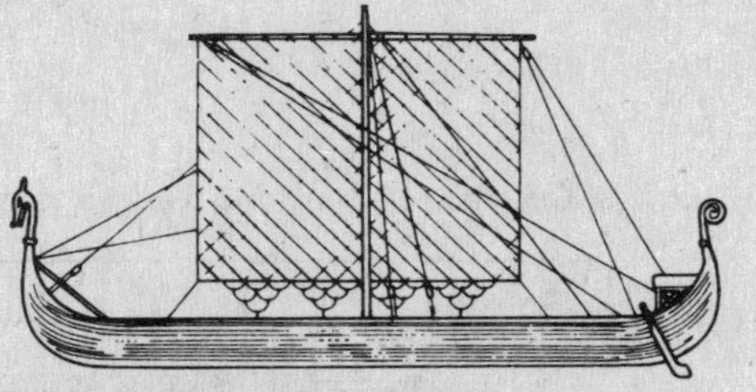

Viking longship (c. 1000 AD) *The clinker-built, double-ended longship, propelled by oars and sail, was used mainly to transport fighting men.*

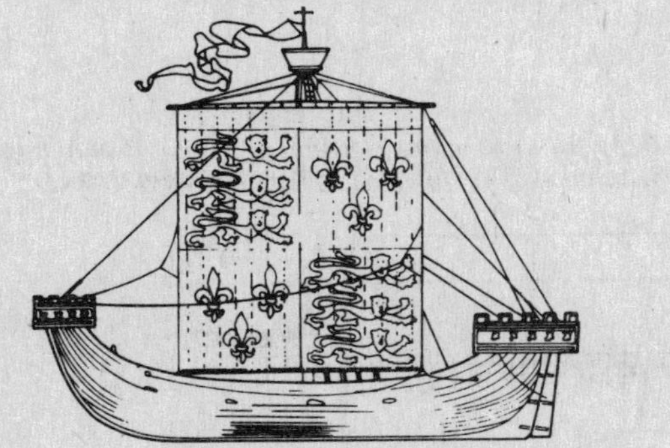

medieval nef (c. 1400) *This single-masted vessel had platforms (castles) for fighting men at either end and one on the mast (topcastle) from which missiles could be hurled.*

Victory (1778) *Nelson's flagship at the battle of Trafalgar (1805), the* Victory *carried 100 guns and a crew of 850. It is now preserved at Portsmouth, England.*

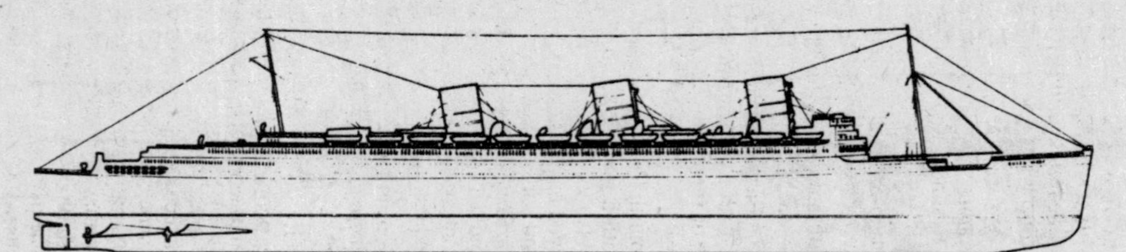

Queen Mary (1934) *In 1938 this British passenger liner captured the Blue Riband for the fastest Atlantic crossing with a time of 3 days 20 hours 42 minutes. In 1967 it was anchored off Long Beach, Calif., as a tourist attraction.*

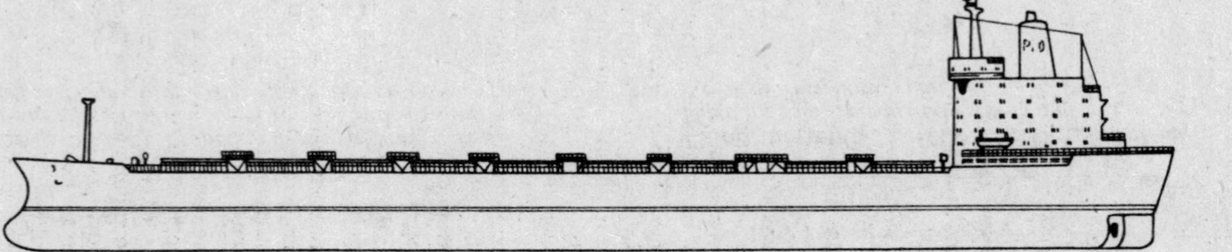

oil tanker (1968) *The largest vessels afloat today, some of these giant ships have a deadweight capacity of over 300,000 tons.*

strength of navies is now calculated in terms of their nuclear-powered submarines armed with long-range missiles.

Since the innovation of steam, the main developments in ships have been the use of *nuclear energy, especially in submarines, and the invention of the *Hovercraft and the *hydrofoil to remove the hull from the water in order to reduce drag.

shipworm A *bivalve mollusk belonging to the family *Teredidae*, also called pileworm. The shell plates of a shipworm are small with sharp ridges used for boring into wooden structures. The resulting burrow is lined with a limy material, encasing the long body (up to 71 in [180 cm]). Shipworms can damage wooden ships, piers, etc.

Shiraz 29 38N 52 34E A city in S central Iran. It is a trading center for the surrounding region and is connected by road to the port of Bushire; Pahlavi University was established there in 1945. Population (1986): 848,300.

shire A district, with a central town, used by the Anglo-Saxons as a unit of local government. Many modern countries in the UK were originally shires.

Shiré Highlands An upland area is S. Malawi, with an average height of about 3000 ft (900 m). Tea and tobacco are cultivated.

Shire horse A breed of draft horse descended from the English warhorse and one of the world's largest horses. It is massively built with characteristic long white hair (called feathering) covering the lower parts of the legs. The coat is gray, bay, or black. Height: about 17 hands (6 ft; 1.73 m).

Shiva The third member of the Hindu trinity, the *Trimurti. He is known as the Destroyer, but also represents the principle of generation symbolized by the lingam or phallus. His female counterpart is Parvati, also known in her more ominous aspects as Kali and Durga. He is often portrayed in human form with four arms, a third eye in the center of the forehead, and sometimes wearing a necklace of skulls. His most famous depiction is as *Nataraja* (king of dancing), his dance symbolizing the cosmic rhythm of creation and destruction. The worship of Shiva is characterized by an asceticism that contrasts with the gentler worship of *Vishnu, the other major sect of modern Hinduism.

Shizuoka 34 59N 138 24E A port in Japan, in SE Honshu on an inlet of the Pacific Ocean. It is the center of Japan's chief tea-producing region. Its university was established in 1949. Population (1991): 472,666.

Shkodër (Italian name: Scutari) 42 03N 19 01E A city in NW Albania, on Lake Scutari. It has been ruled successively by many peoples, including the Turks. Local industries include food canning and the manufacture of cement and weapons. Population (1987 est): 76,500.

shock **1.** A severe condition resulting from failure of the circulatory system, when the blood supply to the tissues is inadequate. The shock may be caused by failure of the heart to pump sufficiently strongly, for example after a heart attack; by loss of blood fluid, for example through *hemorrhage or *burns; or by widening of the blood vessels so that there is not enough blood to fill them, for example after injury or during a very severe infection. The patient is in a state of collapse (possibly unconscious)—pale, sweaty, and nauseated, with low blood pressure and a weak fast pulse. Shock due to hemorrhage is treated with blood transfusions while that due to infection is treated with antibiotics and also often with fluid transfusions. There is no adequate treatment for shock caused by a failing heart. **2.** Injury resulting from electrocution. The extent of the injury depends on the current passing through the body, which is related to the voltage and the skin resistance. As skin resistance is greatly reduced when it is wet, main-line voltage (240 V) can cause a lethal current (about 15 milliamps) to flow through the body if live terminals are touched with wet hands.

Shockley, William Bradfield (1910–89) US physicist, born in England, who shared the 1956 Nobel Prize with John *Bardeen and Walter *Brattain for their discovery of the *transistor while working at the Bell Telephone laboratories in 1948. This discovery revolutionized the electronics and computer industries. He is also known for his controversial views concerning the relationship between race and intelligence.

shock wave A narrow region of a high pressure in a fluid, created when a fast-moving body passes through the fluid. The waves are propagated outward from the body and occur, for example, when an aircraft passes through the *sound barrier.

shoebill A large bird, *Balaeniceps rex*, occurring in papyrus swamps of E Africa; 47 in (120 cm) tall, it has pale-gray plumage, long legs, and a large head with a broad shoe-shaped bill used to probe for lungfish. It is the only member of its family (*Balaenicipitridae*). Order: *Ciconiiformes* (herons, storks, etc.).

shofar A Jewish ceremonial trumpet used in the synagogue. It is made of a ram's horn, flattened and bent by a steaming process. Its use as a prelude to proclamations and to sound the alarm is recorded in the Old Testament.

shogi A board game for two players, a Japanese form of chess. Each player starts with 20 flat pieces distinguished by size and markings. As in chess the pieces have prescribed moves and the object is to checkmate the enemy king, but unlike chess captured pieces may be used in the game by the player who captures them.

shogun A military title held hereditarily by the heads of three families; they were successively the actual rulers of Japan, although the emperors retained formal sovereignty. The shogunate was secured for the Minamoto from the emperor in 1192 after *Minamoto Yoritomo's victory over the Taira league. From 1338 to 1573 the Ashikaga family held the title and in 1603 *Tokugawa Ieyasu, who claimed Minamoto ancestry, revived it. The last shogun was Tokugawa Keiki (1827–1913; ruled 1867–68).

Sholapur 17 43N 75 56E A city in India, in Maharashtra. It is a major cotton textile center. Population (1991): 603,870.

Sholes, Christopher Latham (1819–90) US inventor of the typewriter, which he patented, with two others, in 1868. After spending several years perfecting his inventory, he sold his patent to Eliphalet *Remington's company in 1873.

Sholokhov, Mikhail (1905–84) Soviet novelist. After service with the Red Army during the Civil War he returned to his native village in the Don Cossack region, the setting for his first major novel (1928–40), translated in two parts as *And Quiet Flows the Don* and *The Don Flows Home to the Sea*. His authorship of this novel has been questioned by Solzhenitsyn and others. He won the Nobel Prize in 1965.

shooting Discharging a weapon at a target or at game. The two main categories of **target shooting** for rifles are small bore (.22 caliber) at ranges of 27–219 yd (25–200 m), and full bore (7.62 caliber) at ranges of 200–1200 yd (183–1097 m); full-bore courses are fired from standing, sitting, kneeling, and prone (lying down) positions. Weapons for pistol shooting range from the .177 air pistol to the .45 pistol, at ranges of 10–50 yd (9–45 m). In **clay-pigeon shooting** (*or* trapshooting) clay disks are mechanically flung into the air and fired at with shotguns.

shop steward Part-time *labor-union officials, who represent the union members with whom they work. The function of the shop steward is to represent his fellow workers in negotiations with management and in talks with other labor-union officials.

shorthand Any form of writing designed to be written quickly, especially for the transcription of spoken language. Most forms of shorthand are based on the principle of recording only as many letters or sounds as are necessary for reasonably accurate reading back, generally in simplified characters that are fast to write. In the Pitman System, for example, the characters are based on segments of a circle or straight lines; vowels are indicated only where the writer thinks it necessary, by a system of dots in descending order; voicing of consonants is indicated by thickening strokes. The most popular US system is that invented by John Robert Gregg (1867–1948). In these systems speeds of up to 300 words per minute can be achieved. **Speedwriting**, devised in the US in the 1920s, uses ordinary Roman alphabet characters, omitting all but the essential ones. **Stenotypy** is a form of machine shorthand using a limited keyboard; it is widely used for reporting court proceedings. The use of shorthand is of great antiquity; for example, Cicero's secretary Tiro had devised a Latin shorthand system in the 1st century BC.

Shoshoni A group of North American Indian tribes of the Great Basin region who spoke a language of the Uto-Aztecan family. They lived by gathering wild fruits and insects and trapping small game. Some acquired horses and moved onto the Plains to hunt buffalo and adopted much of the culture of this region. One such group was the *Comanche.

Shostakovich, Dmitri (1906–75) Russian composer. He was a pupil of Glazunov at the St Petersburg conservatory. His first symphony, written when he was 18, was very successful. Subsequent works, especially the operas *The Nose* (1927–28) and *Lady Macbeth of Mtsenk* (1930–32), brought allegations of formalism and decadence from the Soviet press. Shostakovich regained official favor with his fifth symphony (1937), subtitled "A Soviet artist's reply to just criticism." His compositions also include 10 subsequent symphonies, including the wartime seventh symphony (*The Leningrad*; 1941), two concertos each for piano, violin, and cello, 15 string quartets, and much other music.

shotgun A smoothbore firearm with pump or automatic-repeating action. It may have one or two barrels and fires shot (small pellets) into a pattern covering a broad target. Guns with tapered barrels gain range but reduce the pattern area. Shot is used against small game, while lead slugs and balls are used against deer.

shot put (*or* putting the shot) A field event in athletics, in which an iron or brass sphere is thrown as far as possible. It weighs 16 lb (7.26 kg) for men and 8.8 lb (4 kg) for women. It is thrown, or put, one-handed from in front of the shoulder and the putter must stay within a circle 7 ft (2.1 m) in diameter.

shoulder The part of the body to which the *arm is attached. The skeleton of the shoulder consists of the scapula (shoulder blade), which forms a ball-and-socket joint with the humerus, permitting free movement of the arm. It is also the site of attachment of muscles of the arm and back. It is braced by the clavicle.

shoveler duck A *duck, *Spatula clypeata,* found in the N hemisphere, having a large bill specialized for feeding on water plants and invertebrates on the surface of fresh water; 20 in (50 cm) long, it has a pale-blue wing flash; the male has a dark-green head, white breast, and chestnut underparts and the female is speckled brown.

show jumping Competitive jumping of horses, often against the clock, over a series of artificial obstacles of varying severity. Penalties are given for knocking down or refusing fences. Since World War II it has become a major international sport.

Shrapnel, Henry (1761–1842) British army officer, who invented the shrapnel shell. First used in 1804, the shell comprised a projectile that sprayed bullets when activated by a timing device.

SHOVELER DUCK *Distinguished from all other ducks by its large spatulate bill with fringed edges, seen in this male.*

Shreveport 32 30N 93 40W A city in Louisiana, on the Red River. It is the industrial center of a large oil and natural-gas region. Timber, cotton, and metal are also important products. Population (1990): 198,525.

shrew A small insectivorous mammal belonging to the family *Soricidae* (265 species), found all over the world except Australasia and the Polar regions. The dwarf shrew (*Suncus etruscus*) is the smallest mammal in the world, weighing only 0.07 oz (2 g) and measuring 2.8–3.1 in (7–8 cm). Shrews are very active: the common shrew (*Sorex araneus*) eats its own weight in food every 24 hours in order to meet its energy requirements. Order: **Insectivora*.

Shrewsbury 52 43N 2 45W A city in W central England, on the Severn River. It achieved importance as a gateway to Wales, and a castle was built in 1070. Shrewsbury is a market town for the surrounding agricultural area, with engineering and malting industries; market gardening is also important. Population (1985): 87,300.

shrike A fierce predatory songbird belonging to a family (*Laniidae*; 74 species) occurring in Eurasia, Africa, and North America and also called butcherbird. Shrikes range from 6–14 in (15–36 cm) in length and have soft black, gray, or brown plumage. They dive on insects and small vertebrates from the air, killing them with their hooked falconlike bills, often impaling prey on thorns.

shrimp A *crustacean, usually 1.6–3.1 in (4–8 cm) long, belonging to a worldwide suborder (*Natantia*; about 2000 species) that occurs in fresh and salt water. Shrimps have a semitransparent body with long slender legs (the first pair are pincerlike), a fanlike tail, and whiplike antennae, nearly as long as the body. Shrimps swim backward by rapid flexions of the abdomen and tail and they feed on small animals or plants. Many species, including the European *Crangon vulgaris*, are commercially important as food. Order: **Decapoda*.

shrimp plant A popular ornamental plant, *Beloperone guttata*, native to warm regions of the Americas. About 18 in (45 cm) high, it has inconspicuous white flowers enclosed by reddish-brown leaflike bracts, so that the whole flower cluster resembles a shrimp. Family: *Acanthaceae*.

Shropshire A county in the West Midlands of England, bordering on Wales. The Severn River separates the lowlands in the N and E from the uplands in the S and W. Area: 1348 sq mi (3490 sq km). Population (1987): 397,000. Administrative center: Shrewsbury.

Shroud of Turin A relic believed to be the linen cloth used to wrap Christ's body for burial. It bears impressions of a human body marked with wounds consonant with Christ's at the crucifixion. It has been kept in Turin since 1578, but there are gaps in its history prior to the 14th century. It has been subjected to a number of tests, some with surprising results, although none can be said to have confirmed or disproved its authenticity.

Shrove Tuesday The day before the beginning of Lent (*see* Ash Wednesday), so called from the "shriving" (i.e. confession and absolution) of the faithful that was customary before the Lenten season. In many countries carnivals are held, including New Orleans' famous Mardi Gras (Fat Tuesday) celebration.

Shula, Don(ald Francis) (1930–) US professional football player and coach who, in November 1993, broke George Halas's National Football League (NFL) record, when he won his 325th regular-season game. After college, he played professional football for the Cleveland Browns, Baltimore Colts, and Washington Redskins. Retiring from play in 1957, he coached at several colleges and then took a coaching position with the Detroit Lions. In 1963, he became head coach of the Baltimore Colts and, in 1970, took over the struggling Miami Dolphins. He led the Dolphins to the Super Bowl five times (1972, 1973, 1974, 1983, 1985) and won twice, in 1973 and 1974.

Shute, Nevil (N. S. Norway; 1899–1960) British novelist. He combined novel writing with his professional career as an aeronautical engineer. He settled in Australia after World War II. His many popular novels include *A Town Like Alice* (1950) and *On the Beach* (1957), which concerns the destruction of mankind in an atomic war.

sial The earth's continental crust, which is composed of granitic rocks rich in silicon (Si) and aluminum (Al). It is less dense than the underlying layer of *sima and much thicker.

Sialkot 32 29N 74 35E A city in Pakistan. The shrine of the first Sikh guru, Nanak, is situated there. Industries include textiles, surgical instruments, and sporting goods. Population (1981): 302,009.

Siam. *See* Thailand.

Siam, Gulf of An arm of the South China Sea, about 310 mi (500 km) wide and 435 mi (700 km) long, bordering on Thailand, Cambodia, and Vietnam.

siamang The largest of the *gibbons, *Hylobates syndactylus*, found in Malaya and Sumatra. Up to 35 in (90 cm) tall, with arms spanning 60 in (150 cm), siamangs have a large naked vocal sac on the throat, which expands to give volume to their cries.

Siamese cat A breed of short-haired cat, originating from SE Asia. The Siamese has a graceful slender body, a wedge-shaped head with slanted blue eyes and large pointed ears, and a long slim tapering tail. The fur on the body is cream-colored or off-white, shading into one of several colors (seal-brown, blue-gray, chocolate, lilac, tabby, or red) on the ears, mask, paws, and tail (the "points"). The seal-pointed and blue-pointed varieties are probably the most popular.

Siamese twins Identical twins who are fused together, usually at the head or along the trunk. They may have developed equally or unequally; in the latter case, one baby is fairly normal but is attached to a wasted remnant of a fetus. Siamese twins can sometimes be surgically separated, providing that vital organs are not involved in the point of union. The original Siamese twins, Chang and Eng (1811–74), were born in Siam; they were joined at the hip and remained fused, despite which they each married and fathered children.

Sian. *See* Xi An.

Sibelius, Jean (Johan Julius Christian S.; 1865–1957) Finnish composer. He began to compose as a child and studied at the Helsinki conservatory and in Berlin and Vienna. In 1897 the government made him a grant for 10 years to enable him to compose full time. Many of his works have Finnish associations and many were inspired by the epic poem the *Kalevala.* His works include seven symphonies, the symphonic poems *Kullervo* (choral; 1892), *En Saga* (1892), *The Swan of Tuonela* (1893), *Finlandia* (1899–1900), and *Tapiola* (1925), a violin concerto, a string quartet entitled "Voces Intimae," and many songs.

Siberia A region in Russia. Corresponding to N Asia, it is bordered on the W by the Ural Mountains, on the N by the Arctic Ocean, on the E by the Pacific Ocean, and on the S by Mongolia and China. Siberia comprises three geographical areas—the West Siberian Plain, the Central Siberian Plateau, and the Soviet Far East. It is notorious for its long harsh winters, during which the lowest temperatures anywhere in the world have been recorded. Its outstandingly rich mineral resouces include coal, especially in the *Kuznetsk Basin, petroleum, diamonds, and gold. Forestry is also important and Siberia's many rivers (notably the Ob, Yenisei, and Lena) are harnessed for hydroelectric power. The Russian settlement of Siberia began in 1581 but was intermittent until the building (1891–1905) of the Trans-Siberian Railroad. Siberia was long a place of exile for Russian criminals and political prisoners. Area: about 5,330,896 sq mi (13,807,037 sq km).

Siberian Husky. *See* Husky.

Sibiu 45 46N 24 09E A city in central Romania. An important center for Transylvania in the 15th century, it possesses the Brukenthal Museum, one of the oldest in Europe, and much medieval architecture. It is now a major industrial center, manufacturing machinery, textiles, and food products. Population (1992): 169,696.

Sibyl In Greek and Roman mythology, any of various divinely inspired prophetesses, the most famous of which was the Sibyl of Cumae, near Naples. Three books of these Sibylline prophecies were preserved in the Temple of Jupiter on the Capitoline hill at Rome and were consulted in national emergencies.

Sica, Vittoria De. *See* De Sica, Vittoria.

Sichuan (Ssu-ch'uan *or* Szechwan) A province in central China, on the Yangtze River, surrounded by mountains. The center is a plateau and the E a fertile plain. Warm and humid and China's most productive rice area, it is prosperous and densely populated, with several ethnic groups. Besides rice, produce includes corn, sugarcane, wheat, cotton, and forest products. The W is good grazing land, exporting pig bristles. Salt, gas, oil, coal, and other minerals are produced. Despite great difficulties with transport because of it mountainous surroundings, it has flourishing industries. It is also known for its crafts. *History*: it was among the first areas settled by the Chinese, important from the 3rd century BC, when China's oldest irrigation system was constructed there. A kingdom in the 3rd century AD, separatism often flourished because of the area's self-sufficiency and impenetrable position; it became the center of the Nationalist government during the Sino-Japanese War (1937–45). Economic development was stimulated at this time by migration from the coasts and has again speeded up since the 1950s. Area: about 220,000 sq mi (569,800 sq km). Population (1990): 107,218,173. Capital: Chengdu.

Sicilian Vespers (1282) The massacre of 2000 French residents of Palermo that began the Sicilian revolt, backed by Pedro III of Aragon (1236–85; reigned 1276–85), against the oppressive regime of the Angevin *Charles I. General war ensued between the Aragonese, Sicilians, and Italian Ghibellines on one side and the Angevins, French, and Italian Guelfs, supported by the papacy, on the other. Aragonese control was finally established in 1302 under Pedro's son Frederick II (1272–1337). *See also* Guelfs and Ghibellines.

Sicily The largest island in the Mediterranean Sea, which together with adjacent islands comprises an autonomous region of Italy. It is separated from the mainland by the Strait of Messina. Sicily is largely mountainous, rising to over 5,900 ft (1800 m) with its highest point at Mount Etna. Although most of the population is concentrated in urban centers, the region is underdeveloped and there is much poverty. The service sector is important, as is the mining industry, especially oil. The region's farmers produce citrus fruits, vegetables, wheat, rye, olives, and wine. Manufacturing industries include oil refining, petrochemicals, chemicals, pharmaceuticals, and food processing. *History*: settled by the Greeks in the 8th century BC, it was later occupied by the Carthaginians and between 241 and 211 BC it became a Roman province. It was conquered by the Arabs in the 9th century AD and in 1060 the Norman conquest of Sicily began. In 1266 Charles I became the first Angevin king of Sicily, which was conquered by Aragon in 1284 following the revolt called the *Sicilian Vespers. In 1734 Don Carlos of Bourbon became Charles IV (*see* Charles III of Spain) of Naples and Sicily, which formally became the Kingdom of the Two Sicilies in 1815 under *Ferdinand I. After conquest by Garibaldi (1860) Sicily was united with the rest of Italy. Since then Sicily's history has been one of trouble and discontent as a result of an ailing economy and the persistence of widespread poverty, which has not been helped by the island's social structure, the *Mafia, and other conservative forces on the island presenting an obstacle to reform. Area: 9927 sq mi (25,710 sq km), with adjacent islands. Population (1991): 4,989,871. Capital: Palermo.

Sickert, Walter Richard (1860–1942) British impressionist painter and etcher, born in Munich of Danish and Irish parentage. He studied under *Whistler and *Degas. His paintings of Venice and Dieppe (1895–1905) and scenes from the music hall and domestic life are distinguishable from French *impressionism chiefly by their somber colors.

sickle-cell disease A condition resulting from the production of an abnormal form of hemoglobin (the pigment of red blood cells). The disease is hereditary and affects only blacks. When the blood is deprived of oxygen the abnormal hemoglobin crystallizes and distorts the red cells into a sickle shape: these sickle cells are removed from the blood by the spleen, which leads to *anemia. Children affected with the severest form of the disease do not usually survive until adulthood; those less severely affected do survive and even tend to have some built-in resistance to malaria, which may partly explain the persistance of this harmful gene in the population.

sidereal period The time taken by a planet or satellite to return to the same point in its orbit, i.e. to complete one revolution, with reference to the background stars. It can be determined from the body's *synodic period.

sidewinder A small nocturnal *rattlesnake, *Crotalus cerastes*, occurring in deserts of the SW US and Mexico, that has a sideways looping method of locomotion enabling it to move quickly over loose sand; 18–30 in (45–75 cm) long, it is usually pale brown or gray with indistinct darker spotting and a hornlike scale above each eye.

Sidgwick, Henry (1838–1900) British moral philosopher. Sidgwick's major academic work, *The Methods of Ethics* (1874), was a comparative study of moral philosophy, which focused on *hedonism and *utilitarianism. As a university teacher, he worked for the abolition of religious tests at Cambridge and the admission of women students. He was the first president of the Society for Psychical Research (1882–85).

Sidi-Bel-Abbès 35 12N 0 42W A city in NW Algeria. An old Moorish town, it was the headquarters of the French Foreign Legion until 1962. It lies in a fertile area renowned for its wine. Population (1987): 152,778.

Sidmouth, Henry Addington, 1st Viscount. *See* Addington, Henry, 1st Viscount Sidmouth.

Sidney, Algernon (1622–82) English politician, who was beheaded for complicity in a plot against Charles II and the king's brother James, duke of York. In exile after the Restoration of Charles in 1660, he returned in 1677 and became prominent in attempts to exclude the Roman Catholic James from the succession.

Sidney, Sir Philip (1554–86) English poet and courtier. A man of letters and man of action, he typified the Renaissance ideal of the complete gentleman. His works include the prose romance *Arcadia* (1580), the sequence of Petrarchan sonnets, *Astrophel and Stella* (1591), and an important work of critical theory, *The Defense of Poesy* (1595). A gifted linguist, he served as a diplomat in Europe and was killed while fighting the Spanish in the Netherlands.

Sidon (*or* Saida) 33 32N 35 22E A small seaport in S Lebanon. It was an important Phoenician city, several references are made to it in the Bible, and it was greatly damaged during the Crusades. It is now the terminus of an oil pipeline from Saudi Arabia.

Siegen 50 52N 8 02E A city in NW Germany, in North Rhine-Westphalia. A former center for the mining of iron ore, its manufactures now include office equipment and computers. It is the birthplace of Rubens and has a university (1972). Population (1991 est): 107,039.

Siegfried A hero of Germanic legend, who also appears in early Scandinavian legend as Sigurd. The two best-known versions of his story are the Germanic **Nibelungenlied* and the Old Norse *Volsungasaga*. In the former, Siegfried wins *Brunhild for his brother-in-law Gunther, but a quarrel between Brunhild and Siegfried's wife Kriemhild leads to Siegfried's death by treachery. In the *Volsungasaga*, Sigurd is betrothed to Brynhild (the Old Norse version of her name) but is tricked (by a magic potion) into forgetting her and marries Gudrun. He then wins Brynhild for his brother-in-law Gunnar; later Brynhild incites Gunnar to kill him. Siegfried is the hero of the last two operas of *Wagner's *The Ring of the Nibelung*.

siemens (S) The *SI unit of conductance equal to the conductance between two points on a conductor when a potential difference of one volt between the points causes a current of one ampere to flow. Named for Ernst Werner von *Siemens.

Siemens, Ernst Werner von (1816–92) German electrical engineer, who opened a telegraph factory in 1847 and, a year later, laid a government telegraph line from Berlin to Frankfurt. Together with his brother **Karl Siemens** (1829–1906), he established telegraph factories in a number of European cities. A third brother **Sir William Siemens** (Karl Wilhelm S.; 1823–83) moved to England in 1844. He invented the open-hearth method of making steel in 1861, which was based on the principle of heat regeneration previously patented by a fourth brother **Friedrich Siemens** (1826–1904).

Siena 43 19N 11 19E A city in central Italy, in Tuscany. Founded by the Etruscans, it was an important commercial and artistic center in the Middle Ages. Its many fine buildings include a 13th-century gothic-romanesque cathedral, a university (1240), and several palaces, especially the Palazzo Pubblico (1297–1310) with its slender tower 328 ft (100 m) high. There are horse races through the main square during the annual Palio festival. Tourism is Siena's main source of revenue. Population (1990 est): 58,300.

Sienkiewicz, Henryk (1846–1916) Polish novelist. His only novel generally known outside Poland is *Quo Vadis* (1896), a historical epic set in Rome under the emperor Nero; it has been the subject of many films. He also wrote a trilogy celebrating Poland's military struggles during the 17th century. He won the Nobel Prize in 1905.

Sierra Leone, Republic of A country in West Africa, on the Gulf of Guinea. Coastal plains, fringed by mangrove swamps, rise to higher land in the interior reaching heights of almost 6500 ft (2000 m). The majority of the population is African, the main groups being Mende and Temne. *Economy*: chiefly agricultural, organized mainly in small farms. The principal food crop is rice and cash crops include palm kernels, cocoa, coffee, and ginger. Livestock is important, particularly cattle in the N, and there has been considerable recent development in the fishing industry as well as in forestry. Minerals, including diamonds, iron ore, and bauxite, are the main exports and the country has important deposits of rutile, which are being exploited. *History*: in 1787 local chiefs ceded to Britain a piece of land along the coast for the settlement of slaves freed in the colonies. In 1896 the region became a British protectorate, gaining independence within the Commonwealth in 1961. In 1967 a military coup and countercoup took place and after further upheaval civilian rule was restored in 1968. In 1971 Sierra Leone became a republic. In 1977 one-party government (by the All-People's Congress) was introduced. Dr. Siaka Stevens, who had led the country since 1961, retired in 1985 and was succeeded by Joseph Momoh. Economic reforms in 1990 did little to bolster the economy. Liberian rebels invaded Sierra Leone in 1991; neighboring African troops aided the army in repulsing the invasion. In 1992, Momoh was overthrown by a military coup, whose leaders formed an interim government. Official language: English; Krio is widely spoken. Official currency: leone of 100 cents. Area: 27,925 sq mi (73,326 sq km). Population (1990 est): 4,168,000. Capital and main port: Freetown.

Sierra Madre The chief mountain system of Mexico. It extends for about 1500 mi (2500 km) SE from the US border, reaching 18,697 ft (5699 m) at Citlaltepetl. It comprises the Sierra Madre Oriental (E), the Sierra Madre del Sur (S), and the Sierra Madre Occidental (W).

Sierra Maestra A mountain range in Cuba. It extends along the extreme SE coast reaching 6476 ft (1974 m) at the Pico Turquino. Fidel *Castro established his guerrilla base there in the 1950s.

Sierra Morena A mountain range in S Spain, extending about 250 mi (400 km) E–W between the Guadiana and Guadalquivir rivers.

SIENA *The cathedral.*

Sierra Nevada A mountain range in the US. It extends generally NW–SE through California, reaching 14,495 ft (4418 m) at Mount Whitney. It contains Yosemite National Park.

Sierra Nevada A mountain range in S Spain. It rises to 11,421 ft (3481 m) at Mulhacén, the highest point in Spain.

Sieyès, Emmanuel Joseph (1748–1836) French churchman, who was a leading figure in the *French Revolution. His pamphlet *Qu'est-ce que le tiers état?* (*What Is the Third Estate?*, 1789) greatly influenced the revolt of the Third Estate at the start of the Revolution. He voted for the execution of the king but withdrew from politics during the Jacobins' ascendancy. In 1799 he became a member of the *Directory and helped to bring about the coup that established Napoleon Bonaparte in power. His influence thereafter declined.

sifaka A *prosimian primate belonging to the genus *Propithecus* (2 species), of Madagascar. About 20 in (50 cm) long, with a tail the same length, sifakas have long white fur with red or orange and black markings. They have long hind legs and are mainly arboreal, feeding on leaves, buds, fruit, and bark. Family: *Indriidae*.

Siger of Brabant (c. 1240–c. 1284) French theologian. A teacher at Paris University, Siger was accused of heresy (1276) on account of his criticisms of Aristotle, in which he appeared to dissent from doctrines of immortality and the afterlife. *Aquinas wrote a treatise against him, but Dante placed him among the 12 sages.

Sigismund (1368–1437) Holy Roman Emperor (1411–37; crowned 1433) and king of Hungary (1387–1437) and of Bohemia (1419–37). He conducted two unsuccessful crusades against the Turks (1396; 1428) and was largely responsible for the summoning of the Council of *Constance to heal the Great Schism. Implicated in the treacherous burning of John *Hus in 1415, he fought the *Hussites throughout the 1420s.

Sigismund (I) the Old (1467–1548) King of Poland (1506–48). Sigismund gained control of E Prussia (1525) after defeating the *Teutonic Knights. He encouraged the development of the Renaissance in Poland.

Sigismund II Augustus (1520–72) King of Poland (1548–72); the last of the Jagiellon dynasty. Sigismund's reign saw the Union of *Lublin (1569), which united Poland with Lithuania, and the expansion of the Polish Reformation.

Sigismund III Vasa (1566–1632) King of Poland (1587–1632) and Sweden (1592–99). Sigismund was deposed from the Swedish throne by his uncle, later *Charles IX of Sweden, and failed in his subsequent attempts to regain the crown. Charles's son *Gustavus II Adolphus conquered Poland's Livonian territory (1621). Sigismund had some success against Russia, capturing and holding Moscow (1610–12).

Siglo de Oro The Golden Age of Spanish literature that lasted from about 1550 to 1650. The literature of this period was characterized by patriotism and new attitudes of critical realism. Leading writers included the dramatist Lope de Vega, the novelist Cervantes, and the poet Luis de Góngora.

Signac, Paul (1863–1935) French painter and art theorist associated with *pointillism. A disciple of *Seurat, he is known chiefly for his mosaic-like paintings of European harbors and his treatise *D'Eugène Delacroix au Néo-impressionisme* (1899).

Signorelli, Luca (c. 1441–1523) Italian Renaissance painter, born in Cortona. Probably the pupil of *Piero della Francesca, he worked in Florence, Perugia, and in the Vatican, where he painted a fresco for the Sistine Chapel (c. 1481). He completed frescoes in Orvieto Cathedral begun by Fra *Angelico and painted his masterpiece, *The Last Judgment*, there (1499). His studies of muscular nudes were admired by and influential on Michelangelo.

signoria (Italian: lordship) A form of government in late medieval Italian city-states following the collapse of communal government caused by factional struggles. Control was given (sometimes voluntarily) to a *signore* (lord), who formed a more or less despotic government. *Signori* established dynasties, especially in N Italy (e.g. the *Visconti and *Este), which often gained reputations for good government and artistic patronage.

Sigurdsson. *See* Sverrir.

Sihanouk, Norodim, Prince (1923–   ) King (1941–70; 1993–   ) of Cambodia. When the Japanese occupation ended in 1945, Sihanouk, after much opposition and factional strife, achieved Cambodia's independence from France (1953). Abdicating in 1955, he continued to dominate Cambodian politics as prime minister until 1970, when his regime was overthrown by a military coup and he went into exile in China. After the victory of the Khmer Rouge guerrillas (1975) he again became head of state but retired in 1976. He continued in exile his efforts to regain control of the Cambodian government and was reinstated on the throne in 1993.

sika A deer, *Cervus nippon*, also called Japanese deer, native to S Asia, Japan and Taiwan and introduced to New Zealand and Europe. Gray-brown in winter and chestnut with white spots in summer, its shoulder height is 27.5–40 in (70–100 cm). Stags have slender eight-pointed antlers about 32 in (80 cm) long.

Sikhism The religion of some nine million Indians, mostly inhabiting the Punjab. Founded in the 15th century by the Guru *Nanak, Sikhism combines Hindu and Islamic ideas. The Hindu concepts of *karma and rebirth are accepted, but the caste system is rejected. Sikhs believe that god is the only reality and that spiritual release can be obtained by taming the ego through devotional singing, recitation of the divine name, meditation, and service. The guidance of the *guru is essential. The concept of Khalsa, a chosen race of warrior-saints, is central, as are the so-called five Ks: *kangha* (comb); *kacch* (shorts); *kirpan* (sword); *kara* (steel bracelet); and *kes* (uncut hair and beard). *See also* 'Adi Granth. The Sikhs came to world attention in 1984 with the occupation of their holy temple at Amritsar by Indian troops, which was followed a few months later by the assassination of Indian prime minister Indira Gandhi by her Sikh bodyguards. Violent reprisals against Sikhs took place throughout India.

Sikh Wars 1. (1845–46) The war caused by the invasion of British India by the Sikhs from their territory in the Punjab. The Sikh defeat resulted in the loss of territory that included Kashmir. **2.** (1848–49) The war that developed from a Sikh revolt at Multan. Following the Sikh defeat, by Gough at Gujarat (Feb 22, 1849), the Punjab was annexed by the British.

Sikkim A state in NE India, in the Himalayas E of Nepal. Low valleys rise to Mount Kangchenjunga, 8598 m (28,208 ft), providing a tremendous range in climate and vegetation. The world's biggest cardamom producer, Sikkim also grows mandarin oranges, grains, potatoes, pulses, and ginger. Copper is mined and the jungle exploited for timber. A variety of people, most of whom are Buddhists, inhabit Sikkim. *History*: ruled by a Buddhist dynasty, Sikkim passed under British and then Indian protection (1947). Following a plebiscite Sikkim became the 22nd state of India in 1975. Area: 2817 sq mi (7298 sq km). Population (1991): 405,505. Capital: Gangtok.

Sikorski, Władysław (1881–1943) Polish general and statesman. Sikorski was prime minister (1922–23) and then minister of military affairs (1924–25). After Poland's collapse in 1939, he became prime minister of the Polish government-in-exile in London. The circumstances of his death, in an airplane crash near Gibraltar, are the subject of a controversial play by Rolf *Hochhuth.

Sikorsky, Igor Ivan (1889–1972) Russian-born US aeronautical engineer, who invented the helicopter. He began experimenting with helicopter designs in 1909 but his early models failed and he turned to the design and construction of aircraft, producing the S-1 biplane in 1910. In 1919 he moved to the US, returning to the problem of helicopters in the 1930s and completing the first successful model, the VS-300, in 1939.

silage A cattle food produced from a fresh fodder crop, usually grass or a green cereal crop, that has been preserved by controlled bacterial fermentation. The crop is placed in an airtight structure (silo) and allowed to ferment; the organic acids produced "pickle" the crop and prevent further decay, resulting in highly digestible and nutritious food. Silage making is a rapid and versatile method of fodder conservation.

Silchester (Latin: Calleva Atrebatum) An ancient capital of the British tribe of Atrebates in S England. Rebuilt after the Roman conquest, Silchester was inhabited until the 6th century AD. The Roman town wall (c. 200 AD) is still visible.

Silenus In Greek mythology, an elderly *Satyr, companion of the god *Dionysus. He was famed for his wisdom and prophetic powers as well as his drunkenness. The Sileni were his fellow nature spirits.

Silesia A region of E central Europe now in NE Czech Republic, SE Germany, and SW Poland. Because of its geographical position, mineral wealth, and industrial potential, Silesia has been disputed territory since the 17th century, when it was claimed by both Austria and Prussia. Its seizure by Frederick the Great of Prussia, which precipitated the War of the *Austrian Succession, was finally recognized by Austria in 1763, after the *Seven Years' War. After World War I it was divided between Czechoslovakia, Germany, and Poland and after World War II, between Czechoslovakia and Poland.

silhouette In art, a profile image or portrait in black on a white background or vice versa. Named for the French finance minister Étienne de Silhouette (1709–67), who made paper cut-outs of silhouettes, this type of portrait was very popular in the late 18th and early 19th centuries until it was supplanted by photography.

silica The mineral silicon dioxide, SiO_2, the most abundant of all minerals. There are three main forms of silica: *quartz, tridymite, and cristobalite, the last two occurring in acidic volcanic rocks. Cryptocrystalline silica is *chalcedony; amorphous silica is *opal. Creosite is a high-pressure variety, found near meteorite craters. Lechatelierite is a natural silica glass. Silica content is used to classify igneous rocks into acidic (over 65% silica), intermediate (52–66% silica), basic (45–52% silica), and ultrabasic (under 45% silica) varieties. Since these terms do not reflect pH value, another classification based on silica content is also frequently used; in it, igneous rocks are classified as oversaturated (containing free silica), saturated (all silica combined with no unsaturated minerals, e.g. feldspathoids), or undersaturated (containing unsaturated minerals). *See also* silicate minerals.

silicate minerals A group of minerals that constitute about 90% of the earth's crust and one-third of all minerals. They consist of silicates of calcium, magnesium, aluminum, or other metals, in varying degrees of complexity. They are classified according to their atomic structure; all are based on the tetrahedral unit SiO_4. *Feldspar and *quartz (which is chemically an oxide but resembles the silicates more closely in many properties and is usually included in this group) are the most common. *See also* amphiboles; clay; garnet; micas; olivine; pyroxene.

silicon (Si) The second most abundant element in the earth's crust, after oxygen. It is a major constituent of almost all rock-forming minerals (*see* silicate minerals). The element was discovered by J. J. Berzelius in 1824 and is extracted by reduction of the oxide (silica; SiO_2) with carbon in an electric furnace. Pure silicon is now of great importance in the electronics industry as a semiconductor. It is prepared by decomposition of trichlorosilane ($SiCl_3H$). Silicates have been important for centuries as the main constituents of pottery, glasses, and many building materials. Silicon carbide (*see* carborundum) is a widely used abrasive, refractory, and semiconductor. Organic silicon compounds are known as *silicones. At no 14; at wt 28.086; mp 2573°F (1410°C); bp 4275°F (2355°C).

silicon chip. *See* integrated circuit.

silicones Synthetic polymers consisting of chains of alternating silicon and oxygen atoms, with organic groups attached to the former. The chains can be cross-linked to varying degrees. Silicones include fluids, greases, rubbers, and resins. All have similar chemical properties: stability to heat, oxidation, many chemicals, and oils. The main applications are in adhesives, paints, elastomers, and waterproofing agents.

silicosis A lung disease caused by prolonged inhalation of silica dust: an occupational disease of stonecutters, quarry workers, etc. Silica causes more damage than an equivalent amount of coal dust: the air sacs of the lungs become thickened and scarred, causing breathlessness and coughing in the patients. There is no specific treatment and prevention by use of masks and other safety measures is essential. *See also* pneumoconiosis.

silk The thread produced by the caterpillar of the *silkworm moth and the fabric woven from it. The cocoons are unraveled and the filaments from several twisted together; processing this raw silk includes combining these strands, washing away the sticky sericin secretion, and sometimes adding metallic salts for weight. China, where silk production was first practiced, and Japan are the leading producers of pure silk; wild silk, produced by silkworms that feed on leaves other than mulberry or by uncultivated silkworms, includes a coarser brown Indian silk. Lustrous, elastic, absorbent, and very strong, silk remains a luxury fabric considerably superior to its synthetic imitations.

silk-cotton tree. *See* kapok.

Silk Road A trade route, 4000 mi (6400 km) long, that connected China with the Mediterranean. It was most used in antiquity, when silk was taken westward and wool and precious metals eastward, but was again traveled in the later Middle Ages, notably by Marco Polo.

silkworm A caterpillar that spins a silken cocoon, especially one that is suitable for commercial silk production. The commonest is the Chinese silkworm (*Bombyx mori*), which feeds on mulberry leaves. The pupae are killed by heat and the silken thread, up to 2,953 ft (900 m) long, is then unwound. 50,000 cocoons are needed to produce 2.2 lb (1 kg) of silk. The Japanese oak silkmoth (*Antherea yamanai*) and the Chinese species *A. pernyi* are also used. Some American moths, such as the *cecropia and *io, also produce silk.

silky oak One of two species of Australian trees. *Grevillea robusta*, found in forests of E Australia, grows to a height of 115 ft (35 m) and has fernlike leaves. It is widely cultivated in the tropics as an ornamental or shade tree. The northern silky oak (*Cardwellia sublimis*) is an important timber tree, its pinkish soft wood being used in furniture manufacturing and for building purposes.

silky terrier A breed of toy dog developed in Australia by crossing the Australian terrier with the Yorkshire terrier. Formerly called the Sydney silky, it has a compact body with short legs. The long fine glossy coat is blue and tan or gray-blue and tan. Height: 9–10 in (23–25 cm).

sill A horizontal or near-horizontal sheetlike mass of intrusive igneous rock, lying parallel to the layering of the rock into which it is intruded. Most sills consist of medium-grained hypabyssal rock, the commonest being dolerite. *Compare* dike.

Sillitoe, Alan (1928–) British novelist. He won immediate success with his first novel, *Saturday Night and Sunday Morning* (1958), about the violent and alienated life of a Nottingham factory worker. This was followed by a book of short stories, *The Loneliness of the Long Distance Runner* (1959). His many later books include the semiautobiographical *Raw Material* (1972), and additional short stories, *The Second Chance* (1981). He also wrote the novel, *Her Victory* (1982) and *Life Goes On* (1985).

SILK ROAD

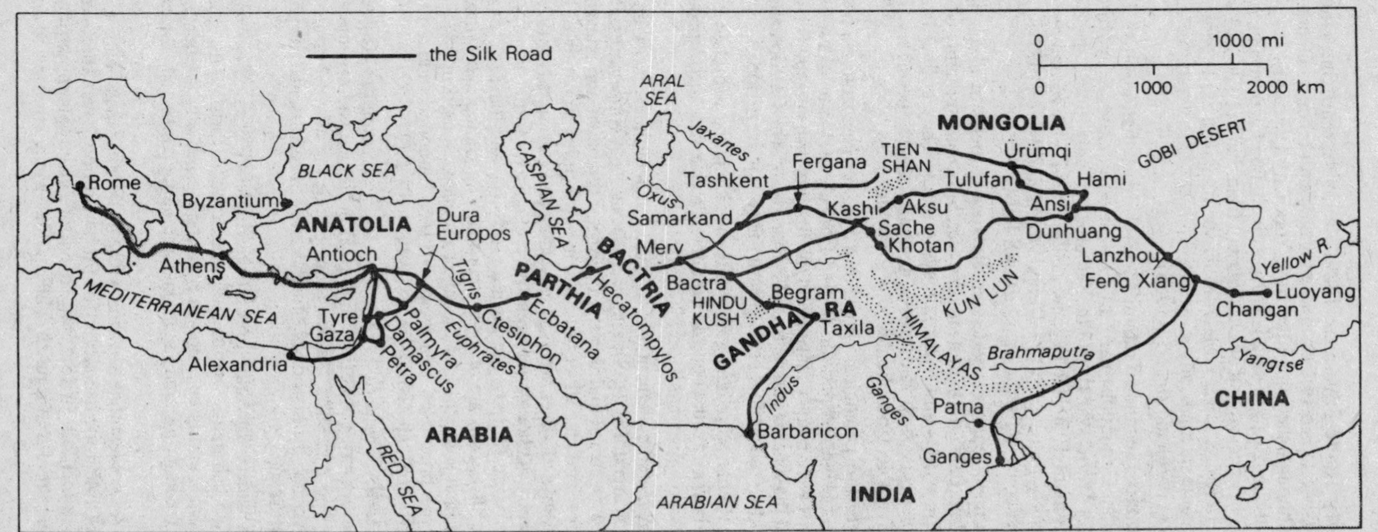

SILK ROAD *Between the 1st century* BC *and the 3rd century* AD, *Chinese silks traveled westward to the Mediterranean in exchange for precious metals.*

Sills, Beverly (Belle Silverman; 1929–) US soprano. She sang with the Philadelphia Civic Opera in 1948 and with the San Francisco Opera Company (1953–55). Although she joined the New York City Opera in 1955, it was not until 1966 that she began to sing lead roles, including Cleopatra in *Julius Caesar*. She made her guest debut at La Scala in Milan, Italy (1969) and at the Metropolitan Opera House (1975). Meanwhile, she remained at the New York City Opera and became its managing director (1980–88). She wrote two autobiographies, *Bubbles* (1976) and *Beverly* (1988).

Silone, Ignazio (Secondo Tranquilli; 1900–78) Italian novelist. He helped found the Italian Communist party in 1921, lived in exile in Switzerland from 1930 until after World War II, and then returned to Italy to lead the Democratic Socialist party until 1950. He became disillusioned with communism, but his novels, especially *Fontamara* (1930) and *Bread and Wine* (1937), express his strong socialist concern for the peasants of S Italy.

silt A fine-grained sedimentary deposit, the rock particles of which range from 0.0008–0.002 in (0.002–0.06 mm) in diameter. Silts consist mainly of clay minerals, with iron oxides and hydroxides and silica. They collect in sheltered marine environments, such as estuaries, making dredging necessary if the estuary is to be navigable. Consolidated silts form siltstones.

Silurian period A geological period of the Lower Paleozoic era between the Ordovician and Devonian periods, lasting from about 445 to 415 million years ago. Conditions were mainly marine and the first true fish appeared. The first evidence of land plants also comes from Silurian rocks. The Caledonian period of mountain building reached its peak toward the end of the period.

Silvanus A Roman woodland god, sometimes identified with the Greek *Pan. He was usually portrayed as an old countryman. He was worshiped at sacred groves or trees.

silver (Ag) A metallic element, known since ancient times. It occurs in nature as the metal, as argentite (Ag_2S), and in lead, zinc, and copper ores. Pure silver has the highest electrical and thermal conductivity known and is used in some printed electrical circuits. Silver tarnishes in air, forming a coating of black sulfide (Ag_2S). Alloys of silver are used as solders and sterling silver (92.5% pure) is used for jewelry. Although not a reactive metal, silver forms many compounds including the oxide (Ag_2O), the nitrate ($AgNO_3$), and halides (for example, AgCl, AgBr). Silver salts are of great importance in photography since they are light sensitive, and some 30% of the silver produced is used in this way. Silver iodide (AgI) has been used in attempts to seed clouds to induce rainfall. At no 47; at wt 107.868; mp 1765°F (926°C); bp 4017°F (2212°C).

Silver Age, Latin The period (18–c. 130 AD) succeeding the *Golden Age of *Latin literature. During this time rhetorical brilliance and ornamentation became prized for its own sake. Major writers include the satirist *Juvenal, the epigrammatist *Martial, the historians *Tacitus and *Suetonius, and the philosopher and dramatist *Seneca.

silverfish A widely distributed primitive wingless □insect, *Lepisma saccharina*, also called fish moth. One of the three-pronged *bristletails, it is covered with silvery scales and is common in buildings, especially kitchens, bakeries, and libraries, feeding on starchy materials, including books and fabrics. Family: *Lepismatidae*.

silverplate Any object that is plated with silver rather than being solid silver. The first substitute for pure silver for tableware, etc., was the invention of *Sheffield plate in 1742. In 1840 the advent of *electroplating brought silverplated domestic articles to a much wider public. Many silverplated articles are marked EPNS (electroplated nickel silver)—nickel silver itself is an alloy of copper, nickel, and zinc and contains no silver; in this process a layer of silver is electroplated onto the nickel-silver base.

silverside A fish, also called sand smelt or whitebait, belonging to a family (*Atherinidae*) found in fresh and coastal waters of warm and temperate regions. Its small slim body, up to 28 in (70 cm) long, bears a silvery band along each side and two dorsal fins. Order: *Atheriniformes*.

sima The earth's oceanic crust, which is composed of basaltic rocks rich in silica (Si) and magnesium (Mg). It is denser than the *sial of the continental crust and is believed to continue beneath it.

Si-ma Qian (*or* Ssu-ma Ch'ien; c. 145–c. 85 BC) Chinese historian, astronomer, and calendar reformer. He succeeded his father as historian to the Han emperor Wu, but he offended the emperor and was castrated and imprisoned. He later became palace secretary. His *Records of the Historian*, the first major Chinese historical work, included the entire documented history of China to that date.

Simenon, Georges (1903–89) Belgian novelist. The best-known of his several hundred novels are his detective stories featuring the Parisian *commissaire de police*, Maigret, who first appeared in 1931. His other novels, written in a brisk colloquial style and with intuitive psychological perception, include *La Neige était sale* (1948) and the semiautobiographical *Pedigree* (1948).

Simeon, tribe of One of the 12 *tribes of Israel. It claimed descent from Simeon, the son of Jacob and Leah. The territory allocated to the tribe was S of that of Judah, W and SW of the Dead Sea. It was eventually assimilated into Judah.

Simeon Stylites, St (c. 390–459 AD) Syrian monk and hermit, who lived for over 35 years on a small platform on top of a tall pillar (Greek, *stylos*). His many imitators were known as stylites. Feast day: Jan 5.

Simferopol 44 57N 34 05E The capital of Ukraine's Crimean *oblast* (autonomous region). It has food-processing, engineering, and consumer-goods industries. Population (1991 est): 353,000.

simile A figure of speech in which two things are compared in order to emphasize a particular feature or quality they share. A simile differs from a *metaphor in being an explicit comparison, usually using the words *as* or *like*, for example "He fought like a lion."

Simla 31 07N 77 09E A city in India, the capital of Himachal Pradesh situated in the foothills of the Himalayas. It was the summer capital of India (1865–1939). Population (1981): 70,604.

Simms, William Gilmore (1806–70) US novelist. He wrote many historical romances concerning life in the South, including *Guy Rivers* (1834) and *The Yemassee* (1835). He edited various southern magazines, defended slavery, and suffered personal ruin in the Civil War.

Simnel, Lambert (c. 1475–1535) English impostor whom the Yorkists tried to pass off as Edward, earl of Warwick (1475–99), a Yorkist claimant to the throne, in a plot to overthrow Henry VII. Simnel was captured in 1487 and subsequently worked in the king's kitchens.

Simon, St In the New Testament, one of the 12 Apostles. He is surnamed the Canaanite or Zelotes, which possibly means that he was one of the *Zealots. He preached in Egypt and joined St *Jude in Persia, where, according to one tradition, he was martyred by being cut in half with a saw. Feast day: Oct 28.

GEORGES SIMENON

Simonov, Konstantin (1915–79) Soviet novelist, playwright, poet, and journalist. His writings, which focus chiefly on World War II, include the poem "Wait for Me" and the novels *Days and Nights* (1945), on the defense of Stalingrad, and *Victims and Heroes* (1959).

simple harmonic motion Any oscillation performed by a body about some reference point so that the restraining force is directly proportional to its displacement from that point. Examples of simple harmonic motion include a *pendulum swinging through a small angle and a vibrating string. The maximum displacement of the system is known as the amplitude and the time taken for one complete oscillation, the *period. The displacement, x, at a time t is simply represented by the equation $x = A\sin\omega t$, where A is the amplitude and ω the angular frequency, which is related to the period T by $\omega = 2\pi/T$. Thus a graph of the displacement x plotted against time t has the shape of a sine wave, i.e. it is sinusoidal.

Simplon Pass An alpine pass linking Brig in Switzerland with Iselle in Italy. It was built between 1800 and 1807 on Napoleon's orders and reaches a height of 6590 ft (2009 m). The **Simplon Tunnel** to the NE is, at 12 mi (20 km), the longest rail tunnel in the world. Built in 1890 by Alfred Brandt (1846–99), it was opened in 1906.

Simpson, George Gaylord (1902–) US paleontologist, noted for his contributions to knowledge of the early history of mammals and the intercontinental migration of species. Simpson studied mammalian fossil remains in both North and South America and, in *the Meaning of Evolution* (1949), discussed the philosophical implications of evolutionary theory.

Simpson Desert (*or* Arunta Desert) A desert of central Australia, mainly in Northern Territory. It consists of an arid region covered by parallel sand dunes, which extend to 100 mi (160 km) in length. Area: about 29,723 sq mi (77,000 sq km).

Sinai A desert peninsula in Egypt, bounded by Israel and the Gulf of Aqaba to the E and the Gulf of Suez and mainland Egypt to the W. Mount Sinai, 7497 ft (2285 m) high, is in the mountain range in the S. According to the Old Testament it was on this mountain that Moses received the tablets of the law from Jehovah (Exodus 24). The N half of the desert is plateau. The chief resources of the region are manganese and the oil deposits in the W, based on Sudr; agriculture is practiced on the Mediterranean coast. Sinai was occupied by Israel in 1956 and again in the 1967 Arab-Israeli War and following the 1973 war Egyptian and Israeli lines were established on either side of a UN buffer zone. Under the 1979 Egyptian-Israeli agreement a large proportion of the area was returned to Egypt, with Israeli withdrawal completed in 1982.

Sinatra, Frank (Francis Albert S.; 1915–   ) US singer and film actor, who recorded his first hit, "All or Nothing at All," in 1943. His nonsinging role in the film *From Here to Eternity* (1953) earned him an Oscar; he subsequently appeared in such films as *Guys and Dolls* (1955) *The Manchurian Candidate* (1962), and *The First Deadly Sin* (1980). He recorded such hits as "Strangers in the Night" (1966) and his concerts continue to be very popular.

FRANK SINATRA *He is seen (left) in a comic scene with Bing Crosby (center) and Dean Martin.*

Sinclair, Upton (1878–1968) US novelist. A committed socialist, he used the profits from *The Jungle* (1906), a novel of social protest, to establish a cooperative for left-wing writers and to finance several unsuccessful political campaigns. The best-known of his many polemical novels are the 11-volume Lanny Budd series known as *World's End* (1940–53).

Sind A province in SE Pakistan, on the Arabian Sea. From the broad Indus lowland it extends E into the Thar Desert and W into rocky hills. Grains, other crops, and livestock are raised. Important industries include textiles, chemicals, and cement. *History*: Sind's history goes back 5000 years. Islam was introduced in 711–12 AD and British rule established in 1843. Area: 54,407 sq mi (140,914 sq km). Population (1983 est): 20,312,000. Capital: Karachi.

Singapore, Republic of A republic in SE Asia, off the S tip of Peninsular Malaysia, consisting of the island of Singapore and over 50 islets. The city of Singapore, located in the S, occupies a substantial part of the island's area. The majority of the diverse population is Chinese with minorities of Malays, Indians, and others. *Economy*: Singapore is the largest port in SE Asia and one of the largest in the world, its importance being as an entrepôt port on a major searoute. It is a major commercial center and in recent years industry has been expanded and diversified. The chief industries are oil refining (it has the third largest refining complex in the world), shipbuilding and repairing, textiles, and electronics. The fishing industry is being developed, ornamental fish being an important export. The main exports are rubber, oil and oil products, machinery, and transport equipment. *History*: although a prosperous commercial center in the Middle Ages, the island was largely uninhabited in 1819 when Sir Stamford Raffles established a station of the British East India Company there. In 1824 it was ceded to Britain as part of the *Straits Settlements. During World War II it was occupied by the Japanese, the British defense forces having surrendered in 1942. It became a separate British colony in 1946 and gained its independence in 1959. It joined the Federation of Malaysia on its formation (1963) but broke away in 1965, following conflict with the predominantly Malay central government, and formed an independent republic. *Lee Kuan Yew, prime minister since 1959, officially retired in 1990 but remained influential as a senior cabinet minister. Goh Chok Tong, who followed as prime minister, spearheaded the movement to revise the constitution in 1991, which led in 1993 to the country's first direct presidential election, won by Ong Teng Cheong, who had greater power than his predecessors. President: Ong Teng Cheong. Prime Minister: Goh Chok Tong. Official languages: Chinese, English, Malay, and Tamil. Official currency: Singapore dollar of 100 cents. Area: 232 sq mi (602 sq km). Population (1992 est): 2,800,000.

Singer, Isaac Bashevis (1904–91) US novelist and short-story writer. Born into a rabbinical Jewish family in Poland, he emigrated to the US in 1935. His novels and collections of stories, written in Yiddish and frequently dramatizing themes from Jewish life in Poland, include *Gimpel the Fool* (1957), *Shosha* (1978), *Old Love* (1979), and *The Collected Stories of Isaac Bashevis Singer* (1982). He won the Nobel Prize in Literature, 1979.

Singer, Isaac Merrit (1811–75) US inventor, who in 1857 designed and built the first commercially successful domestic sewing machine. It was a great improvement on Elias *Howe's machine and incorporated a number of innovations, such as continuous stitching, that remain the basis of all modern sewing machines.

singing The use of the human voice as a musical instrument, involving the control of a column of air sent from the lungs through the larynx, where it activates the vocal cords, and the subsequent resonance of the sounds produced within the sinus and mouth cavities. Styles of singing vary enormously in an art that covers many traditional folk techniques as well as those cultivated in Europe for opera and art song. The greatest European school of singing was the lyrical *bel canto (Italian: fine singing) style taught by the Italians in the 17th and 18th centuries. In the 19th century singers developed more dramatic and declamatory techniques in order to be heard over the increasingly large orchestra. In the 20th century singers have made use of microphones to amplify the voice, particularly in pop music. *See also* alto; baritone; bass; contralto; countertenor; soprano; tenor.

Sing Sing. *See* Ossining.

Sinhalese The major ethnic group in Sri Lanka. They speak an *Indo-Aryan language that has been much influenced by *Pali and the Dravidian languages, particularly *Tamil. They are descended from migrants from Bengal, who colonized Sri Lanka during the 5th century BC. An agricultural people, they base their social organization on caste and practice Theravada Buddhism.

sinkhole (*or* sink) A saucerlike hollow in the ground surface, typical of chalk and limestone areas. It may form through the solvent action on limestone of rain containing dissolved carbon dioxide; alternatively it may be due to a rock collapse. Sinkholes often act as channels down which water seeps into underground drainage systems.

Sinkiang Uigur. *See* Xinjiang Uygur Autonomous Region.

Sinn Féin (Irish: Ourselves) An Irish nationalist party organized by Arthur Griffith in 1905. In 1918, under Eamon *De Valera, it won a majority of the Irish seats in the British Parliament and achieved the creation of the Irish Free State in 1922. Sinn Féin exists today as the political wing of the republican movement. *See also* Irish Republican Army.

Sino-Japanese Wars **1.** (1894–95) The war between China and Japan resulting from rivalry in Korea. War was declared after the Japanese sank the *Kowshing*, which was transporting Chinese reinforcements to aid the Korean king in suppressing the Tonghak uprising. Japan inflicted a crushing defeat on China, which was forced to pay a large indemnity and cede Taiwan, the Pescadores, and the Liaodong peninsula. **2.** (1937–45) The war between China and Japan brought about by Japanese expansion into China in the 1930s. The Japanese had established a puppet state in Manchuria (*see* Manchukuo) in 1932 but only after the negotiation of a Nationalist-Communist *United Front against Japan did full war break out. The Japanese took Shanghai and Nanchang in 1937 and Wuhan and Canton in 1938. Their position remained strong until the US entered World War II (1941) and gave China assistance. After Japan's surrender (1945) China regained Manchuria, Taiwan, and the Pescadores.

Sinop 42 02N 35 09E A port in central N Turkey, on the Black Sea. Ancient Sinope was the most important Greek colony on the Euxine (Black) Sea and flourished under Mithridates the Great, during whose reign fine buildings and a harbor were constructed. It became part of the Ottoman Empire in 1458. Population: 15,096.

Sino-Tibetan languages A group of languages spoken in E Asia. It includes all the *Chinese dialects (which use the same alphabet but differ substantially in sound), the Tibeto-Burman languages (Tibetan, Burmese, and many related languages spoken in the valleys of the Himalayas), and probably the Tai languages, such as Siamese, Laotian, and Shan. The main characteristic that justifies this large grouping is the monosyllabic nature of the vocabulary of all these languages and their use of tonality to differentiate otherwise similar words. They are all isolating languages, that is they use word order, not inflection, to determine grammatical relations.

sintering The heating without melting of powdered substance, usually metal or plastic, so that it becomes a solid mass. *See also* powder metallurgy.

Sintra (former name: Cintra) 38 48N 9 22W A city in central Portugal. Its beauty has been celebrated by several literary figures, including Byron in his *Childe Harolde*. The many notable buildings include the royal palace (14th–15th centuries) in Moorish and gothic styles. It is a tourist and agricultural center. Population (1987 est): 289,000.

Sinŭiju 40 04N 124 25E A port in North Korea, on the Yalu River opposite Andong, China. Its industrial development began during the Japanese occupation (1910–45) and its principal industries include sawmills and the manufacture of paper. Population (1967 est): 165,000.

sinus A hollow cavity, especially one in a bone. The term usually refers to the air sinuses of the head, which are cavities in the facial bones; all have connections to the nasal cavity and they are susceptible to infection (*see* sinusitis). The term is also used for a pus-filled channel leading from an infected organ or tissue to a surface (usually the skin).

sinusitis Inflammation of the sinuses—the spaces in the skull that are connected to the nose. They commonly become infected when a patient has a cold or similar infection, causing pain in the face and prolonging the original illness. Sinusitis can also be caused by an allergic reaction. If the inflammation persists the affected sinuses may need to be surgically drained or washed out.

Siouan languages A family of North American Indian languages including Dakota *Sioux, *Crow, and several others. Most are spoken by Plains tribes. Some experts classify the Siouan languages as a branch of a larger family called Macro-Siouan, which includes the Iroquoian and Caddoan languages.

Sioux A confederation of North American Plains Indian tribes, also known as the Dakota. They fought fiercely against white encroachments upon their territories and defeated General Custer at the battle of the *Little Bighorn (1876) under their leaders Sitting Bull and Crazy Horse. The last conflict with the whites resulted in the massacre of a group of Sioux at *Wounded Knee (1890).

Sioux City 42 30N 96 28W A city in Iowa, on the Missouri River. An agricultural trading center, it has a large livestock market and many food-processing plants. Population (1990): 80,505.

Sioux Falls 43 34N 96 42W A city in South Dakota, on the Big Sioux River. Founded in 1857, it has one of the country's largest sheep and cattle markets and is an important wheat center. Manufactures include farm machinery and electrical components. Population (1990): 100,814.

Siqueiros, David Alfaro (1896–1974) Mexican painter, one of the leaders in the Mexican Revolution of 1910 and one of the founders of modern Mexican art. A committed socialist from the start of his career, Siqueiros is best known for his monumental murals that reflect his intimate knowledge of the Mexican people. His first major murals were painted in collaboration with *Rivera and *Orozco in the National Preparatory School, Mexico City; perhaps the most impressive is *The March of Humanity*, measuring 50,000 sq ft (4600 sq m), which Siqueiros painted while he was in prison for his political activities. From the 1950s he was internationally recognized as one of Mexico's greatest artists.

siren An eel-like *salamander belonging to a North American family (*Sirenidae*; 3 species). Sirens have no hind legs, very small forelegs, and permanent gills. They hunt for worms, snails, etc., in ponds and swamps. The largest species is the 24 in (60 cm) mud-colored great siren (*Siren lacertina*) and the smallest is the gray mud siren (*Pseudobranchus striatus*), about 8 in (20 cm) long.

Sirens In Greek mythology, female creatures, sometimes portrayed with bird-like features, who lured sailors to their island by their singing and then destroyed them. *Odysseus saved himself by tying himself to the mast of his ship and filling the ears of his crew with wax. The *Argonauts were protected by the superior singing of *Orpheus.

Sirius (*or* Dog Star) The brightest star in the sky, with an apparent magnitude of −1.47. It occurs in the constellation Canis Major and can be found by following the descending line of Orion's Belt. It is also one of the nearest stars, lying 8.7 light years away. It forms a visual *binary star with **Sirius B**, which was the first *white dwarf to be detected, in 1925.

sirocco (*or* scirocco) A southerly wind occurring in N Africa, Sicily, and S Italy. Hot and dry on the N African coast, it picks up moisture as it crosses the Mediterranean Sea bringing extensive clouds to S Italy.

sisal A perennial plant, **Agave sisalana*, native to central America and cultivated throughout the tropics for its fiber. The plant, the stem of which grows to a height of only 35 in (90 cm), matures three to five years after planting and yields fiber for seven to eight years. Sisal fiber is obtained by crushing the leaves to a pulp and then scraping the pulp from the fiber, which is washed and dried. It is used in shipping, general industry, and agriculture.

SISAL *The fiber is obtained from the leaves of the plant, which are up to 6 ft (1.8 m) long. Mature plants produce flower stalks, up to 20 ft (6 m) high, bearing yellow flowers.*

siskin A Eurasian *finch, *Carduelis spinus*, occurring in N forests and at high altitudes in the S. It is about 5 in (12 cm) long with a dark yellow-green plumage, paler streaked underparts, bright-yellow wingbars, and in the male a black chin and crown. Siskins feed on small seeds, particularly those extracted from alder cones.

Sisley, Alfred (1839–99) Impressionist painter, born in Paris of British parents. In 1862, he met *Monet and *Renoir and later exhibited with them. In the 1870s he produced some of his best landscapes, for example *Misty Morning* (Louvre), and three pictures of the *Floods at Port-Marly*. Unable to sell his works, he spend his last years in poverty.

Sistine Chapel The principal chapel of the Vatican, so called because it was built for Pope Sixtus V (1473) by Giovanni dei Dolci. It is the meeting place for the College of Cardinals but is chiefly famous for its Renaissance interior decoration, with murals by *Perugino, *Botticelli, and *Ghirlandaio and the roof and ceiling by *Michelangelo.

Sisyphus A legendary Greek king of Corinth. For various offenses he was condemned in the underworld eternally to roll a boulder to the top of a hill, from whence it always rolled down again.

sitar An Indian long-necked *lute with a resonating body made from a large gourd, seven metal strings stopped against movable arched frets, and a series of sympathetic strings. The distinctive pitch distortions of sitar music are achieved by pulling and easing the strings over the raised frets. □musical instruments.

sitatunga A spiral-horned antelope, *Tragelaphus spekei*, of central African swamplands, also called marshbuck or water kodoe. Long-legged and up to 48 in (120 cm) high at the shoulder, it is deep brown with white markings on the face, chest, and back. The female lacks horns. Sitatungas feed on shrubs and aquatic plants.

Sitka 57 05N 135 20W A port in Alaska, on Baranof Island. Founded in 1799, it was the capital of Russian America until 1867 and is the site of a Russian Orthodox cathedral (1848). It was an important US naval base during World War II. The main industries are fishing and timber. Population (1990): 8558.

Sitting Bull (c. 1834–93) Chief of the Northern Sioux Indians. Early in his career he acquiesced to the demands of the Army that his people be resettled on the North Platte River (1868), but when the terms of the treaty were violated, he led a confederation of Indian forces in active opposition to the army. Following the massacre of Gen. George A. *Custer and his troops at the Battle of the *Little Big Horn, Sitting Bull fled with his men into Canada. After an amnesty (1881), he settled on a Dakota reservation but was killed during further hostilities in the 1890s.

Sitwell, Edith (1887–1964) British poet and writer. A lighthearted aestheticism characterizes her early experimental poetry, especially *Façade* (1923), and *Gold Coast Customs* (1929). Her brother **Sir Osbert Sitwell** (1892–1969) wrote poems, short stories, and novels, notably *Before the Bombardment* (1926), but his best-known works are his nostalgic autiobiographical memoirs. Both he and his sister gave encouragement to a number of writers, artists, and musicians. The youngest brother **Sir Sacheverell Sitwell** (1897–1988) is best known as an art critic, especially of baroque art, and as a travel-book writer.

SI units (Système International d'Unités) An international system of units, based on the *m.k.s. system, used for all scientific purposes. It has seven base units (meter, kilogram, second, ampere, kelvin, candela, and mole) and two supplementary units (radian and steradian). All physical quantities are expressed in these units or in derived units consisting of combinations of these units, 17 of which have special names and agreed symbols. Decimal multiples of all units are expressed by a set of prefixes. Where possible a prefix representing 10 raised to a power that is a multiple of 3 is used.

Sivaji (1627–80) Emperor of India (1647–80), who founded the Maratha dynasty. Born and reared in Poona (later the Maratha capital), he raised a guerrilla force and soon took control of a large part of Maharashtra. A strong opponent of the Mogul Empire, he was crowned as independent king in 1647 and spread his dominion into S India, leaving a powerful legacy for his successors.

Sivas 39 44N 37 01E A city in central Turkey. It is a trading center for grain, wine, and minerals and has 13th-century Seljuq buildings and a university (1973). Population (1990): 221,512.

Six, Les Six French composers: Auric, Louis Durey (1888–1979), Honegger, Milhaud, Poulenc, and Germaine Tailleferre (1892–1983). These composers came briefly under the influence of Cocteau and Satie in the 1920s; their chief common feature was protest against lingering romanticism and impressionism in French music. They each developed an individual style, however, and did not long remain a group.

SITTING BULL *Chief of the Sioux who led the victorious Indian forces against Custer at the Little Big Horn in 1876.*

Six Nations US Indian tribes of the Iroquois group, mainly in N New York and W Massachusetts and Connecticut. Originally five in number—the Mohawk, Cayuga, Oneida, Seneca, and Onondaga nations—they were joined by the Tuscarora nation in 1722.

Sixtus IV (Francesco della Rovere; 1414–84) Pope (1471–84), notorious for his nepotism, especially in his support of his nephew, the future *Julius II, and for political intrigue, especially against the Medici in Florence. A patron of arts and learning, he instigated the building of the Sistine Chapel and founded its choir.

Sixtus V (Felice Peretti; 1521–90) Pope (1585–90), who reformed papal administration and taxation. He issued a revised version of the Vulgate and was a notable patron of the arts, instigating the building of the Vatican Library and Lateran Palace.

Sjælland (English name: Zealand; German name: Seeland) The largest of the Danish islands, bounded by the Kattegat, the Sound, the Baltic Sea, and the Great Belt. Predominantly low lying and undulating, its fertile soil is important for both arable and dairy farming. Area: 2709 sq mi (7016 sq km) Chief town: Copenhagen.

Skagerrak A channel in N Europe, lying between Denmark and Norway and connecting the Kattegat to the North Sea.

skaldic poetry Old Norse poetry originally recited by skalds (professional bards generally attached to a princely or noble retinue). In contrast to the heroic poetry of the Eddaic tradition (*see* Eddas), it was descriptive and occasional, characterized by elaborate alliteration, internal rhyming, convoluted word order, and highly allusive, often riddling phrases called "kennings." It apparently originated in 9th-century Norway, but its outstanding practitioners were Icelanders (*see* Icelandic literature).

Skalkottas, Nikos (1904–49) Greek composer. He was a pupil of Kurt Weill and Schoenberg. His works include two piano concertos, 36 Greek dances for orchestra, four string quartets, and a ballet suite *La Mer grecque* (1948).

Skanda (Kumara *or* Karttikeya) In Hindu mythology, a battle god. In one account he is the son of *Shiva, born to defend the gods against the demons. He is represented with six heads and 12 arms and rides on a peacock.

Skanderbeg (George Kastrioti; c. 1404–68) Albanian national hero. Brought up in Islam as a hostage of the Turkish sultan, Skanderbeg led (1444–68) the Albanian resistance movement against Turkey. The use of guerrilla tactics aided by Albania's mountainous topography and a series of alliances with the great powers of Europe ensured his success but after his death the movement collapsed.

Skåne (*or* Scania) A peninsular area in S Sweden, on the Baltic Sea and the Sound. It is known as the "granary of Sweden," its fertile plains producing wheat, rye, barley, oats, potatoes, and sugar beet. Area: 4230 sq mi (10,957 sq km).

Skara Brae A late Neolithic village in Scotland, in Mainland, Orkney, dating to about 2000 BC. The houses were built of dry stone with stone slabs for furniture, all very well preserved. An artificial mound of refuse heaped over the entire settlement, helped to preserve it.

skate A large *ray fish belonging to the family *Rajidae* (over 100 species), especially the genus *Raja*; 20–80 in (50–200 cm) long, skates have a diamond-shaped flattened body with spiny or thorny structures on the upper surface and often an extremely long snout. They lay eggs and some have weak *electric organs on the tail.

skateboarding The recreation and competitive sport of riding on a board about 2.3 ft (70 cm) long to which two pairs of roller-skate wheels are attached. The sport began in about 1960 in California and combines surfing, skiing, and roller-skating techniques. Speeds of up to 66 mph (107 km per hour) have been attained. The first world championships were staged in 1966.

skeleton The rigid supporting framework of an animal's body. In such animals as arthropods it lies outside the body (exoskeleton) and must be shed periodically during growth. Vertebrates, including man, have a skeleton (endoskeleton) of *bones and cartilage that is entirely within the body and grows with age. The human skeleton is made up of over 200 bones, which are connected to each other at *joints and held together by ligaments. The skeleton protects and supports the soft tissues of the body and provides a firm surface for the attachment of muscles and a system of levers that are essential for movement.

Skelton, John (c. 1460–1529) English poet. He was court poet to Henry VII and tutor to the future Henry VIII. His poems include *Speke Parot* (1521), *Colin Clout* (1522), and other satires, several of them attacks on Cardinal *Wolsey. Essentially medieval in form and theme, the most interesting of his poems are often written in short rhyming lines of doggerel verse, known as Skeltonics.

skepticism The philosophical tradition that absolute certainty or knowledge cannot be attained. It began perhaps with ancient Greek skepticism about the senses (*see* Pyrrhon). Sometimes the skeptic's claim was that any knowledge attained must go unrecognized; sometimes he systematically suspected certain subjects, such as reality, religious beliefs, or moral principles, on the grounds, for example, of the relativity or subjectivity of such beliefs.

skiing A recreational and competitive sport consisting of sliding over snow on a pair of specially shaped runners (skis) attached to the feet. Skis have been used in Scandinavia since the Stone Age, but skiing for pleasure did not develop until the late 19th century. It is divided into **Alpine** (*or* downhill) **skiing**, which includes the events of downhill (straightforward racing), slalom (a winding course through "gates"), and giant slalom (faster and less winding than slalom) and **Nordic skiing**, comprising cross-country (or *langlauf*) skiing, which involves self-propulsion and requires lighter equipment than Alpine skiing, and ski jumping. Alpine and Nordic competitions are controlled by the International Ski Federation. There is also freestyle skiing (downhill skiing that is both balletic and gymnastic), skijoring (being towed on skis by a horse or vehicle), and ski flying, which is *hang gliding on skis. Recreational skiing has become a vast vacation industry, the most notable skiing areas of the world being the Rockies and the Alps.

Skikda (former name: Philippeville) 36 58N 6 51E A port in NE Algeria, on the Mediterranean Sea. Occupying the site of the Roman port of Rusicade, it has the remains of a Roman theater. It receives natural gas from the Sahara and exports iron ore. Population (1987): 128,747.

skimmer A black-and-white bird belonging to a family (*Rhynchopidae*; 3 species) occurring chiefly around western Atlantic coasts and African and Asian rivers. The skimmer fishes by flying close to the water, shearing the surface with the lower mandible and snapping the bill shut as soon as a fish is caught.

skin The tissue that covers the body. The outer layer (epidermis) consists of several layers of cells: the outermost layer contains dead cells made of keratin, which are constantly sloughed off and replaced by the deeper layers of continuously dividing cells. The inner layer of skin (dermis) contains *connective tissue with blood vessels, sensory nerve endings, *sweat glands, sebaceous glands (which secrete an oily substance, sebum, that protects the skin surface), and *hair follicles. The skin has several important functions. It protects the body from external injury and desiccation; it assists in regulating body temperature (e.g. by sweating); and it is sensitive to touch, temperature, and pain. The branch of medicine concerned with the diagnosis and treatment of skin disorders is called **dermatology**. Skin grafting is one of the most important and successful *transplantation operations.

skink A lizard belonging to the family *Scincidae* (600 species), occurring throughout the tropics and in temperate North America. Skinks are well adapted for burrowing: up to 20 in (50 cm) long, they have cylindrical streamlined bodies with smooth scales, internal eardrums, a transparent covering over the eye, and often reduced limbs. Many skinks have an elongated tail and move with sideways undulations of the body. They feed on insects or plant material and many bear live young. □reptile.

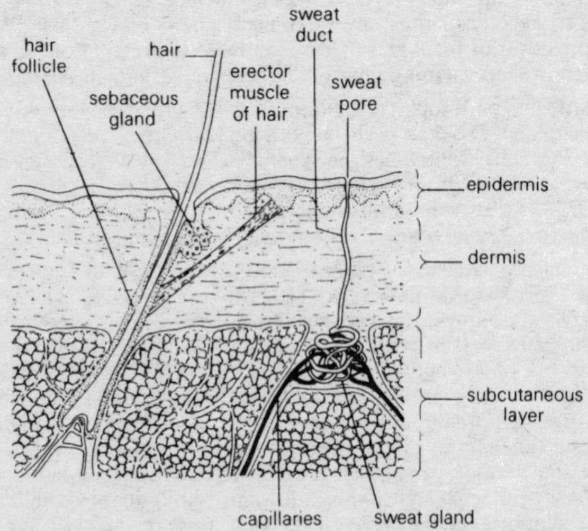

SKIN *A vertical section through the human skin shows its microscopic structure. The subcutaneous layer of fat cells provides insulation.*

Skinner, Burrhus Frederic (1904–90) US psychologist and advocate of *behaviorism. Many of Skinner's experiments involved teaching animals (such as rats and pigeons) by reinforcing the desired action, when achieved, with rewards of food. He developed equipment, including the Skinner box, in order to standardize the teaching of simple actions to small animals and applied his principles to human educational aids. His novel *Walden Two* (1948) describes a utopian society based on his behaviorist principles. His other works include *The Behavior of Organisms* (1938), *Science and Human Behavior* (1953), and *Beyond Freedom and Dignity* (1971).

Skinner, Cornelia Otis (1901–79) US actress and writer. From a theatrical family, she first acted with her father Otis Skinner (1858–1942) in *Blood and Sand* (1921). After touring the US and Europe doing monologues she had written, she appeared in *Major Barbara* (1956) and *The Pleasure of His Company* (1958), which she coauthored. Her essays are collected in *Excuse It, Please* (1936), *Nuts in May* (1950), *The Ape in Me* (1959), and *Elegant Wits and Grand Horizontals* (1962). She also wrote *Our Hearts Were Young and Gay* (1942) with Emily Kimbrough, *Family Circle* (1948), and *Madame Sarah* (1967).

skipjack A *tuna fish, *Euthynnus pelamis*, also called ocean bonito, found in all warm seas. It has four to seven dark horizontal stripes along its belly and grows to about 28 in (70 cm) long.

skipper A butterfly belonging to the widely distributed family *Hesperiidae* (about 3000 species). The adults are small and have a stout body and head resembling a moth and a swift darting flight. The caterpillars feed on plants and pupate in cocoons made of silk and leaves.

Skopje (Turkish name: Usküb) 42 00N 21 28E A historic city in and the capital of Macedonia, on the Vardar River. It became the capital of Serbia in the 14th century and was occupied by the Turks (1392). It was burned down in 1689 to stop a cholera epidemic and almost completely destroyed by an earthquake in 1963. It has a university (1949) and varied industries, including cement, brick, glass, and steel. Population (1991 est): 563,000.

skua A large hook-billed seabird belonging to a family (*Stercorariidae*; 4 species), also called jaeger, breeding in Arctic and Antarctic regions and wintering in warmer latitudes; 20–23 in (52–58 cm) long, skuas are strong fliers and have a dark plumage with two long central tail feathers. They scavenge around seabird colonies, feeding on eggs, chicks, and food scraps. Order: *Charadriiformes* (gulls, plovers, etc.).

skull The skeleton of the head, made up of 22 bones of varying shapes and sizes. The cranium consists of 8 flat platelike bones that surround and protect the brain. Some of these contribute to the formation of the facial skeleton. The remaining 14 bones, including the mandible (*see* jaw), form the face: the mandible is the only movable bone in the skull; the rest are connected by immovable joints called sutures. Numerous holes puncture the skull to allow blood vessels and nerves to pass to and from the brain. The largest of these is the foramen magnum at the base of the skull, through which the spinal cord passes.

skunk A black-and-white carnivorous mammal of the family **Mustelidae* that is known for its defensive habit of ejecting a foul-smelling fluid. The nine species are found in North, South, and Central America. The best known is the North American striped skunk (*Mephitis mephitis*), which inhabits woodland, feeding at night on insects, mice, and fruit.

skydiving (*or* freefalling) The sport of jumping from an airplane with a parachute and performing maneuvers before opening it. During this period of "free fall" the parachutist positions his body to glide or performs, rolls, turns, or other stunts. In a team event divers pass a baton to each other or form a star pattern by joining hands. *See also* parachuting.

Skye The largest and most northerly island of the Inner Hebrides group, off the W coast of Scotland. The island's economy is based chiefly on crofting and tourism; sheep and cattle are also raised. Area: 670 sq mi (1735 sq km). Chief town: Portree.

Skye terrier A bread of dog originating on the Scottish island of Skye and used to flush foxes and badgers from cover. It has a long body, short legs, and a large head with erect or drooping ears. The soft undercoat is covered by a long straight outer coat which may reach the ground. Colors are gray, fawn, cream, or black. Height: 10 in (25 cm).

Skylab A US manned space station launched into earth orbit in May 1973. Three groups of three US astronauts were conveyed to and from the orbiting laboratory by modified Apollo spacecraft (*see* Apollo moon program). They remained on board for a total of 513 man days during the period May 1973, to February 1974. In a weightless environment, they conducted a variety of experiments and observations (especially of the sun). Physical and psychological fitness were carefully monitored. Skylab's orbit eventually became unstable and it crash-landed in July 1979, in Western Australia.

skylark A *lark, *Alauda arvensis*, occurring in Eurasia and N Africa and noted for its sustained warbling flight song. It is about 7 in (17 cm) long and has a streaked brown plumage, a small crest and a white stripe above the eye. Skylarks were a delicacy in the 19th century and are still trapped in parts of Europe.

Skyros (Modern Greek name: Skíros) A Greek island in the central Aegean Sea, the largest of the Northern Sporades. Area: 79 sq mi (205 sq km).

skyscraper A multistory building. Skyscraper building was stimulated by the commercial need for space in cities where land was scarce and land rents high. The first skyscraper, the Equitable Life Assurance Society, was built in New York City in 1868. Architecturally it was made possible by the development of high-speed elevators in the 1850s, although it was only the introduction of a metal frame in Chicago in the 1880s that made further advances possible. The Empire State Building (1930–32) in New York was the tallest in the world until the completion in the 1970s, in the same city, of the World Trade Center, which is 1353 ft (412 m) high. In 1974 the Sears Tower in Chicago rose even higher, to 1454 ft (473 m), to become the world's tallest skyscraper.

Slade, Felix (1790–1868) British art collector, who bequeathed his collection of books, glass, and engravings to the British Museum. He also endowed professorships of art at the Universities of Oxford and Cambridge and at University College, London. The Slade School of Fine Art is named for him.

slander. *See* defamation.

Slánský, Rudolf (1901–52) Czechoslovak statesman, who was the victim of an anti-Semitic purge. Slánský was secretary general of the Communist party in Czechoslovakia's postwar government. In 1951 he and nine other Jews were executed for espionage. He was posthumously absolved.

slate A fine-grained rock produced by the low-grade metamorphism of mudstone, siltstone, or other argillaceous sediments. Its perfect cleavage is due to the parallel alignment of platy crystals of mica and chlorite. Slate is used as a construction material, formerly for roofs but now mainly for facing and ornamental purposes.

Slater, Samuel (1768–1835) US industrialist and inventor; born in England. He emigrated to the US in 1789 and, from memory, recreated the Arkwright spinning frame for an American textile manufacturer in Rhode Island and soon became an owner of the company. He also formed his own company for the manufacture of cotton thread, another firm that specialized in building textile plants (1798), and several other mills and factories throughout New England. *See also* Arkwright, Sir Richard.

slave-making ant An *ant, confined to the N hemisphere, that raid colonies of other ants to capture larvae and pupae, which develop into worker "slaves." Genera: *Harpagoxenus, Formica, Polyergus, Anergates*. *See also* Amazon ant.

Slave River A river in W Canada, flowing N from Lake Athabasca (Alberta) to Great Slave Lake (Mackenzie district); part of the *Mackenzie River system. Length: 258 mi (415 km).

slavery The condition in which human beings are owned by others as private property. Slavery was common throughout the world from earliest times. In ancient Greece and Rome, captives from conquered lands were the chief source of slaves. While most were forced to perform heavy labor, others, with special skills, were often well treated and sometimes freed. The condition of slaves in later Roman times worsened until the deteriorating economy led to the virtual disappearance of slaves and the emergence of *serfs in the Middle Ages. The slave trade again became a lucrative business in the 16th century, when European traders began to transport thousands of Africans to the Americas. By the early 19th century, English humanitarians, such as William *Wilberforce, attacked slavery on moral grounds and it was abolished in all British territories by 1834. In the US, the *abolition movement, headed by such leaders as William

Lloyd *Garrison, and Frederick *Douglass, campaigned agaisnt slavery in the South. The issue of slavery eventually became one of the central causes of the *Civil War. In 1863, Pres. Abraham *Lincoln issued the *Emancipation Proclamation, which officially liberated all slaves in southern states. The 13th Amendment to the Constitution, ratified in 1865, officially abolished the institution of slavery in the US.

Slavonic languages A subgroup of the *Indo-European language family. Slavonic languages are native to E Europe and NW Asia. They are often classified into three groups: South Slavonic (languages of Yugoslavia Bosnia-Hercegovina, Croatia, Macedonia, Slovenia, and Bulgaria, including *Serbo-Croat, Slovene, *Bulgarian, and Macedonian); West Slavonic (languages spoken in Czechoslovakia, Poland, and E Germany, including Czech, *Slovak, Sorbian, and Polish); and East Slavonic (Russian, Belorussian, and Ukrainian). The similarities and differences between languages of the three groups are not as clearcut as the geographical classification suggests. All the dialects can be related to each other historically and all developed from a common ancestor, Proto-Slavonic. Russian is a common language for most Slavs, many of whom learn it as a second language.

Slavs Peoples of E Europe and parts of W Asia. They may be divided into three groups: Eastern Slavs (including Russians, Ukrainians, and Belorussians); Western Slavs (including Poles, Czechs, Slovaks, and Sorbs or Wends); and Southern Slavs (including Serbs, Croats, Slovenes, Macedonians, and Bulgarians). The *Slavonic languages form a branch of the Indo-European family. Migrating from Asia, these peoples settled in this region during the second or third millennium BC. The present Slav nations began to emerge around the 5th and 6th centuries AD, when there was further westward movement.

sleep A naturally occurring state of unconsciousness. Orthodox sleep occurs in four stages, which vary in depth. The electrical activity of the brain continues but is more rhythmical than when awake and reacts less to outside stimuli. It is periodically interrupted by paradoxical sleep, in which the eyes move rapidly and the brain is more active, but the muscles are especially relaxed. Paradoxical sleep is particularly associated with *dreams. Sleep is biologically necessary and probably helps to control physical growth; individuals' needs vary widely between three and 10 hours a night. Sleeplessness can be caused by changes of routine, *anxiety, and *depression, and by many drugs (*see also* insomnia). Disorders of sleep include *sleepwalking and night terrors (*see* nightmares).

sleeping sickness A disease caused by infection with a protozoan of the genus *Trypanosoma*, which is transmitted by the tsetse fly and occurs only in East, central, and West Africa: it is the African form of *trypanosomiasis. Initial symptoms are swelling of the lymph nodes and fever, which persists for several months. The brain is then infected, causing lethargy, weakness, and depression: without treatment the patient dies. The drugs pentamidine and suramin can be used to treat the early stages of the disease; arsenic-based compounds are needed when the brain is affected. Attempts to prevent the disease by eradicating the fly have not yet proved successful.

sleepwalking (*or* somnambulism) A disorder of *sleep in which the sleeper walks about and performs complex activities automatically and without regaining consciousness. It is quite common in children and not a sign of illness. In adults it can indicate immaturity or *neurosis.

sleepy sickness A highly infectious viral disease of the brain. Known medically as *encephalitis lethargica, it is marked by drowsiness leading eventually to coma. A worldwide epidemic of the disease occurred between 1917 and 1924.

Slidell, John (1793–1871) US politician and Confederate diplomat. He served in the US House of representatives (1843–45), as US minister to Mexico (1845), and US senator (1853–61). At the outbreak of the Civil War, he left the Senate to become the Confederacy's minister to France. His passage aboard the British ship *Trent* ended in capture by the US Navy and imprisonment until early 1862. When he finally arrived in France, his quest for financial aid for and recognition of the Confederacy failed. *See also* Trent Affair.

slide rule A mathematical instrument for performing multiplication and division. It consists of a rule that slides along a groove in another rule. Both rules are marked with logarithmic scales so that products and quotients can be calculated by effectively adding and subtracting *logarithms in the form of lengths of rule. Slide rules have now been largely replaced by pocket *calculators.

Sligo (Irish name: Contae Shligigh) A county in the NW Republic of Ireland, in Connacht bordering on the Atlantic Ocean. Chiefly hilly, much of the land is devoted to pasture; cattle rearing and dairy farming are important. It possesses some coal, lead, and copper. Area: 693 sq mi (1795 sq km). Population (1991): 54,736. County town: Sligo.

Slim, William Joseph, 1st Viscount (1891–1970) British field marshal. In World War II he became commander of the 14th Army (the "forgotten army") in Burma (1943). After successful operations against the Japanese he became commander in chief of Allied land forces in SE Asia. In 1948 he became chief of the imperial general staff and was then governor general of Australia (1953–60).

slime molds Organisms belonging to the group *Myxomycophyta*, usually regarded as fungi (since they produce fruiting bodies) but having affinities with the protozoa. The so-called true slime molds (*Myxomycetes*) are found beneath logs and in other damp places. They consist of slimy sheets of protoplasm that engulf bacteria, wood particles, etc. The cellular slime molds (*Acrasiales*) are single-celled amoeba-like organisms found in soil. The parasitic slime molds (*Plasmodiophorales*) live in the tissues of plants; the species *Plasmodiophora brassicae* causes *clubroot in cabbages.

slipper orchid A terrestrial *orchid of the tropical Asian genus *Paphiopedilum* (about 50 species) and the related genera *Cypripedium* and *Phragmipedium*. They are characterized by their flowers, which have a pouched slipper-shaped lip and are usually borne singly or in clusters of two or three. *Paphiopedilum* flowers are usually a mixture of white, brown, and green, often with darker markings; the leaves may also be mottled or otherwise marked. Slipper orchids are popular greenhouse ornamentals.

slippery elm Either of two North American trees, *Fremontodendron californica* (family *Bombacaceae*) or *Ulmus fulva* (family *Ulmaceae*). Mucilage extracted from the bark has been used in poultices and to treat diarrhea, dysentery, and other conditions.

Sliven 42 40N 26 19E A city in E central Bulgaria. Its main industry is textiles, the first mill in Bulgaria having been opened there in 1834. Population (1991 est): 112,220.

Sloane, Sir Hans (1660–1753) British physician and naturalist, whose collection of books, manuscripts, pictures, etc., formed the nucleus of the *British Museum. He succeeded Sir Isaac Newton as President of the Royal Society (1727–41).

sloop A □sailing vessel with a single mast set approximately one-third of the boat's length from the bows. Formerly used extensively in coastal fishing, sloops are now a favored rig for yacht racing, since they are the most efficient design for sailing toward the wind. Older sloops were gaff-rigged; more modern vessels are marconi-rigged or Bermuda-rigged. Sloops more than 60 ft (20 m) long are rare because of the number of crew required to handle the large sails. *See also* ketch; yawl.

SLIPPER ORCHID *The flower of a cultivated variety of* Paphiopedilum.

sloth A primitive arboreal *mammal belonging to the family *Bradypodidae* (7 species) of Central and South America, also called ai or unau; 20–25.5 in (50–65 cm) long, sloths are slow-moving and hang upside down from branches, feeding on leaves and fruit. Their grayish-brown fur lies so that rain runs off easily and is often greenish from algae living there, which helps to camouflage them. They cannot walk on the ground. Order: *Edentata*.

sloth bear A shaggy black *bear, *Melursus ursinus*, of S India and Sri Lanka; 5 ft (1.5 m) long and weighing about 220 lb (100 kg), it feeds on bees or termites by tearing open nests with its long claws and sucking up the insects using its long snout.

Slovak A Western Slavonic language, closely related to *Czech, spoken in Slovakia. It is written in the Latin alphabet. There are three distinct dialects.

Slovakia (Czech name: Slovensko) An independent country in central Europe, formerly a province of E Czechoslovakia. Lying mainly within the Carpathian Mountains, it descends SW to the plains of the Danube Valley. It is chiefly agricultural, producing cereals, wine, fruit, and tobacco. *History*: settled by Slavic Slovaks (6th–7th centuries AD), Slovakia was incorporated into Great *Moravia in the 9th century. Conquered by the Magyars in the 10th century, Slovakia was part of Hungary until 1918 when it became a province of the Czechoslovak Republic, remaining as such until 1949, except for a period of independence during World War II. After the communist regime collapsed in 1989, a Slovakian separatist movement grew in strength. Slovakia became independent of the Czech Republic on Jan 1, 1993. Vladimir Meciar, who had championed separatism, became prime minister. Area: 18,930 sq mi (30,300 sq km). Population (1993 est): 5,300,000. Currency: korunna. Capital: Bratislava. *See also* Czech Republic.

Slovenia, Republic of (Serbo-Croat name: Slovenija) A country in SE Europe, a constituent republic of Yugoslavia until 1991. It is mountainous and drained mainly by the Sava and Drava rivers. Agriculture includes livestock raising; potatoes, cereals, and vegetables are grown. The republic possesses important deposits of coal, mercury, and zinc. *History*: it was chiefly under Hapsburg rule from the 14th century until 1918, when it was incorporated into the kingdom of Serbs, Croats, and Slovenes, later renamed Yugoslavia. Declaration of independence in June 1991 triggered a devastating civil war between Serb guerrillas and the Yugoslav government forces on one side and Slovenian forces on the other. Area 7819 sq mi (20,251 sq km). Population (1992 est): 1,985,000. Capital: Ljubljana.

slowworm A legless lizard, *Anguis fragilis*, also called blindworm, occurring in heaths and open woodlands of Europe. It is about 12 in (30 cm) long, usually brown, gray, or reddish, and feeds on snails, slugs, and other soft-bodied invertebrates. Family: *Anguidae* (glass snakes and slowworms).

slug A *gastropod mollusk of the order *Stylommatophora*, widely distributed in moist terrestrial habitats. Slugs have slimy soft bodies with the shell vestigial or absent. They may reach 8 in (20 cm) in length, and can range in color from yellow through red-brown to black. Some are carnivorous or scavenging while others feed on soft plant tissues. Subclass: *Pulmonata. Compare* sea slug.

slump. *See* depression.

Sluter, Claus (c. 1345–1406) Dutch sculptor. Working in Dijon under the patronage of Philip the Bold, duke of Burgundy, he produced his most famous works for the ducal mausoleum in the monastery of Champmol. These included the portal sculptures, the *Well of Moses*, and figures on the duke's tomb. Breaking away form the *international gothic style, Sluter developed a bold realism, which influenced many European sculptors and painters of the 15th century.

Sluys, Battle of (June 24, 1340) A naval battle in the *Hundred Years' War, off the coast of Flanders, in which the French fleet was destroyed by the skillful use of archers by *Edward III's army. The victory gave the English crucial strategic control over the English Channel.

smallage. *See* celery.

small arms Short-range low-weight *firearms, originally defined as capable of being handled by one individual, they included pistols, submachine guns, rifles, grenades, and shotguns. An artificial caliber ceiling of 0.60 in (1.5 cm) or, in some classification systems, 0.78 in (20 mm) has had to be abandoned with the introduction of small rocket antitank guided missiles.

smallpox A highly infectious virus disease marked by a skin rash that leaves permanent pitted scars. Smallpox is transmitted by direct contact; the initial symptoms of fever, prostration, severe headache, and backache are followed by the appearance of the rash on the face and limbs. Secondary infection with staphylococci is often fatal. There is no specific treatment and as recently as 1967 the disease caused two million deaths. After a worldwide vaccination program sponsored by the World Health Organization smallpox was officially declared to have been eradicated in 1979.

smell, sense of. *See* nose.

smelt A slender food fish of the genus *Osmerus* and family *Osmeridae*, occurring in coastal and estuarine waters of Europe and North America. It migrates to fresh water to spawn. The European smelt (*O. eperlanus*), up to about 12 in (30 cm) long, also called sparling, is greenish gray above and silvery below. It has a cucumber-like smell when eaten fresh. Order: *Salmoniformes*.

smelting The extraction of a metal from its ore by heating. The method used depends on the metal, the type of ore, and the melting points of both. The smelting takes place either in a *blast furnace (e.g. to extract iron) or a *reverberatory furnace (e.g. to extract copper).

Smetana, Bedřich (1824–84) Bohemian composer. He studied in Prague and took part in the revolution against Austria in 1848. In 1859 he left Sweden (where he had been conducting) and returned to Prague, joining a group of composers who were establishing a national opera. *The Brandenburgers in Bohemia* (1862–63) and *The Bartered Bride* (1863–66) were composed for it. In 1874 he became totally deaf but continued to compose, writing the four symphonic poems *Má Vlast* (1874–79) and a string quartet "From My Life" (1876). He died insane in an asylum.

smew A sawbilled *duck, *Mergus albellus*, that breeds in N Eurasia and winters south in the Mediterranean. It is 16–17 in (40–44 cm) long, has a short bill, and feeds on fish and crustaceans. Drakes are white with black markings; females are gray with a chestnut head and white throat and cheeks.

Smith, Adam (1723–90) Scottish moral philosopher and political economist. At Edinburgh University (1752–63), he lectured and wrote on moral philosophy. In 1776, he published *An Enquiry into the Nature and Causes of the Wealth of Nations*, an attack on *mercantilism that was to become the bible of the free-trade movement. He held that employment, trade, production, and distribution are as much a part of a nation's wealth as its money. An individual allowed to promote his own interests freely within the law often promotes the interests of society as a whole.

Smith, Alfred E(manuel) ("Al"; 1873–1944) US politician. A Tammany Hall Democrat, he served in the New York state legislature (1903–15) and as governor (1918–20; 1922–28), where he was known for his government reorganization and welfare programs. Thwarted in his quest for the Democratic presidential nomination in 1924, he became the first Roman Catholic nominee in 1928. His religion and opposition to Prohibition, as well as the success of the previous Republican administration, led to his defeat by Herbert *Hoover.

Smith, Bessie (1894–1937) US jazz singer and songwriter, known as "Empress of the Blues," who began her career in traveling shows and carnivals. In the 1920s she made records with Louis Armstrong and Fletcher Henderson (1898–1952). Her popularity declined in the 1930s. She died in an automobile accident.

Smith, David (Roland) (1906–65) US sculptor. After studying art in New York City and Europe, he worked in an automobile factory and, during World War II, in a locomotive factory where he became interested in welding as art. His first series of sculptures, *Agricola*, were spaces outlined by wires and bent rods. His *Tank Totem* and *Sentinel* series of the 1950s used parts from cars or other pieces of machinery. In the 1960s, he turned to large, depersonalized geometrical shapes, welded together at various angles, in his *Zig* and *Cubi* series. He was killed in an automobile accident in 1965.

Smith, Ian (Douglas) (1919–) Prime minister (1964–79) of Rhodesia (now *Zimbabwe). An advocate of white supremacy, he demanded full independence for Southern Rhodesia in 1964 but opposed Britain's stipulation that black majority rule be prepared for. In 1965 he made a unilateral declaration of independence, which he maintained until 1976, when he agreed to the principle of black majority rule. He was a minister in the preindependence government (1979–80).

Smith, John (c. 1580–1631) English colonist. In 1606, he invested in the new Virginia Company, which was granted a charter to settle in North America. On arrival at what became Jamestown, Va., he explored and charted the region. In 1607 he was saved from death at the hands of Indians by *Pocahontas. He returned to England in 1609 and wrote valuable accounts of his experiences, including *Description of New England* (1616), *Map of Virginia* (1612), and *General Historie of Virginia* (1624).

Smith, Joseph (1805–44) US founder of the Church of Jesus Christ of Latter Day Saints (*Mormons). Smith announced in 1827 his discovery of the sacred *Book of Mormon*, which he claimed he had translated from two gold tablets written by a prophet named Mormon. His new church, founded in Fayette, N.Y. (1830), grew rapidly but attracted considerable opposition because of its doctrines. Smith encouraged westward migration and the group established itself in Nauvoo, Ill. (1840), where they were welcomed at first. Smith became mayor. Rumors that the Mormons practiced polygamy spurred opposition. While in jail on charges of conspiracy, Smith was killed by an angry mob. The Mormons continued their migration westward to Utah under Brigham *Young.

Smith, Stevie (Florence Margaret S.; 1902–71) British poet. She published highly original and deceptively simple poetry, the characteristic tone of which was a blend of tenderness, toughness, and humor. The best known of her idiosyncratic novels is *Novel on Yellow Paper* (1936). Her *Collected Poems* (1975) were published posthumously.

Smithsonian Institution A research institution in Washington, D.C. The Institution was founded in 1846 with a bequest from Englishman James Smithson (1765–1829) as "an establishment for the increase and diffusion of knowledge." It has carried out important scientific work and explorations throughout the world, and administers several important history, science, and art museums, including the National Air and Space Museum and the National Collection of Fine Arts.

smog A fog containing a high proportion of smoke (its name is abbreviated from smoke fog) occurring chiefly in urban and industrial areas. Occasionally it may be particularly dense, as it can be in cities such as New York, Los Angeles, London, and Denver, where geography and certain weather conditions intensify its effects. Emissions from automobiles, and the burning of oil and coal are the chief pollutants. Legislation to require the burning of cleaner fuels, and the use of pollution control devices, have reduced the incidence of severe smog.

smoke tree (*or* smoke bush) One of several species of trees and shrubs having a whitish cloudy appearance at some stage of the season. The American smoke tree (*Cotinus obovatus*) grows to a height of 30 ft (9 m) and has a smokelike mass of whitish flower heads, as does the Australian smoke bush (*Conospermum stoechadis*). *Rhus cotinus* is the common smoke bush native to the Mediterranean area and parts of Asia.

Smolensk 54 49N 32 04E A city in W Russia, on the Dnepr River. It has engineering, textile, and consumer-goods industries and several educational institutions. *History*: dating to at least the 9th century, it was sacked by the Tatars (13th century) and was subsequently disputed between Lithuania (and later Poland) and Russia, falling finally to the latter in 1654. It was on the route of Napoleon's retreat from Moscow in 1812 and was badly damaged in World War II. Population (1991 est): 350,000.

Smollett, Tobias (George) (1721–71) British novelist. Born and educated in Scotland, he settled in London in 1744. His picaresque novels, lively in style and unsophisticated and rambling in structure, include *Roderick Random* (1748), *Peregrine Pickle* (1751), and *Humphry Clinker* (1771). He was also a prolific journalist and translator.

smooth snake A widespread Eurasian snake, *Coronella austriaca*, that has smooth glossy scales and is brown or reddish with a pale belly and dark spots along its back and tail. Up to 26 in (65 cm) long, it favors sandy heathlands and feeds on lizards, small snakes, and rodents. Family: *Colubridae*.

smuggling The illegal import or export of goods to evade payment of duties or official restrictions. Trading countries often impose bans, limitations, or taxes on certain goods, the evasion of which provides an incentive for smugglers. Smuggling has flourished from the time of the Greek city-states until the present day. After World War II smuggling of guns, narcotics, gold, diamonds, and illegal immigrants became rife, particularly through international airlines and remote frontier towns. In recent years one of the primary concerns of world customs authorities, the function of which is to detect and prevent smuggling, has been the breaking of international narcotic smuggling networks.

smut A disease affecting flowering plants, particularly the cereals and grasses, caused by various *basidiomycete fungi of the genus *Ustilago*. Infection is not usually apparent until spore formation, when dark powdery masses of spores are released over the flower head. Stinking smuts, or bunts, are caused by fungi belonging to the related genus *Tilletia*. Both types of smut cause reduced yields of grain and are controlled by spraying crops with fungicide and by treating seed before sowing.

Smuts, Jan (Christiaan) (1870–1950) South African statesman and general; prime minister (1919–24, 1939–48). Educated in England, he returned to South Africa in 1895. He was a commando leader in the second *Boer War (1899–1902) but thereafter worked for reconciliation with Britain. He played an important part in the achievement of responsible government for the Transvaal (1906) and the Union of South Africa (1910). He was a member of Britain's imperial war cabinet in World War I and helped establish the League of Nations. He succeeded *Botha as prime minister in 1919 but was defeated in 1924. In 1939 he again became prime minister, advocating South Africa's entry into World War II. His desire to maintain South Africa's links with the British Commonwealth made him unpopular among Afrikaners.

Smyrna. *See* Izmir.

snail A *gastropod mollusk with a spirally coiled shell, including terrestrial, freshwater, and marine forms. The common garden snail (*Helix pomatia*) grows to about 1.2 in (3 cm) and is active at night, feeding on vegetation and sheltering by day in crevices. In dry weather, a temporary covering is secreted over the shell aperture to prevent desiccation. The giant African land snail (*Achatina fulica*) grows up to 5 in (12 cm) long.

JAN SMUTS *On campaign in S Africa in 1914, at the outbreak of World War I.*

snake A legless *reptile belonging to the suborder *Serpentes* (about 3000 species), occurring worldwide but especially common in the tropics. Snakes are long and slender: they range from 0.39–33 ft (0.12–10 m) in length and grow throughout their lives, periodically shedding the skin in one piece. They feed chiefly on other vertebrates and are adapted to swallowing prey whole, having flexible ligaments and joints allowing the two parts of the lower jaw to move apart during swallowing. Prey may be killed by constriction, by engulfing it alive, or by the injection of a potent neurotoxic or hemorrhagic venom by means of hollow or grooved fangs. The major families are the *Boidae* (pythons, boas, etc.), the *Colubridae* (typical snakes, e.g. the grass snake), the *Elapidae* (cobras, coral snakes, etc.), and the *Viperidae* (vipers, etc.). Order: *Squamata* (lizards and snakes).

snakebird. *See* darter.

snakefly An insect of the family *Raphidiidae* (about 80 species), so called because its small head and long slender thorax ("neck") resemble a snake about to strike. It is found in woodland areas of every continent except Australia and uses chewing mouthparts to feed on small insects. Eggs are laid beneath bark. Order: **Neuroptera*.

snake gourd An annual or perennial vine of the genus *Trichosanthes* (about 15 species), especially *T. anguina*, native to tropical SE Asia and Australia. It is widely cultivated for its long tapering green edible fruits, which often exceed 40 in (1 m) in length. Family: *Cucurbitaceae*.

snake-necked turtle A freshwater turtle belonging to the family *Chelyidae* (35 species), found in South America, Australia, and New Guinea. They have a long snakelike neck that is extended to catch prey and breathe air at the surface. It cannot be retracted into the shell but is tucked sideways into a fold of shoulder skin. A South American species, the matamata (*Chelys fimbriata*), has a jagged well-camouflaged shell, 12–16 in (30–40 cm) long, and a pointed head.

Snake River A river in the NW US. Rising in the Yellowstone National Park in Wyoming, it flows W through Idaho to join the Columbia River in Washington. Length: 1038 m (1670 km).

snakeroot Any of various plants the roots of which were formerly reputed to cure snakebites. Snakeroots include the *bistort and several North American species, such as the herbs *Cimicifuga racemosa, Aristolochia reticulata*, and *Eupatorium urticoefolium*.

snapdragon. *See* Antirrhinum.

snapper A carnivorous shoaling fish of the family *Lutjanidae* (about 250 species), found in tropical seas. It has an elongated body, usually 24–36 in (60–90 cm) long, a large mouth, and sharp teeth. Snappers are valuable food fish, especially the red snapper (*Lutjanus blackford*), although others may be poisonous.

snare drum (*or* side drum) A small drum with gut strings (snares) stretched across the lower skin. These make a rattling sound when the drum is played. It is used in the orchestra and in the military band.

sneeze A reflex violent expulsion of air through the mouth and nose caused by irritation of the lining of the nasal cavity. The irritation may be due to inflammation of the nasal passages, such as occurs with a cold and hay fever. Sneezing is the principal means by which colds and similar infections are spread, since it expels a cloud of droplets containing the infective microbes.

Snefru King of Egypt (c. 2600 BC); founder of the 4th dynasty, traditionally noted for his kindliness, in contrast with his son *Khufu. He encouraged shipping to facilitate communications within Egypt and to import materials from abroad. Two pyramids at Dashur are attributed to him.

Snell's law When a ray of light passes from one medium to another the angle (r) between the refracted ray and a line normal to the interface between the media is related to the angle (i) of the incident ray, also taken to the normal, by the equation $\sin i/\sin r = n$, where n is the relative refractive index of the media (*see* refraction). It is named for the Dutch astronomer Willebrord Snell (1591–1626), who discovered it in 1621. It was not published until 1638, when Descartes announced it without crediting Snell.

snipe A *sandpiper belonging to a subfamily (*Scolopacine*; 10 species) occurring in wet areas of warm and temperate regions. Snipe have a long flexible bill used to probe for worms, and a barred and striped brown, black, and white plumage. The common snipe (*Gallinago gallinago*) is 12 in (30 cm) long and a popular gamebird.

snooker A game, deriving from *billiards, that arose among British officers in India (1875). It is played by two players or pairs of players on a billiards table. There are 22 balls: 1 white cue ball, 15 red balls (value 1 point each), and 6 colored balls—yellow (2 points), green (3), brown (4), blue (5), pink (6), black (7). The object is to pocket a red ball and a colored ball alternately, each time returning the colored ball to its prescribed spot on the table. The red balls are not replaced. When all the red balls have been sunk the colors are sunk in order of numerical value.

snoring Noisy breathing occurring during sleep, caused by vibration of the soft palate at the back of the mouth. Snoring generally occurs when sleeping on the back with the mouth open. It is most liable to occur when the nose is blocked (e.g. by a cold) and the person must breathe through the mouth.

snow A solid form of precipitation composed of ice crystals or snowflakes. Ice crystals occur when temperatures are well below freezing point; with temperatures nearer to 32°F (0°C) snowflakes develop through the clustering together of crystals. Snow is usually measured with a graduated ruler, which is inserted into the flat surface of undrifted snow. Approximately 1 ft (0.3 m) of snow is equivalent to 1 in (25 mm) of rainfall.

Snow, C(harles) P(ercy), Baron (1905–80) British novelist and scientist. The moral problems of politics and power are a recurrent theme of his series of novels beginning with *Strangers and Brothers* (1940) and ending with *Last Things* (1970). His lecture *The Two Cultures and the Scientific Revolution* (1959) prompted a lively controversy with the critic F. R. *Leavis. He was married to the writer Pamela Hansford Johnson (1912–81).

snowball tree. *See* guelder rose.

snow bunting A short-billed *bunting, *Plectrophenax nivalis*, of Arctic snowfields, that visits Britain in winter. It is about 6 in (16 cm) long and has a brownish plumage with white underparts and black wingtips. In summer the male is white with an orange bill and black markings. It nests in rock crevices and feeds on seeds and insects.

Snowdon (Welsh name: Eryri) 53 04N 4 05W The highest mountain in Wales, in Gwynedd. The surrounding area, **Snowdonia**, is popular for walking, rock climbing, and mountaineering. Height: 3560 ft (1085 m).

Snowdon, Antony Armstrong-Jones, Earl of (1930–) British photographer. His work includes several television documentaries and photographic books, such as *Venice* (1972). His marriage (1960–78) to Britain's Princess Margaret ended in divorce.

snowdrop A small early spring-blooming herbaceous plant of the genus *Galanthus* (about 10 species) native to Europe and W Asia. They grow from bulbs to produce grasslike leaves and slender stems bearing solitary nodding white flowers, tipped with green or yellow. There are over 50 cultivated varieties, which are easily grown in gardens and survive for years without attention. *G. nivalis* is the common European snowdrop; *G. elwesi* is the giant snowdrop of SW Asia. Family: *Amaryllidaceae*.

snow goose An Arctic *goose, *Anser caerulescens*. It is 28–31 in (70–78 cm) long and is either pure white with black wingtips, pink legs, and a red bill or blue-gray with a white head. Snow geese winter in the southern US, Japan, and China.

snow leopard A big *cat, *Panthera* (or *Uncia*) *uncia*, also called ounce, found in the mountains of central Asia. It is 6.2 ft (1.9 m) long, with a thick ash-gray coat marked with dark rosettes. It hunts mountain goats, sheep, and marmots, catching its prey by stalking.

snow-on-the-mountain A hardy annual plant, **Euphorbia marginata*, native to North America and widely cultivated as a garden foliage plant. Up to 24 in (60 cm) high, it has pale-green pointed leaves, 1.2–3.1 in (3–8 cm) long, with white margins (sometimes the whole leaf is white). Family: *Euphorbiaceae*.

snowshoe hare A *hare, *Lepus americanus*, of N North America, also called varying hare. Up to 28 in (70 cm) long, it has a white winter coat and leaves tracks similar to snowshoes. Populations of snowshoe hares can vary greatly from year to year; similar fluctuations occur in the populations of lynxes—their chief predator.

Snowy Mountains A mountain range in Australia. It lies within the *Australian Alps, and contains Australia's highest mountain, Mount *Kosciusko. The Snowy Mountains Hydroelectric Authority has diverted rivers and constructed dams and reservoirs for irrigation and hydroelectric purposes.

snowy owl A large *owl, *Nyctea scandiaca*, occurring chiefly in Arctic tundra regions; 20–26 in (52–65 cm) long, it has broad wings, a round head, and a snow-white plumage with black barring. It nests on open ground and feeds on lemmings, hares, and birds.

snuff A preparation of tobacco and other ingredients that is sniffed rather than smoked. The character of a particular variety of snuff depends on the coarseness of the tobacco used, the moisture content, and the added ingredients, such as lavender and menthol, which introduce flavor and scent to the mixture.

Spaniards discovered snuff-taking among the natives of the Americas in the 16th century. The habit was fashionable until the early 19th century, when it was largely replaced by the *cigar. Highly decorated snuffboxes were made as valuable items of jewelry.

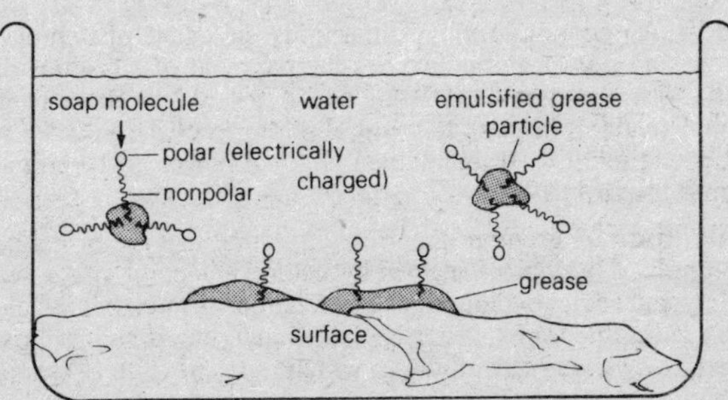

SOAPS *The action of soap in emulsifying grease. The nonpolar hydrocarbon end of the soap molecule attaches itself to the grease. The attraction of the polar end to water breaks up the grease and distributes it throughout the solution.*

soap Salts of *fatty acids. Normal household soap (**hard soap**) is a mixture of sodium stearate, oleate, and palmitate. It is made by the *hydrolysis of *fats with caustic soda (sodium hydroxide), thus converting the glycerides of stearic, oleic, and palmitic acids into sodium salts and glycerol. **Soft soap** is made with potassium hydroxide instead of sodium hydroxide. Soaps have a cleansing action because they contain negative ions composed of a long hydrocarbon chain attached to a carboxyl group. The hydrocarbon chain has an affinity for grease and oil, and the carboxyl group has an affinity for water. Particles of grease or oil are therefore emulsified in soapy water. Insoluble salts of other metals with fatty acids are used as fillers and waterproofing agents and are also called soaps. *See also* detergents.

soapstone. *See* talc.

soapwort A perennial herb, *Saponaria officinalis*, native to Europe and temperate Asia and introduced to North America. The shoots grow to a height of 12–36 in (30–90 cm) and bear pink flowers. The leaves and roots contain a lathering agent (saponin), formerly used for washing clothes. Family: *Caryophyllaceae.*

Soares, Mario (1924–) Portuguese statesman; prime minister (1976–77; 1978; 1983–85); president (1986–). He was a critic of *Salazar and lived in exile from 1970 to 1974, when he became foreign minister in the newly established military government. He became prime minister as leader of the Portuguese Socialist party, and was Portugal's first socialist president.

soccer. *See* football.

So-ch'e. *See* Shache.

Sochi 43 35N 39 46E A city in SW Russia, on the Black Sea. It is a popular resort, where, since 1977, smoking has been forbidden. Population (1991 est): 342,000.

social contract An agreement under which people consent to surrender liberties in return for the guarantee of responsible government. Hobbes saw the contract as one in which citizens surrender the freedom inherent in a state of nature to an absolute sovereign; Locke, however, argued that the sovereign is limited by the obligation to preserve certain fundamental liberties; and Rousseau, the third of the chief theorists of the social contract, believed that governments require the support of the general will of the people.

social credit An economic theory that finds the cause of depression in the lack of purchasing power and advocates the payment of a regular dividend to every citizen. Formulated by C. H. Douglas (1879–1952), a British engineer and economist in Canada, it became the central platform of the Social Credit party, formed in Canada in 1935. It maintained political power in Alberta and British Columbia until the early 1970s.

social Darwinism A group of theories suggesting that the principles governing the evolution of biological species by natural selection also govern the affairs of society and social evolution. Either relations in society are held to be determined by a "struggle for existence" between individuals and groups or history is interpreted as a series of conflicts in which only the "fittest" social systems thrive.

Social Democratic party (SDP) A moderate British political party of the center, formed in 1981 by Labour party dissidents.

socialism A concept that has various meanings, resulting in diverse political movements, but one that generally emphasizes the establishment of cooperation rather than competition among men. The word was first used in the early 19th century to describe the followers of Robert *Owen in England and François Fourier and *Saint-Simon in France. From the beginning two main senses of the word emerged. The first sense was in effect a continuation of liberalism, the emphasis being on reform of the social system to develop liberal values, such as political freedom, and the ending of class privileges. Socialism in the second sense was explicitly contrasted with a competitive individualist form of society; practical cooperation could not be achieved until a society based on private property was replaced by one based on social ownership and control. The resulting controversy between reformists and revolutionaries has been long and bitter. In 1848 Marx and Engels laid down the principles of scientific socialism in *The Communist Manifesto* and *Marxism became the theoretical basis for most socialist thought. The British *Fabian Society (founded 1884) revived a variant of the first sense of the term, which later found political expression in the *Labour party. It was the split in Russia, however, between the revolutionary *Bolsheviks and the reformist *Mensheviks that led to the decisive distinction between the terms *communism and socialism as they are now generally understood, socialists being those who seek change by peaceful reform and communists being those dedicated to change by revolution.

Socialist party US political party formed by the merger of the Socialist Labor party and the Social Democratic party in 1901. The party repeatedly nominated presidential candidates, including Eugene V. *Debs (1900–12; 1920) and Norman M. *Thomas (1928–48), offering government ownership of all businesses necessary to public welfare as an alternative to capitalism.

socialist realism A theory of literary composition decreed by the Soviet authorities in Russia in 1932 to be the official literary doctrine to which all communist writers must adhere. It defined the purpose of literature as the promotion of socialism and resulted in the production of much literature that was little more than political propaganda. Mikhail *Sholokhov is the most notable of the few writers who have managed to transcend its restrictions.

Social Security Act (1935) US law that provided guaranteed benefits for retirement-aged workers (65 or over), based on income and worker and employer contributions. Part of Pres. Franklin D. Roosevelt's *New Deal program, it was, in effect, a pension plan to provide for old age in a nuclear family society. Subsequent amendments provided for dependents of deceased workers, disabled and unemployed workers, and health insurance benefits. The Social Security Administration is the agency in charge of the program.

Society Islands An archipelago in French Polynesia. It consists of two island groups, the **Windward Islands** (including Tahiti and Moorea) and the **Leeward Islands** (including Raiatea and Huahine). The capital of French Polynesia, Papeete, is on Tahiti. Discovered in 1767, they are mountainous and the site of ruined Polynesian stone temples. Copra, vanilla, phosphates, and mother-of-pearl are produced. Area: 616 sq mi (1595 sq km).

Society of Friends. *See* Quakers.

Society of Jesus. *See* Jesuits.

Socinus, Laelius (Italian name: Lelio Francesco Maria Sozini; 1525–62) Italian Protestant reformer. He traveled widely in N Europe, meeting other leading Protestant reformers. His anti-Trinitarian beliefs and his desire to reconcile Christianity with humanism deeply influenced his nephew **Faustus Socinus** (Fausto Paolo Sozini; 1539–1604). He settled in Poland in 1579, where he became leader of an anti-Trinitarian branch of the Reformed Church. Its doctrine, known as Socinanism, contributed to the development of Unitarian theology (*see* Unitarianism).

sociobiology The study of social behavior in animals and man. Sociobiologists believe that such aspects of behavior as aggression, male dominance, and the roles of the sexes have developed through evolution in the same way as structural features. The study was developed in the 1970s.

sociology The systematic study of the development, organization, functioning, and classification of human societies. Its growth was stimulated by the rapid industrial and social change in Europe in the early 19th century, Auguste *Comte (the first to use the term "sociology"), Emile *Durkheim, and Max *Weber being among the founding fathers of the discipline, which was established in several universities by the early 20th century. Precluded from experimental methods, the discipline has employed techniques of participant observation, the systematic comparison of different societies, and surveys of social conditions, attitudes, and behavior. Contemporary sociology is divided into several specialized subdisciplines including demography, political, educational, and urban sociology as well as sociological studies of deviance, religion, and culture.

sockeye salmon A *salmon, *Oncorhynchus nerka*, also called red salmon or blueback, that lives in the N Pacific and spawns in Canadian fresh waters.

Socotra A South Yemeni island in the Indian Ocean, off Somalia. It is generally barren, rising to 4931 ft (1503 m), but in some valleys such crops as dates are grown and livestock is raised. It came under British protection in 1886 but has belonged to South Yemen since 1967. Area: 1197 sq mi (3100 sq km). Chief town: Tamrida.

Socrates (c. 469–399 BC) Athenian philosopher. He wrote nothing himself but his disciples *Plato and *Xenophon stress his intellect, integrity, courage, humor, and sense of divine guidance. *Aristophanes caricatured him in *The Clouds* as an eccentric intellectual. Socrates diverted philosophy from the physical speculations of the *pre-Socratics toward *ethics. His insistence upon thorough critical analysis of ethical concepts also marked the beginning of *logic. The "Socratic method" of teaching was by eliciting answers from interlocutors to reveal inconsistencies in accepted opinions, a method particularly effective against the *Sophists. His resolute stance against tyranny, whether exercised by the mob or oligarchs, brought about his trial on charges of atheism and "corrupting the youth," and he was condemned to die by drinking hemlock. Plato's *Phaedo* is an eloquent account of his death.

Soddy, Frederick (1877–1956) British chemist, who worked under *Rutherford and *Ramsay and went on to win the 1921 Nobel Prize for his discovery of *isotopes. His scientific books included *The Interpretation of the Atom* (1932); he also wrote on economics, his main work being *Cartesian Economics* (1922).

Söderblom, Nathan (1866–1931) Swedish churchman; archbishop of Uppsala (1914–31). A pioneer of the modern ecumenical movement, he made new contacts with Anglican and Eastern Orthodox Churches and was a chief initiator of conferences on "Faith and Order" (Uppsala, 1919) and "Life and Work" (Stockholm, 1925). He received the Nobel Peace Prize in 1930.

sodium (Na) A highly reactive alkali metal, long-recognized in compounds but first isolated as the element by Sir Humphry Davy in 1807 by electrolysis of the molten hydroxide (NaOH; caustic soda). It is now obtained commercially by electrolysis of common salt (NaCl). It occurs naturally in some silicate minerals (for example *feldspars; $NaAlSi_3O_8$), as well as in salt deposits and in the oceans. The metal is soft, bright, and less dense (relative density 0.97) than water, with which it reacts violently, liberating hydrogen. For safety, it has to be stored in mineral oil. It is used in organic chemistry as a reducing agent and in the production of *tetraethyl lead. Sodium forms a low-melting-point (−12.3°C) alloy with potassium, but liquid sodium itself is used as the coolant in fast-breeder nuclear reactors. It is a highly electropositive element, forming many ionic salts of great importance, such as the chloride (common salt; NaCl), the carbonate (soda ash; Na_2CO_3), the bicarbonate (baking-soda; $NaHCO_3$), various phosphates, the nitrate ($NaNO_3$), and many others. *Soap is usually the sodium salt of fatty acids (e.g. sodium stearate). Sodium gives a strong yellow color to flames. At no 11; at wt 22.9898; mp 208.2°F (97.8°C); bp 1622.8°F (882.9°C).

sodium bicarbonate (sodium hydrogen carbonate *or* bicarbonate of soda; $NaHCO_3$) The white soluble powder that is a constituent of *baking powder and is used to make fizzy drinks and as an antacid in medicine. It is made from *sodium carbonate by passing *carbon dioxide through a saturated solution.

sodium carbonate (Na_2CO_3) A white soluble salt. The commercial form (**soda ash**) is a white anhydrous powder and is used in making glass, soap, paper, as well as other chemicals. **Washing soda**, its hydrated form ($Na_2CO_3.10H_2O$), is a white crystalline solid used as a domestic cleanser and water softener.

sodium hydroxide (*or* caustic soda; NaOH) A white solid that is strongly alkaline in aqueous solution and is very corrosive to organic tissue. It is made by electrolysis of salt solution and is used in making rayon, paper, detergents, and other chemicals.

Sodom and Gomorrah In the Old Testament, two cities of Palestine, known as the "cities of the plain," S of the Dead Sea in the area in which Lot, the nephew of Abraham, settled. According to Genesis (18, 19), they were destroyed by fire and brimstone from heaven because of the utter depravity of their inhabitants.

Sofia (Bulgarian name: Sofiya) 42 40N 23 18E The capital of Bulgaria, situated on a plateau in the W of the country. Industries include engineering, metals, textiles, and food processing. It contains some ancient churches, including that of St Sofia (6th–7th centuries), as well as two mosques. The university was founded in 1888. *History*: a Roman town (known as Serdica) from the 1st to the 4th centuries AD, it was destroyed by the Huns in 447. It came under the Byzantine Empire in the 6th century and was taken over by the Bulgars in the 9th century. Under Turkish rule from 1382, it was liberated by the Russians in 1878 and became the national capital (1879). Population (1991 est):1,141,142.

soft-shelled turtle A freshwater turtle belonging to the family *Trionychidae* (20–25 species), occurring in North America, Africa and Asia. They have a flat almost circular shell covered by a leathery skin instead of horny plates, a long neck with a small head, and webbed feet. They are carnivorous and often lie buried in mud but can be fast-moving and aggressive. Chief genus: *Trionyx*.

software The *programs written to set up a computer system for operation, as distinct from the physical equipment or hardware. Computer manufacturers generally supply machines complete with most of the basic software, which is regarded as an integral part of the computer. It includes the programs that convert high-level programming languages to low-level or assembly languages and programs that translate assembly language into the machine code, the code the machine itself can follow.

Sogne Fjord The longest and deepest fjord in Norway, extending 127 mi (204 km) inland N of Bergen. It is flanked by spectacular mountain scenery. Depth: about 4000 ft (1220 m).

soil The mixture of unconsolidated mineral particles, derived from weathered rock, and organic matter (humus), derived from the breakdown of plant tissue by living organisms, that covers much of the earth's land surface and provides a medium for plant growth. Soil formation (pedogenesis) depends on the nature of the parent material, the climate and topography of the region, the organisms present in the soil, and the time that has elapsed since pedogenesis began on a bare surface. Soils are characterized by their texture, which depends on particle sizes (*see* sand; silt; clay), and their structure, which depends on the way the particles are bound into aggregates (e.g. crumbs, granules, flakes, etc.). These are important factors in determining the fertility of the soil, particularly its moisture and air content, susceptibility to leaching (the removal of nutrients to deeper levels by percolating water), and ease of cultivation. Soils are also classified according to their profiles—the arrangement of the layers (horizons) between the ground surface and the bedrock. *See also* chernozem; loam; podzol.

Soissons 49 23N 3 20E A city in France, in the Aisne department on the Aisne River. Strategically situated on the NE approaches to Paris, it has been sacked many times. It has a fine 13th-century cathedral. Soissons is a market town and has metallurgical industries. Population (1982): 32,000.

Sokoto 13 02N 5 15E A city in NW Nigeria. It is a major trade center for livestock and agricultural products. The University of Sokoto was founded in 1975. Population (1992 est): 185,500.

sol. *See* colloid.

Solanaceae A family of herbaceous plants and shrubs (about 2000 species), widely distributed but chiefly tropical. Their flowers have five fused sepals and petals and are usually pollinated by insects. The family includes several commercially important species (e.g. the potato, tomato, pepper, and tobacco) and some ornamentals (e.g. *Petunia*); various other members are poisonous (e.g. the nightshades).

solar cell. *See* solar power.

solar constant The total amount of solar energy passing perpendicularly through unit area per unit time at a particular distance from the sun. It is about 1.36 kW m^{-2} at the earth's mean orbital distance.

solar flare A sudden brightening, within minutes, of areas in the sun's atmosphere, resulting from an explosive release of energetic particles and radiation. Flares occur in regions of intense localized magnetic field, often above *sunspot groups, and take up to an hour to fade. Large flares affect radio transmission on earth and produce *auroras.

solar power The use of the sun's energy to provide heating or to generate electricity. A vast amount of solar energy (about 3×10^{24} joules) falls on the earth every year. This energy can be converted into heat, the commonest method being by direct heating of water flowing through special panels on the roof of a building. The temperature rise produced is fairly small but it reduces the energy required from other sources for hot water and space heating. Higher temperatures, sufficient to form steam for electricity generation, are possible using mirrors to collect and focus the sun's rays. It is estimated that 7000 square meters of mirror is required to generate 1 megawatt of electricity by boiling water to drive a turbogenerator. Direct conversion of solar radiation into electrical energy is possible with **solar cells**. These devices consist of semiconductor junctions in silicon crystals that are sensitive to the *photovoltaic effect. The method is used mainly in small-scale specialized applications, for example powering remote monitoring equipment, spacecraft, marine beacons, etc. For this method to have widespread commercial applications the cost of solar cells would need to be reduced by a factor of about 10. Intense research to make economical use of solar energy is progressing in a number of countries.

solar prominences Immense clouds of gas in the solar atmosphere, visible, usually only spectroscopically, as flamelike projections beyond the sun's limb. They show great diversity in structure. **Quiescent prominences** persist for possibly several months at high solar latitudes, reaching, typically, a height and length of 25,000 mi (40,000 km) and 125,000 mi (200,000 km). **Active prominences** are short lived in comparison and may alter their shape considerably in minutes.

SOLAR PROMINENCES *A photograph of the solar eclipse on May 29, 1929, showing a solar prominence.*

solar system A system comprising the *sun and the astronomical bodies gravitationally bound to the sun, that is the nine major *planets, their *satellites, and the immense numbers of *minor planets, *comets, and *meteoroids. Almost all the mass of the solar system (99.86%) resides in the sun. The planets orbit the sun in the same direction and, with the exception of Pluto, move in paths close to the earth's orbit (i.e. close to the *ecliptic) and the sun's equator. This and other information is taken as evidence of the common origin of the sun and planets, some 4600 million years ago, following the contraction and subsequent flattening of a rotating cloud of interstellar gas and dust.

solar wind An almost radial outflow of charged particles discharged from the sun's corona into interplanetary space. The particles, mainly protons and electrons, are moving at speeds between 125–559 mi (200–900 km) per second in the vicinity of the earth's orbit and although low in density (about 8 per cubic centimeter) can still interact with the earth's magnetosphere.

solder An *alloy that is melted to form a joint between other metals or, occasionally, nonmetals. The surfaces to be joined are heated by a soldering iron or by a flame, but are not melted. **Soft solder** is usually made of lead and tin and melts in the range 392–482°F (200–250°C). Because the solder itself is not very strong, it is not used for joints that have to stand up to stress or heat, but is used for making secure electrical connections. **Brazing**, also called **hard soldering**, uses a harder alloy with a higher melting temperature (1563–1654°F; 850–900°C), usually a *brass with 60% zinc and 40% copper. **Silver solder** originally contained silver and was used for jewelry. It has a slightly lower melt-

SOLAR SYSTEM

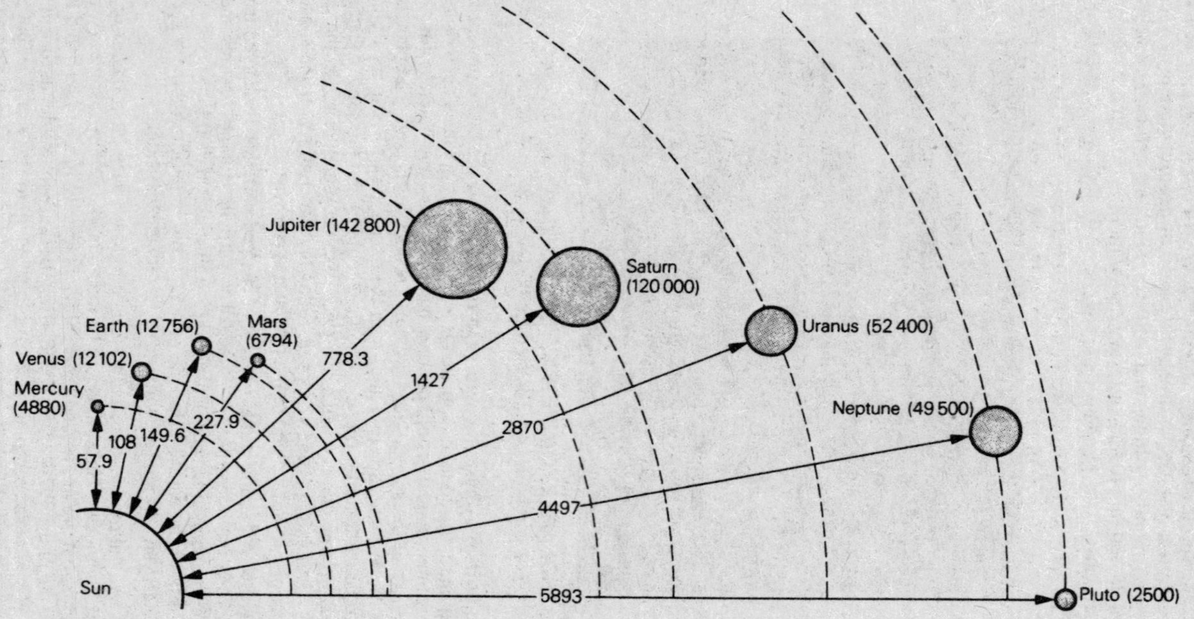

SOLAR SYSTEM *The planets with their equatorial diameters in kilometers (in brackets after the planet's name) and their distance from the sun in millions of kilometers (not to scale).*

ing point (1167–1527°F; 630–830°C) than brass, and often contains antimony or other metals but no silver. Like brazing, its strength makes it useful in engineering applications. A flux of zinc chloride or a resin is applied to the hot surfaces before soldering to clean them and to enable the solder to flow. In some solders (resin-cored) the flux is contained inside the solder.

soldier beetle A slender soft-bodied beetle with hairy wing cases, belonging to a small but widely distributed family (*Cantharidae*; 3500 species). Brightly colored and 0.20–0.59 in (5–15 mm) long, the adults are attracted to flowers, particularly those of the parsley family (*Umbelliferae*), although most feed on small insects. The larvae are found in soil and moss.

sole An elongated *flatfish of the family *Soleidae* (over 100 species), found in temperate and tropical seas. The common European sole (*Solea solea*), also called Dover sole, is a valuable food fish and has a blotchy brown body, up to 20 in (50 cm) long, with a black spot on each pectoral fin. *See also* lemon sole.

solenodon A shrewlike insectivorous mammal belonging to the family *Solenodontidae* (2 species) found in Cuba and Haiti. Solenodons measure 11–12.5 in (28–32 cm) and have a long naked tail and a long snout with large upper incisor teeth. They feed chiefly on insects, using their long claws to tear open rotten wood. Order: **Insectivora*.

solenoid A coil of wire usually forming a long cylinder. When electric current flows through it a *magnetic field is created. This field can be used to move an iron rod placed on its axis. Solenoids are often used to operate mechanical valves attached to the iron rod by switching the current on or off. In most cars a solenoid is used to operate the heavy-current switch that supplies energy to the starter motor.

solfeggio. *See* solmization.

Solferino, Battle of (June 24, 1859) An indecisive battle between Austria on one side and Sardinia-Piedmont and France on the other. As the Austrians withdrew, Solferino was technically a French victory but the French emperor Napoleon III, alarmed by unrest in Paris and the strength of the Austrians, made peace at Villafranca less than three weeks after the battle. The heavy casualties (about 30,000 dead) led an eyewitness, Henri *Dunant, to campaign for the establishment of the International *Red Cross.

solid state One of the four states of matter and that to which all substances, except helium, revert at sufficiently low temperatures. It is distinguished from the other states by being the only one in which matter retains its shape, as a result of the stronger intermolecular forces.

solid-state devices Electronic devices made with solid *semiconductor components. They have no moving parts and depend for their operation on the movement of charges within a crystalline solid. Solid-state devices are smaller, lighter, physically more robust, and more easily mass-produced than *thermionic valve equipment, which they have now superseded for most uses. *See also* semiconductor diode; thyristor; transistor.

solifluction A process of mass movement of soil and rock debris, associated with areas bordering on ice sheets in which *permafrost is a feature. During the summer season the top layer of soil thaws but as the ground below remains frozen the water is unable to drain away. The soil therefore becomes saturated and on slopes will flow downhill.

Solingen 51 10N 7 05E A city in NW Germany, in North Rhine-Westphalia. Its reputation for blades and cutlery dates to the Middle Ages. It was severely damaged in World War II. Population (1991 est): 162,928.

solipsism The philosophical view that the human mind has no logical justification for believing in the existence of anything other than itself. It is thus an extreme form of *idealism in which the outside world exists only in the mind of the observer. Many philosophers have tried to refute the theory and some have concluded that it is irrefutable. Modern critics, including *Wittgenstein, regard it as incompatible with the existence of a language capable of expressing the view.

solmization A method of teaching sight-singing that eliminates learning to read music notation from the stave. The tonic sol-fa system derived from the hexachord invented by *Guido d'Arezzo. It was systematized in the 1840s by John *Curwen: the notes of the rising major scale are represented by the syllables doh, ray, me, fah, soh, lah, ti, and doh. The system can be applied in any key, and modulation to a different key simply involves shifting doh to another pitch. Vocal exercises on solmization syllables are known by the Italian word solfeggio.

Solo. *See* Surakarta.

Solomon In the Old Testament, the third king of Israel, son of *David and Bathsheba, who reigned in the 10th century BC. During his peaceful reign several foreign alliances were formed (notably with Phoenicia and Egypt), trade and commerce were expanded and the *Temple at Jerusalem as well as many palaces were built. To realize his schemes he had to impose heavy taxation and use compulsory labor, which resulted in the revolt of N Israel. He was famous for his wisdom, and much of the "wisdom" literature of the Old Testament, such as the Song of Solomon, Proverbs, and Ecclesiastes, is attributed to him.

Solomon Islands, State of A country in the Pacific Ocean, E of New Guinea. It consists of a 900 mi (1450 km) chain of numerous small islands, the largest of which are *Guadalcanal, Malaita, San Cristobal, New Georgia, Santa Isabel and Choiseul. *Bougainville, within the Solomon Islands archipelago, is part of Papua New Guinea. The larger islands are mainly forested and mountainous, with some active volcanoes. Most of the population are Melanesian, with Polynesian and Micronesian minorities. *Economy*: the chief product is copra, which, with timber, is the main export. Oil palms, forestry, and fishing are being developed. *History*: the islands were discovered by the Spanish in 1568. The four main islands became a British protectorate in 1893 and others were added in 1898–99. During World War II they were the scene of fighting between the Japanese and Allied forces. They achieved self-government in 1976 and became independent within the Commonwealth of Nations in 1978. Prime Minister: Francis Hillyo. Official language: English. Official currency: Australian dollar of 100 cents. Area: 11,500 sq mi (29,785 sq km). Population (1990): 314,000. Capital and main port: Honiara.

Solomon's seal A hardy perennial herbaceous plant of the genus *Polygonatum* (about 25 species), native to moist shady woods of the N hemisphere, especially *P. multiflorum*. Its arching stem, 12–31 in (30–80 cm) long, bears two rows of broad spindle-shaped leaves, 2–5 in (5–12 cm) long, in the axils of which grow clusters of 2–5 greenish-white tubular flowers followed by red berries. The plant has a fleshy white underground stem (rhizome) marked with prominent scars (hence, probably, the name). Family: **Liliaceae*.

Solon (6th century BC) Athenian statesman, who laid the foundations of Athenian democracy. As archon (c. 594–593), Solon cancelled debts for which land or liberty was the security and introduced a new coinage and system of weights and measures. He also reformed the constitution, dividing the citizens into four classes, and issued a more lenient legal code.

Solothurn (French name: Soleure) 47 13N 7 32E A town in NW Switzerland. It has a cathedral (1762–73) and a former arsenal containing an excellent collection of armor and old weapons. Industries include watchmaking and precision instruments. Population: 17,708.

solstice Either of two points on the *ecliptic, midway between the *equinoxes, at which the sun reaches its greatest angular distance above or below the celestial equator (*see* celestial sphere). In the N hemisphere the sun's northernmost position occurs at the **summer solstice**, usually on June 21, when daylight hours are at a maximum. Its southernmost position occurs at the **winter solstice**, usually on December 21, when daylight hours are minimal.

Solti, Sir Georg (1912–) Hungarian-born, British conductor and pianist. He studied in Budapest with Kodály and Dohnányi and was conductor of Britain's Royal Opera (1961–71). He became conductor of the Chicago Symphony Orchestra in 1969. From 1979 until 1983, he was also principal conductor of the London Philharmonic Orchestra.

solution A homogenous liquid mixture of two or more substances. Solutions, unlike *colloids, contain no identifiable particles of different substances. The components mix as single molecules, ions, or atoms. When a solid or gas is dissolved in a liquid, the liquid is known as the solvent and the dissolved material, the solute. If the components are all liquid, the one in excess is the solvent. In a **solid solution**, molecules, atoms, or ions of one component occupy positions in the crystal structure of the other.

Solutrean A culture of the Upper *Paleolithic succeeding *Gravettian. Named for the site of Solutré near Mâcon (E France), it existed in W Europe from about 18,000 to 15,000 BC in the warmer climate that followed the Wurm *glaciation. It is characterized by symmetrical pressure-flaked flint and other stone points of laurel- and willow-leaf (foliate) shape, which foreshadow the concern for aesthetic expression more fully realized in the subsequent *Magdalenian culture.

Solvay process An industrial process for the production of sodium carbonate from salt, limestone, and ammonia. Limestone is first heated strongly to produce calcium oxide and carbon dioxide: $CaCO_3 \rightarrow CaO + CO_2$. The carbon dioxide gas is passed through brine saturated with ammonia, precipitating sodium hydrogen carbonate ($NaHCO_3$). This, on mild heating, yields sodium carbonate and some carbon dioxide, which is recycled. The ammonia is also recovered from the supernatant liquor from the second step, by the action of lime produced in the first step. Named for E. Solvay (1833–1922).

Solway Firth An inlet of the Irish Sea between Dumfries and Galloway Region in SW Scotland and Cumbria in NW England. Length: about 35 mi (56 km).

Solzhenitsyn, Aleksandr (1918–) Russian novelist. After distinguished service in World War II, he was arrested and held in prison camps until his rehabilitation in 1956. The cultural liberalization heralded by the publication of *A Day in the Life of Ivan Denisovich* (1962), dealing with life in the Stalinist labor camps, was short lived and in 1974 he was forced to leave the Soviet Union and eventually settled in Vermont. His major works, published first in the West, include *The Cancer Ward* (1966), *The First Circle* (1968) and *The Gulag Archipelago* (1974–78). He won the Nobel Prize in 1970. His memoirs, *The Oak and the Calf*, appeared in 1980.

soma A plant of uncertain identity. In the Vedic religion of India its intoxicating or hallucinogenic juice was used in sacrifices, especially to *Indra. It is also personified as a god in a number of hymns in the *Rigveda*.

Somali An E African people occupying Somalia, Djibouti (where they are called Issas), Ethiopia, and NW Kenya. There are many tribes, which are divided into patrilineal clans headed by a chief chosen by the senior men. Among the nomadic herdsmen of the interior blood feud is common. Dwellers in towns and along the coast are traders and farmers. All are at least nominally Muslims. Their language belongs to the Cushitic branch of the *Hamito-Semitic family.

Somalia (official name: Somali Democratic Republic) A country in East Africa, occupying most of the Horn of Africa between the Gulf of Aden and the Indian Ocean. Coastal plains rise in the N to a plateau reaching heights of over 6000 ft (1800 m). Most of the inhabitants are nomadic *Somalis with minorities of Sab, Bantu, and others. *Economy*: chiefly agricultural, with livestock raising (including sheep, goats, cattle, and camels) being especially important. There is some crop growing in the S, including sugar, maize, sorghum, bananas, and other fruit. The limited mineral resources are being exploited and include tin, iron ore, gypsum, and uranium. Fishing is being encouraged, and industry concentrates mainly on leather and food processing. Communications are difficult; there are no railroads, but an extensive road-building program is being carried out with Chinese and other aid. The main exports are livestock, hides and skins, and fruit (especially bananas). *History*: colonized by Muslims from the 7th century AD, the region was occupied in the 19th century by the French, British, and Italians (*see* Somaliland). The former British and Italian territories gained independence in 1960 (while the French territory of the Afars and Issas became independent Djibouti in 1977). In 1969, after a military coup, a Supreme Revolutionary Council was established in Somalia under Gen. Mohamed Siad Barré. The country has had serious territorial disputes with Ethiopia (*see* Ogaden), which has a considerable Somali population. In the early 1980s northern dissident expatriates, claiming neglect and political inequities on the part of the southern-based government, launched attacks from Ethiopia on southern Somalia. A peace accord was signed with Ethiopia in 1988, but the civil war continued, culminating in the ouster of Barré in 1991, when the capital was captured by the rebels. Ali Mahdi Mohamed formed an interim government, but the country remained divided despite a truce accord signed in March 1992 and a UN peacekeeping force sent in April to monitor the cease-fire. Famine conditions were prevalent by mid-1992, and the UN sent peacekeeping troops, including contingents of US soldiers. Official language: Somali; Arabic, Italian, and English are used extensively. Official religion: Islam. Official currency: Somali shilling of 100 centesemi. Area: 270,000 sq mi (700,000 sq km). Population (1990 est): 8,415,000. Capital and main port: Mogadishu.

Somaliland A region corresponding to present-day Somalia and Djibouti. Between the 7th and 12th centuries AD the coastal region was occupied by Muslim traders while the N was settled from the 10th century by nomadic Somalis. During the 19th century the region was divided between France, Britain, and Italy. Italian Somaliland was united with Ethiopia by Mussolini to form Italian East Africa (1935) and was acquired by Britain in World War II. British Somaliland became independent as Somalia in 1960 and the French territory, Afars and Issas, as Djibouti in 1977.

Somerset A county of SW England, bordering on the Bristol Channel. It consists mainly of a flat plain enclosed by the Quantock Hills and Exmoor in the W, the Blackdown Hills in the S, and the Mendip Hills in the NE. It is predominantly agricultural; dairy farming is especially important. The few scattered industries include food processing and textiles. Tourism is an important source of revenue. Area: 1335 sq mi (3458 sq km). Population (1986): 450,800. Administrative center: Taunton.

Somerset, Edward Seymour, 1st Duke of (c. 1500–52) English statesman, who was ruler of England (1547–49) during the minority of Edward VI. Seymour's advancement was facilitated by the marriage of his sister Jane Seymour to Henry VIII, on whose death he became Protector of England and a duke. He defeated the Scots in 1547 and furthered the Protestant *Reformation with the first Book of Common Prayer (1549). He fell from power in 1549 and was subsequently executed.

Somme River A river in N France, rising in the Aisne department and flowing mainly W through Amiens and Abbeville to the English Channel. It was the scene of extensive fighting in *World War I (1916). Length: 152 mi (245 km).

Sommerfeld, Arnold Johannes Wilhelm (1868–1951) German physicist, who did his most important work on atomic structure while he was professor at Munich (1906–31). His modifications of the *Bohr atom included the introduction of elliptical orbits for the electrons and azimuthal and magnetic *quantum numbers. He also worked on *wave mechanics and the theory of electrons in metals.

sonar. *See* echo sounding.

sonata (Italian: sounded, as opposed to *cantata*, sung) A piece of music for one or more instruments. The name has been used of a variety of abstract musical forms, including baroque works for one or more instruments and continuo, the one-movement keyboard sonatas of Scarlatti, and the piano sonatas of Haydn and Mozart. **Sonata form**, the normal structure of the first movement of the classical sonata, was based on the exposition, development, and recapitulation of two contrasting themes. It was applied to the first movement of the *symphony and of *chamber music compositions as well as the sonata proper. Beethoven and his successors enlarged the formal boundaries of the sonata; Liszt evolved a single-movement form out of the three or four movements of the classical sonata. In the 20th century sonata form has been adapted in a variety of ways and new formal patterns have been evolved by such composers as Bartók, Hindemith, Stravinsky, and Tippett.

Sondheim, Stephen (Joshua) (1930–) US composer, who studied lyric writing with Oscar Hammerstein II and composition with Milton Babbitt. He wrote the lyrics for the musicals *West Side Story* (1957), *A Little Night Music* (1973), *Sweeney Todd* (1979), *Into the Woods* (1987), and *Sunday in the Park with George* (1989); *Side by Side by Sondheim* (1976), a successful revue in New York and London, contains many of his songs.

son et lumière (French: sound and light) A nighttime, open-air dramatization of the history of a building, town, etc., using theatrical lighting effects with a synchronized sound track of music and speech. It was developed in 1952 at the Château de Chambord, France, by the Château's curator, Paul Robert-Houdin.

song A short composition for one or more singers, with or without accompaniment. Song is usually regarded as the foundation of music and is certainly the oldest form of musical expression. Besides the folk song traditions of every race, solo song has been a significant part of established musical tradition. In Western music the French chansons of the 15th century, the Italian *frottola, the lute songs of the Elizabethans, operatic *arias, German *Lieder* (as treated by Schubert, Schumann, and Wolf), and the French tradition of *mélodies* (as treated by Duparc and Fauré) are all of great importance. A **song cycle** is a group of songs intended to be performed in sequence: the texts are either thematically related, or are all by the same poet.

Song (*or* Sung) (960–1279) A Chinese dynasty that may be divided into the Northern and Southern Song periods. It was founded in N China by Zhao Guang

Yin (*or* Chao K'uang Yin; 927–76), who reunited the war-torn country but, despite a strong administration, was never able to control the *Juchen. These tribes forced the Song south in 1127 and founded their own dynasty in the N. The Southern Song established a new capital at Hangzhou, where a great flourishing of Chinese poetry, painting, and pottery occurred. The Song were overthrown by the Mongols under Kublai Khan in 1279.

Song, T. V. (*or* T. V. Sung; 1894–1971) Chinese banker and politician. He was finance minister (1925–31) and foreign minister (1942–45) in the Chinese Nationalist Government. After 1949 he lived in the US. His elder sister **Song Qing-Ling** (*or* Sung Ch'ing-ling) married *Sun Yat-sen (1914) and herself became a revolutionary leader and later a member of the Chinese Communist party. His younger sister **Song Mei-ling** (*or* Sung Mei-ling) married *Chiang Kai-shek, fleeing with him to Taiwan in 1949.

songbird A *passerine bird belonging to the suborder *Oscines* (about 4000 species), in which the vocal organ (syrinx), at the junction of the trachea (windpipe) and bronchi, is highly developed. The flow of air vibrates the vocal membranes; muscles alter their tension and so produce the different notes. Bird song communicates the identity and whereabouts of an individual to other birds and also signals alarm and sexual intentions; it is especially important in birds that feed or migrate in flocks.

Songhai A West African people inhabiting the region of the Middle Niger River S of Timbuktu. Adopting the Islamic religion in the 11th century AD and influenced by Muslim traders from Africa, the Songhai became prosperous and cultured traders. Between about 1350 and 1600 their kings developed a vast commercial empire, based on the gold and salt trade, which extended from the West African coast to Lake Chad and absorbed the earlier empire of Mali. After the Moroccan invasion of 1591, the Songhai empire collapsed.

Songhua River (*or* Sungari R.) A river in NE China, rising in *Jilin province and flowing roughly NE to the Heilong (*or* Amur) River on the border with Russia. Length: over 800 mi (1300 km).

Song of Solomon An Old Testament book, also known as the Song of Songs or Canticles. It was traditionally ascribed to *Solomon but was probably written in the 2nd century BC. Written in extravagantly erotic language, it is a series of oriental love poems concerning a bridegroom and his bride, "the Shulamite." Both Jews and Christians interpreted the work allegorically as describing the relation between God and Israel or, for Christian commentators, between Christ and the Church.

song thrush A Eurasian thrush, *Turdus philomelos*, about 9 in (22 cm) long and having a brown back, pale breast streaked with brown, and orange underwings. Its song is loud and distinctive, each phrase being repeated several times. It feeds on invertebrates and smashes snails against a stone before eating them.

sonic boom. *See* sound barrier.

sonnet A poem of 14 lines originating in Italy in the 13th century and introduced into England in the 16th century by Sir Thomas *Wyatt. Its two principal variations are the Petrarchan sonnet, usually divided into an octet rhyming *abbaabba* and a sestet rhyming *cdecde*, and the Shakespearean sonnet, usually rhyming *abab cdcd efef gg*. Sonnets have been written by Milton, Wordsworth, and G. M. Hopkins and it remains one of the few traditional forms still employed by major 20th-century poets. *See also* rhymes.

Soochow. *See* Suzhou.

Sophia (1657–1704) Regent of Russia (1682–89) for her brother Ivan V (1666–96) and half-brother *Peter the Great. She was overthrown by Peter and forced to retire to a convent, where she died.

Sophia (1630–1714) Electress of Hanover (1658–1714), in whom the Act of *Settlement (1701) vested the English crown. Sophia, the wife of Elector Ernest Augustus (1629–98; ruled 1692–98), was the granddaughter of James I of England and the daughter of Frederick the Winter King, of the Palatinate. Her son succeeded to the British throne as George I.

Sophists The Greek sages of the 5th and early 4th centuries BC who were itinerant experts on various subjects including public speaking, grammar, ethics, literature, mathematics, and elementary physics. They were not a clearly defined school, but they did have certain interests in common. In philosophy they attacked the *Eleatics' account of reality and tried to explain the phenomenal world. Their educational program centered on the belief that virtue can be taught. From their opponent *Plato, they acquired a bad name as philosophical tricksters, more interested in money and prestige than in truth. In Roman times the term "sophist" came to mean simply a teacher of rhetoric.

Sophocles (c. 496–406 BC) Greek dramatist; with Aeschylus and Euripides, one of the three great Athenian tragic dramatists. He developed the more static drama of Aeschylus by introducing a third actor and reducing the role of the chorus. Of his 123 plays, seven survive: *Ajax, Women of Trachis, Electra, Philoctetes*, and his three most famous plays dealing with Thebes, *Oedipus Rex, Oedipus at Colonus*, and *Antigone*. He led an active public life, being a friend of Pericles and holding several important civil and military administrative posts.

soprano (Italian: upper) The highest female singing voice. Range: middle C to the C above the treble stave. The **mezzo-soprano** voice lies between the soprano and the contralto. Range: A below middle C to F an octave and a sixth above.

Soranus of Ephesus (2nd century AD) Greek physician, whose works were a major influence on gynecology and obstetrics until the 17th century. He described contraception, abortion, and procedures during childbirth and also wrote about fractures and diseases.

Sorbonne One of the oldest parts of the university in Paris, France, founded by the theologian Robert de Sorbon (1201–74) in about 1257. The present site of the Sorbonne, off the Boulevard Saint-Michel, dates from 1627 and was the scene of the first confrontations between students and police in the riots of May 1968.

Sorel, Georges (1847–1922) French social philosopher. As a political activist, Sorel believed that socialism could only come about through a general strike (*see* syndicalism). His theory of the "social myth," which held that the proletariat could be manipulated by propaganda, was, ironically, most successfully proved by the fascist dictators.

Sorghum A genus of annual or perennial *grasses (about 30 species), native to Africa, especially *S. vulgare*, of which there are several varieties, such as sweet sorghum, *durra, and *kaffir corn, widely cultivated as cereal crops. Usually growing up to 8 ft (2.5 m) high, they have rigid stalks, sometimes containing a sweet sap, long flat leaves, and terminal flower clusters bearing 800 to 3000 starch-rich seeds. The seeds are used as grain for making bread, etc., and as a source of edible oil, starch, and sugar. The stalks are used as fodder or sometimes for syrup manufacture.

Sorocaba 23 30S 47 32W A city in S Brazil, in São Paulo state on the Río Sorocaba. It is a major industrial center; manufactures include textiles, fertilizers, and wine. Population (1980): 254,718.

sorrel A perennial herb, *Rumex acetosa,* common throughout temperate Eurasia and North America. It grows to a height of 40 in (1 m) and bears numerous small red flowers. The tangy-tasting leaves are used as a culinary flavoring and in salads. Family: *Polygonaceae. See also* wood sorrel.

Sorrento 40 37N 14 23E A seaport in SW Italy, in Campania. A resort since Roman times, it is the birthplace of the poet Tasso. Oranges and lemons are grown. Population (1981): 17,301.

Sosigenes of Alexandria (1st century BC) Greek astronomer, about whom little is known except that, on his advice, Julius Caesar reformed the calendar and added an extra day every four years to produce the modern system of leap years. This system is known as the Julian *calendar.

Sosnowiec 50 16N 19 07E A town in S Poland. It is a metallurgical center; other industries include engineering, chemicals, and the manufacture of textiles. Population (1992 est): 259,500.

Sotho A large group of Bantu-speaking peoples of S Africa. The term applies in a general sense to the peoples of Botswana, Lesotho, and the Transvaal (South Africa), but, more specifically, to one of the four main divisions of these peoples, the Sotho of Lesotho. The other branches are the Tswana, Pedi, and Venda, each with many tribes. All live by combined agriculture and animal husbandry and have a broadly similar culture, now disintegrating under the impact of urbanization.

Soto The largest Japanese school of Zen Buddhism, founded in China in the 9th century AD and brought to Japan by *Dogen in 1227. Soto emphasizes meditation and morality. Adherents strive to live as what they hope to become, perfect Buddhas.

Soto, Hernando de (?1496–1542) Spanish explorer. After exploration in Central America, he set out in 1539 to conquer Florida. He landed with 600 men at Tampa Bay and journeyed circuitously through what became the S US in search of gold. In 1541 he crossed the Mississippi, the first white man to do so, but died on the return journey.

Soufflot, Jacques Germain (1713–80) French architect. After training in Italy (1731–38), Soufflot became the leading French exponent of *neoclassicism. Apart from the Hôtel Dieu in Lyons (1841–48), his most famous building is the Church of St Geneviève in Paris (begun in 1757), now called the *Panthéon.

Soult, Nicolas Jean de Dieu, Duc de Dalmatie (1769–1851) French general in the Revolutionary and Napoleonic Wars. A sergeant at the outbreak of the French Revolution, he rose to the rank of general in 1794 and later commanded in the Peninsular War. He became president of the council (1832–34, 1839–40, 1840–47) under Louis Philippe.

sound A disturbance propagated through a medium by longitudinal waves. The term strictly applies only to those waves that are audible to the human ear, i.e. with frequencies between about 20 and 20,000 hertz, those with frequencies above 20,000 hertz being called ultrasound and those below 20 hertz infrasound. Sound is propagated by vibrations of molecules in the medium, producing fronts of compression and rarefaction. Sound waves are longitudinal as the molecules vibrate in the direction of propagation; the velocity of sound in air at 0°C is about 332 meters per second (760 mph at 32°F). The three principal characteristics of a sound are its pitch (the frequency of the wave), loudness (the amplitude of the wave), and *timbre (the extent to which it contains harmonics of the fundamental frequency). However, there is a relationship between pitch and loudness (*see* sound intensity). *See also* acoustics.

Sound, the (Danish name: =Øresund; Norwegian name: Öresund) A sea channel in N Europe, between Denmark (Sjælland) and Sweden, linking the Kattegat and the Baltic Sea. Length: 70 mi (113 km). Narrowest point: 2.5 mi (4 km).

sound barrier An obstacle experienced by subsonic *aircraft attempting to fly at or above the speed of sound. Drag increases sharply, lift falls off, and the aircraft becomes difficult to control (*see* aeronautics). At subsonic speeds the pressure waves created by the aircraft as it flies through the air are able to move ahead of the aircraft; at supersonic speed they cannot escape in a forward direction as the source is moving faster than the pressure waves themselves. Thus shock waves build up on the aircraft's wings and fuselage, creating an apparent barrier to supersonic flight. The barrier was overcome for the first time by the US Bell X1 rocket aircraft in 1947. Since then many aircraft capable of supersonic flight have been built (including Concorde) by greater streamlining, sweptback wings, and more powerful engines. As these aircraft cross the sound barrier a **sonic boom** is heard. This is created by a shock-wave cone with the nose of the aircraft as its vertex. In level flight the intersection of this cone with the ground produces a hyperbola at all points along which the boom is heard.

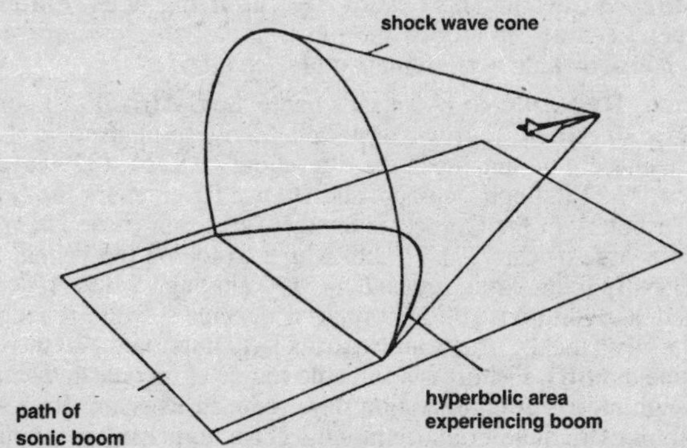

SOUND BARRIER *As an aircraft passes through the sound barrier the sonic boom is heard along a hyperbolic area on the ground.*

sound intensity The rate at which sound energy is propagated through a unit area perpendicular to the direction of propagation. It is measured in watts per square meter. The intensities of two sound levels are compared by a unit called the *decibel. The intensity of sound is not the same as its loudness, the latter being the magnitude of the sensation produced by the human ear, which is dependent on the frequency of the sound.

Souphanouvong, Prince (1912–) Laotian statesman; president (1975–86). In the civil war in Laos (1953–73) he led the revolutionary Pathet Lao and, on its conclusion, joined the coalition government established in 1974. In 1975, however, Pathet Lao forces seized complete control and Souphanouvong became president, a post he held until his resignation due to health problems in 1986.

soursop An evergreen tree belonging to the tropical American genus *Annona*, especially *A. muricata*, widely cultivated in the Old World tropics. It grows to a height of 26 ft (8 m) and produces large oval spiny green fruit, the flesh of which can be eaten or used as an ingredient of soft drinks, ice cream, etc., Family: *Annonaceae*.

Sousa, John Philip (1854–1933) US composer and bandmaster. In 1880 he was appointed leader of the Marine Corps Band and in 1892 formed his own band, which toured the world. He wrote military marches including "The Stars and Stripes Forever," "The Washington Post," "Semper Fidelis," and "Liberty Bell" and invented the **sousaphone**, a tubalike band instrument with a forward-facing bell.

souslik (*or* suslik) A nocturnal *ground squirrel belonging to the genus *Citellus* (34 species), of E Europe, Asia, and North America (where it is sometimes called a gopher). The European souslik (*C. citellus*) is yellowish brown with large eyes and small ears and lives in burrows in dry open country, feeding on seeds, nuts, and bulbs. *See also* chipmunk.

Soustelle, Jacques (Émile) (1912–90) French anthropologist and politician. A member of the *Free French during World War II, he became secretary general of de Gaulle's Rassemblement du Peuple français in 1947. He was governor general of Algeria (1955–56) and subsequently opposed the policies of successive French governments toward Algeria, living in exile from 1961 to 1968. He then became director of the prestigious École pratique des hautes Études. His books include *Arts of Ancient Mexico* (1967).

South Africa, Republic of (Afrikaans name: Suid-Afrika) A country occupying the S tip of Africa. Narrow coastal plains rise to plateaus in the interior, with the Drakensberg mountains in the E reaching 10,822 ft (3299 m). The N is mainly desert. The Limpopo, Molopo, and Orange Rivers mark the N boundary. The Vaal, a tributary of the Orange, is another important river. The majority of the inhabitants are Africans (71%) with white, Coloured (an official category) and Asian (mostly Indian) minorities. *Economy*: although South Africa is highly industrialized, agriculture is still important, with cereals, fruit growing, and cotton, as well as livestock. Citrus fruit is particularly important and there is a considerable wine industry. Fishing is a valuable source of income and whaling continues although efforts at conservation have reduced its scale. Rich and varied mineral resources include gold, diamonds, chrome, platinum, uranium, coal, manganese, phosphates, and iron. South Africa leads the world in the production of gold, gem diamonds, antimony, and vanadium. Hydroelectricity is a valuable source of power. Well-developed and diverse industry includes metals, machinery, and chemicals, as well as light industry, such as food processing and textiles. Main exports include metals (especially gold), citrus fruits, sugar, wines, and textiles. *History*: originally inhabited by San (Bushmen) and Khoikhoi peoples. Bantu-speaking tribes moved southward to present-day South Africa between 1000 and 1500. The Portuguese under *Dias first sighted the Cape of Good Hope (1488) but made no permanent settlement there. The Dutch East India Company settlement (1652) at Table Bay (Cape Town) expanded into a colony that spread into the interior, meeting little resistance from the *Khoisan inhabitants. After Louis XIV revoked the Edict of Nantes (1685), Huguenot refugees augmented the white settlers. During the Napoleonic Wars Britain acquired the Cape Colony for strategic reasons, a possession confirmed in 1814. In the 1830s increasing numbers of Dutch farmers (or Boers, forebears of the modern Afrikaners) moved in vast numbers E and N to escape British rule (*see* Great

Trek). Bloody warfare (primarily with the Zulus) ensued as the *Bantu peoples who were migrating southward clashed with the Boers. The Boers founded two independent republics, the Orange Free State and the Transvaal (*see* Sand River Convention), but their republic in Natal was soon annexed by the British (1843), who were also expanding the eastern boundaries of the Cape Colony (*see* Cape Frontier Wars). *Kruger's assertion of Boer independence led to war (1880–81), which broke out again between the Boers and the British after the discovery of gold (1886) in the Transvaal had led to hostility between the Boers and the immigrant gold-diggers (*see* Boer Wars). The need for cooperation led the two former Boer republics and the two British colonies to combine in the Union of South Africa (1910). The Depression of the 1930s saw the emergence of both African and Afrikaner nationalism as unskilled laborers from both groups were forced into the cities to compete for jobs. In 1913 a segregation policy was instituted to safeguard South Africa as a white country; the creation of the Bantustans or African homelands ensued, thus ensuring the forcible exclusion of Africans from the political and social life of the country. All of South Africa's "people of Colour" became subject to discriminatory laws, although Coloureds and Asians were granted somewhat broader privileges. In both World Wars South Africa, under J. C. *Smuts, enthusiastically supported Britain, but anti-British Afrikaner interests grew steadily stronger. In 1948 Smuts was ousted by the Afrikaner National party and the even harsher segregationist policy known as apartheid or "separate development" became official. A program of Bantu self-government, whereby 10 Bantustans, or black homelands, were to achieve independence was enacted. (In 1976 *Transkei became the first Bantu homeland to receive independence.) In 1961 because of disapproval on the part of the Commonwealth nations South Africa became a republic outside the Commonwealth. From the 1950s the African movement against apartheid intensified, leading to numerous clashes between blacks and the government, in which many blacks died. Under Pres. Pieter Botha the South African government moved to modify some of its apartheid laws and in 1983 revised its constitution for the first time. Protests by the black majority against the regime escalated from 1985, leading to the government's imposition of a state of emergency, which curtailed civil rights, in 1986. President Botha resigned in 1989 and was succeeded by F. W. de Klerk, who proved moderate and conciliatory. In 1990, the South African government recognized the opposition African National Congress (ANC) and released its leader, Nelson *Mandela, who had been jailed for 26 years. By early 1992, legislation that abolished apartheid was in place. In February 1993, the government and ANC leaders agreed to establish a "government of national unity" that would manage the transition ending rule by the white minority. The first elections in which blacks were able to vote were in 1994. Increased international acceptance has followed South Africa's reforms, and then-President F. W. *de Klerk and Mandela shared the 1993 Nobel Peace Prize. State president: Nelson Mandela. Official languages: Afrikaans and English. Official currency, since 1959: rand of 100 cents. Area: 472,359 sq mi (1,221,042 sq km). Population (1990 est): 39,500,000. Capitals: Pretoria (administrative), Bloemfontein (judicial), Cape Town (legislative).

South America The fourth largest continent, lying chiefly in the S of the W hemisphere between the Pacific and Atlantic Oceans. Roughly triangular in shape and tapering in the S, it is linked to the continent of North America by the Isthmus of Panama. An ancient shield occupies much of the NE part of the continent and forms the Brazilian and Guiana Highlands. These are separated by the vast basins of the Orinoco, Amazon, and Paraná–Paraguay river systems. In the extreme W, beyond a series of plains, rise the mountains and high plateaus of the *Andes, the world's longest mountain system. The Andes rise to their highest point at Mount *Aconcagua and contain Lake *Titicaca, the continent's largest lake. South America's climate varies considerably, largely because of its length, but much is tropical with vast areas of tropical rain forest (selva). The population consists chiefly of the indigenous Indians, Europeans (especially Spanish and Portuguese), and mestizos together with large numbers of Negroids. *History*: much archeological evidence remains of the flourishing kingdoms of South America (such as those of the *Incas and *Chibchas), which were vanquished by the Spanish conquistadors. The entire continent was divided—Portugal taking the NE portion (now Brazil) and Spain the remainder—during the 16th century. With the collapse of the Spanish Empire during the early 19th century, there followed struggles for independence under national leaders, who included *Bolívar and *San Martin. Large-scale European immigration (including German and Italian) occurred in the 19th century. During the 20th century the constitutent nations have become increasingly industrialized and seen rapid rises in their populations. Area: 17,767,331 sq km (6,858,527 sq mi). Population (1990 est): 304,000,000.

South American languages The indigenous languages of South America, the Antilles, and parts of Central America, many of which are now extinct. Brought originally from North America by migrating Indians, the languages are extremely diverse in nature. The number of speakers is currently estimated at 11,200,000, the majority in the central Andes. The classification of the six hundred documented languages, based on lexical and syntactic similarities, presents no clear picture. Although linguists agree that the languages probably shared a common source, there is no consensus on their relationships.

Southampton 50 55N 1 25W A city in S England, an inlet of the English Channel. It is the UK's principal passenger port, used by the largest transatlantic liners. Southampton's industries include marine engineering, electrical equipment, and yacht building. The University of Southampton was established in 1952. Population (1981): 204,406.

South Australia A state of S central Australia, bordering on the Indian Ocean. It consists chiefly of low-lying plains with the *Great Victoria Desert in the W, rising in the NW to the Musgrave Ranges and in the SE to the Flinders Range. The only major river is the Murray. Lake Eyre is frequently only an immense salt flat. Intensive agriculture is restricted to the S. Its vineyards produce almost half of Australia's wine. Mineral resources include iron ore from the Middleback Ranges, low-grade coal at Leigh Creek, large natural gas fields in the N, and opals. Industry, concentrated in Adelaide, includes the manufacture of motor vehicles, textiles, and chemicals. Area: 380,070 sq mi (984,377 sq km). Population (1992 est): 1,459,000. Capital: Adelaide.

South Bend 41 40N 86 15W A city in Indiana on the St Joseph River. Industries include the manufacture of aircraft, motor-vehicle parts, and machinery. The University of Notre Dame is there. Population (1990): 105,511.

South Carolina A state in the SE, on the Atlantic coast. It is bounded on the S and E by the Atlantic Ocean, on the S and W by Georgia, and on the N by North Carolina. Lowlands make up two-thirds of the state, rising to uplands (the Piedmont Plateau) culminating in the Blue Ridge Mountains in the extreme NW. Major rivers include the Savannah. Although the population is predominantly rural (55%) with African Americans comprising 31% of the total, South Carolina is undergoing a transition from a basically agrarian economy to one dominated by industry. The large areas of woodland supply the furniture industries and the large textile and clothing industries are based on the region's cotton crop. Other leading manufactures include chemicals, machinery, and food products. South Carolina's beaches along the NW coast (the most famous being

Myrtle Beach) and the popular Sea Islands (including Cumberland Island and Hilton Head) with wildlife sanctuaries and resort areas, are tourist attractions. Charleston, a major US port of entry, is famous for its charming antebellum homes, flowering gardens, and picturesque winding streets. *History*: what was perhaps the first but short-lived white settlement in North America was founded by the Spanish in 1526 at an unknown site in present-day South Carolina. French Huguenots later attempted to colonize the area but were thwarted by the Spanish, whose missions dotted the SW coast from Florida to what is now Charleston. With the arrival of the English during the reign of Charles II (for whom Charleston was named), Carolina was settled as a proprietary colony (1670). Dissatisfaction with the despotic rule of the small group of proprietors resulted in revolt by the colonists, and in 1719 the Carolinas were made a royal colony with a royal governor. South Carolina was made a separate colony in 1729. White immigration was encouraged to offset the growing population of imported black slaves. Sectionalism began to emerge with the poor lowland farmers in the NW demanding political equality with the wealthy plantation lords in the S. The Stamp Act and the Townshend Acts transformed sentiments in South Carolina to favor revolution. After the American Revolution the invention of the cotton gin and the subsequent glut in the cotton market by growing cotton production in the W states precipitated a decline in prosperity. South Carolina's John Calhoun, defending the doctrine of states' rights, became the philosophical founding father of much of the political and intellectual basis of the Confederacy. South Carolina was the first state to secede from the Union and shots fired at Fort Sumter signaled the outbreak of the Civil War. Regarded as the birthplace of secession, South Carolina suffered severe, deliberate, and devastating reprisals at the hands of Union soldiers, culminating in the burning of Columbia. During Reconstruction, South Carolina also experienced great hardship and corruption, emerging as a state in which white political supremacy prevailed but whose agrarian economy had been virtually destroyed. In the 1920s Jim Crow laws were instituted. Hard hit by the Depression and a serious boll weevil infestation, the state rallied with state work programs provided by the New Deal. The political and legal position of African Americans, now a minority, underwent gradual improvement into the 1980s. Population (1990): 3,486,703. Capital: Columbia.

South Caucasian languages A group of languages, also known as the Kartvelian languages, spoken by the people of W Transcaucasia and adjacent regions. It includes *Georgian, Svan, Mingrelian, and Laz. Only Georgian possesses a literary tradition and is used for literary purposes by speakers of the other languages.

South China Sea (Chinese name: Nanhai) A section of the W Pacific Ocean, between SE Asia, Borneo, the Philippines, and Taiwan. A monsoon area, it is heavily fished.

South Dakota One of the Plains states in the N central part of the country. It is bordered by North Dakota on the N, by Iowa and Minnesota on the E, by Nebraska on the S, and by Montana and Wyoming on the W. The Missouri River separates the arid Badlands, the Black Hills, and the Great Plains in the W from the flat fertile prairie in the E, which forms the basis of South Dakota's predominantly agrarian economy. Livestock and livestock products are the chief source of revenue. Although it has the largest gold mine in the US, mineral extraction is minimal. *History*: home of the nomadic Sioux and the sedentary Arikara, the area was partially explored (1742–43) by the French. It was part of the Louisiana Purchase (1803) and was explored by the Lewis and Clark expedition shortly thereafter. Early settlement was spurred by the fur trade and the subsequent development of farms, but it was Col. George Custer's confirmation of the existence of gold in the Black Hills (1874) that lured hordes of prospectors. The Indians were gradually subdued, ending with the massacre at Wounded Knee (1890). The arrival of the railroads stimulated the development of ranching and farming and the years 1880 to 1890 saw a tripling of Dakota Territory's population. In 1889 the lines between North and South were drawn and both states entered the Union. From this time until after World War II, South Dakota was severely harmed by droughts and economic depressions. A new prosperity emerged after the war as a result of the establishment of hydroelectric projects, control of the Missouri River, growth of industry and tourism, and mechanization of farms. Area: 77,047 sq mi (199,551 sq km). Population (1990): 696,004. Capital: Pierre.

Southeast Asia Treaty Organization (SEATO) An organization formed to protect SE Asia from possible communist aggression. It was analogous to the *North Atlantic Treaty Organization. The treaty was signed in Manila in 1954 by Australia, France, New Zealand, Pakistan, the Philippines, Thailand, the UK, and the US. Pakistan withdrew in 1973 and the organization was formally ended in 1977. *See also* Association of Southeast Asian Nations.

Southend-on-Sea 51 33N 0 43E A resort in SE England, on the lower Thames estuary. It is the nearest seaside resort to London and has the world's longest pleasure pier. Population (1981): 156,683.

Southern Alps The highest range of mountains in New Zealand. It extends SW–NE through South Island and contains many peaks over 10,000 ft (3000 m), including Mount *Cook. Glaciers, fed by the central snowfields, flank the mountains and include Tasman Glacier. It is an important winter sports area.

Southern Christian Leadership Congress (SCLC) US civil-rights organization founded by Martin Luther *King, Jr. in 1957. Advocating a policy of nonviolence, he hoped to bring about equal rights in the South. It backed the successful desegregation of public facilities (1963) and the March on Washington (1963). After King's assassination (1968), it was led by Ralph *Abernathy and then Joseph Lowery, but its influence declined.

Southern Cross. *See* Crux.

Southern Rhodesia. *See* Zimbabwe, State of.

southernwood A perennial herb, *Artemisia abrotanum*, also called lad's love, native to S Europe and Asia and cultivated for its aromatic leaves, which can be used to make a beverage. Family: **Compositae*. *See also* wormwood.

Southey, Robert (1774–1843) British poet and writer. He was a close associate of *Wordsworth and *Coleridge and in 1803 settled in the Lake District. He became poet laureate in 1813. His poetry lacks originality and was overshadowed by the work of his greater contemporaries. He wrote several historical books, notably *The Life of Nelson* (1813).

South Georgia An island in the S Atlantic Ocean, a dependency of the Falkland Islands. King Edward Point is a base for members of the British Antarctic Survey. With the Falkland Islands, it was invaded by Argentina in April 1982, but was recaptured by British forces the same month. Area: 1450 sq mi (3755 sq km).

South Holland (Dutch name: Zuid-Holland) A province in the W central Netherlands, on the North Sea. Its S part consists of several islands. It is densely populated and agriculture, especially cattle raising and flower bulbs, is the chief occupation. The extensive trading and shipping industry is centered on the port of Rotterdam. Tourism is also important. Area: 1287 sq mi (3333 sq km). Population (1990 est): 3,219,839. Capital: The Hague.

South Island The larger of the two principal islands of New Zealand, separated from North Island by Cook Strait. It is generally mountainous, rising over 11,483 ft (3500 m) in the *Southern Alps in the W, with coastal plains. Population (1991): 877,235.

Southland Plain A low-lying area of New Zealand, on SE South Island bordering on the Pacific Ocean. Sheep rearing and dairying are important.

SOUTHLAND PLAIN

South Orkney Islands A group of islands within the British Antarctic Territory, in the S Atlantic Ocean. A dependency of the Falkland Islands until 1962, their major importance is as a whaling base. They are also claimed by Argentina.

South Ossetia An autonomous region (*oblast*) in Georgia. Its inhabitants comprise chiefly Orthodox Christian Ossetians, a Caucasian people. Timber is produced and its many rivers are used to generate hydroelectric power. Livestock are raised in the higher regions. Area: 1500 sq mi (3900 sq km). Population (1981 est): 97,000. Capital: Tskhinvali.

South Sea Bubble (1720) The collapse of the British market in South Sea stocks that had far-reaching political repercussions. The South Sea Company was founded in 1711 to trade with Spanish America. A boom in South Sea stock was followed by collapse and the subsequent inquiry revealed corruption among ministers and even touched the king. The day was saved by Sir Robert *Walpole, who transferred the South Sea stocks to the Bank of England and the East India Company.

South Shetland Islands An uninhabited archipelago within the British Antarctic Territory, in the S Atlantic Ocean. Until 1962 they were a dependency of the British Falkland Islands.

South West Africa. *See* Namibia.

Soutine, Chaim (1893–1943) Lithuanian-born painter, who emigrated to Paris in 1913. There influenced by *expressionism, he achieved recognition in the 1920s despite his reluctance to exhibit his work. Using thickly applied paint, intense color, and distorted and writhing forms, he was, together with *Chagall, the leading representative of French expressionism.

Sovetsk (name until 1945: Tilsit) 55 02N 21 50E A city in W Russia, on the Nemen River. Founded by the Teutonic Knights in 1288, it was there that the Treaties of *Tilsit were signed (1807) between Napoleon and, respectively, Prussia (which held the town until 1945) and Russia. Industries include food processing and the manufacture of pulp. Population (1988 est): 41,000.

soviet A government council in the former Soviet Union. Soviets originated as committees of workers' deputies in the *Revolution of 1905 and were again established in the *Russian Revolution of 1917, which established the *Soviet Union. The Supreme Soviet was in theory the supreme organ of government in the Soviet Union and soviets were also elected at the local, provincial, and republican levels. Candidates, one for each deputy, were selected by the Communist party.

Soviet Far East. *See* Siberia.

Soviet Union (officially: Union of Soviet Socialist Republics) Formerly the world's largest country and its third most populous, covering N Eurasia and bordering on the Pacific and Arctic Oceans and the Baltic, Black, Caspian, and Aral Seas. It was a federal state comprising 15 constituent republics; the Armenian, Azerbaidzhan, Belorussian, Estonian, Georgian, Kazakh, Kirghiz, Latvian, Lithuanian, Moldavian, Russian Soviet Federal, Tadzhik, Turkmen, Ukrainian, and Uzbek Soviet Socialist Republics. Administrative subdivisions included 20 autonomous Soviet Socialist Republics and, within some of these, eight autonomous regions (Russian *oblast*, region). The area W of the River Yenisei consists of vast plains and depressions, dissected by the Ural Mountains, while the E consists mainly of mountains and plateaus. The mountain belt along the S border includes the Carpathian, Caucasus, Pamir, and Sayan Mountains, the Stanovoi Range, and the Tien Shan. The rivers mainly flow N to the Arctic Ocean. The population included over a hundred national groups, for whom many of the country's subdivisions were established. The most numerous were the Russians, Ukrainians, Uzbeks, Belorussians, Tatars, and Kazakhs. Population was most dense W of the Urals, where most of the large industrial cities are situated. *Economy*: based on the system of state ownership, it was controlled through Gosplan (the State Planning Commission) and Gosbank (the State Bank). It was directed from 1928 by a series of *five-year plans and the economy became the largest and strongest after the US. Its main asset was the country's vast natural resources and the Soviet Union was the world's leading producer of oil, coal, iron ore, cement, and steel; manganese, gold, natural gas, and other minerals were also of major importance. Industry was long concentrated after 1928 on the production of capital goods through metalworking, machine manufacture, and the chemical industry, and relatively few consumer goods were produced. During the 1960s and 1970s the latter received slightly more emphasis. Agriculture, organized in a system of state and collective farms, was on a large scale and was highly mechanized but not highly productive, hampered in many areas by the climate and by a shortage of resources. The Soviet Union was one of the world's greatest producers of cereals, although bad harvests (as in 1972 and 1975) necessitated imports and hampered the economy. The 1976–80 five-year plan shifted resources to agriculture, and 1978 saw a record harvest. Fishing, forestry, and dependent industries were also important; the country was the world's greatest producer of timber. Largely self-sufficient, it traded little in comparison to its economic strength, although trade with noncommunist countries increased greatly during the 1970s. Fuels, metals, machinery, and timber were exported, while machinery, consumer goods, and occasionally grain were imported. *History*: the area has been populated for three to four millenniums, although little is known of its history until the 8th century AD, when European and

Middle Eastern traders began its exploration. Control of the area between the Baltic and Black Seas was established by Scandinavian adventurers by 1000. Dominated by Kiev from the mid-10th to mid-11th centuries, these Varangian principalities submitted (after 1223) to the overrule of the Golden Horde. By the time of the Horde's collapse in the 14th century, Moscow, ruled by Rurik princes, had emerged as a powerful principality, becoming the capital of a united Russia under Ivan the Great in the 15th century. Contact with W Europe was established in the late 17th century by Peter the Great, who also established the Russian bureaucracy and educational system and built a new capital, St Petersburg (later called Leningrad). By the 19th century Russian territories had been greatly extended but, although a force to be reckoned with in the world, Russia was industrially far behind the UK, Germany, and the US, its bureaucracy had grown unwieldy and oppressive, and its Romanov emperors (tsars) were opposed to any political change. Revolutionary activity began with the Dekabrists' conspiracy, uncovered in 1825, and, although serfdom was abolished in 1861, its abolition was achieved on terms unfavorable to the peasants and served to encourage revolutionaries, a group of whom assassinated Alexander II in 1881. Bloody Sunday (Jan 22, 1905), on which several hundred workers were killed during a demonstration in St Petersburg, was followed by great disorder (*see* Revolution of 1905). A parliament, the *Duma, was established in 1906, but political unrest continued and was aggravated during World War I by military defeat and food shortages. The February and October Revolutions (*see* Russian Revolution) were followed by a period of civil war (1918–22), after which communist control was complete. After Lenin's death (1924) Stalin had emerged as leader by 1928, having ousted Trotsky. Under Stalin, who replaced Lenin's New Economic Policy with five-year plans and collective farms, the Soviet Union (established 1922) became a major industrial power but a totalitarian state, with effective political opposition eliminated during the 1930s by purges. World War II established the Soviet Union as one of the two major world powers, a position maintained since then through military strength, aid to developing countries, and scientific research, especially into weaponry and space technology. Relations with the other superpower, the US, improved after the *Cold War, with agreements on *disarmament, although the Soviet invasion of Afghanistan (1979) provoked US condemnation. Internal dissension was still viewed as a threat, as shown by the trials of human-rights activists. Dissension within the communist bloc (*see* Warsaw Pact) provoked a similar response from the Soviet Government, which intervened in the Hungarian Revolution (1956) and the Czechoslovakian liberalization program (1968) and which directed the suppression of the Solidarity labor movement in Poland in 1981. Strained relations with the US were marked by the US boycott of the 1980 Olympics in Moscow and the Soviet boycott of the 1984 Olympics in Los Angeles, but more importantly by the breakdown in 1983 of nuclear arms control talks. US-Soviet summit meetings in 1986 and 1987 and a Gorbachev-Reagan meeting in late 1988 brought about arms cuts in Europe and promoted Soviet *glasnost* (openness) and *perestroika* (economic restructuring). The reunification of Germany and the disintegration of Communist regimes throughout E Europe in 1989–90 eventually triggered a peaceful evolution in the Soviet Union in 1991. As the country's economy appeared ready to collapse and as various republics declared their independence, the Russian republic's Boris Yeltsin eclipsed Soviet leader Mikhail Gorbachev in power. The Soviet Union declared its dissolution on Dec 25, 1991, with the former republics recognized as independent. A looser confederation, called the Commonwealth of Independent States (CIS), with 11 of the former republics as members, replaced the Soviet Union's governmental structure. Official language: Russian. Area: 8,647,675 sq mi (22,402,200 sq km). Population (1988):

284,500,000. Capital: Moscow. *See also* articles on individual countries: Armenia, Azerbaijan, Belarus, Estonia, Georgia, Kazakhstan, Kyrgyzstan, Latvia, Lithuania, Moldova, Russia, Tajikistan, Turkmenistan, Ukraine, Uzbekistan.

Soweto 26 10S 28 02E A large urban area in South Africa, in the Transvaal forming a suburb of Johannesburg. It is inhabited solely by black Africans and comprises 36 townships. In June 1976, in serious rioting by African students, over a hundred people died. Population (1983): 915,872.

soybean An annual plant, *Glycine max*, widely cultivated for its seeds. The many commercial varieties grow to heights of 8–79 in (20–200 cm) and produce clusters of pods, each containing two or three seeds. The ripe seeds contain 35% protein. Soybean oil is extracted for use in making margarines, cooking oils, resins, and paints and for many other foods, chemicals, and textiles. The meal residue is an important protein food for livestock and a meat substitute for man. The beans are also eaten whole, ground into soy flour, and used to make many by-products, including soy sauce. Family: **Leguminosae.*

Soyinka, Wole (1934–) Nigerian dramatist and poet, winner of the Nobel Prize for literature (1986). He was educated in Nigeria and England. His works, characterized by a lively and often satirical style, include the play *The Lion and the Jewel* (1963); the novels *The Interpreters* (1965), *The Man Died* (1973), and *Aké* (1982); and the fictionalized memoir, *Isarà* (1989). He edited the literary journal *Black Orpheus* (1960–64) and was imprisoned during the Nigerian civil war (1967–69). Diaries and poems from this period are collected in *A Shuttle in the Crypt.*

Spa 50 29N 5 52E A town in SE Belgium. It is a tourist resort, renowned since the 14th century for its mineral springs. Population (1981): 10,000.

Spaak, Paul Henri (1899–1972) Belgian statesman, the first socialist prime minister of Belgium (1938–39, 1947–50) and foreign minister (1936–38, 1939–46, 1954–57, 1961–65). He negotiated the Treaties of Rome, which established the EEC, and was president of the EEC assembly in 1949. From 1957 to 1961 he was secretary general of NATO.

spacecraft A vehicle designed to be launched into space and to function effectively for a considerable period in the hostile conditions of space. Due to the immense expense and the difficulties involved in prolonged space travel, most spacecraft are unmanned. Their instruments are powered by arrays of solar cells (*see* solar power), for craft out to Mars's orbit, and can be controlled by ground stations. Their information is sent back to earth as radio transmissions. Unmanned craft include several thousand *satellites of diverse functions and numerous *planetary probes. In manned craft, such as the *Skylab and *Salyut orbiting space laboratories and the vehicles taking part in the *Apollo moon program, the weightless conditions require the careful monitoring of physiological and psychological reactions both during and after the flight.

space exploration The space age began with the launching of the Soviet satellite Sputnik I on Oct 4, 1957. The first manned flight, one earth orbit, was made by the Soviet cosmonaut Yuri *Gagarin on Apr 12, 1961. Man first flew round the moon in December 1968, aboard the US Apollo 8 and first landed on the lunar surface in the lunar module of Apollo 11 in July 1969 (*see* Apollo moon program). Although manned exploration of space has at present gone no further than the moon, unmanned *planetary probes have been sent to every planet as far as Saturn, reached by Pioneer 11 in September 1979. Voyager 2 passed Uranus in 1986 and approached Neptune in 1990. Most probes have made a close fly-by of targeted planets.

space shuttle A manned reusable US space transportation system developed by *NASA. It consists of a delta-wing orbiter that has three powerful rocket engines, a large cargo bay in which satellites, etc., are carried into earth orbit, and passenger and crew space. It is launched by rocket propulsion. Although its two externally mounted rocket boosters can be recovered after they detach shortly after launch, the huge external propellant tank is discarded. The first two-day test flight of the Columbia shuttle, crewed by John Young and Robert Crippen, took place in April 1981. Subsequent flights were frequent until January 1986, when the explosion of the *Challenger* just after liftoff killed seven astronauts and interrupted the program until late 1988.

space-time continuum A coordinate system that has four dimensions, three representing physical space and the fourth time. The four-dimensional space-time continuum is used in *relativity to define an event. For example, an event occurring on the sun would be observed at different times on earth and on Jupiter, as light from the sun takes some 35 minutes longer to reach Jupiter than to reach the earth. Thus the concept of simultaneity requires a four-dimensional coordinate system to define events without ambiguity.

spadefoot toad A nocturnal burrowing *toad belonging to a widely distributed family (*Pelobatidae*). Spadefoot toads survive in arid regions by digging themselves deep holes in sand or mud with a special horny structure on the foot. The European spadefoot (*Pelobates fuscus*) exudes a garlic-smelling secretion when harmed.

Spain, Kingdom of A country in SW Europe, occupying over four-fifths of the Iberian Peninsula. The Balearic and Canary Islands are also part of Spain. It consists mainly of a high plateau, rising over 10,000 ft (3000 m) in the Pyrenees in the NE. *Economy*: traditionally agricultural, the industrial sector had begun to predominate by the early 1970s. After many years of economic stagnation, there was a remarkable improvement in the 1960s with the development of the motor-vehicle, machine-tool, ship building, and chemical industries. Tourism, an important source of foreign currency, began to flourish again by late 1976. There is both livestock and crop farming and varied crops include wheat, barley, citrus fruit, and vegetables (especially potatoes, onions, sugar beet, and tomatoes). There is a thriving wine industry. Forestry is important, as well as fishing (sardines, tuna, and cod), and rich mineral resources include coal, lignite, anthracite, and iron ore. Hydroelectricity is a valuable source of power. The hosting of the 1992 Summer Olympics and World Fair drew world attention and money to Spain. *History*: remains of Neanderthal man have been found at Gibraltar, Valencia, and Gerona, and Spain was subsequently inhabited by Iberians, Celts, Phoenicians, and Greeks. In the 3rd century BC the Carthaginians under Hamilcar Barca conquered most of the Iberian peninsula but were expelled by the Romans in the second *Punic War (218–201 BC). Christianity was introduced in the 1st century AD and by the 5th century the Romans had given way to German tribes, including the Vandals and then the Visigoths. The Visigothic kingdom collapsed (711) in the face of Muslim invaders, who dominated most of the central and S parts of the peninsula under a series of powerful dynasties (*see* Umayyads; Abbadids; Almoravids; Almohads). The reconquest of Muslim Spain was pursued throughout the Middle Ages by the Christian kingdoms in the N and was completed in 1492 with the conquest of Granada by Ferdinand of Aragon and Isabella of Castile. The union of Spain, begun by the union of Aragon and Castile following the marriage of Ferdinand and Isabella, was now complete. The year 1492 also saw the expulsion from Spain of the Jews, who were followed, after much persecution, by the Muslims (1609); the influence of both peoples on Spanish culture was enormous. The 16th century was Spain's golden age. Overseas exploration led to the formation of an empire in the New World, which brought great wealth to Spain. The country's prestige and power, as well as its possessions, in Europe were furthered by the Hapsburg kings Charles I (who as *Charles V was also Holy Roman Emperor) and his son Philip II, but the latter's reign witnessed the beginnings of decline. The *Revolt of the Netherlands against Spanish rule led to the secession (1581) of the northern Dutch provinces and in 1588 Spain suffered the humiliating defeat of the Armada by the English. Following the Thirty Years' War Spain lost to France its position as the leading European power (1659). The death in 1700 of the last Hapsburg king (Charles II), without an heir, led to the War of the *Spanish Succession (1701–14). This confirmed the Bourbon succession and also deprived Spain of the Spanish Netherlands, Milan, Naples, Sardinia, and Sicily. In the second half of the 18th century Spain's decline was arrested by reform, especially under *Charles III, but in 1808 Napoleon established his brother Joseph Bonaparte on the Spanish throne.

The Spanish resistance to their French conquerors contributed to the defeat of Napoleon (*see* Peninsular War) and in 1814 the Bourbon Ferdinand VII was restored. *Carlism and conflict between monarchists and republicans (the latter achieved short-lived victory in 1873–74) dominated the 19th century, during which Spain also lost its last American possessions. It was neutral in World War I, following which *Primo de Rivera established a military dictatorship that undermined the position of the monarchy. In 1931 Alfonso XIII abdicated and the Second Republic was established. The electoral victory of the Popular Front under Azaña in 1936 precipitated a military revolt led by General *Franco that became the *Spanish Civil War (1936–39). Franco's victory initiated over three decades of Nationalist dictatorship. Following Franco's death in 1975, the monarchy was restored and Prince Juan Carlos de Borbón became king and head of state. After widespread demonstrations and industrial conflict Carlos Arias Navarro was replaced as prime minister by Adolfo Suárez and the return to a more democratic form of government proceeded more rapidly. In 1978 provisional regional self-government was granted to Catalonia, Valencia, the Canary Islands, Aragon, Galicia, and the Basque provinces, although terrorist activities by Basque separatists continued. Spain's first Socialist government in nearly 50 years was elected in 1982 under Felipe González, who had campaigned on a moderate platform and who moved discreetly to reform the armed forces, which contained many Franco Loyalists among its officers. Spain joined the North Atlantic Treaty Organization (NATO) in 1982 and joined the European Community (EC) in 1986. González was reelected in 1986 and 1989 and worked to prepare Spain's somewhat sluggish free-enterprise economy for the EC's 1992 economic reforms. He was successful enough to win reelection again in 1993. Official language: Spanish. Official religion: Roman Catholic. Official currency: peseta of 100 céntimos. Area: 194,883 sq mi (504,879 sq km). Population (1990 est): 39,623,000. Capital: Madrid. Main port: Barcelona.

Spalato. *See* Split.

Spallanzani, Lazzaro (1729–99) Italian physiologist, noted for his studies of microscopic life. Spallanzani demonstrated that microorganisms arose not by spontaneous generation but from spores present in the air. He also studied regeneration, digestion, and spermatozoa. He showed that contact by semen was necessary for development of the egg and he achieved the first successful artificial insemination of a dog.

Spandau 52 32N 13 13E A district in Berlin, at the confluence of the Havel and Spree Rivers. Nazi war criminals were imprisoned in the 16th-century fortress after 1946. It is a main industrial district.

spaniel One of several breeds of sporting dogs developed in Britain and thought to have originated in Spain. The English springer spaniel is typical, having a lean compact body, long muzzle, and long drooping ears. It is longer in the leg than the similar *cocker spaniel but has the same flat wavy weather-resistant coat. It is generally black and white or liver and white, while the smaller Welsh springer spaniel is always red and white.

The white Clumber spaniel is the heaviest breed. The Irish water spaniel has a distinctive curly dark-brown coat and is a strong swimmer. Height: 20 in (51 cm) (English springer); 21–24 in (53–61 cm) (Irish water); 18–19 in (46–48 cm) (Welsh springer). *See also* King Charles spaniel.

Spanish A *Romance language spoken in Spain, Latin America, the Philippines, and elsewhere by about 145 million people. The standard form is based on the Castilian dialect, originally spoken in the Burgos region, and became the official language of Spain in the late 15th century.

Spanish-American War (1898) Conflict between the US and Spain, fought in Cuba and the Philippines over Spanish possessions in the Americas. Spurred by US interests in Spanish-controlled Cuba, Cuban nationalists' desire for independence, stories of Spanish atrocities, and, more immediately, the sinking of the US battleship *Maine* in Havana's harbor, the US demanded withdrawal of Spain from Cuba and planned to blockade all Spanish ports. Spain retaliated with a declaration of war. The few battles involved took place in Cuba and the Philippines. Adm. George *Dewey took Manila in the Philippines, and the Spanish fleet under Adm. Pascual Cervera was defeated while fleeing Santiago de Cuba's harbor. US forces, by scaling the hills surrounding Santiago with the aid of Teddy *Roosevelt and his Rough Riders, were able to take the city. The war was in effect ended, and peace negotiations began, resulting in independence for Cuba and cession of the Philippines, Puerto Rico, and Guam to the US. The US, in turn, paid Spain $20 million. The treaty, signed in Paris, signaled the end of Spanish possessions in the Americas. *See also* San Juan Hill, Battle of.

Spanish Civil War (1936–39) The civil war in Spain precipitated by a military revolt on July 18, 1936, led by the Nationalist General *Franco, against the Republican Government of *Azaña. By the end of 1936 the Nationalists had gained control of most of W and S Spain, while the Republicans held the urban areas of the E and N, including Madrid, Valencia, Barcelona, and Bilbao. During 1937 the Nationalists, with Italian and German help, failed in their attempt to take Madrid but captured Bilbao; in April occurred the indiscriminate bombing by German planes of the town of Guernica, an event commemorated in a famous painting by Picasso. In 1938, however, in spite of the assistance of the *International Brigade and, to a lesser extent, of the Soviet Union, the Republican front was broken and early in 1939 Barcelona, Valencia, and then Madrid fell to the victorious Nationalists. The Republican cause in the war, which claimed some 750,000 Spanish lives, rallied liberals throughout Europe and North America in the fight against fascism.

Spanish fly A golden-green European *blister beetle, *Lytta vesicatoria*, that is the chief source of cantharidin. This chemical can be extracted from its dried body—especially the wing cases—and was formerly used as a blistering agent and diuretic in medicine (it was also reputedly an aphrodisiac).

Spanish Guinea. *See* Equatorial Guinea, Republic of.

Spanish literature The earliest major work of Spanish literature is the heroic epic *Poema de mío Cid*, dating from the 12th century and written in the Castilian vernacular. Catalan poetry flourished during the 15th century, but after the union of Aragon and Castile in 1479, the Castilian language became dominant throughout Spain. Major writers of the *Siglo de Oro, which lasted from about 1550 to 1650, include *Cervantes and *Lope de Vega. After the death of *Calderon, little literature of major importance was produced until the regional novels of Juan Valera (1824–1905) and *Pérez Galdós appeared in the late 19th century. A dominant influence during the early 20th century was the philosopher and novelist Miguel de *Unamuno. The major poets were Ruben *Dario, who introduced modernist theories to Spain from his native Nicaragua, and *Garcia Lorca. Many writers went into exile during the Civil War, and most of the best literature in Spanish in recent years has been produced in Latin America by such writers as *Borges, *Neruda, and *Paz.

Spanish moss **1.** An epiphytic plant, *Tillandsia usneoides* (or *Dendropogon usneoides*), also known as black moss, long moss, and vegetable horsehair, and found in warm regions of America. Its seeds are windblown to trees, where they germinate and grow downward in large silvery-gray beardlike masses, 20–25 ft (6–7.5 m) long. It is covered with hairlike scales, which absorb water from the air. When dried it can be used as packing material or upholstery. Family: *Bromeliaceae*. **2.** A tropical lichen, *Usnea longissima*, which resembles *T. usneoides*.

SPANISH MOSS *This unusual plant grows on trees and resembles a lichen. Dried, it is used like horsehair.*

Spanish Riding School (full name: Imperial Spanish Riding School of Vienna) A center for classical horsemanship in Vienna. Founded in the Hapsburg imperial palace, probably in the late 16th century, it was moved to its present building, designed by *Fischer von Erlach, in about 1730. Here the purest *haute école* *dressage as taught in the 16th and 17th centuries is practiced. The white

*Lipizzaner stallions used here have been bred from horses imported from Spain in the 16th century—hence the title "Spanish." □horse.

Spanish Sahara. *See* Western Sahara.

Spanish Succession, War of the (1701–14) The third of the European wars caused by Louis XIV's attempts to increase French power. The immediate cause of the conflict was the dispute over the succession to the Spanish throne. Following the death of the childless Charles II, Louis proclaimed the succession of his grandson as Philip V. England felt menaced by the prospect of a union of French and Spanish dominions and by French commercial expansion. England, the Dutch Republic, and the Holy Roman Emperor formed an alliance against France in 1701 and were joined by most German states upon the outbreak of general hostilities (1702). Spain, Bavaria, Portugal, and Savoy supported France. The English won a series of brilliant victories under the Duke of *Marlborough but pressed for peace in 1712, when a Spanish-Austrian union threatened. The Treaties of *Utrecht (1713–14) concluded the war, which marked the end of French expansionism under Louis.

Spanish Town 17 59N 76 58W A town in SE Jamaica, on the Rio Cobre. Founded in 1525, it was the capital of Jamaica until 1871.

Spark, Muriel (1918–) British novelist. After several volumes of poetry and criticism, she achieved success with a series of witty satirical novels including *Memento Mori* (1959) and *The Prime of Miss Jean Brodie* (1961). Her later novels include *The Hot House by the East River* (1973), *The Abbess of Crewe* (1974), *The Takeover* (1976), *Territorial Rights* (1979), *Loitering With Intent* (1981), *The Only Problem* (1984), *A Far Cry from Kensington* (1988), and *Symposium* (1990).

spark chamber A device that detects charged particles. It consists of a gas-filled chamber containing a number of thin parallel wires or plates separated by a few centimeters and held at a high voltage. An incoming particle causes a spark to jump from plate to plate across the chamber, enabling the progress of the particle to be photographed.

sparrow A small thick-billed member of the *weaverbird family. Sparrows range from 4–7 in (10–17 cm) in length and are generally brown and gray in color, often with black or bright yellow patches. They are mostly tropical Old World species but also occur in Eurasia and have been introduced to North America where the *house sparrow is a pest. Sparrows eat seeds, feeding on the ground and nesting in holes in river and stream banks and buildings. Many similar small birds, especially buntings and finches, are also called sparrows. Subfamily: *Passerinae.*

sparrowhawk A small woodland *hawk, *Accipiter nisus*, occurring in Eurasia and NW Africa. It has a long tail and short rounded wings and the male (11 in; 27 cm long) is gray with brown-barred white underparts; females (15 in; 38 cm long) are brown above. It hunts small birds.

Sparta 37 05N 22 25E In ancient Greece, the capital of Laconia on the Eurotas River in the S Peloponnese. Developing from Dorian settlements during the 10th century BC, Sparta controlled much of Laconia and Messenia by 700 BC. The indigenous peoples became *helot serfs or semi-independent half-citizens (*perioeci*) and were subject to the governing class of Spartiates. Two hereditary kings ruled, with a powerful body of magistrates (*ephors*) and a council of elders (*gerousia*); there was also a citizen assembly (*apella*). Sparta became an austere militaristic state, where weaker boys were abandoned at birth and those that survived were subjected from the age of seven to a rigid military training. Its military strength brought conflict in the 5th century with Athens, and Sparta's ultimate victory (404) in the consequent *Peloponnesian War brought it a short-lived supremacy in Greece: defeat by the Thebans at *Leuctra (371) marked the beginning of Spartan decline. The ancient city was destroyed by the Visigoths in 396 AD and the modern town S of its ruins dates from 1834. Population (1981): 15,915.

Spartacus Thracian gladiator, who led a revolt against Rome in 73 BC. After defeating the Romans in five separate engagements in Italy, he moved N to Cisalpine *Gaul. When his followers refused to disperse, Spartacus marched S again and was defeated by Marcus Licinius *Crassus (71). He and his followers were crucified.

Spartacus League A German socialist group, founded during World War I, that adopted the name of the leader of a slave revolt in ancient Rome, *Spartacus. Its leaders were Rosa *Luxemburg and Karl *Liebknecht, both of whom were murdered after an attempted uprising in 1919. The German Communist party grew out of the League.

Spartina A genus of *grasses (16 species), known as cordgrass, found on salt marshes and tidal flats of North America, Europe, and Africa. They have stiff erect stems, 0.98 in to 10 ft (0.3–3 m) tall, long narrow grooved leaves, and yellowish flower spikes. Townsend's cord grass (*S. townsendii*), also called rice grass, a natural hybrid, has been used extensively to help reclaim coastal land.

Spassky, Boris (1937–) Soviet chess player. He was world champion from 1969 to 1972, when he lost the title to *Fischer at Reykjavík.

spastic. *See* cerebral palsy.

Speaker of the House Member of the US House of Representatives majority party who is elected by fellow members to preside over the House. His duties include selecting the leaders and members of certain committees and signing documents for the House as a whole. He is second in line, after the vice president, in succession to the presidency.

Spearman, Charles Edward (1863–1945) US psychologist, whose statistical studies of the results from various kinds of intelligence tests led him to postulate a factor of intelligence, G, that is common to all aspects of intelligence. His work led to the development of factorial analysis as an important statistical method.

spearmint An aromatic perennial herb, *Mentha spicata*, native to central and S Europe and widely cultivated as a culinary herb. It grows to a height of 12–36 in (30–90 cm) and has spikes of small lilac flowers. The oil extract from the leaves is used to flavor sweets, toothpastes, chewing gum, etc. Family: **Labiatae*.

Special Drawing Rights (SDRs) The rights of member countries of the *International Monetary Fund to draw on the fund to finance *balance-of-payments deficits. First instituted in 1970, SDRs (unlike normal drawings) do not have to be repaid and therefore form a permanent addition to the drawing country's reserves, functioning as an international reserve currency and supplementing its holdings of gold and convertible currencies. The value of SDRs is computed as a weighted average of 16 currencies. Their advantage over gold and other reserve currencies is that their supply can be controlled and does not depend either on the discovery of mineral deposits or on the US balance of payments.

special education A wide range of facilities that aim to provide suitable education for children with physical or mental disabilities or for exceptionally gifted children. Although special education dates back to the 18th century, it was not until the mid-20th century that mentally and physically handicapped children ceased to be dealt with as a separate group and were regarded like other children as needing an education appropriate to age, aptitude, and ability. Special education is provided either within regular schools or in special schools.

species A unit of classification of animals and plants. Individuals of the same species usually resemble one another closely and can breed among themselves to produce fertile offspring that resemble the parents. Examples of species are the domestic cat, the dog rose, and the field mushroom.

Some species are subdivided into subspecies and varieties. Breeds of domestic animals and cultivated varieties of plants have been specially developed by man for economic or other purposes and are all derived from a few wild species. Those originating from the same species can interbreed, despite obvious differences in character. All breeds of domestic dog, for instance, belong to the same species—*Canis familiaris*—and types as diverse as the poodle, corgi, and greyhound can breed together.

specific gravity. *See* density.

specific heat capacity (c) The quantity of heat needed to raise a unit mass of substance by 1°C. It is measured in *SI units in joules per kelvin per kilogram. For gases, the specific heat capacity at constant pressure (c_p) exceeds that at constant volume (c_v) as heat is required to do work against the surroundings during the expansion. The ratio c_p/c_v (symbol: γ) is 1.66 for monatomic gases, 1.4 for diatomic gases, and about 1 for other gases.

spectacled bear The only South American *bear, *Tremarctos ornatus*, also called Andean bear. Up to 5 ft (1.5 m) long, it is brownish-black with white circles around the eyes and climbs trees to feed on leaves, nuts, and fruit.

spectacles, or **glasses** Lenses worn in frames in front of the eyes to correct defective vision. Convex lenses bend parallel light rays inward; they are used by those unable to focus on close objects (*see* farsightedness). Concave lenses have the opposite effect and are used by those unable to focus on distant objects (*see* nearsightedness). *Astigmatism is treated by wearing lenses that produce a compensating distortion of the light rays. Bifocal spectacles have convex lenses consisting of upper and lower parts of different curvatures, for focusing on distant and near objects, respectively: they are worn for presbyopia. *See also* contact lenses.

spectral type. *See* Harvard classification system.

spectrum In general, the way in which a particular property of a system is distributed over its components. The visible spectrum, for example, is observed in a *rainbow, which shows the distribution of frequencies when sunlight is split up into its components by raindrops. The visible spectrum, however, is only a small part of the *electromagnetic spectrum, which ranges from X-rays to radio waves. **Spectroscopy** is concerned with observing and analyzing the emission and absorption of electromagnetic energy by atoms and molecules.

According to the *quantum theory, atoms and molecules can only emit or absorb energy in discrete amounts, called quanta. When an atom or molecule is heated, bombarded with electrons, etc., it absorbs energy (becomes excited); on falling back to its lower state it emits a photon (a quantum of radiation energy). The energy of this photon is equal to hf, where f is the frequency of the radiation and h is *Planck's constant. Each atom or molecule can only make specific energy transitions. This means that as well as the continuous *black-body radiation produced by thermal agitation, atoms can emit and absorb radiation at particular frequencies, which show up as colored lines in their spectrum. These **line spectra** can be used to identify particular elements. The spectrum formed by atoms or molecules that are emitting radiation is called an **emission spectrum**.

As atoms absorb energy at the same frequency as they emit it, if a substance lies in the path of radiation its atoms will absorb certain of the energy quanta in the radiation, producing dark lines in the spectrum. These dark lines are **absorption spectra**. For example, the sun's spectrum contains many dark lines (called Fraunhofer lines). These are caused by atoms of hydrogen, helium, etc., in the sun's atmosphere absorbing energy from the radiation produced in the center of the sun.

Spectroscopes (*or* spectrometers) are instruments for analyzing a spectrum. They usually consist of a collimator to collect the radiation from the source, a grating or prism to split it into its components and a telescope to view the refracted radiation. A means of recording the spectrum photographically is needed for ultraviolet and infrared radiation.

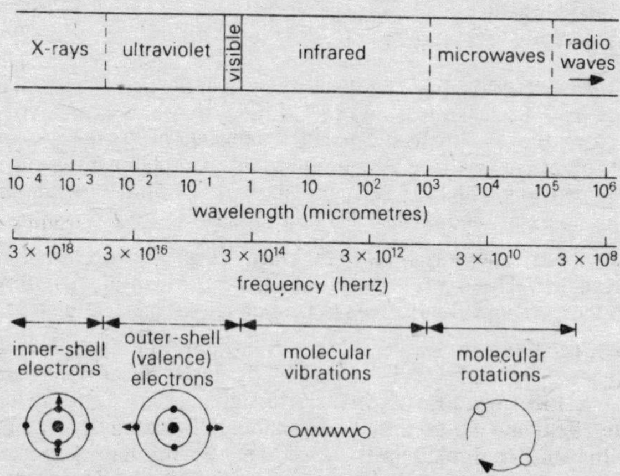

SPECTRUM *Energetic photons in the X-ray region of the spectrum alter the excitation of atomic inner-shell electrons. The ultraviolet and visible photons interact with the outer-shell electrons that participate in chemical reactions. Infrared photons alter the vibrational states of molecules and microwave photons effect molecular rotation.*

speedwell An annual or perennial herbaceous plant of the genus *Veronica* (about 200 species), up to 24 in (60 cm) high, occurring throughout temperate regions. The flowers, borne singly or in clusters in the axils of the simple toothed leaves, are usually blue, sometimes white or pinkish, with four unequal petals. The fruit is a flattened heart-shaped capsule. Two common species are *V. officinalis* and the germander speedwell (*V. chamaedrys*). Family: *Scrophulariaceae*.

speedwriting. *See* shorthand.

Speke, John Hanning (1827–64) British explorer. He accompanied Richard *Burton on the expeditions (1855, 1857–58) to discover the source of the Nile. They discovered Lake Tanganyika and then Speke went on alone to discover Lake Victoria, which, on a second visit in 1860, he established to be the source of the Nile.

speleology The study and exploration of *caves and underground water courses. This includes the survey of caves and the study of their formation, plant and animal life (past and present), and geology. Potholing—or descending through potholes into underground drainage passages in order to follow the course of underground streams—is an increasingly popular although relatively dangerous activity.

spelling The conventional representation of spoken words in an alphabetic writing system. The underlying principle of alphabetic writing is that there should be a consistent one-for-one relationship between speech sounds and written letters but this is rarely fully realized in practice. Inconsistencies arise because a change in pronunciation is not always matched by a corresponding spelling change. In English, for example, an extensive change in the value of vowels took place in the 15th century (*see* Great Vowel Shift), *-e* at the end of a word ceased to be pronounced, and the sound represented by *-gh-* (the sound of *-ch* in Scottish *loch*) dropped out or changed to /f/.

Spencer, Lady Diana *See* Charles, Prince.

Spencer, Herbert (1820–1903) British philosopher. As copy editor of the *Economist* (1843–53), Spencer was an influential exponent of *laissez-faire. His early book *Social Statics* (1851) was strongly tinged with an individualistic outlook, as was his multi-volume *System of Synthetic Philosophy* (1860–96), of which the most important volume was *First Principles* (1862). He believed that state intervention limited progress and he developed this idea fully in his popular *The Man versus the State* (1884). Spencer's other writings include works on psychology, ethics, and sociology. He supported Charles *Darwin's theory of evolution by natural selection, coining the phrase "survival of the fittest," and applied evolutionary ideas to social development.

Spencer Gulf An inlet of the Indian Ocean, in S Australia situated between Eyre Peninsula and Yorke Peninsula, with Port Augusta, Port Pirie, and Whyalla located on its shores. Length: about 200 mi (320 km). Width: about 75 mi (120 km).

Spender, Stephen (1909–) British poet and critic. A friend of W. H. Auden, he published left-wing poetry during the 1930s and was briefly a member of the Communist party. His later poetry, included in *Collected Poems* (1955) and *The Generous Days* (1971), is more personal and lyrical. He has also published several volumes of criticism; an autobiography, *World within World* (1951); and *Journals 1934–83* (1985).

Spengler, Oswald (1880–1936) German philosopher. Spengler's most famous work, *The Decline of the West* (1918), argued that nations and cultures have a natural lifespan and their rise is inevitably followed by their eclipse. His ideas appealed to the German fascists, as he emphasized the individual's duty of obedience to the state.

Spenser, Edmund (c. 1552–99) English poet. He dedicated *The Shepheardes Calendar* (1579), pastoral poems arranged by the months of the year, to Sir Philip Sidney, nephew of his patron the earl of Leicester. In 1580 he was appointed secretary to the Lord Deputy of Ireland, where he became a prominent landowner. His major work, *The Faerie Queene*, a long moral allegory in nine-line "Spenserian" stanzas, was dedicated to Elizabeth I and published in six books in 1590 and 1596. His other works include the sonnet sequence *Amoretti* (1595) and the *Epithalamion* (1595), celebrating his second marriage.

Speranski, Mikhail Mikhailovich (1772–1839) Russian statesman, described by Napoleon as "the only clear head in Russia." Speranski, as Alexander I's chief adviser (1807–12), presented proposals for the reform of the administration and for the drafting of a new constitution. His unpopularity with colleagues led to his exile until 1816. In 1826 he began his greatest achievement, the codification of Russian law.

sperm (*or* spermatozoon) The reproductive cell of male animals, which is formed in the *testis and fertilizes an egg cell during sexual *reproduction. A sperm usually has a head region, containing the genetic material, and a tail, by means of which it swims to the egg. In man, sperms develop and mature in the testes, where the temperature is 3.5°F (2°C) below body temperature. At ejaculation they are mixed with secretions from various glands (including the *prostate gland) to form semen.

spermaceti A *wax obtained from the head cavity and from the oils of whales, dolphins, and porpoises. It is liquid at room temperature and is separated from the oil by chilling. Spermaceti is used in ointments, cosmetics, fine candles, and textile finishing.

spermatophyte Any plant that reproduces by means of *seeds rather than spores. Spermatophytes include the *gymnosperms (conifers, cycads, etc.) and the *angiosperms (flowering plants).

sperm whale A large toothed *whale, cathodon, also called cachalot. It is about 60 ft (18 m) long, gray-blue above and pale beneath, with tiny flippers and large tail flukes. The blowhole is near the tip of the snout and it can dive up to 0.6 mi (1 km) in search of octopus and squid, sometimes staying underwater for over one hour. Family: *Physeteridae.*

Sphagnum A widely distributed genus of mosses (over 300 species), called bog or peat moss, forming dense raised clumps in bogs and other waterlogged places. Green to dark red in color and up to 12 in (30 cm) high, the fine stems bear clusters of threadlike branches, densely clothed with tiny leaves, and globular spore capsules. The ability of the stems and leaves to retain water (up to 20 times the weight of the plant) is responsible for the outstanding ability of these mosses to drain very wet ground and form bogs. The dead remains of the plants accumulate to form *peat—an important fuel and ingredient of horticultural composts. Family: *Sphagnaceae.*

sphalerite (*or* zinc blende) The principal ore of zinc, a sulfide, usually brown or black in color. It frequently occurs with *galena in metasomatic deposits, and in hydrothermal veins and replacement deposits.

spherical coordinates. *See* coordinate systems.

sphinx A mythological creature with a lion's body and a human head, occurring in the art and legends of most ancient Near and Middle Eastern civilizations. The most famous representation is the Great Sphinx at Giza, Egypt, dating from the 3rd millennium BC. In Greek legend, the Sphinx was a female monster that preyed on travelers going to Thebes. She killed those who could not answer her riddle, which was finally solved by *Oedipus.

sphygmomanometer A device for measuring arterial *blood pressure. It consists of an inflatable arm cuff connected via a rubber tube to a column of mercury with a graduated scale or an aneroid device. The cuff is inflated until the pulse can no longer be detected (using a stethoscope) and then slowly deflated until first the systolic and then the diastolic pressure can be recorded as the pulse returns.

Spica A conspicuous blue star, apparent magnitude 0.97 and about 215 light years distant, that is the brightest star in the constellation Virgo. It is an eclipsing *binary star.

Spice Islands. *See* Moluccas.

spices. *See* herbs and spices.

SPHINX *The Great Sphinx at Giza is thought to be a portrait statue of King Khafre (c. 2550 BC).*

spider An *arachnid belonging to the worldwide order *Araneae* (or *Araneida*; over 30,000 species); 0.04–3.5 in (1–90 mm) long, the body of a spider consists of a cephalothorax and abdomen separated by a narrow "waist." There are eight walking legs, up to eight eyes, and several pairs of spinnerets, which produce silk used for making webs, egg cocoons, etc. Spiders are predominantly terrestrial and prey mainly on insects, hunting them or trapping them in their webs. The victims are killed with poison-bearing fangs; in a few species the poison is harmful to man. The female is generally larger than the male, which she sometimes kills and eats after mating. She then deposits the eggs on or near the web, among leaves or twigs, etc., or carries them until they hatch. The young go through a series of molts to reach the adult stage. *See also* black widow; tarantula; water spider; wolf spider.

spider crab A marine *crab belonging to the widely distributed family *Maiidae*, especially one of the genus *Libinia*. It has a thick rounded body, with long spindly legs and generally moves slowly. Most spider crabs are scavengers, especially of dead animals.

spider mite A red or yellow *mite, 0.02 in (0.5 mm) long, also called red spider mite, belonging to the family *Tetranychidae*. It sucks plant juices from foliage and fruits and is a serious pest of orchard trees, crops, and houseplants.

spider monkey A monkey belonging to the genus *Ateles* (4 species), of Central and South American forests. Spider monkeys have very long legs and are 35–60 in (88–150 cm) long including the prehensile tail 20–35 in (50–90 cm), which is capable of supporting their weight. They live in family groups in thick forest, feeding on seeds and leaves. Family: *Cebidae.*

spider plant A plant of the genus *Chlorophytum*, especially *C. elatum*, native to South Africa and widely grown as a house plant. It has narrow green and white striped leaves, 24–36 in (60–90 cm) long, and periodically produces a stem bearing small white flowers or young plantlets. Family: *Liliaceae.*

spider wasp A solitary *wasp belonging to a family (*Pompilidae*) of worldwide distribution. It preys chiefly on spiders, which are also paralyzed and stored in underground nests as food for the larvae. Spider wasps have dark slender bodies (0.2–3 in [5–75 mm] long), long legs, and usually smoky or amber-colored wings.

spiderwort. *See* Tradescantia.

spikenard A perennial Himalayan herb, *Nardostachys jatamansi*, growing to a height of 24 in (60 cm) and bearing tiny purple flower clusters. It is cultivated for an essential oil derived from its roots, which is used for perfumes and various medicines. Family: *Valerianaceae.*

Plowman's spikenard (*Inula conyza*) is a perennial herb of Europe and N Africa with yellow flowers and fragrant roots. Family: **Compositae.*

Spillane, Mickey (Frank Morrison S.; 1918–) US detective-story writer. His numerous crime novels featuring the detective Mike Hammer, the popular success of which was due to the uninhibited description of sex and violence, include *I, the Jury* (1947), *The Twisted Thing* (1966), and *The Day the Sea Rolled Back* (1979).

spin A property possessed by elementary particles as a result of which they possess a constant angular momentum that is independent of their motion. The spin is quantized and labeled by a spin *quantum number (symbol: s), which may be integral or half-integral.

spina bifida A defect, present at birth, in which the backbone fails to fuse properly, leaving the spinal cord and its coverings exposed. Commonly the child has paralyzed legs and disordered bladder and bowel function. The degree of the handicap varies: children who survive and are severely affected require crutches or wheelchairs and need special surgical procedures to help their bladder function. The intelligence of children with spina bifida is often normal, but the condition is frequently associated with *hydrocephalus. Spina bifida can be diagnosed during pregnancy (*see* amniocentesis).

spinach An annual herbaceous plant, *Spinacia oleracea*, native to Asia and widely cultivated as a vegetable. Its edible leaves are rich in iron and vitamins A and C and are boiled as a vegetable and used in salads, soups, soufflés, etc. Family: *Chenopodiaceae.*

spinal cord An elongated part of the central *nervous system, running downward from the base of the brain and consisting of a core of gray matter (nerve cell bodies) surrounded by white matter (nerve fibers). It is surrounded and protected by the spine and is enclosed in membranes (meninges). It gives off spinal nerves, usually in pairs, and ends in a bundle of nerves supplying the legs and lower part of the body. Through it run the nerve fibers between the brain and the body; injury can therefore cause paralysis and loss of sensation.

spindle tree A Eurasian tree or shrub, *Euonymus europaeus*, that grows to a height of about 20 ft (6 m). It produces small white flowers and pink and orange fleshy fruits, 0.4–0.6 in (10–15 mm) across, which yield a yellow food dye. The fine-grained wood has been used to make spindles and clothespins. The winged spindle tree (*E. alatus*) occurs in China. Family: *Celastraceae*. *See also* Euonymus.

spine In anatomy, the backbone, or vertebral column: a series of small bones (vertebrae) that runs up the center of the back. The spine encloses and protects the spinal cord, articulates with the skull, ribs, and pelvis, and provides attachment for muscles of the back. There are 26 vertebrae in the adult spine, which are subdivided as follows: 7 cervical, in the neck; 12 thoracic, in the chest region attached to the ribs; 5 lumbar, in the lower back; 5 sacral, attached to the hip bone (fused into a single bone—the sacrum); and 4 coccygeal (fused into a single bone—the coccyx). The vertebrae are connected by tough disks of cartilage (intervertebral disks), which absorb the shock produced by running and other movements.

spinel A group of oxide minerals, usually occurring as octahedral crystals. The spinel minerals form a compositional series between true spinel ($MgAl_2O_4$) and hercynite ($Fe^2 + Al_2O_4$). Magnetite ($Fe^2 + Fe_2{}^3 + O_4$) is the most common and is an important iron ore. Chromite, a source of chromium, is $Fe^2 + Cr_2O_4$. Spinels occur mostly in metamorphic rocks, especially limestones, and in basic and ultrabasic igneous rocks.

spinet A plucked keyboard instrument of the *harpsichord family that superseded the *virginals in the 17th century. It is wing shaped, the strings (one to each note) being at an angle of 45° to the keyboard.

Spingarn, Joel Elias (1875–1939) US educator and reformer. A professor at Columbia University (1909–11), he wrote *The New Criticism* (1911) and, later, *Creative Criticism* (1917). He served as an adviser (1919–32) at Harcourt, Brace, and Co., a publishing firm he cofounded. Long active in the *National Association for the Advancement of Colored People, he was its president (1930–39); its Spingarn Medal, an annual achievement award given to an African American, is named for him. He was also instrumental in the establishment of African-American officer training programs during World War I.

Spinifex A genus of *grasses (3 species), native to S and E Asia and Australia. They grow on sand dunes and form long underground stems (rhizomes), which stabilize the dunes. The heads of spiny one-flowered spikelets break off and are blown about by wind. The name is also used for other Australian grasses that form spiny hummocks, especially *Triodia hirsuta* and *T. irritans*, also called porcupine grass.

spinning The process of converting cleaned and straightened fibers into yarn by twisting overlapping fibers together; until the 18th century this was a household task. Yarn was made originally by drawing out a length of fiber from the mass and attaching it to a vertically hanging stick (spindle) that was weighted to help it spin around; as it spun, the fiber wound onto it. This process was mechanized first by the spinning wheel (in Europe not until the 14th century, although it was used in India long before). The 16th-century Saxony wheel was an improved version, which could be operated continuously. The inventions of James *Hargreaves, Richard *Arkwright, and Samuel *Crompton in the late 18th century industrialized the process. Modern spinning machines produce thousands of meters of yarn every hour. As applied to synthetic fibers, spinning is the extrusion of viscous solutions to form continuous filaments.

Spinoza, Benedict (*or* Baruch de S.; 1632–77) Dutch philosopher, theologian, and scientist of Jewish parentage. Influenced by the writings of *Descartes, *Hobbes, and *Bruno, Spinoza rejected the concepts of the personal nature of

God and the immortality of the soul. The Jewish community of his native Amsterdam expelled him in 1656 on account of his unorthodoxy and his *Tractatus Theologico-Politicus* (1670) was furiously attacked by Christian scholars. The idea of God as the basis of all things (*Deus sive Natura*—God or Nature—in his phrase) was, however, central to his philosophy. For this reason he is often cited as the herald of modern *pantheism. He maintained that man's highest good is his "knowledge of the union existing between the mind and the whole of Nature." His major work, the *Ethica ordine geometrico demonstrata*, generally known as the *Ethics*, could only be published posthumously in 1677. Both *Schleiermacher and *Hegel were greatly influenced by his writings.

spiny lobster A *lobster, also called sea crayfish or crawfish, belonging to the mainly tropical family *Palinuridae*. Its carapace is covered with spines and it lacks pincers, but the antennae are strongly developed.

spiracle The external opening of a respiratory tubule (trachea) of insects and spiders. The term is also used for the paired gill openings of cartilaginous fishes, such as sharks, and for the respiratory openings of tadpoles and whales.

Spirea A genus of shrubs (about 100 species), widely distributed in N temperate regions. Many are cultivated as ornamentals, including the willow spirea (*S. salcifolia*), which grows to a height of 40–80 in (1–2 m) and bears dense clusters of small pink flowers. Other species and hybrids may have white or crimson flowers. Family: **Rosaceae*.

Spires. *See* Speyer.

spirits Distilled liquor generally defined as having an alcohol content of at least 40%. Spirits are derived from fermented liquids, for example wine (giving brandy); fruit wines (giving fruit brandies, such as slivovitz from plums and *kirsch from cherries); cider (giving calvados or applejack); grain or potatoes (giving *whisky, *gin, *vodka, or *aquavit). These liquids are distilled, i.e. some of the water is removed by vaporization to increase the alcohol content of the remaining liquid.

spiritual A type of religious song developed by US plantation slaves, with texts adapted from the Bible. The spiritual was often extemporized, with a lead singer relating the story in stanzas and a chorus singing the refrain. Harmonized arrangements of spirituals have eliminated the improvisational quality. Famous spirituals include "Steal Away," "Go Down, Moses," and "Deep River."

spiritualism Any theory that emphasizes the direct intervention of spiritual and supernatural forces in the everyday world. The term can cover phenomena as disparate as *extrasensory perception, *telekinesis, and various states associated with religious ecstasy, such as glossolalia (speaking in tongues, or making unintelligible utterances). In Western societies, spiritualism commonly means the practice of communicating with the spirits of the dead through a medium in seances or with a *ouija board. Organizations devoted to *psychical research have amassed considerable evidence for spiritualist phenomena, some occurring under rigidly controlled conditions to preclude fraud, although much of it is not the reproducible kind of evidence that scientists seek.

spirochete A bacterium belonging to the order *Spirochaetales*. Spirochetes are corkscrew-shaped, flexible, and up to 0.01 in (0.5 mm) long; they swim by means of bending and looping motions, achieved by contraction of a bundle of fibrils (the axial filament) within the cell. Some spirochetes cause diseases, including syphilis and yaws in man.

Spirogyra A genus of *green algae, also called mermaid's tresses or pond scum, in the form of threadlike strands of connected cells up to about 12 in

(30 cm) long. Large masses may be found floating near the surface of quiet fresh waters. Reproduction is asexual (by fragmentation) or sexual (*see* conjugation).

spit A linear deposit of sand or pebbles extending from a coastline. It often occurs where the coastline changes direction sharply and is deposited by the movement of beach material by wave action.

Spitsbergen. *See* Svalbard.

spittlebug. *See* froghopper.

spitz One of a group of dog breeds originating in N Eurasia and having a thick coat, small pricked ears, and a brushlike tail carried over the back. The Finnish spitz, bred in Finland as a hunting and guard dog, has a reddish-brown or yellowish-red coat while the Lapland spitz is either white, brown and black, or blackish brown. *Husky breeds also show spitz characteristics. Height (Finnish spitz): 17 in (44 cm) (dogs); 15 in (39 cm) (bitches).

Spitz, Mark (Andrew) (1950–) US swimmer, who won a record seven gold medals in the Munich Olympic Games (1972). In the period 1967–72 he won altogether nine Olympic golds and set 27 individual world records for freestyle and butterfly. He attempted a comeback for the 1992 Olympics but failed.

MARK SPITZ *The swimmer won seven gold medals at the 1972 Olympic Games in Munich. Here (center) he is seen with the silver and bronze medalists at the ceremony following his victory in the men's 200 meter butterfly event.*

spleen A rubbery dark-red organ, about 5.5 in (14 cm) long, situated in the abdomen just beneath the lower border of the left side of the rib cage. The spleen assists in the body's defense mechanisms by producing antibodies in newborn babies and by absorbing and digesting bacteria in the bloodstream. It also removes worn-out and abnormal red blood cells and other particles from the circulation. The spleen becomes enlarged in some diseases, including liver disease and severe infections. The spleen can be removed in adults without any ill effects.

spleenwort A tufted *fern of the genus *Asplenium* (about 700 species), growing on walls and rocks throughout the world. The tapering branched fronds are about 2–12 in (5–30 cm) long, with triangular lobed leaflets bearing oval or spindle-shaped clusters of spore capsules. The name derives from the former use of some species to treat disorders of the spleen and liver. Family: *Aspleniaceae. See also* bird's nest fern.

Split (Italian name: Spalato) 43 31N 16 28N A port city in Croatia on the Adriatic Sea. The vast 3rd-century AD Palace of Diocletian contains the present-day city center, including the cathedral, which was Diocletian's mausoleum. It has a university (1974) and diverse industries. Population (1991): 206,559.

Spock, Benjamin McLane (1903–) US physician and pediatrician, whose books on child care and development have become best-sellers, especially his *Common Sense Book of Baby and Child Care* (1946). He was a prominent opponent of US policy during the Vietnam War.

Spode porcelain Fine tableware and other porcelain made in the Staffordshire, England, factory started by Josiah Spode I in 1770. Josiah Spode II introduced "Feldspar" porcelain and "Stone China" as well as using *creamware. The meticulous decoration used transfer printing and painted Japan patterns enhanced by careful gilding.

Spokane 47 40N 117 25W A city in Washington. It is a trade and shipping center for a four-state area called the Inland Empire, which has mineral deposits and farms producing cattle, wheat, and fruit. Industries include timber and food processing. Population (1990): 177,196.

Spoleto 42 44N 12 44E A city in Italy, in Umbria. Dating from Etruscan times, it has Roman remains and a 12th-century cathedral. Its annual festival of music and drama was founded in 1958 by Gian Carlo *Menotti. There is a textile industry. Population (1990 est): 40,000.

sponge An aquatic invertebrate animal belonging to the phylum *Porifera* (about 5000 species). Most sponges are marine, found attached to rocks or the sea bed, and measure up to several meters across: they may be treelike, cylindrical (*see* Venus's flower basket), or flat irregular masses. Sponges have an internal skeleton of lime, silica, or a fibrous protein (spongin). Bath sponges are spongin skeletons without the living animals. The simplest type of sponge has a vase-shaped body with a pore at the top and smaller pores in the sides. The inside is lined with flagellated collar cells, which maintain a flow of water in through the side pores and out at the top. Food particles in the water are extracted by the collar cells; other cells in the body wall digest food, secrete the skeleton, and produce eggs and sperm. Fertilized eggs are dispersed in the water current and the free-swimming larvae eventually settle and become new sponges. The animals can also reproduce asexually, by budding or fragmentation.

spontaneous generation (*or* abiogenesis) The theory that living organisms arise from nonliving materials. It was widely upheld for many centuries, based on such observations as the appearance of tadpoles from mud and maggots in decaying meat. Belief in the spontaneous development of microorganisms continued until the 19th century, when Louis *Pasteur proved that, like higher organisms, they were capable of reproduction.

spoonbill A long-legged wading bird belonging to a subfamily (*Plataleinae*; 6 species) occurring around estuaries and lakes in tropical and subtropical regions worldwide; 24–32 in (60–80 cm) long, spoonbills are usually entirely white, often with a naked head. They feed on fish and crustaceans picked up by sweeping the large spatulate bill from side to side in mud or shallow water. Family: *Threskiornithidae* (ibises and spoonbills); order: *Ciconiiformes* (herons, storks, etc.).

Spooner, William Archibald (1844–1930) British clergyman and academic. Spooner became famous for his frequent transposition of the first letters of words; for example "a well-oiled bicycle" became "a well-boiled icicle." Such a transposition became known as a **Spoonerism**.

Sporades Two groups of Greek islands in the Aegean Sea, the **Northern Sporades**, which include Skyros, and the **Southern Sporades**, which, with the exception of Sámos and Ikaría, constitute the *Dodecanese.

spore The small, often single-celled, reproductive unit of plants, protozoa, and bacteria, which may serve either as a rapid means of propagation or as a dormant stage in the life cycle. Spores may be produced sexually or asexually, i.e. fusion of sex cells (gametes) may or may not occur before their formation. In plants exhibiting an *alternation of generations spores are formed by the sporophyte following meiosis and give rise to the gametophyte, which produces the sex cells. In some algae and fungi spores are produced following cell division (*see* mitosis) and thus give rise to an exact replica of the parent.

sporophyte. *See* alternation of generations.

Sporozoa A phylum of microscopic single-celled animals (*see* Protozoa), all of which are parasites with complex life cycles involving asexual and sexual forms of reproduction. They are often found in the intestinal tracts or blood of animals and form resistant spores or cysts, which can remain dormant until entering a suitable host. The phylum includes the malaria parasite (*see* Plasmodium).

sprat A small food fish, *Clupea* (*Sprattus*) *sprattus*, also called brisling, that is similar and related to the herring. Up to 7 in (17 cm) long, it lives in shoals in the E Atlantic, N Mediterranean, and British coastal waters. The young are known as *whitebait.

spring An emission of water from the ground. Springs occur where the water table intersects the surface or where a subsurface stream flowing over an impermeable rock stratum reaches the ground surface. Small outfows of water (seepages) may create a small localized marsh or bog. *See also* hot spring.

spring balance A device for measuring weights. The simplest form consists of a helical spring fixed at its upper end; from the lower end the load is suspended, extending the spring in direct proportion to its weight (according to *Hooke's law).

springbok A rare antelope, *Antidorcas marsupialis*, inhabiting arid regions of S Africa. About 32 in (80 cm) high at the shoulder, the springbok has a white face with a black line along each side of the muzzle, a fawn body with dark flank hairs, and a patch of white hairs on the rump, which can be flashed as an alarm signal. It is the national emblem of South Africa. □mammal.

Springfield 39 49N 89 39W The capital city of Illinois, on the Sangamon River. Abraham Lincoln lived there from 1837 until 1861 and is buried nearby; his home is preserved as a national historic site. Situated in an agricultural area, Springfield is an administrative, commercial, and medical center with varied industries. Population (1990): 105,227.

Springfield 42 07N 72 35W A city in S central Massachusetts, on the Connecticut River. The arsenal operating there from 1794 until 1966 developed the Springfield and Garand rifles. Industries include chemicals and plastic. Population (1990): 156,983.

Springfield 37 11N 93 19W A city in Missouri, in the Ozark Mountains. The commercial center for an agricultural region, its industries include railroad engineering and the manufacture of furniture and textiles. Population (1990): 140,494.

springhaas A nocturnal kangaroo-like rodent, *Pedetes capensis*, inhabiting the grasslands of eastern and southern Africa. Also called the Cape jumping hare, it is about 14 in (35 cm) long with yellowish-brown fur and a long bushy black-tipped tail. The springhaas uses the long claws on its forelimbs for excavating burrows and digging up the roots and tubers on which it feeds.

Springs 26 15S 28 26E A city in South Africa, in the S Transvaal. Founded in 1885, it became the center of extensive goldfields and today is a mining and manufacturing center producing gold and uranium. Population (1980 est): 153,974.

springtail An eyeless wingless □insect of the worldwide order *Collembola* (about 3500 species); 0.12–0.40 in (3–10 mm) long, it has a forked appendage on the abdomen, which is used for jumping. Springtails crawl about in moist soil and leaf litter or on water or snow and feed on decaying vegetable material, sometimes becoming minor pests of garden crops.

spring tide A □tide of relatively large range that occurs near the times of full and new moon. Low tides are lower and high tides higher than normal, and flooding may occur if strong onshore winds coincide with high water. *Compare* neap tide.

sprinkler system A safety system often installed in hotels, warehouses, factories, etc., for *fire prevention. It consists of a set of sprinkler valves connected to a water supply and an initiating alarm mechanism sensitive to heat or smoke. This may be a thin alloy bar in each sprinkler that bends at a low temperature or a sophisticated electronic sensor.

spruce A coniferous □tree of the genus *Picea* (about 50 species), widely distributed in the N hemisphere. Its needles grow in spirals and leave peglike projections on the shoots when they fall. The woody cones, 2–6 in (5–15 cm) long, hang down from the branches. An important and widely grown timber tree is the Norway spruce (*Picea abies*), of which the timber is used for paper pulp, roofing, barrels, boxes, etc. This conifer can reach a height of 131 ft (40 m), but young specimens are used as Christmas trees. Family: *Pinaceae*.

sprue A disease of the lining of the small intestine in which food is not properly absorbed. It is common in the tropics, often affecting people who have moved from temperate regions. Symptoms include diarrhea, anemia, and weight loss, and patients are treated with antibiotics, vitamin preparations, and a special diet.

spurge An annual or perennial herb of the genus **Euphorbia*, especially the hardier temperate species, which have been used as purgatives. Many are weeds but some are cultivated as ornamentals, including the Cypress spurge (*E. cyparissias*). Family: *Euphorbiaceae*.

spurrey One of several annual or perennial herbs that are found on sandy soils and salt marshes, chiefly in N temperate regions. The corn spurrey (*Spergula arvensis*) grows to a height of 2.8–16 in (7–40 cm) and has long thin leaves and white flowers. The sand spurreys (genus *Spergularia*; about 20 species) are smaller and usually have pinkish flowers. Family: *Caryophyllaceae*.

Spurs, Battle of the (Aug 16, 1513) The battle in which Henry VIII of England defeated the French at Guinegate, near Thérouanne (N France). The battle was so called because of the speed of the French retreat. The English victory led to the capture of Tournai.

Sputnik A series of Soviet unmanned satellites, the first of which was the first spacecraft to be launched (Oct 4, 1957). It burned up in the atmosphere after 92 days. Sputnik 2, launched Nov 3, 1957, carried the first animal, the dog Laika, into space.

Squanto (?–1622) American Indian of the New England Pawtuxet tribe. Before the Pilgrims landed, he had lived in England and been enslaved in Spain; he became the friend of and interpreter for the Pilgrims in Plymouth, Mass., in 1620. He taught them how to live in their new land and made possible treaties of friendship with surrounding tribes.

Square Deal (1901–09) A program of economic and social reform introduced by Pres. Theodore *Roosevelt to benefit the "plain man." In addition to its strict enforcement of antitrust laws, it sponsored federal supervision of big business, including federal wage and hour standards, and established the Food and Drug Administration (1906) to regulate the quality of processed foods and pharmaceuticals.

square root. *See* root.

squash The fruit of certain plants, some of which grow on bushes, others on trailing or climbing vines, most prominently *Cucurbita pepo* or summer squash. It is probably native to the Americas and includes several varieties widely cultivated as vegetable crops. Squashes bear yellow or orange cup-shaped flowers and large elongated fleshy fruits, which have orange, green, or yellow skins and are eaten as cooked vegetables. Winter squashes, *C. maxima*, include hubbard and butternut. Zucchini are a variety of squash eaten when small and immature (up to 6 in [15 cm] long). Family: *Cucurbitaceae*.

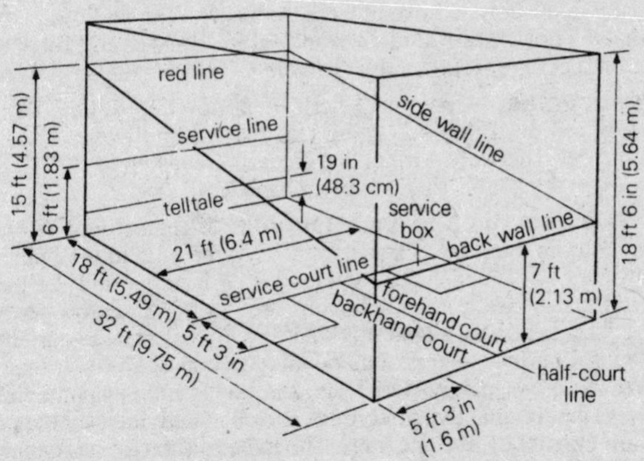

SQUASH RACKETS *The dimensions of the court.*

squash rackets A racket-and-ball game played in a four-walled court. It originated from an older English game (rackets), played at Harrow School, London, in the mid-19th century. Players hit a small ball of synthetic rubber with the object of making a shot that the opponent cannot return. (When the ball is played it must hit the front wall of the court and may hit any other wall.) The service each time goes to the winner of the previous point. The US version is a singles or doubles game, in which either side may score and the game goes to 15 points.

squid A *cephalopod mollusk of the order *Decapoda*. Surrounding the mouth, squids have 10 arms bearing suckers; two are long retractile tentacles used for capturing prey. Their cylindrical tapering bodies have fins on either side and a reduced internal stiffening shell. Squids feed on fish and mollusks, using a siphon to produce a jet of water to dart forward. The giant squid (genus *Architeuthis*) can reach 65 ft (20 m) in length. □oceans.

squill A perennial herbaceous plant of the genus *Scilla* (100 species), native to temperate Europe and Asia. Growing from bulbs, they produce long narrow leaves and blue, white, or purple flowers borne in a cluster on a leafless stalk. Some species, including *S. nonscripta* and *S. sibirica* are cultivated as garden ornamentals. Family: *Liliaceae.*

squint (*or* strabismus) A condition in which both the eyes cannot focus on the same object at the same time. This may be caused by paralysis of one of the nerves moving the eye, in which case the squint is often temporary. Nonparalytic squints are often seen in children and may be corrected by special lenses, eye exercises, or surgery.

squirrel A *rodent belonging to the family *Sciuridae*, which includes *ground squirrels, *flying squirrels, and tree squirrels, distributed worldwide.

The gray squirrel (*Sciurus carolinensis*), native to North America but now found in most parts of the world, is a typical tree squirrel, being an agile climber with a long bushy balancing tail and grasping hands. Gray squirrels feed chiefly on nuts, berries, and buds and have become a pest of orchards and gardens. They do not hibernate, but store food for the winter. *See also* red squirrel.

squirrel monkey A long-tailed monkey, *Saimiri sciureus*, common in Amazonian forests. Squirrel monkeys are 24–32 in (60–80 cm) long including the tail (14–17 in; 35–43 cm) and live in large troops, feeding on flowers, fruits, and small animals. They have tufted ears and white rings round their eyes with greenish fur and orange feet. Family: *Cebidae.*

squirting cucumber A perennial herb, *Ecballium elaterium*, native to the Mediterranean region. It has spreading hairy stems and leaves and its yellow flowers produce elastic-walled fruits that eject the seeds up to a distance of several meters when the fruit is ripe. Family: *Cucurbitaceae.*

Sri Lanka, Democratic Socialist Republic of (name until 1972: Ceylon) An island country in the Indian Ocean, to the E of the S tip of the Indian subcontinent, from which it is separated by the Gulf of Mannar and the Palk Strait. Broad coastal plains rise to a mountainous area in the S central part of the island. Sri Lanka is primarily a land of villages, with less than a quarter of the inhabitants living in urban centers. The population consists of two main groups: the Sinhalese, who are mainly Buddhists, and the Tamils, who are chiefly Hindus. *Economy*: predominantly agricultural, the chief activities are the processing and export of tea, rubber, and coconuts. The industrial sector has expanded considerably in recent years and the main products include cement, paper, ceramics, leather goods, chemicals, textiles, steel, and fertilizers. There is little mineral wealth, the most valuable deposits being graphite and gemstones. *History*: according to tradition an Indian prince, Vijaya, conquered the island in the 6th century AD and became the first king of the Sinhalese. In 1505 the Portuguese established settlements in the W and S, which passed to the Dutch in the mid-17th century and to the British in 1796. In 1802 the whole of the island was made a separate crown colony. Following World War II Ceylon became a dominion (1948) within the British Commonwealth and in 1972 Sri Lanka became a republic. Conflict between the Buddhist Sinhalese and Hindu Tamil communities has been a continuing problem. Following the 1977 general election, in which the United National party (UNP) was victorious, the Tamil United Liberation Front (TULF) emerged for the first time as the main parliamentary opposition. The government of President Jayawardene was confirmed in the first election under the presidential system established in 1978. Serious violence between Sinhalese and Tamils preceded the election. From 1985, Sinhalese-Tamil violence was so frequent that government stability was threatened, and India became involved in the conflict to protect the Tamil minority, which is numerous in S India. After Jayawardene's retirement, Ranasinghe Premadasa succeeded to the presidency in January 1989. The economy slowed in 1990, one reason being the repatriation of thousands of Sri Lankan workers from Kuwait during Iraq's annexation of Kuwait. The loss of income from tea exports to Iraq and the rise in oil prices during the Persian Gulf War also burdened the economy, as did continuing civil war between Tamil separatists and the government. Premadasa was assassinated by a suicide bomber in May 1993 and was succeeded by Banda Wijetunge. Head of state: President: Banda Wijetunge. Official language: Sinhala (Tamil and English are both recognized as national languages). Official currency: Sri Lanka rupee of 100 cents. Area: 25,332 sq mi (65,610 sq km). Population (1990 est): 17,135,000. Capital: Colombo.

Srinagar 34 08N 74 50E A city in India, the summer capital of Jammu and Kashmir on the Jhelum River. It has numerous museums, palaces, mosques, and a fortress, and is the site of the University of Jammu and Kashmir (1948). Industries include carpets, silver, silk, and leather. Population (1991): 586,038.

SS (German: *S*chutz*s*taffel, Defense Squad) The elite Nazi military corps, created in 1925 as Hitler's bodyguard and commanded by Heinrich Himmler from 1929. The SS, or Blackshirts, by the mid-1930s controlled the Nazis' security system, including the *Gestapo, *concentration camp guards, and the Waffen SS, an elite corps of combat troops in World War II. After the German defeat Himmler committed suicide and the activities of the SS were condemned at the Nuremberg trials (1946).

Ssu-ma Ch'ien. *See* Si-ma Qian.

St. Names beginning St are listed under Saint.

stabilizers (ship building) Adjustable finlike devices, projecting from the hull of a vessel, that reduce the vessel's motion in a heavy sea. They are operated automatically by a heavy gyroscope and are often called gyrostabilizers.

stadtholder (*or* stadholder) The ruler of the United Provinces of the Netherlands. Originally a provincial governor responsible to the central government of the Netherlands' Burgundian and then Spanish rulers, following the *Revolt of the Netherlands in the 16th century the secessionist United Provinces elected *William the Silent as their stadtholder. The office was traditionally held by the House of Orange until the fall of the republic in 1795.

Staël, Anne Louise Germaine Necker, Madame de (1766–1817) French writer, daughter of the financier *Necker. Her Paris salon became a center of liberal intellectual opposition to Napoleon, with whom she quarreled and consequently, after 1803, was forced to live in exile, mostly at her chateau on Lake Geneva. She traveled widely in Europe, studied with Schiller and Goethe in Weimar, and returned to Paris after the Bourbon restoration in 1814. Her most important literary work was *De l'Allemagne* (1810), which introduced German literature to France. She also wrote two novels featuring unconventional young heroines, *Delphine* (1802) and *Corinne* (1807).

Staffa 56 26N 6 21W An uninhabited island off the W coast of Scotland, in the Inner Hebrides. Composed largely of basalt columns, it is famous for its spectacular coast and caves, including *Fingal's Cave.

Staffordshire A county in the Midlands of England. It consists mainly of gently undulating lowlands rising to moorlands in the N, with the River Trent flowing SE. Agriculture is important, especially dairy farming. Industries include the pottery industry, which became famous during the 18th century, especially through the work of Josiah *Wedgwood. Area: 1049 sq mi (2716 sq km). Population (1987): 1,028,000. Administrative center: Stafford.

Staffordshire bull terrier A breed of dog developed in England from a bulldog-terrier cross as a pit dog. It is stockily built with a broad deep head and a short smooth coat that is pure white; red, fawn, black, or blue; or any of these colors in combination with white. Height: 14–16 in (35–40 cm) (English); 17–19 in (43–48 cm) (American).

stag beetle A beetle belonging to a family (*Lucanidae*; about 900 species) occurring mostly in the tropical regions. The males have well-developed mandibles that in many species resemble antlers—sometimes equal to the length of the body (which is about 0.31–1.5 in [8–40 mm] long). They are used during combat with other males. Most stag beetles are black or brown, although tropical species are often more colorful. The scavenging larvae develop from eggs laid in rotten wood.

STAG BEETLE *Two males of the European species* Lucanus cervus *using their enormous mandibles to fight for a female.*

stagecoach A large four-wheeled carriage drawn by four or six horses and used for scheduled long-distance transport services from the mid-17th century until the advent of railroad travel. The journey was divided into stages; horses, kept at strategically sited stops, were changed after each stage. The coach usually had seats for six inside and poorer passengers rode on the roof. After 1784 mails were carried by coach. In the US stagecoaches remained important auxiliaries to the developing railroad systems throughout the 19th century.

staghorn fern A *fern of the genus *Platycerium*, which grows upon other plants but is not a parasite. The fronds fork repeatedly into long pointed leaflets, resembling antlers, and the spore capsules are borne on their undersides. The fern, which is native to most warm regions, is cultivated as a pot plant. Family: *Polypodiaceae.*

staghound A *foxhound used for hunting wild deer. *See also* deerhound.

Stahl, Georg Ernst (1660–1734) German physician and chemist, who in about 1700 formulated the *phlogiston theory of combustion. Stahl had an alchemical disregard for quantitative measurement and consequently the phlogiston theory does not take into account changes of mass on combustion. Stahl's work in physiology was equally unscientific in modern terms, relying on a vitalist approach.

stained glass Colored glass panels formed of fragments of glass cut to shape according to a pictorial or abstract design and held together by "H" section lead strips. The earliest surviving stained-glass windows date from the 12th century AD, but this principle of embellishing buildings was known much earlier. The glass used was either colored throughout by the addition of metallic oxides (e.g. copper oxide [CuO] for ruby red) while molten or dipped into molten colored glass to obtain a fine film of color on both sides (flashed glass). From the 16th century painted glass displaced the more expensive colored glass. The 12th century saw considerable production of religious stained glass windows in N Europe. Much survives in France. Less exuberant colors and a classical restraint marked the post-Renaissance use of stained glass until leading designers exploited its decorative potential in the 19th century. Modern stained glass employs abstract patterns in secular as well as ecclesiastical surroundings.

stainless steel An alloy *steel containing up to 20% chromium and 10% nickel. It is corrosion resistant because the oxide that forms on the surface remains intact and protects the metal, unlike other steels in which it flakes off. Stainless steel is used in a wide variety of engineering applications where this property is important, as well as in kitchen utensils. It is more expensive to produce than ordinary carbon steel and more difficult to machine.

Stakhanovite A member of a Soviet labor movement that strove to increase industrial production. Named for Aleksei Grigorievich Stakhanov (1906–77), a coal miner who in 1935 reorganized his work gang to increase its daily production sevenfold, the movement failed because quality could not be maintained.

stalactites and stalagmites Deposits of calcium carbonate in limestone caves; stalactites are conical or cylindrical projections from the cave roof, while stalagmites grow upward from the floor and are generally more stumpy. They sometimes meet to form a continuous column. They are gradually formed from water containing calcium bicarbonate dripping from the roof. When the water evaporates a solid residue of calcium carbonate is left.

Stalin, Joseph (J. Dzhugashvili; 1879–1953) Soviet statesman. Born in Georgia, Stalin became a Marxist in the 1890s and was expelled from a theological college for his revolutionary activity (1899). In 1903 he joined the *Bolsheviks under Lenin and in the years preceding the Russian Revolution (1917) was repeatedly imprisoned and exiled. In 1921 he became commissar for nationalities and in 1922, general secretary of the Communist party. After Lenin's death in 1924 Stalin struggled to eliminate his rivals, above all *Trotsky, and emerged as supreme dictator in 1929. He abandoned Lenin's *New Economic Policy, initiating a series of five-year plans to enforce, with great brutality, the collectivization of industry and agriculture. The 1930s saw the reign of terror, culminating in the great purge, in which Stalin sought to enhance his power by the removal of his real, or imagined, rivals. In World War II, Stalin became chairman of the Council of People's Commissars and, following Hitler's invasion of the Soviet Union (1941), reversed the German alliance of 1939. He attended Allied conferences at *Tehran (1943) and at *Yalta and Potsdam (1945), where his negotiating skills were noted by Roosevelt and Churchill. In the postwar years, when

Stalin's autocracy intensified, he pursued a foreign policy of imperialism toward the communist countries of E Europe together with unremitting hostility toward the noncommunist world.

Stalinabad. *See* Dushanbe.

Stalingrad. *See* Volgograd.

Stalingrad, Battle of (1942–43) A battle in World War II, in which the German 6th Army under *Paulus, having entered Stalingrad (now Volgograd), was forced to surrender to the Russians under *Zhukov. The Germans lost 200,000 men.

Stalinsk. *See* Novokuznetsk.

Stamboul. *See* Istanbul.

stamen The part of a flower that produces the *pollen (male gametes). It comprises an anther, a lobed structure consisting of four pollen sacs, borne on a stalk (filament). The pollen develops within the sacs, which split open to release it. In self-pollinated flowers, the stamens open inward, toward the pistil, but in cross-pollinated flowers they open outward. *See also* flower. □plant.

STALIN

Stamford 41 03N 73 32W A city in SW Connecticut, on Long Island Sound. Settled in 1641, it changed from a farming to an industrial center in the mid-

1800s with the coming of the railroad. Industries include chemical, drug, electrical, and optical research as well as food processing, business machinery, and cosmetics. Population (1990): 108,056.

Stamford Bridge 53 59N 0 55W A village in N England, in Humberside on the Derwent River. Here King Harold defeated Tostig and King Harald of Norway in 1066, three weeks before his own defeat at Hastings by William the Conqueror.

stammering A disorder of the rhythm of speech, known medically as dysphemia. The normal flow of speech is interrupted by hesitations, repetitions of syllables, and sometimes by grimaces. Stammering is common in children, especially if speech is slow to develop, and does not indicate any illness. It is often made worse by anxiety and can become persistent; even then it usually improves with speech therapy.

Stamp Act (1765) The first British Act that imposed direct taxes on the American colonies, requiring that a stamp be affixed to all documents, newspapers, and dice. The revenue was to be used to finance the troops stationed in the colonies. Groups such as the Sons of Liberty organized to resist the act. Parliament was forced by colonial hostility to repeal the act but asserted its right to impose laws on the colonies (Declaratory Act, 1766), thus aggravating the opposition that led to the *American Revolution.

standard deviation. *See* variance.

standardwing A *bird of paradise, *Semioptera wallacei*, discovered in 1858 in the Moluccan Islands. The male is about 10 in (25 cm) long and has two long white ribbonlike feathers at each shoulder, which are erected over the back during its courtship display.

Standish, Myles (c. 1584–1656) English colonist in America. He sailed to America on the **Mayflower*, becoming military leader of the first settlement in New England, at Plymouth.

Stanford, (Amasa) Leland (1824–93) US businessman and politician. He served as governor of California (1861–63), during which time he helped to organize the Central Pacific Railroad and served as its president (1861–93). Eventually, through merger and construction of railroads, he headed the Southern Pacific Company, the parent company of a transcontinental line. Stanford University at Palo Alto was founded by him (in memory of his son) as Leland Stanford Junior University in 1885.

Stanford, Sir Charles (Villiers) (1852–1924) Irish composer. Among his compositions are six operas, seven symphonies, concertos, chamber music, songs, and Anglican church music.

Stanhope, James, 1st Earl (1673–1721) British soldier and statesman; George I's chief minister (1717–21). He served in the War of the Spanish Succession (1701–14) and helped suppress the *Jacobite uprising (1715). His grandson **Charles, 3rd Earl Stanhope** (1753–1816) was a politician and scientist. Becoming a member of Parliament in 1780, he urged parliamentary reform and supported the French Revolution. His inventions included two calculating machines and a microscope lens; he also experimented with electricity.

Stanislavsky, Konstantin (K. Alekseyev; 1863–1938) Russian actor and theater director. As director of the Moscow Art Theater, which he founded in 1898 with Nemirovich Danchenko (1859–1943), he developed an innovative style of naturalistic production. His theories about acting, published in *My Life in Art* (1924) and *An Actor Prepares* (1926) and later developed in the US as "method" acting at the *Actors' Studio, emphasized the value of ensemble playing and of the actor's complete identification with the character he played.

Stanisław I Leszczyński (1677–1766) King of Poland (1704–09, 1733–35) and Duke of Lorraine (1735–66). Stanisław was placed on the throne by *Charles XII of Sweden, after whose defeat Stanisław was deposed. He regained the throne by election but lost the subsequent War of the Polish Succession and became duke of Lorraine.

Stanisław II Poniatowski (1732–98) The last king of Poland (1764–95). Stanisław became a favorite of Catherine the Great of Russia, who secured his election to the throne and dominated his reign. In 1772 parts of Poland were annexed by Russia, Prussia, and Austria; in 1793 it was again partitioned (by Russia and Prussia). After the failure of *Kosciuszko's rebellion, and the third partition of Poland, Stanisław abdicated.

Stanisław, St (*or* Stanislaus; 1030–79) The patron saint of Poland. Of noble birth, he was elected bishop of Cracow in 1072. He was implicated in a plot against Bolesław II and murdered in mysterious circumstances. Feast day: May 7.

Stanley 51 45S 57 56W The capital of the Falkland Islands, in NE East Falkland Island on the Atlantic Ocean. A whaling base, it exports wool, skin, tallow, and seal oil. It was the focal point of the Falklands War of 1982. Population (1980 est): 1000.

Stanley, Sir Henry Morton (1841–1904) British explorer and journalist. He went to the US in 1859, joined the *New York Herald*, and in 1871 was sent by James Gordon *Bennett to search for David □Livingstone in Africa. Having found him at Ujiji, the two men explored Lake Tanganyika together. On a second expedition (1874–77) Stanley followed the Congo River (now Zaïre River) to its mouth. By obtaining Belgian sponsorship for exploration in the Congo he was instrumental in securing Belgian sovereignty over the Congo Free State. His last African expedition (1886–89) relieved *Emin Paşa in the S Sudan.

Stanley Falls. *See* Boyoma Falls.

Stanley Pool. *See* Malebo Pool.

Stanleyville. *See* Kisangani.

Stanovoi Range A mountain range in SE Russia extending about 500 mi (800 km) E–W. It rises to 8143 ft (2482 m) and forms part of the watershed between the Arctic and Pacific Oceans.

Stanton, Edward McMasters (1814–69) US lawyer and statesman. From 1836 he practiced law in Ohio, Pennsylvania, and Washington, D.C., before being appointed attorney general (1860–62). In 1862 he became secretary of war, a position he held through the Civil War and Reconstruction period under Presidents Abraham *Lincoln and Andrew *Johnson until 1868. A Radical Republican, he was often at odds with President Johnson, who ultimately tried, unsuccessfully, to force his resignation. He was appointed to the US Supreme Court in 1869, but died before he could take his seat.

Stanton, Elizabeth Cady (1815–1902) US reformer and pioneer in the women's rights movement. Frustrated in her attempts to obtain education open to males only, she married abolitionist Henry Brewster Stanton in 1840. Settling in Seneca Falls, N.Y., by 1846, she and Lucretia *Mott held the *Seneca Falls Convention (1848). She later worked closely with Susan B. *Anthony in advancing women's rights and served as president of the National Woman Suffrage Association (1869–90) and the *National American Woman Suffrage Association from 1890.

Staphylococcus A genus of spherical bacteria, some of which are disease-causing parasites of animals and man. *S. aureus* is responsible for boils and mastitis, *S. pyogenes* infects wounds, and certain strains cause acute food poisoning.

star A luminous ball of gas that is visible in the night sky. The sun is a typical star: stellar mass ranges from about 0.005 to 50 times the sun's mass. A star's mass determines its *luminosity, surface temperature, size, and other properties as well as its evolutionary path and lifetime: the higher the mass, the brighter, hotter, and larger the star and the shorter its life.

During the course of their history stars evolve, a process called stellar evolution. Young stars, recently evolved from the *protostar stage, generate energy by the thermonuclear fusion of hydrogen to form helium. This continues for some 10^{10} years for stars of solar mass but for only a few million years for the most massive stars. When the hydrogen is exhausted, stars evolve into *red giants. Further thermonuclear reactions occur involving fusion of helium and possibly the heavier elements in more massive stars. A low-mass star finally evolves to a *white dwarf. More massive stars explode as *supernovae, the surviving cores possibly forming *neutron stars or *black holes depending on mass. Stars are not distributed uniformly throughout the *universe, but are grouped into enormous clusters, called *galaxies, as a result of gravitational forces. The sun forms part of the *Galaxy (written with a capital G), often known as the Milky Way system. The nearest galaxy to ours is some 16×10^5 light years away and the nearest star to the sun within the Galaxy is about 4 light years away.

star apple An evergreen tree, *Chrysophyllum cainito*, native to the West Indies and Central America. Growing to a height of 50 ft (15 m), it has purplish-white flowers and bears sweet-tasting smooth-skinned fruits that resemble apples, red to yellow in color with star-shaped cores. Family: *Sapotaceae*.

Stara Zagora 42 25N 25 37E A city in central Bulgaria. The city was rebuilt after its destruction by the Turks in the late 19th century and has grown much since World War II. Fruit, in particular, is grown in the surrounding area. Population (1991 est): 164,553.

starch A carbohydrate that is an important storage product of many plants. Chemically it consists of linked glucose units in the form of two polysaccharides, amylose and amylopectin, which are present in varying proportions. Starch occurs naturally as white powdery granules that are insoluble in cold water but form a gelatinous solution in hot water. Plants manufacture starch by photosynthesis and it is a major constituent of seeds, fruits, roots, and tubers, and a major source of dietary energy for animals and man. It is also used in the paper and textile industries.

Star Chamber, Court of A court, originating in the king's council of medieval England, that met in the Star Chamber at Westminster Palace. It was concerned chiefly with breaches of the peace. Its misuse by Charles I to enforce his unpopular policies led to its abolition (1641).

star cluster A group of physically associated stars that shared a common origin. **Open** (*or* galactic) **clusters** are diffuse asymmetrical groupings of up to a few hundred stars and occur in the disk of our *Galaxy. **Globular clusters** are compact spherical groupings containing many thousands of very old stars and occur in the Galactic halo.

starfish A marine invertebrate animal, also called sea star, belonging to a worldwide class (*Asteroidea*; 1800 species) of *echinoderms. Its fleshy star-shaped body is covered with a spiny skin and has five or more radiating arms. Starfish occur on shores and ocean floors and move slowly, using saclike tube feet on the underside of the arms. They feed mainly on mollusks, crustaceans, and other invertebrates.

stargazer A fish belonging to either of the families *Uranoscopidae* (electric stargazers; about 25 species) or *Dactyloscopidae* (sand stargazers; about 24 species), found in tropical and temperate seas. Stargazers have a tapering body, up to 12 in (30 cm) long, a vertically slanting mouth, and eyes on top of the head. They lie buried in sand awaiting prey. Order: *Perciformes.*

starling A noisy sharp-winged songbird, *Sturnus vulgaris*, having a black plumage speckled with iridescent purple, green, and white. It is a versatile bird, common on farmland, where it probes the soil for insects, and also in cities, where it is a scavenger. It is gregarious and commonly nests in flocks in buildings and trees, sometimes becoming a serious crop and environmental pest. Family: *Sturnidae.*

star-of-Bethlehem A spring-blooming perennial plant, *Ornithogalum umbellatum*, native to the Mediterranean and grown in gardens. Growing from a bulb, it has grasslike basal leaves and a slender stalk, up to 12 in (30 cm) tall, bearing clusters of star-shaped white flowers striped with green. Family: *Liliaceae.*

star of David (Hebrew *magen David*: shield of David) A six-pointed star or hexagram, composed of two equilateral triangles. Widely used from antiquity as an ornament or magical sign, it has been regarded since the 17th century as a Jewish symbol and was imposed on the Jews as a "badge of shame" by the Nazis. In 1897 it was officially adopted as an emblem of Zionism and it now appears on the flag of Israel.

Starr, Ringo (Richard Starkey; 1940–) British rock musician, former drummer of the *Beatles. After the Beatles disbanded, Starr acted in such films as *The Magic Christian* (1970) and made solo albums.

Star-Spangled Banner, The National anthem of the US. The words, written (1814) by Francis Scott *Key during the War of 1812, were set to the music *To Anacreon in Heaven* (1780) of John Stafford Smith. Long sung in the US, it was adopted as the national anthem in 1931.

START II (Strategic Arms Reduction Treaty) A nuclear arms pact signed (Jan 3, 1993) by US president George Bush and Russian president Boris N. Yeltsin in the wake of the end of the Cold War. It called for reducing each country's long-range nuclear arsenals by two-thirds within 10 years. It also disallowed any land-based, multiple-warhead missiles.

Star Wars. *See* Strategic Defense Initiative.

State, Department of US cabinet-level agency that advises the president in the formulation and execution of foreign policy. Headed by the secretary of state, the department determines and analyzes US overseas interests, makes recommendations regarding policy, and represents the US in the UN, other international organizations, foreign countries, and negotiations for treaties. Established in 1789, the department includes the Foreign Service, which oversees US embassies and consulates.

Staten Island An island in New York, one of the five boroughs of New York City. Largely residential, it is the least densely populated of the city's boroughs. Area: 57 sq mi (148 sq km). Population (1990): 378,977.

States General **1.** In France, the assembly of representatives of the three estates—clergy, nobility, and the Third Estate or commons. First summoned by Philip the Fair in 1302, the States General did not meet after 1614 until summoned by Louis XVI in 1789 on the eve of the *French Revolution. The Third Estate declared itself a National Assembly, which replaced the States General. **2.**

In the Netherlands, the assembly of provincial representatives created by its Burgundian rulers in the 15th century. Following the *Revolt of the Netherlands against Spain, it became (1579) the chief organ of the United Provinces' central government.

states of matter Any of three distinct physical states: solid, liquid, and gas. A fourth state, *plasma, is often added. The different states are distinguished by the strength of the intermolecular forces compared to their random thermal motion. For example, in a solid the intermolecular forces are sufficiently strong to hold the molecules to an approximately fixed position, whereas in a gas the intermolecular forces have hardly any effect on the random movements of the atoms and molecules. Liquids represent an intermediate state.

states' rights The rights of the individual US states in relation to the power of the federal government. The issue arose in debates over the *constitution (1789), which established a strong federal government. Subsequent assertion of states' rights, especially that of secession from the Union, led eventually to the *Civil War.

static electricity The effects created by electrical charges at rest. Current electricity is an effect resulting from a flow of electrons; in static electricity electrons from one object are pulled onto another object, usually by rubbing them together, but they do not flow. The effect can be observed with many nonconducting materials, for example a comb passing through dry hair or a leather sole on a nylon carpet. A force exists between two charged bodies (*see* electric field), attractive if they have opposite charges, repulsive if the charges are similar; the magnitude of the force is given by *Coulomb's law. Static electricity can often cause problems (*see* lightning) but can be useful in electrostatic precipitators. *See also* electroscope; electrostatic generators.

statics. *See* mechanics.

Stations of the Cross A series of 14 pictures or images depicting the final events of the life of Christ, beginning at Pontius *Pilate's house, where he was condemned to death, and concluding at the sepulcher. They are usually arranged on the walls of a church and form the basis of a devotion in which prayers are recited as each station is visited in turn. The devotion was popularized in the Middle Ages by the Franciscans but derived from the early custom of pilgrims who followed the Way of the Cross in Jerusalem.

statistics The study of methods for collecting and analyzing quantitative data. The data measure certain characteristics of a group of people or objects, called the population; usually the whole population cannot be observed, often because it is too large, so data are collected from a representative sample of the population (*see* random sampling). The sample is analyzed and conclusions are inferred about the whole population, using *probability theory because the inferences cannot be certain. A population that has what is called a normal or Gaussian distribution (named for Karl *Gauss) varies randomly about a mean value. The standard deviation, the root-mean-square deviation from the mean value, is a measure of the spread in the population. The higher the standard deviation, the larger the sample size needed to be representative of the population. In binomial distributions the population consists of only two possible outcomes, as in tossing a coin, and in this case different statistical methods are used. In descriptive (*or* deductive) statistics, data for a group are collected and analyzed without conclusions being drawn about a larger group.

Statue of Liberty US national monument. A statue of a woman 152 ft (46 m) high holding a torch in her raised right hand, on Liberty Island in New York harbor. Designed by the French architect *Bartholdi, it was given to the Americans by the French in 1884 to commemorate the French and American Revolutions. Unveiled and dedicated in 1886, it has been a US national monument since 1924. In the 1980s it underwent a complete renovation.

Staudinger, Hermann (1881–1965) German chemist, who was professor at Freiburg University. He won the 1953 Nobel Prize for his work on the molecular structure of polymers. Staudinger showed that polymer molecules consisted of chains of repeated units and not a random distribution of such units as was previously thought. His work was of great importance to the developing plastics industry.

Stauffenberg, Claus, Graf von (1907–44) German army officer, who attempted to assassinate Hitler in 1944. Stauffenberg served in N Africa, where he was badly wounded. He tried to eliminate Hitler by bombing his headquarters at Rastenburg. He and his fellow conspirators were executed.

Stavanger 61 32N 5 12E A seaport in SW Norway. Its 12th-century cathedral was built by Bishop Reinald from Winchester. Its industries include fish canning and ship building. Stavanger is also the center of Norway's North Sea oil industry. Population (1986 est): 95,000.

Stavisky affair A French political scandal. In 1933 the fraudulent dealings of financier Serge Alexandre Stavisky (c. 1866–1934) were revealed and shortly afterward he was found dead. Attempts by the government to hush up the affair encouraged rumors that Stavisky had been murdered to prevent him from exposing the involvement of public figures in his affairs. Consequent right-wing riots led to the replacement of the left-wing government with a broad-based coalition.

Stavropol **1.** 45 03N 41 59E A city in SW Russia. The center of a fertile agricultural region, it has food-processing industries. It possesses several educational institutions. Population (1991 est): 328,500. **2.** *See* Togliatti.

steady-state theory A cosmological theory (*see* cosmology) proposed in 1948 by *Bondi, *Hoyle, and T. Gold in which the universe is regarded as having always existed in a steady state. The *expansion of the universe is compensated by the continuous creation of new matter. On the present evidence this theory has largely been discredited in favor of the *big-bang theory.

steam engine A □heat engine in which heat from a furnace is used to raise steam, the expansion of which forces a piston to move up and down in a cylinder to provide mechanical energy. A primitive steam engine was invented in 1698 in England to pump water from mines. In 1711 *Newcomen improved on this design but still relied on cooling the cylinder with a jet of water after each stroke. *Watt's single-acting steam engine, patented in 1769, was the first to use a separate condenser. Watt went on to invent the double-acting engine, the crank and crosshead mechanism, and the governor. Thus by the end of the 18th century man had, for the first time, a reliable source of power that did not rely on muscles or the wind. It was largely this engine that created the *industrial revolution. In 1808 Richard *Trevithick made the first use of a steam engine to drive a carriage, but it was not until the end of the century that steam-driven automobiles were in use—and they were quickly replaced by automobiles using Otto's gasoline engine. The steam engine, however, was the supreme prime mover of *railroads throughout the world from 1829 (when *Stephenson built his first *locomotive) until World War II, when steam was largely replaced by electric and diesel-electric trains. From the beginning of the 19th century steam engines were also widely used in place of sails in *ships. Moreover, it was the steam engine that drove the first electricity generators for public supply. The more compact and efficient steam *turbine, however, has now replaced the steam engine for this purpose.

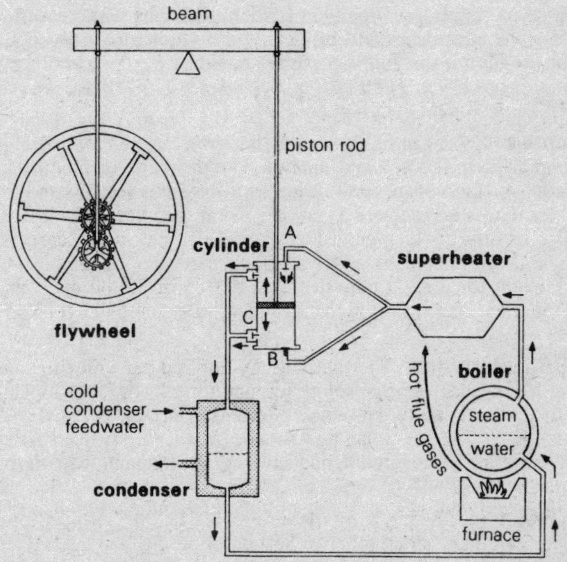

STEAM ENGINE *The principle of a double-action beam engine of the kind patented by James Watt. During the first half of the cycle, valve A opens, steam flows in and pushes the cylinder down, and steam flows out to the condenser through valve C. During the second half of the cycle, B opens and the steam pushes the piston the other way.*

steatite. *See* talc.

steel An *alloy of iron containing a small carefully controlled proportion of carbon, usually less than 1%. Carbon steels contain principally iron and carbon. Alloy steels have other metals added. Steel products form the basis of modern technology and steel production is therefore a key factor in the world economy. The uses of steel range from steel girders in bridges and buildings to kitchen utensils. For many engineering products the starting material is **mild steel**, a carbon steel with between 0.2% and 0.8% carbon and sometimes a little manganese or silicon. It can be further improved by *heat treatment. Alloy steels, such as *stainless steel, are usually more expensive to produce. They are used where special hardness, strength, or corrosion resistance are needed.

Steel is made by *smelting iron ore in a blast furnace to produce pig iron, which is added to melted down scrap iron before being further purified in an open-hearth furnace, *Bessemer converter, or *electric-arc furnace.

Steele, Sir Richard (1672–1729) British essayist and dramatist. Born in Dublin, he served in the English army from 1692 to 1705 and wrote a number of successful sentimental comedies, beginning with *The Funeral* (1701). He edited the *London Gazette* (1707–10), the official government journal. He is best remembered for his essays in *The Tatler* (1709–11) and the *Spectator* (1711–12), periodicals that he founded and on which he collaborated with Joseph *Addison.

Steen, Jan (c. 1626–79) Dutch painter. After training under Adriaen Van *Ostade and Jan van *Goyen, whose daughter he married, he worked in The Hague,

Delft, and Haarlem, but principally in Leiden, where he kept a tavern. Although he painted some landscapes and biblical and mythological subjects, he is best known for his humorous and sometimes bawdy tavern and domestic scenes. Representative works are *The Feast of St Nicholas* (Rijksmuseum, Amsterdam) and *The Morning Toilet* (Buckingham Palace).

steeplechase **1.** A form of horse race that grew out of *foxhunting, in which horses jump artificial hedges and ditches. The difficulty of the obstacles varies between courses and between countries. Hurdling is a less taxing version over lower lighter fences and shorter distances. The horses used are either trained for the purpose or turn to steeplechasing after their *flat-racing careers are over. Point-to-points are steeplechases for amateur riders, run by the local hunt clubs. **2.** A track event for men in athletics over a 1.85 mi (3000 m) course that includes 28 hurdles 3 ft (91 cm) high and seven water jumps 12 ft (3.66 m) across per lap.

Stefan-Boltzmann law The total energy emitted per unit time and per unit area by a *black body at an absolute temperature T is proportional to T^4. The constant of proportionality, known as Stefan's constant, is equal to 5.6697×10^{-8} W $m^{-2}K^{-4}$. The law is named for the Austrian physicist Joseph Stefan (1835–93) who first discovered it, and Ludwig *Boltzmann, who derived it thermodynamically.

Stefan Dušan (1308–55) King of Serbia (1331–55). Serbia's foremost medieval ruler, Stefan Dušan established Serbian supremacy in the Balkans by conquering Macedonia, Albania, and parts of Greece; in 1346 he was crowned Emperor of the Serbs and Greeks. He introduced a new legal code.

Stegodon A genus of long-legged extinct *elephants that lived in Asia and Africa between 12 and 1 million years ago. The first of the true elephants, it gave rise to the now extinct *mammoths and to the Indian and African elephants.

STEGOSAURUS *It was originally thought that the plates on the back of this dinosaur were erect and probably functioned as weapons. Recent theories, however, postulate a horizontal arrangement of plates, which acted as heat exchangers.*

Stegosaurus A dinosaur of the late Jurassic period (about 150–135 million years ago); 23 ft (7 m) long and weighing 1.75 tons, it had a double row of large triangular plates arranged in pairs along its back and two pairs of spikes at the end of its tail. *Stegosaurus* had a small head and fed on soft plants. Order: **Ornithischia*.

Steichen, Edward (1879–1973) US photographer; born in Luxembourg. From the early 1900s he was involved in photography, serving as head of the army's Air Service photographic division during World War I and as head of navy combat photography during World War II. His Gallery 291, run with Alfred Stieglitz, opened in 1905; from 1923 to 1938, his work was devoted to photographing the rich and famous. He directed photography (1947–62) at the Museum of Modern Art, where he assembled his well-known *Family of Man* exhibit (1955).

Stein, Sir (Marc) Aurel (1862–1943) British explorer and archeologist of Hungarian birth. Stein made expeditions to India, Persia, Turkistan, and the Far East, which resulted in many discoveries, including the Cave of the Thousand Buddhas near Dun-Huang (W China), with its paintings and documents. His books include *Ancient Khotan* (1907) and *Innermost Asia* (1928).

Stein, Gertrude (1874–1946) US writer. From 1903 she lived in Paris, where she presided over the American expatriate literary community, including Hemingway and Fitzgerald. Her experiments in prose, which include *Three Lives* (1909) and *Tender Buttons* (1914), were influenced by the cubist theories of Picasso, Braque, and other painters whom she helped. Her most accessible work is *The Autobiography of Alice B. Toklas* (1933).

Stein, Karl, Freiherr vom (1757–1831) Prussian statesman. He became first minister to Frederick William III in 1807, after serving as finance minister (1804–07), and introduced major administrative and economic reforms that helped Prussia to recover from its defeat by Napoleon. Dismissed in 1808, he then became adviser to Alexander I of Russia.

Steinbeck, John (1902–68) US novelist. First receiving national attention for his realistic novel *Tortilla Flat* (1935), Steinbeck later wrote *In Dubious Battle* (1936), *Of Mice and Men* (1937), and *The Grapes of Wrath* (1939). This latter work, for which he was awarded the Pulitzer Prize in literature in 1940, has been widely acclaimed as an epic account of the lives of a group of migrant farm workers during the Depression and deals frankly with the difficult social and economic conditions of Steinbeck's native California. Among his later works were the novels *Cannery Row* (1945), *The Pearl* (1947), *East of Eden* (1952), *The Winter of Our Discontent* (1961), and an autobiographical work, *Travels with Charley* (1962). In recognition of his dedication to portraying the plight of the poor and disenfranchised elements of American society, Steinbeck was awarded the Nobel Prize in literature in 1962.

steinbok A small solitary African antelope, *Raphicerus campestris*, inhabiting long grass or thinly forested areas. Steinboks are about 20 in (50 cm) high at the shoulder with a reddish-brown coat; males have small horns.

Steiner, Rudolf (1861–1925) Austrian-born founder of *anthroposophy. Steiner rejected the Oriental associations of *theosophy, with which he was originally associated, and aimed in his system to reintegrate man with the world of the spirit. He founded his first school in 1919 and his teachings are now propagated in over 70 Rudolf Steiner schools, which aim to develop the child's whole personality, not only his intellect.

Steinmetz, Charles Proteus (1865–1923) US electrical engineer, born in Germany, who developed the mathematical theory of *alternating current, introducing both real and imaginary components. This work greatly stimulated the development of devices running on alternating current. Steinmetz also discovered the law of *hysteresis and made some 200 inventions in electrical engineering, including a high-voltage generator.

Steinway, Henry (Engelhard) (Heinrich Steinweg; 1797–1871) German-born US piano maker. He emigrated to the US in 1849 and founded the piano firm of Steinway and Sons in New York, branches of which were opened in London (1875) and Hamburg (1880).

stela (*or* stele) A free-standing oblong slab, used in ancient Greece and the Near East as a grave or boundary marker. The Greek grave stelae were usually inscribed and ornamented with relief sculptures of the dead. The *Maya of Central America set up stelae with calendrical information.

stellar evolution. *See* star.

Stendhal (Henri Beyle; 1783–1842) French novelist. Between 1799 and 1813 he became acquainted with social life in Paris and also served with Napoleon's armies in Italy, Germany, Russia, and Austria. From 1814 to 1821 he lived in Italy and returned there as consul in 1830. His two major novels, *Le Rouge et le noir* (1830) and *La Chartreuse de Parme* (1839), are notable for their blend of romantic vigor with dispassionate and often ironical psychological analysis. He also wrote works of literary, artistic, and musical appreciation.

sten gun A 0.35 in (9 mm) submachine gun designed during World War II. Some four million of these simple weapons were produced. They were dangerously short and sometimes unreliable but some are still in use among terrorists.

Steno, Nicolaus (*or* Niels Stensen; 1638–86) Danish anatomist and geologist, who established that fossils were the petrified remains of ancient living organisms and that the layers (strata) of rocks represented stages in their deposition. Originally a physician, he discovered the duct of the parotid salivary gland; he later became a bishop.

Stentor A genus of tiny single-celled animals (*see* Protozoa) occurring in fresh water. Up to 0.08 in (2 mm) long, they are trumpet-shaped, with tracts of hairlike cilia over the body surface, and are often attached by a stalk to the substrate. They feed by wafting currents of water containing bacteria, algae, and protozoans into the funnel-shaped gullet entrance. Class: **Ciliata*.

Stephanotis A genus of evergreen climbing shrubs (5 species), also called Madagascar jasmine, native to Madagascar, and including some ornamental species. *S. floribunda* is a popular greenhouse plant with small fragrant white waxy flowers. Family: *Asclepiadaceae.*

Stephen (c. 1097–1154) King of England (1135–54); grandson of William the Conqueror. Stephen seized the throne from Henry I's daughter Matilda, who invaded England in 1139. The civil war that followed proved Stephen a brave soldier but revealed his lack of political sense. In 1152, after much of the country had been ravaged in factional fighting and the royal administration had broken down, Stephen recognized Matilda's son Henry (later Henry II) as heir to the throne.

Stephen I, St (?975–1038) The first king of Hungary (997–1038). Stephen was crowned on Christmas Day, 1000, allegedly with a crown sent by Pope *Sylvester II—the St *Stephen's Crown. Stephen's promotion of Christianity led to his canonization in 1083.

Stephen, St In the New Testament, the first Christian martyr. According to Acts 6, he was one of the seven deacons appointed by the Apostles to provide charity for the Greek-speaking widows in the Christian community. Also a preacher and miracle worker, he was accused of blasphemy and stoned to death by the Jews. Feast day: Dec 26.

Stephen Báthory (1533–86) King of Poland (1575–86). Stephen defeated *Ivan the Terrible of Muscovy in the *Livonian War but his plan to conquer Muscovy was cut short by his death.

Stephens, Alexander Hamilton (1812–83) US politician; Confederate vice president. He graduated from the University of Georgia (1832), taught school (1832–34), and became a lawyer (1834). He served in the US House of Representatives (1843–59) before being elected vice president of the Confederacy in 1861. After the Civil War he again served in the House of Representatives (1873–82) and as governor of Georgia (1882–83).

Stephenson, George (1781–1848) British engineer, who developed a greatly improved steam □locomotive. Stephenson became interested in locomotives in 1813. Two years later he built the *Blucher*, which could draw 30 tons of coal at 4 mph. He went on to construct a number of improved models, culminating in his most famous locomotive, the *Rocket*, built in 1829. It carried passengers at a speed of 36 mph on the new Liverpool–Manchester line and stimulated railroad development throughout Europe and in North America.

steppes The midlatitude grasslands of Eurasia extending in a broad belt from the Ukraine to SW Siberia. They correspond to the prairies of North America and consist chiefly of level, virtually treeless, plains.

steradian (sr) The *SI unit of solid angle equal to a solid angle that encloses a surface on a sphere equal to the square of its radius.

stere A metric unit of volume equal to one cubic meter.

stereochemistry. *See* isomers.

stereophonic sound Sound reproduction in which two signals are used to give a directional quality. It results in more realistic reproduction than a single signal system (monophonic sound) because the brain distinguishes the direction by assessing the difference between the sound in each ear. For recording, either two directional *microphones at right angles in one place or two separated microphones are needed. Playback requires at least two *loudspeakers, one for each signal.

sterility Inability to produce offspring by sexual reproduction. Sterility, or infertility, in men may be caused by various conditions in which the sperms are deficient in numbers or defective in quality. It may also result from psychological problems causing *impotence. In women sterility may be due to disease of the womb, blockage of the Fallopian tubes leading from the ovaries to the womb, or failure of the ovaries to produce egg cells. Generalized illness can also affect fertility. Numerous methods of treatment are possible depending on the cause; if the underlying condition cannot be treated, the couple may consider *artificial insemination. Sterility can also be deliberately induced (*see* sterilization).

sterilization The surgical technique or any other means used to induce *sterility. Surgical sterilization may be performed for contraceptive purposes or when pregnancy would damage the health of the woman. For men, the operation—vasectomy—involves cutting and tying the duct (vas deferens) that conveys sperm from the testicle. In women the Fallopian tubes are clipped or tied (tubal ligation), which prevents the passage of the egg cells to the womb. This operation is now performed, using a fiberoptic laparoscope, through a minute incision in the abdominal wall. Neither operation affects sexual desire or the ability to satisfy it. Sterilization should be considered as irreversible. *See also* castration.

sterling **1.** The currency of the UK. The pound sterling is named for the Norman *steorling*, a coin with a star (*steorra*) on one face. **2.** Sterling silver is a silver alloy containing at least 92.5% silver.

Sterling Heights 44 02N 84 02W A city in SE Michigan, on the W shore of Lake Saint Clair, NE of Detroit. The city's economy centers around the automobile industry. More recently, the aerospace industry has become important, and some missiles are manufactured. Population (1990): 117,810.

Stern, Isaac (1920–) Russian-born US violinist. He was taken to the US as a young child and studied and made his debut in San Francisco. He is a world-famous soloist and has toured extensively.

ISAAC STERN *He is shown (center) with Yehudi Menuhin and Leonard Bernstein (at the harpsichord), rehearsing Bach's double-violin concerto at Carnegie Hall, New York.*

Stern, Otto (1888–1969) US physicist who won the Nobel Prize in physics in 1943. Born in Germany, he did most of his work there on methods for studying the magnetic characteristics of atoms using molecular beams. The Stern-Gerlach experiment (with Walter Gerlach) established the validity of space quantization, a valuable piece of evidence in favor of the quantum theory. In opposition to Hitler, he came to the US in 1933.

Sternberg, Josef von (J. Stern; 1894–1969) US film director, born in Austria. He directed films noted for their pictorial quality, the best known being a series starring Marlene *Dietrich, including *The Blue Angel* (1930), *Blonde Venus* (1932), *Shanghai Express* (1932), and *The Scarlet Empress* (1934). He wrote the scripts for most of his films and published an autobiography, *Fun in a Chinese Laundry* (1965).

Sterne, Laurence (1713–68) British novelist. Born in Ireland, he was educated at Cambridge and became a clergyman in England. After the publication of the first two volumes of *Tristram Shandy* (1759), an eccentric comic novel consisting largely of sentimental rhetoric and witty digressions, he was lionized by London society. His second novel, *A Sentimental Journey* (1768), was based on his travels on the Continent undertaken for health reasons. He also published several volumes of sermons.

sternum. *See* thorax.

steroids A class of organic chemical compounds with a basic structure of three six-membered carbon rings joined to a five-membered ring. Steroids and their hydroxy derivatives (**sterols**) fulfill many biological roles in plants and animals and include the *sex hormones, *corticosteroids, *bile acids, *vitamin D, and molting hormones in insects. *Cholesterol is an important precursor in the synthesis of many steroids.

stethoscope An instrument widely used by doctors to listen to sounds within the body (*see* auscultation). The first stethoscope was invented by R. T. H. *Laënnec. Modern instruments consist of two earpieces joined by two tubes to a head, which is placed on the body. The head usually has a diaphragm (for high-pitched sounds) and a bell (for low-pitched sounds). More sophisticated stethoscopes are fitted with electronic amplification devices.

Stettin. *See* Szczecin.

Steuben, Frederick William, Baron von (1730–94) US soldier; born in Prussia. He came to the US (1777) after serving in King Frederick II's Prussian army. By 1778 he was major general and was appointed inspector-general of George *Washington's army. He fought with distinction throughout the American Revolution and played a key role in molding the untrained American troops. He wrote *Regulations for the Order and Discipline of the Troops of the United States* (1780), a US Army manual. After the war he became an American citizen and settled in New York state.

Stevenage 51 55N 0 14W A city in SE England, in Hertfordshire. The first of the new towns (1946) to be developed after World War II, it is now an important industrial center manufacturing aircraft, electrical, and plastic goods. Population (1981): 74,365.

Stevens, John Paul (1920–) US jurist; associate justice of the Supreme Court (1975–). He graduated from law school at Northwestern University (1947) and then served as a law clerk to Wiley B. *Rutledge, Jr., an associate justice of the Supreme Court. Appointed judge of the seventh circuit US Court of Appeals (1970–75), Stevens was chosen by Pres. Gerald *Ford to replace William O. *Douglas on the Supreme Court. He basically held moderate views.

Stevens, Thaddeus (1792–1868) US politician. Against slavery and an advocate of public education, he served in the US House of Representatives (1848–53; 1858–68), first as a Whig and then as a Republican, where he chaired the powerful ways and means and appropriation committees. Always urging equality of men, he was in favor of, and attempted to legislate, strong Reconstruction policies after the Civil War. Opposed to the more lenient Reconstruction policies of Pres. Andrew *Johnson, Stevens headed impeachment proceedings against the president.

Stevens, Wallace (1879–1955) US poet. He worked as an insurance executive and wrote most of his poetry after the age of 50. In many of his best-known poems, such as "The Man with the Blue Guitar," he explores the relationship between reality and imagination. His poems are collected in *Ideas of Order* (1936), *Notes Toward a Supreme Fiction* (1942), *Transport to Summer* (1947), *Collected Poems* (1954), which won a Pulitzer Prize, and *Opus Posthumous* (1957) and his essays in *The Necessary Angel* (1951).

Stevenson, Adlai E(wing) (1900–65) US politician. Trained as a lawyer, Stevenson spent much of his early career in private practice in Chicago (1927–41), but he served briefly during the Roosevelt administration as special counsel to the *Agricultural Adjustment Administration (1933–34). During World War II, he was appointed special assistant to the secretary of the navy (1941–44), and after the war he was a member of the US delegation to the *United Nations (1945–47). In 1948, Stevenson was elected governor of Illinois and, during his four years in office, achieved reforms in civil service, police, and public education. In 1952 and 1956 he received the Democratic presidential nomination, but was defeated in both elections by the Republican candidate, Dwight D. *Eisenhower. Stevenson later served as US ambassador to the UN during the Kennedy and Johnson administrations (1961–65).

Stevenson, Robert Louis (1850–94) British novelist. In 1880 he married Fanny Osbourne, whom he had met in France and followed to her native California. Returning to his native Scotland, he published several books, which established his reputation and which remain among the best-known works of fiction in the language: the classic adventure tale *Treasure Island* (1883), *Kidnapped* (1886), set in Scotland after the 1745 Jacobite rebellion, and *The Strange Case of Dr Jekyll and Mr Hyde* (1886). Constantly troubled by respiratory disease, he returned to the US in 1887 and finally settled on the island of Samoa in 1890. His other works include the novel *The Master of Ballantrae* (1889) and the unfinished *Weir of Hermiston* (1896).

Stewart, James (Maitland) (1908–) US film actor. He began his Hollywood career in 1935 and established himself as an incorruptible hero with a distinctive drawl in numerous films, including *Mr Smith Goes to Washington* (1939), *Destry Rides Again* (1939), *The Philadelphia Story* (1940), *The Glenn Miller Story* (1953), *Shenandoah* (1965), and *Airport 77* (1977).

Stewart, Potter (1915–85) US jurist; associate justice of the Supreme Court (1958–81). After filling various public positions in Ohio, he was appointed to the sixth circuit, US Court of Appeals (1954–58). He was appointed to the Supreme Court by Pres. Dwight D. *Eisenhower and was considered a moderate who treated each case individually and who was often called upon to cast the deciding vote.

Stewart Island (Maori name: Rakiura) 47 00S 168 00E A volcanic island of New Zealand, separated from S South Island by Foreaux Strait. Area: 670 sq mi (1735 sq km).

Stewarts. *See* Stuarts.

stibnite An ore mineral of antimony, SbS_3. It is a lead-gray color with a metallic luster and often occurs as distinctive radiating crystals. It is found in low-temperature hydrothermal veins and in replacement deposits.

stick insect An □insect, also called walking stick, belonging to the family *Phasmidae*. Up to 12.6 in (320 mm) long, it has a twiglike body and long spindly legs and the wings are reduced or absent. Males are rare; the females live in trees or shrubs, producing eggs that drop to the ground and develop without fertilization (*see* parthenogenesis). Order **Phasmida*.

stickleback A fish of the family *Gasterosteidae* (about 12 species), found in both fresh and salt water in temperate regions of the N hemisphere. Up to 7 in (17 cm) long, sticklebacks have a row of spines along the back. The male builds a nest for the eggs and guards the young. Order: *Gasterosteiformes.*

Stieglitz, Alfred (1864–1946) US photographer. He is famous for his promotion of European and US modern art in the US and his technical innovations in and development of photography as an art form. His famous Photo-Secession gallery in New York (1905–17), known as 291, put on exhibitions of Matisse (1908), children's art (1912), and *Brancusi (1914). Among his most admired photographs are those of his wife, the painter Georgia *O'Keeffe, his studies of New York City, and a series on clouds.

Stiernhielm, Georg Olofson (1598–1672) Swedish poet and scholar, known as the father of Swedish poetry. Believing that Swedish was man's original language, he tried to purify it by excluding loan words. His greatest work is the didactic epic poem *Hercules* (c. 1647).

stigma The part of the pistil of a flower that is specialized to receive *pollen. In insect-pollinated flowers the stigma is sticky, whereas wind-pollinated flowers have large feathery stigmas.

stigmata (Greek: marks) Marks appearing on the body of a living person that resemble the five wounds (in the hands, feet, and side) that Christ received at the crucifixion. There have been more than three hundred reported cases, typically involving devoutly religious persons. The stigmata are unknown before the 13th century, St *Francis of Assisi being the first saint to receive them. A number of natural explanations have been advanced, and the Roman Catholic Church takes a cautious view of the phenomenon, which does not constitute grounds for canonization.

Stijl, de (Dutch: the style) A group of 20th-century Dutch artists and architects, who launched the art periodical *De Stijl* (1917–28). Prominent members were the painters *Mondrian and Theo van Doesburg (1883–1931) and the architects J. J. P. Oud (1890–1963) and Gerrit Rietveld (1888–1964). The group adhered to the principles of Mondrian's neoplasticism, an abstract style that sought to establish a harmonious and universal means of expression applicable to all branches of art. This would be achieved by reducing form to horizontals and verticals and colors to the three *primary colors and black, white, and gray. In architecture and design neoplasticism was seen at its purest in Rietveld's Schröder house at Utrecht (1924) and in his furniture. Many of its principles were influential at the *Bauhaus.

Stilicho, Flavius (d. 408 AD) Roman general under *Theodosius I, who appointed him guardian of his son *Honorius. On Theodosius's death in 395, Honorius was proclaimed western emperor but Stilicho ruled in effect, ruthlessly removing opposition. He repulsed invasions by the Visigoths under Alaric and by the Ostrogoths but his political intrigues with Alaric and others eventually brought about his execution on Honorius's orders.

still life A branch of painting concerned with the representation of inanimate objects. Although still life was used in religious paintings and portraits, it did not appear as an art form until the 16th century and then only in the Netherlands. Particularly popular were still lifes of objects symbolizing the transience of life—skulls, guttering candles, etc. Still lifes of food and drink became the favorite subjects of such noted painters as *Zurbaran, *Chardin, *Cézanne, and *Braque, while specialists in flower pieces have included Jan *Brueghel and Pierre *Redouté.

stilt A wading bird belonging to the family *Recurvirostridae* (avocets and stilts); 14–18 in (35–45 cm) long, stilts occur in warm wet regions, where they probe in mud for small aquatic animals. The common stilt (*Himantopus himantopus*) has black-and-white plumage, pink legs, and red eyes.

Stilwell, Joseph Warren (1883–1946) US general. Fluent in Chinese, Stilwell was an uncompromising military commander who became popularly known as "Vinegar Joe." He graduated from West Point in 1904. In 1941, Stilwell was appointed *Chiang Kai-shek's chief of staff and in the following year, after US entry into World War II, he was named chief of staff of Allied forces in China, India, and Burma. Later in the war, however, his personal differences with the British commander Lord Louis *Mountbatten and with Chiang resulted in his recall in 1944. After the surrender of Japan, Stilwell served as commander of the US 10th Army in the Pacific.

Stimson, Henry Lewis (1867–1950) US lawyer and statesman. After serving as US attorney (1906–09) in New York City, he was appointed secretary of war (1911–13) under William Howard *Taft. He was governor of the Philippines (1927–29) and then secretary of state (1929–33), during which time he formulated the Stimson Doctrine, a refusal to recognize the Japanese takeover of Manchuria. Again secretary of war (1940–45), under Pres. Franklin D. Roosevelt, he directed US forces and policy during World War II.

stimulants A large group of drugs that stimulate activity of the nervous system. Caffeine (in tea and coffee) and nicotine (in cigarettes) are stimulants used widely to reduce feelings of tiredness and to improve concentration. *Hallucinogens, *amphetamine, and *cocaine are also stimulants. Stimulants may affect other parts of the body, particularly the heart.

stimulated emission. *See* laser.

stingray A round or diamond-shaped *ray fish belonging to a family (*Dasyatidae*; 89 species) found mainly in warm shallow ocean waters. Most species have a whiplike tail armed with one or more saw-edged venomous spines, which can inflict an intensely painful wound causing paralysis and occasionally death. Live young are born.

stink bug. *See* shield bug.

stinkhorn A fungus of the order *Phallales*, producing a phallus-shaped fruiting body. This consists of a stout whitish stalk arising from a basal egg-shaped structure and bearing a thimble-shaped cap containing spores. When the spores are ripe the cap produces a strong-smelling secretion that attracts flies, which disperse the spores. The common stinkhorn (*Phallus impudicus*) reaches a height of 4–8 in (10–20 cm). Class: **Basidiomycetes*.

stinkwood One of several species of trees with unpleasant-smelling timber, including *Gustavia augusta* of tropical America and the African species *Celtis kraussiana* and *Ocotea bullata* (black stinkwood). The wood can be used in furniture making.

Stirling, James (1692–1770) Scottish mathematician, best known for the widely used mathematical formula named for him. Stirling's formula gives the approximate value for the factorial of a large number. It was in fact first derived by Abraham de Moivre (1667–1754).

stitchwort A perennial herb belonging to the widely distributed genus *Stellaria* (85 species), having white starlike flowers. The greater stitchwort (*S. holostea*) is a common woodland and roadside plant of Europe, N Africa, and W Asia, growing to a height of 6–24 in (15–60 cm). Family: *Caryophyllaceae*.

stoat A small carnivorous mammal, *Mustela erminea*, of Europe, Asia, and North America. About 14 in (35 cm) long, with a long sinuous body, flattish head, and short legs, it can be distinguished from a *weasel by its black-tipped tail. Stoats prey mainly on rabbits. *See also* ermine.

stock One of several herbaceous plants of the genus *Matthiola* that are cultivated as ornamentals. Many garden varieties, including 10-week stocks and Brompton stocks, are derived from the European biennial *M. incana*, which grows to a height of 12–24 in (30–60 cm) and has clusters of purple flowers. The night-scented stock (*M. bicornis*) has small lilac flowers that emit their fragrance at night. Family: **Cruciferae*.

stock-car racing A form of *automobile racing that originated in the US in the 1920s, when cars were modified for transporting illegally made whiskey, for which speed was all-important. Stock cars are specially built steel-bodied cars weighing around 4400 lb (2000 kg); they withstand frequent accidents. They are raced on oval tracks at speeds up to about 200 mph (320 km per hour).

STOCK-CAR RACING *The Permatex 300 event at Daytona Beach, Florida.*

stock exchange A market in which securities are bought and sold. The three largest stock exchanges are in New York City, London, and Tokyo. A stock exchange is an essential part of the capital market, providing capital for industry and a form of investment for savers.

Stockhausen, Karlheinz (1928–) German composer, a pupil of Messiaen and Milhaud. From 1953 he worked at the West German Radio Studio for electronic music in Cologne. His early works employed serialism but he later rejected traditional forms and techniques, developing a concept of music as a sequence of sound "events" in such works as *Gruppen* (for three orchestras; 1955–57), *Zyklus* (for solo percussionist; 1959), and *Kontra-Punkte* (for 10 instruments; 1962). Later works, such as *Stimmung* (for six singers; 1968) and *Mantra* (for two pianos and percussion; 1970) were influenced by Indian mysticism and Stockhausen's "rediscovery" of tonality.

Stockholm 59 20N 18 95E The capital of Sweden, built on several islands between Lake Mälar and the Baltic Sea. It is the country's second largest port and its varied industries include shipbuilding, engineering, sugar refining, and brewing. The old town contains many buildings erected in the Middle Ages and in the 16th and 17th centuries, including the Royal Palace and Storkyrkan, Stockholm's cathedral. Its university was established in 1877. *History*: a settlement from very early times, it developed in the 13th century around a fortress erected to protect the entrance to the trading centers of Lake Mälar. It became the capital in 1436 and enjoyed great prestige and influence in the 17th century. Population (1992 est): 679,364.

Stockport 53 25N 2 10W A town in N England, in Greater Manchester on the River Mersey. Traditionally a textile town (particularly for cotton), Stockport also manufactures hats and caps, textile and electrical machinery, paper, plastics, and chemicals. Population (1981): 136,496.

Stockton 37 59N 121 20W A city and port in California, on the San Joaquin River. It can accommodate oceangoing vessels and is a distributing and processing center for the fertile San Joaquin Valley. Population (1990): 210,943.

Stockton-on-Tees 53 34N 1 19W A city in NE England, on the River Tees. The first passenger railroad was built from there to Darlington in 1825, and it was once an important port. Engineering and ship repairing are major industries. Population (1981): 154,585.

Stoicism The philosophical school founded about 300 BC in the Painted Porch (Greek: Stoa Poikile) at Athens by *Zeno of Citium. Stoics believed that God (identified with reason) was the basis of the universe, that human souls were sparks of the divine fire, and that the wise man lived "in harmony with nature." Knowledge of virtue was all-important. Stoicism was subsequently modified to stress the primacy of active virtue and duty. *Epictetus (55–135 AD) taught that all men were brothers. Stoicism appealed strongly to many prominent Romans, including Marcus *Brutus and *Marcus Aurelius, and its doctrines influenced many later thinkers.

Stoke-on-Trent 53 00N 2 10W A city in England, on the River Trent. Formed in 1910 by the amalgamation of five towns, the area is known as the Potteries and is the center of the British ceramic industry. There are also engineering and tire and cable manufacturing industries. Population (1981): 252,351.

Stoker, Bram (Abraham S.; 1847–1912) Irish novelist. He worked as a civil servant (1867–77), wrote drama criticism, and became secretary and manager to the actor Henry *Irving in 1878. Stoker is chiefly remembered as the author of *Dracula* (1897), a horror story in the *Gothic novel tradition. *See also* Dracula, Count; vampires.

Stokes, Sir George Gabriel (1819–1903) British physicist and mathematician, who was professor of mathematics at Cambridge University. He discovered the law concerning the terminal velocity of a sphere falling through a viscous fluid (*see* Stokes' law). He also attempted to deduce a mathematical model of the luminiferous ether, the medium in which light was at that time thought to vibrate.

Stokes' law The resisting force acting on a sphere, radius r, moving through a fluid under gravity with velocity v is $6\pi r\eta v$, where η is the *viscosity of the fluid. The law is used in the determination of viscosity. Named for Sir George *Stokes.

Stokowski, Leopold (1882–1977) British-born US conductor. An ardent supporter of modern music, Stokowski also became well known for his orchestral transcriptions of Bach's organ music, as well as his flamboyant style. He conducted many of the leading US orchestras, including the Cincinnati Symphony Orchestra (1909–12) and the Philadelphia Orchestra (1912–38).

Stolypin, Petr Arkadievich (1863–1911) Russian statesman. Tsarist Russia's last gifted politician, Stolypin became prime minister in 1906. He promoted many reforms, notably the land reforms that enabled many peasants to live an economically independent life. He became unpopular with both Right and Left owing to his disregard of the views of the Duma and his harsh treatment of revolutionaries; he was assassinated in Kiev.

stomach A muscular sac, just beneath the diaphragm, that opens from the esophagus (gullet) and leads to the duodenum (part of the small intestine). The stomach secretes gastric juice, containing hydrochloric acid and the enzyme *pepsin, which continue the digestion of food that started in the mouth. Release of acid is triggered by the *vagus nerve and by a hormone (gastrin) secreted by the stomach in response to the presence of food. The churning action of the stomach ensures constant mixing of the food and its secretions.

Stone Age The cultural phase during which man relied on stone, supplemented by wood, bone, or antler, as material for weapons and tools. It is the earliest phase in the system devised (1816) by Christian Thomsen (1788–1865) for classifying human technological progress (*compare* Bronze Age; Iron Age). The Stone Age is subdivided into: Old (*see* Paleolithic), Middle (*see* Mesolithic), and New (*see* Neolithic).

stone bass. *See* wreckfish.

stonechat A small *chat, *Saxicola torquata*, occurring in Eurasia and N Africa and feeding chiefly on insects and their larvae. Measuring about 5 in (12 cm) long, the male has a dark-brown head and back, chestnut underparts, and white rump; the female is a drabber brown. Stonechats favor dry heathland regions.

stonecrop An annual or perennial herb belonging to the genus *Sedum* (600 species), found chiefly in warm N temperate regions and also in Central and South America. They have small thick fleshy leaves and clusters of white, pink, or yellow flowers. Some are popular ornamentals, including autumn glory (*S. spectabile*), which grows to a height of 12–18 in (30–45 cm). Family: *Crassulaceae*.

stone curlew A ground-nesting bird belonging to a widely distributed family (*Burhinidae*; 9 species) characterized by thickened tarsal joints, also called thickknee. They are typically nocturnal, living in stony barren regions and feeding on beetles, worms, and other small animals. Order: *Charadriiformes* (gulls, plovers, etc.).

Stone, Edward Durell (1902–78) US architect. Noted for his functional, and later decorative, style, he designed Washington, D.C.'s John F. Kennedy Center for the Performing Arts (1972). Other well-known structures include New York's Museum of Modern Art (1939) and Huntington Hartford Museum (1962), New Delhi's US Embassy (1958), and the US pavilion at the Brussels World's Fair (1958).

stonefish A fish, belonging to the genus *Synanceja*, that occurs in shallow waters of the Indian and Pacific Oceans. It has a robust body, up to 14 in (35 cm) long, covered with wartlike lumps and fleshy flaps, a large head, and poisonous dorsal fins. It lies camouflaged and motionless among rocks or coral to await its prey. Family: *Synancejidae*.

stonefly An insect of the order *Plecoptera* (3000 species), 0.24–2.4 in (6–60 mm) long with long antennae and two pairs of membranous wings. The short-lived adults rarely feed and are found near fresh water. The aquatic *nymphs, which favor fast-flowing streams with stony bottoms, feed on plants, decaying organic material, or other insects.

Stone, Harlan Fiske (1872–1946) US lawyer and jurist; Supreme Court chief justice (1941–46). He was dean of Columbia Law School (1910–23) before being appointed US attorney general in 1924. The next year he was appointed to the Supreme Court. As an associate justice (1925–41) and chief justice, he was generally a conservative, but was strongly in favor of civil rights. He supported most of Pres. Franklin D. Roosevelt's *New Deal programs.

Stonehenge A famous megalithic structure, the focus of a cluster of ceremonial sites on Salisbury Plain in Wiltshire, England. Scientific study and excavation over many years have revealed a complex history with three main phases of modifications (c. 2500–1500 BC) contributing to the Stonehenge seen today. Sarsens and bluestones, the latter brought from S Wales, are set upright in concentric circles and horseshoes the orientation of which suggests one purpose as being sun and moon observation. The alleged "Druid" connection is entirely spurious, dating only from the 18th century AD. *See also* megalith.

Stone, Lucy Blackwell (1818–93) US reformer and pioneer in the woman's rights movement. After graduating from Oberlin College (1847), she initiated a woman's rights convention in Worcester, Mass, in 1850. She, with the help of her husband, Henry Brown Blackwell, was responsible for organizing various woman's suffrage associations throughout New England and in New Jersey; and she was instrumental in the formation of the American Woman Suffrage Association, which later became part of the *National American Woman Suffrage Association in 1890. She and her husband established *Woman's Journal* in 1870.

stone pine A *pine tree, *Pinus pinea*, native to SW Europe and Asia but planted throughout Mediterranean regions since Roman times for its edible seeds. Up to 100 ft (30 m) high, it has spreading branches and an umbrella-shaped crown, needles grouped in pairs, and cones about 5 in (12.5 cm) long. The oily seeds are eaten raw or roasted or are used to flavor stews, etc.

stoneworts *Green algae of the class *Charophyceae*, many of which contain stony deposits of calcium carbonate. The plants have an erect stemlike axis with whorls of branches and rootlike threads (rhizoids), by which they are anchored to muddy bottoms of fresh or brackish waters.

Stoppard, Tom (1937–) British dramatist, born in Czechoslovakia. After working as a journalist, he achieved international success with his play *Rosencrantz and Guildenstern Are Dead* (1967), using characters from Shakespeare's *Hamlet*. In his later plays, such as *Jumpers* (1972), *Travesties* (1975), *Night and Day* (1978), *The Real Thing* (1982), and *Hapgood* (1988), he explored philosophical and political ideas with wit and great verbal facility.

storax A tree or shrub belonging to the genus *Styrax* (130 species), occurring in warm and tropical regions. They have small white star-shaped flowers and several species are cultivated as ornamentals, including the Japanese snowbell (*S. japonicum*), which grows to a height of 30 ft (9 m), and *S. officinalis*, from which the vanilla-scented resin known as storax was formerly obtained. The storax used today in cough mixtures, pastilles, etc., is extracted from trees of the genus *Liquidambar*. The Sumatran species *S. benzoin* is a source of *benzoin. Family: *Styracaceae*.

stork A large long-legged bird belonging to a widely distributed family (*Ciconiidae*; 17 species) occurring in warm and temperate regions; 24–60 in (60–150 cm) tall, storks have a long neck and a long heavy bill and are mostly white with black markings. They feed chiefly on fish, frogs, mollusks, and in-

2433

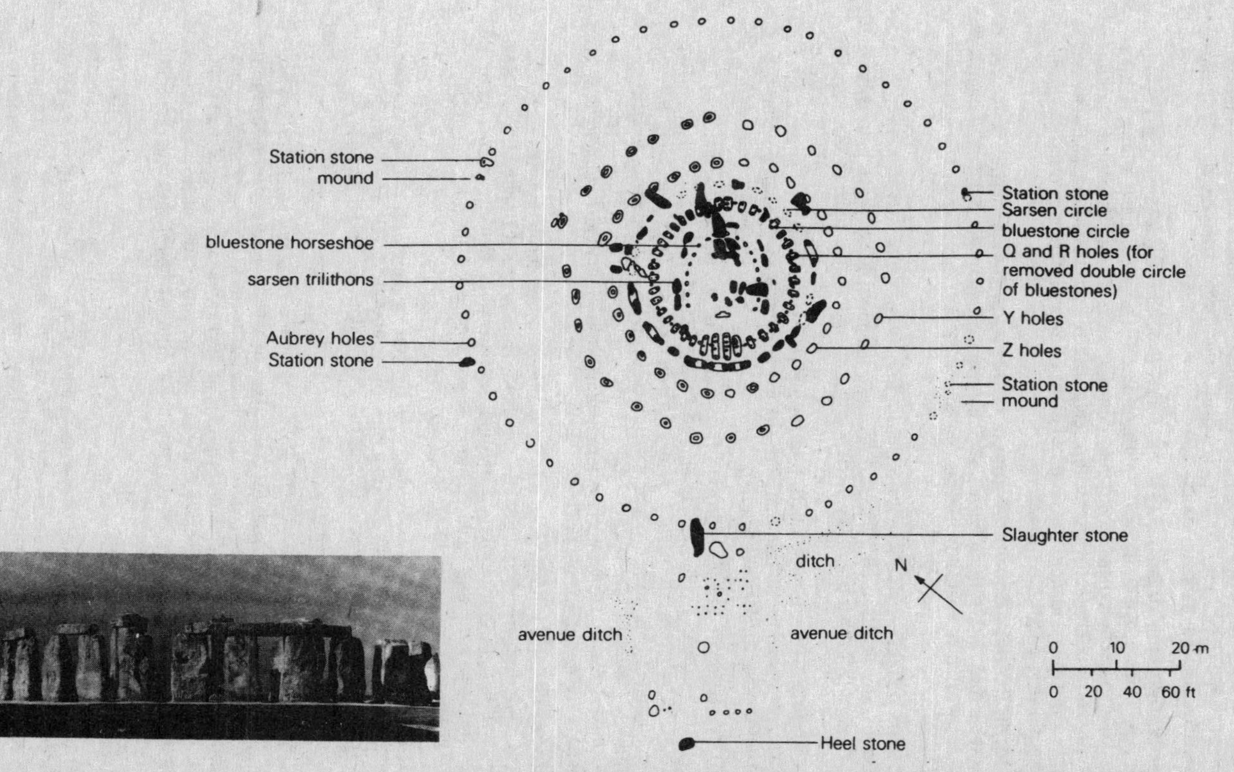

STONEHENGE *The plan reveals features of consecutive building phases that may no longer be visible to the visitor to the site.*

sects—caught in shallow waters or grasslands—and build a large nest platform of twigs in a tree or on a rooftop. Order: *Ciconiiformes* (herons, storks, flamingos). *See also* adjutant stork; marabou.

storksbill An herb belonging to the genus *Erodium* (about 90 species) occurring in Eurasia, Australia, and South America. The seeds have a long slender beaklike projection (hence the name) that is spirally twisted at maturity and unwinds when in contact with a damp surface to release the seeds. The common storksbill (*E. cicutarium*) grows to a height of 24 in (60 cm) and has purplish-pink flowers. Family: *Geraniaceae*.

Storm, (Hans) Theodor Woldsen (1817–1888) German writer. A lawyer, he spent most of his life in his native Schleswig, which inspired the chief themes of his works, in such novellas as *Immensee* (1849) and *Der Schimmelreiter* (1888).

storm petrel A small seabird belonging to a family (*Hydrobatidae*; 20 species) occurring in all oceans; 5–10 in (13–25 cm) long, storm petrels have dark-gray or brown plumage, often with paler underparts. Species of southern oceans have square tails, long legs, and short toes and feed by "walking" on the water with wings outstretched, picking up plankton. Northern species have longer wings and a forked or wedge-shaped tail and feed by swooping on fish. Order: *Procellariiformes* (petrels).

Story, Joseph (1779–1845) US jurist and scholar; associate justice of the Supreme Court (1811–45). He served in the US House of Representatives (1808–09). Appointed by Pres. James *Madison to the Supreme Court, he was the youngest ever to serve and was instrumental in establishing federal supremacy (*Martin* v. *Hunter's Lessee*, 1816) and the illegality of the slave trade (*Amistad Case). He wrote law commentaries that included *Bailments* (1832) and *Equity Jurisprudence* (1836).

Stoss, Veit (c. 1445–1533) German gothic sculptor and wood-carver. Working chiefly in Nuremberg but also in Poland, Hungary, and Bohemia, Stoss developed a style that combined Flemish realism with swirling draperies and expressive gestures and faces. His most important work is the altar of the *Life of the Virgin* for the Church of St. Mary, Cracow.

Stourbridge 52 27N 2 09W A city in central England, on the River Stour. Dr. Johnson attended the grammar school (founded 1552). There are glass-manufacturing and iron-working industries. Population (1981): 54,661.

stout. *See* beer and brewing.

Stowe, Harriet Beecher (1811–96) US novelist. A school teacher, she was a member of a prominent Calvinist family and wrote frequently on religious themes. *Uncle Tom's Cabin*, published in serial form in 1851–52 and in book form in 1852, with its graphic descriptions of the harshness of slavery, had a significant effect on antislavery feeling. It was an international best-seller and greatly stimulated the *abolition movement. She also published another antislavery novel, *Dred* (1856).

strabismus. *See* squint.

Strabo (c. 64 BC–c. 21 AD) Greek geographer, born at Amaseia (now Amasya, Turkey). His *Geography*, in 17 books, is an invaluable source of information about the ancient world. After a survey of previous geographers and a discussion of mathematical geography and maps, Strabo describes the Europe-Asia-Africa land mass clockwise around the Mediterranean, from Spain to N Africa. He marshals the evidence of other writers and his own observations into a comprehensive account, and is a master of historical and political geography, notably when describing the growth of the Roman Empire.

HARRIET BEECHER STOWE *Writer whose best-selling novel* Uncle Tom's Cabin, *a cry for an end to slavery, greatly angered the South.*

Strachey, (Giles) Lytton (1880–1932) British biographer and essayist. He was a leading member of the *Bloomsbury group. His irreverent attitude toward his subjects (Thomas Arnold, Florence Nightingale, Cardinal Manning, and others) in *Eminent Victorians* (1918) revolutionized the ponderous Victorian tradition of biography. His other biographical studies include *Queen Victoria* (1921) and *Elizabeth and Essex* (1928).

Stradivari, Antonio (?1644–1737) Italian violin maker. He was a pupil of Niccolò *Amati. From 1666 he and two of his sons made outstanding violins, violas, and cellos at their workshop in Cremona. Stradivari signed his instruments with the Latin form of his name, Stradivarius.

Strafford, Thomas Wentworth, 1st Earl of (1593–1641) English statesman, one of the chief administrators of Charles I's unpopular personal rule (1629–40). As lord deputy of Ireland (1633–39) his policy ruthlessly strengthened royal power and brought him enormous unpopularity that was intensified by his attempt to suppress the *Bishops' Wars (1639–40) in Scotland. He was impeached by the *Long Parliament and executed on the eve of the Civil War.

strain In physics, the deformation of a body when it is subjected to a *stress. **Longitudinal strain** is the extension per unit length when a body is stretched; **bulk strain** is the volume change per unit volume when a body is compressed; and **shear strain** is an angular measure of deformation. *See also* elasticity.

Straits Settlements A former British crown colony on the Strait of Malacca founded in 1867 and comprising the settlements of Penang, Singapore, Malacca, and Labuan. In 1946 Singapore became a separate crown colony, Labuan was incorporated in North Borneo, and Penang and Malacca joined the Malayan Union. In 1963 all became part of Malaysia. Singapore subsequently became independent.

Strailsund 54 18N 12 58E A city and port in N Germany, on an inlet of the Baltic Sea. Founded in 1209, it became an important Hanseatic port. Industries include ship building, fish processing, and the manufacture of machinery. Population (1989 est): 75,500.

strangeness A property of matter, expressed as a *quantum number (*s*), postulated to account for the unusually long lifetime of some *hadrons. In the quark model (*see* particle physics) strange hadrons contain the strange quark or its antiquark. Strangeness is conserved in *strong interactions and *electromagnetic interactions.

Strasbourg (German name: Strassburg) 48 35N 7 45E A city in NE France, the capital of the Bas-Rhin department on the Ill River. An important inland port, it trades in wine, iron ore, and potash; it has varied industries, including chemicals, oil refining, and textiles as well as the long-established printing and publishing industries. It is famous for its *pâté de foie gras*. Notable buildings include the cathedral (11th–15th centuries) and the university (1538). *History*: made a free imperial city in the 13th century, it was ceded to France in 1697. Captured by the Germans (1871), it was returned to France after World War I. Population (1990): 255,937.

Strategic Arms Limitation Talks (SALT). *See* disarmament.

Strategic Defense Initiative (SDI, *or* Star Wars) US defense plan to protect against a nuclear ballistic missile attack. Based upon satellites that would give early warning of an attack and advanced techniques including lasers and particle beams, SDI was supported by Pres. Ronald Reagan and was opposed for technical and political reasons.

Stratford 43 22N 81 00W A city in E Canada, in SW Ontario. Founded in 1831, it houses the Stratford Festival (1953), an important Shakespearean event. Population (1986): 26,451.

Stratford-on-Avon 52 12N 1 41W A city in central England, on the River Avon. It is famous as the birthplace of William Shakespeare. The Royal Shakespeare Theatre (opened in 1932) is devoted mainly to Shakespeare's plays. Tourists visit Shakespeare's birthplace (now a museum) and other buildings associated with him. Population (1981): 20,858.

stratification The layering of sedimentary rocks in approximately horizontal beds, known as strata. (Certain volcanic deposits also show stratification). The bed is the smallest division of stratified sedimentary rocks, being a single distinct sheetlike layer of sediment separated from overlying and underlying beds by a surface (the bedding plane), which marks a break in sedimentation. An unconformity is a surface representing a gap in the stratigraphic succession caused by changing conditions; it shows a period of erosion or nondeposition.

stratigraphy The branch of geology concerned with the formation, composition, sequence in time, and spatial correlation of the stratified rocks. **Lithostratigraphy** involves the lithological features and spatial relations of rock units. **Biostratigraphy** utilizes fossils in calibrating rock successions. **Chronostratigraphy** involves placing rock bodies in a time scale according to the time of their formation (*see* geological time scale).

stratocumulus cloud (Sc) A low type of *cloud composed of dark gray globular masses, often forming extensive sheets.

stratus cloud A low type of *cloud generally forming below 7900 ft (2400 m), having a low base and a gray uniform appearance; it may actually occur at ground level as hill fog. Precipitation, if any, is usually no more than a fine drizzle.

Strauss, Richard (1864–1949) German composer and conductor. He studied in Munich and Berlin and conducted opera at Munich, Bayreuth, and Vienna. Strauss was much influenced by Wagner, whose use of *leitmotifs he adopted, both in opera and orchestral works. From 1887 to 1899 Strauss wrote a series of symphonic poems, including *Death and Transfiguration* (1889), *Till Eulenspiegels lustige Streiche* (1894–95), *Also sprach Zarathustra* (1895–96), *Don Quixote* (1897), and *Ein Heldenleben* (1898). He then turned to opera, writing 15 works, including *Salome* (1905), *Elektra* (1906–08), *Der Rosenkavalier* (1909–10), and *Ariadne auf Naxos* (1912). His compositions also include two concertos for horn, one for oboe and one for violin, many songs, and *Metamorphosen* for 23 solo strings (1944–45).

Strauss the Younger, Johann (1825–99) Austrian violinist, conductor, and composer. He led his own dance ensemble from the age of 18 and was conductor of the Vienna court balls (1863–70). He wrote a great many dance pieces, including such waltzes as "The Blue Danube," "Vienna Blood," and "Tales from the Vienna Woods," as well as polkas and marches. He also wrote 16 operettas, including *Die Fledermaus* (1874), *A Night in Venice* (1883), and *The Gipsy Baron* (1885).

His father **Johann Strauss the Elder** (1804–49) played in the orchestra of the popular composer Joseph Lanner (1801–43), before forming his own, with which he toured abroad. He was made conductor of the Vienna court balls in 1845, and composed 152 waltzes as well as quadrilles, marches (including the "Radetzky March"), galops, etc. Strauss and Lanner are credited with the creation of the Viennese waltz.

Stravinsky, Igor (1882–1971) Russian-born composer. He became a US citizen in 1945. His father was an opera singer and Stravinsky was a pupil of Rimsky-Korsakov in St Petersburg. He became famous with the series of ballet scores commissioned by Diaghilev for the Ballets Russes, including *The Firebird* (1910), *Petrushka* (1911), and *The Rite of Spring* (1913), which was extremely modern in its use of rhythm and dissonance; it provoked demonstrations at its premiere and had a strong influence on 20th-century music. Stravinsky subsequently developed a neoclassical style in which he attempted to revive baroque and classical composition in a modern form. His works in this style include a piano concerto (1924), the oratorio *Oedipus Rex* (1927), the ballet *Apollon Musagète* (1928), and the opera *The Rake's Progress* (1951). Toward the end of his life Stravinsky adopted *serialism in such works as *Canticum Sacrum* (1955).

strawberry A perennial herb belonging to the genus *Fragaria* (15 species), native to N temperate regions and widely cultivated for its edible □fruit. Most of the commercial varieties are hybrids derived from the European hautbois strawberry (*F. moschata*), the Chilean strawberry (*F. chiloensis*), and the North American scarlet strawberry (*F. virginiana*). The plants are low growing, with creeping stems and small clusters of usually white flowers. It is the flower base (receptacle) that develops into the red fleshy "fruit": the true fruits (achenes) appear as "seeds" embedded in its surface. Strawberries are consumed fresh or used for canning, freezing, and jam making. Family: **Rosaceae*.

strawberry tree. *See* Arbutus.

strawflower. *See* everlasting flower.

streamlining The process of shaping the contours of a body so that it presents the least resistance to motion through a fluid. The mathematical study of these contours is part of *aerodynamics and *hydrodynamics. Streamlining must take into account drag forces, which are always present in real fluids, and is important in the design of aircraft, especially for supersonic flight (*see* sound barrier). *See also* turbulence.

stream of consciousness A technique used by novelists in which the flow of impressions, thoughts, and feelings are recorded as they pass through a character's mind. The term was first used by William *James in *Principles of Psychology* (1890). The technique was used by James *Joyce in *Ulysses* (1922) and also by Virginia *Woolf and William *Faulkner.

Streep, Meryl (1949–) US actress, known for her versatility. The winner of two Academy Awards (Best Supporting Actress, *Kramer vs. Kramer*; Best Actress, *Sophie's Choice*), she graduated from Vassar College and Yale Drama School. Before *Kramer vs. Kramer*, she had been nominated for a Best Supporting Actress Oscar for *The Deer Hunter*. Before *Sophie's Choice*, she won a Best Actress nomination for *The French Lieutenant's Woman* and after was nominated for *Silkwood, Out of Africa, Ironweed, A Cry in the Dark,* and *Postcards from the Edge*.

Streicher, Julius (1885–1946) German Nazi journalist, who spread anti-Semitic propaganda. A collaborator in Hitler's Munich Putsch (1923), he was then editor of *Der Stürmer* (1923–45). He was hanged as a war criminal.

Streisand, Barbra (1942–) US singer and actress. She has performed on stage and in film musicals including *Funny Girl* (1968), for which she received an Academy Award, *Hello Dolly* (1969), *The Way We Were* (1973), and *A Star is Borne* (1976). She also acted in comedy films, such as *What's Up, Doc?* (1972). She both directed and starred in later films, including *Yentl* (1983) and *Prince of Tides* (1991).

Streptococcus A genus of spherical anaerobic bacteria many of which live as parasites in the respiratory and digestive systems of animals and man. *S. pyogenes* causes scarlet fever in man, *S. agalactiae* is responsible for bovine mastitis, and *S. lactis* produces lactic acid and causes souring of milk. *See also* pneumococcus.

streptomycin An *antibiotic, obtained from the bacterium *Streptomyces griseus*, that revolutionized the treatment of tuberculosis. It is usually administered (by injection) in combination with other antibiotics, such as isoniazid, as bacteria soon become resistant to it. In some patients it may cause serious side effects, resulting in deafness and disturbance of balance.

Stresemann, Gustav (1878–1929) German statesman; chancellor (1923) and foreign minister (1923–29) of the Weimar Republic. He brought about a rapprochement in Anglo-German and Franco-German relations after World War I, negotiating the *Locarno Pact and securing the admittance (1926) of Germany to the League of Nations. He shared the Nobel Peace Prize with Briand in 1926.

stress (physics) An effect that causes a deformation (or *strain) in a body, equal to the force causing the effect divided by the area over which it acts. **Tensile stress** tends to stretch a body; **bulk stress** tends to compress it; and **shear stress**, which acts tangentially, tends to twist it. *See also* elasticity.

stress (psychology) Any condition or circumstance that endangers the well-being of an individual and upsets his or her psychological equilibrium. Prolonged stress causes initial alarm, followed by attempts at coping; if these are not successful, then physical and mental symptoms appear. These symptoms are also known as stress and they vary from person to person. Stress can lead to *anxiety, *depression, and *psychosomatic disorders and it can trigger an episode of mental illness in vulnerable people.

strike A form of industrial action in which a group of employees, usually organized in a labor union (or unions), withdraws its labor in order to achieve its demands. A strike is the last resort in the process of *collective bargaining: it may prompt a settlement either because it proves that neither side is bluffing or because the costs involved (in terms of lost pay and profits) force a compromise. As future orders and job security may be jeopardized by a strike, which is contrary to the long-term interests of both sides, responsible unions only resort to the measure in extreme cases.

An authorized strike is one that is recognized by a labor union, whereas an unofficial (or wildcat) strike is a walkout organized by workers without official union backing. *See also* picketing; *compare* lockout.

AUGUST STRINDBERG

Strindberg, August (1849–1912) Swedish dramatist and writer, born in Stockholm. After 1883 he lived chiefly in Berlin and Paris. His unhappy childhood and three unsuccessful marriages gave rise to mental instability and a violent hatred of women. This is reflected in the plays *The Father* (1887) and *Miss*

Julie (1888), the autobiographical prose work *Confessions of a Fool* (1912), and a study of mental illness entitled *Inferno* (1897). Returning to Sweden in 1898, Strindberg began work on a cycle of history plays and the dramatic religious trilogy *To Damascus* (1904). The other major works of this period are *The Dance of Death* (1900), on marital tensions, the symbolic *Easter* (1901), and *A Dream Play* (1901), in which Strindberg abandoned the naturalism that had figured in his earlier plays. His late chamber plays, such as *The Ghost Sonata* (1907), combine irrational elements with realistic settings; they anticipated and were highly influential on many of the later innovations of 20th-century drama.

stringed instruments Musical instruments in which notes are produced by the vibration of stretched strings. The strings may be plucked, as in the guitar, lyre, harp, lute, balalaika, zither, banjo, and ukulele; bowed, as in the violin family and viol family; plucked mechanically, as in the harpsichord; struck mechanically, as in the clavichord and piano; or played with hammers, as in the dulcimer and cimbalom. *Compare* drums; percussion instruments; wind instruments.

stroboscope An instrument used to study periodic motion using a flashing light of known frequency. For example, if a disk revolving at 50 revolutions per second is illuminated by 50 hertz alternating-current mains lighting, it will appear to be stationary. This is because the eye, for any particular flash, sees the disk in exactly the same position as it was for the previous flash. Strobe lighting is used in discotheques to accentuate the music's beat, with which it flashes in time.

Stroheim, Erich von (Hans Erich Maria Stroheim von Nordenwall; 1885–1957) US film director and actor, born in Austria. His films as director include *Greed* (1923), *The Wedding March* (1927), and *Queen Kelly* (1928). As an actor, he specialized in the roles of villains and German officers, as in *La Grande Illusion* (1937). In *Sunset Boulevard* (1950) he played a director from Hollywood's past.

stroke (*or* apoplexy) Sudden loss of consciousness with weakness or paralysis of one side of the body, caused by interruption of the blood supply to the brain. This may be due to a blood clot in one of the arteries of the brain (*see* embolism; thrombosis) or to the rupture of a blood vessel in the brain (cerebral hemorrhage). The underlying causes include untreated atherosclerosis and hypertension (high blood pressure) and diseases affecting the valves of the heart. With careful nursing and physiotherapy to restore the function of paralyzed limbs many patients recover completely.

Stromboli An Italian island in the Tyrrhenian Sea, in the *Lipari Islands. Its active volcano produces a stream of lava.

strong interaction One of the four basic forces in the universe; it occurs between the class of elementary particles called hadrons (*see* particle physics). It is the strongest of the four (being 100 times stronger than the electromotive interaction) but is effective only over a very short range of about 10^{-15} meter. It is the force that holds the protons and neutrons together in the nucleus. *Compare* weak interaction.

strontium (Sr) A reactive *alkaline-earth metal, discovered by Sir Humphry Davy in 1808 and named for Strontian, a town in Scotland where the carbonate ($SrCO_3$) is found. It also occurs as the sulfate, celestine ($SrSO_4$). It is a highly reactive metal, being more electropositive than calcium and reacting vigorously with water to liberate hydrogen. It imparts a strong red color to flames and is used in fireworks. The isotope ^{90}Sr is produced in nuclear fallout. It emits high-energy beta-rays and has a half-life of 28 years; it consequently presents a serious health hazard as, owing to its chemical similarity to calcium, it can become incorporated into bone. At no 38; at wt 87.62; mp 1418°F (769°C); bp 2526°F (1384°C).

Strophanthus A genus of trees, shrubs, and vines (about 60 species), native to tropical regions of Africa and SE Asia. The petals of some species have long threadlike extensions. The bark and seeds yield the drug strophanthin, which resembles *digitalis and is used medicinally as a heart stimulant. Family: *Apocynaceae.*

structuralism An approach to the study of culture and society that seeks to uncover underlying patterns and structures and the basic elements from which such patterns are constructed. The leading figure of this school is the French social anthropologist Claude *Lévi-Strauss, whose work on kinship, art, myth, ritual, and religion has been concerned also with the elucidation of universal laws of human thought through the analysis of its underlying structure. This approach was stimulated by the structural school in *linguistics.

Struve, Otto (1897–1963) US astronomer, born in Russia, who discovered the existence of interstellar clouds and observed that they contain hydrogen and calcium. He also noticed that certain stars, including our own sun, rotate much more slowly than others and suggested that this is because they possess planetary systems.

strychnine An alkaloid poison derived from plants of the genus *Strychnos*. It acts on the central nervous system, causing convulsions and ultimately death. Strychnine has been used in "tonics" and is still used as a poison for pests (such as moles).

Stuarts (*or* Stewarts) The ruling dynasty of Scotland from 1371 to 1714 and of England from 1603 to 1714. The family originated in the 11th century in Brittany and in the 12th century entered Scottish royal service with the appointment of Walter (d. 1177) as steward to David I. The sixth steward, Walter (1293–1326), married (1315) Marjory, the daughter of Robert the Bruce, and their son became Robert II in 1371. The direct male line ended with the death of James V in 1542, when the throne passed to his daughter Mary, Queen of Scots, and following her abdication (1567) to her son James VI, who inherited the English crown (1603) as James I. He was succeeded by Charles I (executed 1649), Charles II, James II, Mary II (and her husband William III), and Anne (d. 1714). The crown then passed to the Hanoverians (*see* Settlement, Act of) but the Stuart claim was kept alive by *James Edward Stuart the Old Pretender, and his son, *Charles Edward Stuart the Young Pretender. The last royal Stuart was Henry Stuart, Cardinal York (d. 1807), the younger son of the Old Pretender.

Stuart, Gilbert (Charles) (1755–1828) US portrait painter. At 19, he went to London and studied (1777–82) with Benjamin *West. Returning to the US (1793), he set up his studio in Philadelphia, where he did his most famous works, three life portraits of Pres. George Washington. At his studio in Washington, D.C., (1803–05) he painted portraits of the famous, including Thomas Jefferson and James Madison.

Stuart, James Ewell Brown ("Jeb;" 1833–64) US Confederate general. He commanded cavalry troops at the Battles of *Bull Run; just before the second battle (1862), he accurately gathered information about the enemy by traveling completely around the Union troops over a period of three days. He fought bravely at *Fredericksburg and *Chancellorsville and continued his scouting work for the Confederate Army. He was fatally wounded at Yellow Tavern while defending Richmond.

Stubbs, George (1724–1806) British animal painter. Largely self-taught as an artist, Stubbs studied anatomy and his earliest works included illustrations for a midwifery textbook (1751) and *The Anatomy of the Horse* (1766), for which he made dissections. He is best known for his horse paintings, such as *Mares and Foals in a Landscape*, but he also painted portraits and farming scenes. His meticulous observation of nature reflects his maxim that nature is always superior to art.

stupa A Buddhist shrine in the form of a mound or dome with a central projection. An early example (c. 100 AD) at Sanchi in N central India is a solid brickwork mound surrounded by a carved stone railing. Some fine later stupas survive in Sri Lanka. When modified to become a reliquary the stupa evolved into the *pagoda.

sturgeon A *bony fish belonging to a family (*Acipenseridae*; about 24 species) found in N temperate fresh and salt waters. Sturgeons have a large sharklike body, up to 27.5 ft (8.4 m) long, with five longitudinal rows of sharp bony plates, a small ventral mouth, and four sensory barbels. They feed near the bottom on small animals and plants. Eggs are laid in fresh water and are commercially important as caviar. *See also* beluga. □fish.

Sturluson, Snorri (1178–1241) Icelandic poet, who was also the author of the *Prose Edda* (*see* Eddas). A leading Icelandic nobleman, Sturluson visited Norway (1218, 1237) and intrigued against King Haakon, who intended to invade Iceland. Haakon had Sturluson murdered in 1241. His work includes a life of St Olaf and the *Heimskringla* (1223–35), a series of sagas about the Norse kings.

Sturm und Drang (German: Storm and Stress) A German literary movement of the late 18th century that anticipated many aspects of romanticism. Its influence is most notable in the drama, characterized by epic scale and the rejection of structural conventions. Goethe and Schiller were leading writers of this movement during their early careers.

Stuttgart 48 47N 9 12E A city in SW Germany, the capital of Baden-Württemberg on the Neckar River. It became the capital of Württemberg in 1482. It was largely destroyed in World War II. One of the country's main industrial centers, its manufactures include electrical goods, cars, and metallurgical goods. It is also a center for banking, exhibitions, and publishing. It has a university (1967). Population (1991 est): 570,700.

Stuyvesant, Peter (c. 1610–72) Dutch colonial administrator; governor of New Netherland (1647–64). His unpopular autocratic rule, which denied religious and political freedom, ended when the British forcibly took over the colony, dividing it into New York and New Jersey.

stye A small abscess at the root of an eyelash. Styes, which commonly occur in crops, are usually treated with warm compresses to drain the pus.

stylops A minute insect of the order *Strepsiptera* (about 400 species), which is parasitic on bees and other insects, affecting their reproductive systems and secondary sexual characteristics. The grublike female lives permanently inside the host's body; the winged male, often less than 0.16 in (4 mm) long, leaves its host to find and fertilize a female. After hatching, the larvae complete their development in a larval host.

Styria (German name: Steiermark) A federal state in SE Austria, bordering on Slovenia. It possesses important mineral resources and the Erzberg is Austria's chief source of iron ore; other minerals include lignite and magnesite. Area: 6326 sq mi (16,384 sq km). Population (1987): 1,181,000. Capital: Graz.

Styron, William (Clark, Jr.) (1925–) US novelist. He wrote *Lie Down in Darkness* (1951), *The Long March* (1953), and *Set This House on Fire* (1960) before receiving a Pulitzer Prize (1968) for *The Confessions of Nat Turner* (1967), a fictional account as told by leader Nat *Turner of the 1831 slave uprising. He also wrote *Sophie's Choice* (1979; film, 1982), *This Quiet Dust* (1982), and the autobiographical *Darkness Visible: A Memoir of Madness* (1990).

Styx In Greek mythology, the main river of Hades across which the souls of the dead were ferried by *Charon. It was sometimes personified as the daughter of Oceanus. After she helped Zeus in his war against the Titans, oaths sworn in her name were held to be inviolable.

Suarez, Francisco de (1548–1617) Spanish Jesuit theologian. He is known for his synthesis of Thomist and Aristotelian philosophy. He developed the theological system of congruism, the reconciliation of grace and free will. In *De legibus* (1612), he expounded the principles of natural and divine law.

subconscious. *See* unconscious.

sublimation In chemistry, the evaporation of a solid without melting. For any substance the liquid phase only occurs within certain limits of temperature and pressure—if the pressure is low enough, heating a solid will result in sublimation. Substances that sublime at atmospheric pressure include carbon dioxide (dry ice) and iodine.

submachine gun A light short-range *small arm developed from the infantry light machine gun. Submachine guns became militarily popular after 1918, filling the gap between the pistol and the rifle, by offering greater fire-power than either. They are also more accurate than the pistol and smaller than the rifle. The first successful type was the *tommy gun, but now all major armies have their own designs. Almost all use 0.35 in (9 mm) ammunition, fire automatically, and depend on blowback action (i.e. use the expanding gas of the ammunition to activate the reloading mechanism).

submarine A warship designed for sustained operation under water. The earliest record of a submarine craft is that developed by Cornelis Drebbel (1572–1634) of Holland in 1620, demonstrated before England's James I in 1624 in the Thames estuary. A more practical model, the "Turtle," was invented by David Bushnell (1742–1824) of Connecticut in 1776, and saw limited use in the American Revolution. Submarines, called **U-boats** (German name: *Unterseeboot*, undersea boat), were first used extensively by the German navy in World War I. They became an important armament in World War II, when the German navy sank millions of tons of Allied ships, especially supply ships in convoy from the US to the UK and the Soviet Union. The US navy used submarines to advantage against the Japanese, when 63% of all Japanese merchant shipping exceeding 1000 tons of cargo weight was sunk and 276 war vessels of various kinds were destroyed. Modern submarines may be powered by nuclear reactors, which require no air for recharging batteries and, hence, can remain submerged for months at a time. These vessels also carry one or more guns mounted on deck, torpedoes for firing underwater, and surface-to-air or surface-to-surface missiles that can be launched when the submarine is submerged.

Subotica 46 04N 19 41E A city in N central Yugoslavia, in Vojvodina near the Hungarian border. It has a large Hungarian minority and is an agricultural trading center. Its manufactures include metal goods, chemicals, and food products. Population (1991 est): 151,000.

subsidence The sinking of part of the earth's surface relative to the surrounding area. On a large scale it may result from crustal movements (e.g., rift valleys). On a small scale it may result from collapsed mining excavations, collapsed roofs of limestone caves, etc. Subsidence involves vertical movement and lacks the horizontal component of landslides, etc.

substitution reaction A type of chemical reaction in which one atom or group of atoms is displaced by another. An example is the reaction of methyl chloride (CH_3Cl) with hydroxide ions (OH^-) to give methanol (CH_3OH) and chloride ions (Cl^-). The hydroxide ion, in this case, is referred to as the substituent. *See also* addition reaction.

succession In ecology, the process of continual change that takes place in the composition of a *community of organisms occupying a particular habitat from the time of its initial colonization to the establishment of a stable *climax community. Succession is influenced by many factors, principally the nature of the habitat, climatic changes, and the effects of colonization on the habitat.

Suckling, Sir John (1609–42) English Cavalier poet and dramatist. Famous for his wit, generosity, and his taste for gambling, he was a loyal supporter of Charles I at the beginning of the Civil War. He was later discovered to be involved in a plot (1641) to free the imprisoned earl of *Strafford and was forced to flee to Paris, where he committed suicide. He wrote four plays and many elegant short lyrics.

Sucre 19 00S 65 15W The capital of Bolivia, in the S at an altitude of 9153 ft (2790 m). It was founded by the Spanish in 1538 on the site of an Indian settlement. The center of the revolutionary movement against Spain, it became the capital in 1859. The seat of government was moved to La Paz in 1898. The St Francis Xavier University was established in 1624. Population (1989 est): 106,000.

Sucre, Antonio José de (1795–1830) South American revolutionary, born in Venezuela. The most able of *Bolívar's generals, Sucre defeated the Spaniards at the decisive battle of Ayacucho (1824) and established the republic of Bolivia. He was its president from 1826 to 1828, when he resigned after a rebellion. The capital city, Sucre, is named for him.

sucrose (cane sugar *or* beet sugar *or* saccharose) A carbohydrate consisting chemically of one molecule each of *glucose and *fructose linked together. It is commercially the most important of the *sugars, being used as a sweetener in foods and drinks. When heated to 160°C it forms barley sugar and at 200°C it becomes caramel.

Sudan, Democratic Republic of the A large country in NE Africa, bordering on the Red Sea. It consists chiefly of a vast plateau rising to mountains in the S and W, reaching heights of over 10,000 ft (3000 m). The main rivers are the Blue Nile and White Nile, which join at Khartoum and provide the country's main source of water. About half the population are Arabs, and there are minorities of *Dinka, Nubians, and others. *Economy*: chiefly agricultural, the main cash crop and export being cotton; other crops include sorghum, sugar, and groundnuts, and production is being increased by means of irrigation schemes, such as the *Gezira irrigation scheme. Livestock rearing is also important. Forest products include gum arabic, of which the Sudan is the world's main producer. Mineral resources include iron ore, gold, and manganese. *History*: the NE was part of ancient *Nubia, which dominated Egypt (c. 730–670 BC). The region was Christianized in the 6th century and resisted invasion from the N until the 13th century, after which it was converted to Islam. In 1821 it was conquered by the Egyptians, against whom a revolt under the Mahdi (*see* Mahdi, al-) took place in 1881. In 1898 an Anglo-Egyptian force under Kitchener subdued his followers and in 1899 an Anglo-Egyptian condominium was established. In 1956 the Sudan became an independent republic. After a coup in 1958 it was ruled by a military government until 1964, when civilian rule was restored. Another coup in 1969 brought Col. Jaafar al Nemery to power. A revolt in the S against the domination of the N lasted from 1955 until 1973, when a new constitution gave the S a certain measure of self-government. In 1985, al-Nemery, who had failed to solve economic problems and renewed N-S conflict, was ousted in a coup. Sadiq al-Mahdi became prime minister in 1986 and ran the government until he was ousted in 1989 by Brigadier General Omar Hassan al-Bashir. Bashir and a 15-member Revolutionary Command Council for National Salvation ruled by Islamic law and was closely associated with the National Islamic Front. Attempts to end the civil war failed as rebels in the south advocated a secular government and the federal government became more Islamic in nature. In 1994 crop failures and famine further distressed the country. Official language: Arabic; English is widely spoken. Official currency: Sudanese pound of 100 piastres and 1000 millièmes. Area: 967,500 sq mi (2,500,000 sq km). Population (1990 est): 25,164,000. Capital: Khartoum. Main port: Port Sudan.

Sudbury 46 30N 81 01W A city in E Canada, in Ontario. Established in 1883, it is one of the world's greatest mining cities, especially for nickel and copper. A distribution and commercial center for NE Ontario, Sudbury has important timber and tool industries. Population (1991): 92,884.

sudden infant death syndrome (SIDS *or* crib death) Sudden death of an infant, up to one year old, from unknown causes, usually occurring while the infant is sleeping. A respiratory virus is suspected, and research has shown certain abnormalities in the central nervous system, adrenal glands, and pulmonary arteries.

Sudetenland A region in N Czech Republic, in the Sudetic mountains. The Sudetenland, incorporated in Czechoslovakia in 1919, formed a defensible frontier with Germany, with which its predominantly German population wanted reunion. Nazi pressure resulted in the *Munich Agreement of 1938, which permitted German reoccupation of the area. After World War II, Czechoslovakia regained the Sudetenland and expelled the Sudeten Germans. It was included in the Czech Republic when the country divided in 1993.

Su Dong Po (*or* Su Tung-p'o; 1036–1101) Chinese poet, essayist, and painter, whose father Su Hsün (*or* Su Xun; 1009–66) and brother Su Tse-yu (*or* Su Ze-yu; 1039–1112) were also famous writers. An imperial official, he was imprisoned and exiled on several occasions for his satirical verses and criticisms of government policies. His poems introduced more varied meters and subjects into the traditional verse forms of his period.

Sue, Eugène (Joseph Marie S.; 1804–57) French novelist. He worked as a ship's doctor until 1829. He achieved popular success with his novels about the Parisian underworld, notably *Les Mystères de Paris* (1842–43). *Le Juif errant* (1844–45) expressed his socialist sympathies.

Suetonius (Gaius Suetonius Tranquillius; c. 69–c. 140 AD) Roman historian and biographer. He was a friend of Pliny the Younger and served as secretary to the emperor Hadrian. Of his many works only *Lives of the Twelve Caesars* and fragments of *Lives of Famous Men* survive. His work is especially informative about the private lives of his subjects.

Suez (Arabic name: As-Suways) 29 59N 32 33E A port in Egypt, on the Gulf of Suez near the mouth of the Suez Canal. An important refueling station, it was virtually deserted following the Arab-Israeli War of 1967 and its oil refineries were damaged. Since the reopening of the Suez Canal (1975), rebuilding has taken place. Population (1986 est): 265,000.

Suez Canal A canal in Egypt connecting the Mediterranean Sea and the Red Sea. Running between Port Said in the N and Suez in the S (via the Great and Little Bitter Lakes), it is 103 mi (165 km) long. It is of great importance to much of the world's shipping. It was designed by the French engineer Ferdinand de Lesseps and was opened in 1869. In 1888 it became a neutral zone, with Britain the guarantor of its status. In 1956, following the withdrawal of British troops, President Nasser nationalized the canal, provoking an Anglo-French attack on Egypt. However, they withdrew within a few days in the face of international censure. The canal was closed from 1967 to 1975 because of Arab-Israeli hostilities and was not opened to Israeli ships until April 1979. It was recently deepened to take the much larger oil tankers now in use.

Suffolk A county in E England, bordering on the North Sea. It consists of undulating lowlands. It is mainly agricultural, producing cereals and sugar beet, and is noted for its horse breeding. Industries are generally related to agriculture. Fishing is centered on Lowestoft. Area: 1467 sq mi (3800 sq km). Population (1981): 596,354. Administrative center: Ipswich.

Sufism (Arabic *sufi*: wearer of a woolen cloak, mystic) A mystical movement arising within Islam in the 8th and 9th centuries AD. The goal of the Sufis was mystical union with God achieved by fervent worship. Later Sufism shows the influence of Neoplatonism and some devotional practices, such as rhythmical body movements, may derive from Hindu asceticism. Sufi thought has influenced leading Arabic and Persian poets. As it evolved, Sufism divided into different orders or brotherhoods, a number of which survive at present and have been introduced into the West. *See also* dervishes.

Sugar Act (*or* Revenue Act; 1764) British revenue-raising law imposed on the American colonists. A duty collected by British customs officers was put on each gallon of West Indian molasses traded for American lumber. The molasses, made into rum and traded for African slaves to be sold in the West Indies, was an integral part of the triangular trade carried on by America, the West Indies, and Africa. These early restrictions ultimately contributed to the start of the *American Revolution.

sugar beet A biennial herb derived from the European sea *beet (*Beta vulgaris*). Sugar beet is widely cultivated for the sucrose content of its large roots, which is over 20% by weight in modern commercial varieties. Sugar was first extracted from beet in the 18th century and the plant is now a major source of sugar, especially in Europe. Family: *Chenopodiaceae*.

sugarcane A perennial grass of the tropical genus *Saccharum* (5 species), especially *S. officinarum*, which is cultivated in tropical and subtropical regions for its sugar content. The clumps of stalks (canes), 10–26 ft (3–8 m) high, have lance-shaped leaves and may bear dense woolly clusters of female flowers. Usually, the canes are cut before flowering and crushed between rollers to extract the sugary liquid. This is concentrated and refined to produce sucrose crystals for table sugar, etc. The remaining liquor (molasses) is used for animal feedstuffs, industrial alcohol, etc., and is fermented to make rum. The fibrous residue (bagasse) is used as fuel and for papermaking, cattle feed, etc.

sugars A class of sweet-tasting *carbohydrates, classified chemically as *monosaccharides or *disaccharides. The sugar widely used to sweeten food, drinks, and confectionery is the disaccharide *sucrose, some 70–80 million tons of which are produced annually. Half of this total is derived from the stems of sugarcane (11–15% sucrose) and half from the roots of sugar beet (17% sucrose).

Sugar manufacture is believed to have originated in India (Sanskrit *sarkara*, sand) around 3000 BC, the method traveling westward through Arab countries (*sukkar*), Greece (*sákharon*), Italy (*zucchero*), and France (*sucre*). It was taken to the New World by Christopher Columbus in 1493. Until the mid-18th century it was an expensive luxury, used primarily as a medicinal sedative.

Sucrose is extracted from raw sugarcane by pressure, the extract being crystallized by evaporation. It is extracted from beet by hot water. Raw cane sugar and beet sugar are further refined to produce the granulated, caster, icing, and cube sugars familiar to commerce. By-products from sugar processing include molasses and sugar-beet pulp, both of which are used in animal feedstuffs.

Suger of Saint-Denis (1081–1151) French abbot and statesman. Suger was educated at the Abbey of Saint-Denis, becoming abbot in 1122. He introduced reforms based on the example of St. *Bernard of Clairvaux. As adviser to both Louis VI (1081–1137; reigned 1108–37) and Louis VII (c. 1121–80; reigned 1137–80), Suger wielded considerable political influence.

Suharto (1921–) Indonesian statesman and general; president (1968–). He gained prominence in the struggle for Indonesian independence from the Netherlands, becoming chief of the army staff in 1965. He came to power in the gradual overthrow (1965–68) of Sukarno. He was reelected at five-year intervals from 1968.

suicide Intentional self-destruction. Condemned by Christianity, Judaism, and Islam, suicide is a criminal offense in some societies. In many traditional societies suicide, whether voluntary or an honorable obligation, is an accepted practice. Compulsory suicide may be performed out of loyalty to a dead master or spouse, derived from the once widespread custom of immolating wives and servants, or in the interest of the group as a whole, such as self-murder by elderly members of a community no longer able to provide for their own subsistence. In certain instances suicide might be offered to a privileged few as an alternative to execution, as among the Greeks (*see* Socrates), the Roman nobility, and the feudal Japanese aristocracy. With the breakdown of traditional practices, especially in industrial societies, the causes of suicide become less clear. Since Durkheim's classic statistical study *Suicide* (1897) sociologists have sought to relate the incidence of suicide to social pressures and the importance of social integration (*see* anomie). Psychologists have emphasized the importance of guilt, anxiety, and loneliness; they have also distinguished between attempted suicide (when death is intended but averted) and parasuicide (when self-injury but not death is intended). *See also* Samaritans.

Sukarnapura. *See* Jajapura.

Sukarno (1901–70) Indonesian statesman, the first president of Indonesia (1945–65). He helped to found the Indonesian Nationalist party in 1927 and was Indonesia's leader during the Japanese occupation (1942–45). When Indonesia was declared independent he became president. In 1957 with popular and military support, he introduced so-called Guided Democracy. A military coup deposed him gradually (1965–68).

Sukhumi 43 01N 41 01E A port in the SW Republic of Georgia, on the Black Sea. It occupies the site of the ancient Greek colony of Dioscurias and is a popular resort. Population (1991 est): 120,000.

Sukkur 27 42N 68 54E A city in Pakistan, on the Indus River. Nearby is the major irrigation project, the Sukkur (or Lloyd) Barrage (1923–32). Industries include textiles and cement. Population (1981): 190,000.

Sulawesi (former name: Celebes) An island in Indonesia, off E Borneo. Irregularly shaped, it is mountainous and forested, with rich mineral deposits. It is Indonesia's chief producer of copra and nickel. Area, including adjacent islands:

72,986 sq mi (189,033 sq km). Population (1971): 8,535,164. Chief towns: Ujung Padang and Menado.

Suleiman (I) the Magnificent (?1494–1566) Ottoman sultan (1520–66), under whom the Ottoman Empire reached its peak. Suleiman captured Belgrade in 1521 and Rhodes in 1522. In 1526 he defeated the Hungarians at *Mohács and annexed large parts of Hungary. In 1529 he besieged Vienna. In campaigns against Persia he made many conquests, including Baghdad (1534), and the Ottoman navy, under *Barbarossa and others, controlled the E Mediterranean. To the Turks Suleiman is known as the Lawgiver because of the many regulations issued during his reign.

sulfonamides (*or* sulfa drugs) A group of drugs derived from sulfanilamide, that prevent the growth of bacteria and were first used in 1936, to treat infections associated with childbirth. Sulfonamides are used to treat a wide variety of infections, particularly those of the urinary tract (e.g. sulfamethiazole) and the eye (e.g. sulfacetamide). Sulfonamides are also combined with trimethoprim (*see* cotrimoxazole), which improves their effectiveness. The sulfonamide sulfasalazine helps the treatment of ulcerative colitis and Crohn's disease. In some patients sulfonamides may cause severe allergic disorders.

sulfur (S) A yellow nonmetallic solid element, occurring in various crystalline and amorphous forms. Sulfur was known in ancient times as brimstone. It is found near volcanoes and in large deposits associated with oil trapped against salt domes, from which it is extracted commercially. Extraction is by the Frasch process, in which the sulfur is melted with superheated steam and pumped to the surface. Sulfur reacts readily with many elements to form sulfides, sulfates, and oxides. Common compounds include sodium sulfide (Na_2S), zinc sulfide (ZnS), the poisonous gas hydrogen sulfide (H_2S), copper sulfate ($CuSO_4$), and calcium sulfate ($CaSO_4$). The oxides SO_2 and SO_3 are acidic gases that dissolve in water to form sulfurous acid (H_2SO_3) and *sulfuric acid (H_2SO_4). At no 16; at wt 32.06; mp 236°F (113°C); bp 833°F (444.6°C).

sulfuric acid (H_2SO_4) A colorless oily liquid that has a great affinity for water and is used as a drying agent. Mixing with water must be carried out carefully because of the heat produced. H_2SO_4 is made by the contact process, in which sulfur dioxide is heated and passed through columns of platinized asbestos catalyst to produce sulfur trioxide (SO_3). The SO_3 is then dissolved in water to form H_2SO_4. Adding further SO_3 to H_2SO_4 produces fuming sulfuric acid (oleum; $H_2S_2O_7$), a fuming liquid that forms a crystalline solid on cooling.

Sulfuric acid is one of the most important industrial chemicals, being used in the manufacture of fertilizers, paints, rayon, explosives, and many other products, as well as in oil refining and car batteries.

sulky A two-wheeled vehicle drawn by a horse, consisting of a light springy frame bearing a single seat for the driver and supported on wheels like bicycle wheels. Used now in *harness racing, this type of cart was used in the 19th century by doctors and others needing to travel alone.

Sulla, Lucius Cornelius (c. 138–78 BC) Roman dictator, associated with the aristocratic party; an opponent of *Marius and *Cinna. Nicknamed Felix (Lucky), he enjoyed early success. Enraged because his command against *Mithridates was transferred to Marius, he stormed Rome (87), forcing Marius and Cinna to flee. Although outlawed when his rivals returned, he successfully concluded the campaign against Mithridates and in 83 invaded Italy and took Rome. Elected dictator, Sulla butchered his political opponents. After legislating to restore the Senate's constitutional powers, he retired into private life (79).

Sullivan, Sir Arthur (1842–1900) British composer. He is best known for his collaboration with the librettist W. S. *Gilbert in such comic operas as *The Pirates of Penzance* (1879), *The Mikado* (1885), and *The Yeomen of the Guard* (1888). He also composed the grand opera *Ivanhoe* (1891).

Sullivan, John Lawrence (1858–1918) US boxer, generally considered the first modern world heavyweight champion (1882–92). He lost his title to Jim Corbett (1866–1933) in the first championship fought under the Queensberry Rules (*see* boxing).

Sullivan, Louis Henry (1856–1924) US architect. Working principally in Chicago, Sullivan was one of the leading figures of the modern architectural movement. His work, begun in the classical style, was modified by *Art Nouveau and developed into a form of *functionalism, the basic tenet being "form follows function." He was among the first to design skyscrapers, such as the Wainwright building, St Louis (1890), the Transportation Building at the Columbian Exposition in Chicago (1893), and the Carson store, Chicago (1899), in both of which the structural framework is clearly visible.

Sully, Maximilien de Béthune, Duc de (1560–1641) French statesman; chief minister to *Henry IV. Sully's financial reforms were fundamental in restoring prosperity after the *Wars of Religion. He retired (1611) following Henry's assassination.

Sully-Prudhomme, René François Armand (1839–1907) French poet. His early verse was lyrical and subjective, but his involvement with the *Parnassians, who favored greater impersonality, led to his attempts in *La Justice* (1878) and other works to write epical philosophic verse. He won the Nobel Prize in 1901.

Sulu Archipelago An island group in the SW Philippines, between Borneo and Mindanao. The most important of its 400 volcanic and coral islands are Basilan and Jolo. Area: 1087 sq mi (2815 sq km). Chief town: Jolo.

sumac (*or* sumach) A tree or shrub of the genus *Rhus* (250 species), native to warm temperate and subtropical regions. The leaves of the Sicilian sumac (*R. coraria*) yield a substance used in tanning and dyeing. Several species are cultivated as garden ornamentals: the stag's-horn sumac (*R. typhina*) of North America grows to a height of 23–39 ft (7–12 m) and has a crimson or orange autumn foliage. Some species are poisonous and irritate the skin on contact, particularly the American *poison ivy and poison sumac (*R. vernix*). Family: *Anacardiaceae. See also* lacquer tree.

Sumatra (*or* Sumatera) The second largest Indonesian island, separated from Peninsular Malaysia by the Strait of Malacca. The mountainous volcanic spine descends in the NE to swamps. Producing over 75% of the country's exports, it is Indonesia's chief rubber and oil producer and also possesses large natural gas deposits and other minerals. Crops include coffee, tea, and pepper. *History*: the Buddhist kingdom of Sri Vijaya (7th–13th centuries) was based in Palembang, spreading through Indonesia and the Malay Peninsula. During the 15th century the Islamic influence became dominant, resisting Dutch domination in the N until 1908. Since 1949 there has been considerable separatist activity directed against the Java-based government. Area: 202,311 sq mi (524,097 sq km). Chief towns: Palembang and Medan.

Sumer The area in S Mesopotamia in which the earliest civilization evolved during the 4th millennium BC. The fertile natural environment encouraged settlements that grew into such cities as *Ur and *Eridu with all the prerequisites of civilized life: a writing system (*see* cuneiform), accumulation of wealth through trade, specialist organization of labor, and sophisticated crafts and architecture. Politically Sumer was a collection of independent city-states, each with its own patron deity. Centralized control was temporarily asserted by neighboring *Akkad (c. 2300 BC) and after 2000 BC Sumer was gradually absorbed into *Babylonia.

summer cypress Either of two annual herbaceous plants, *Kochia scoparia* or *K. trichophylla*, native to temperate Eurasia and cultivated as ornamentals. They form compact bushes, 40–60 in (1–1.5 m) high, and the foliage assumes an attractive red-bronze color in autumn. Family: *Chenopodiaceae.*

Sumner, Charles (1811–74) US politician and reformer. Elected to represent Massachusetts in the US Senate in 1851, he fought against slavery, especially the *Fugitive Slave Law of 1850, and the *Kansas-Nebraska Act of 1854. Attacked by a southern congressman, angered over Sumner's antislavery stance, Sumner was incapacitated for three years (1856–59), but he kept his seat in the Senate. In 1861 he was appointed chairman of the Senate Foreign Relations Committee, a post he held until 1871. He advocated a strong Reconstruction policy and supported impeachment proceedings against Pres. Andrew *Johnson.

Sumter, Fort A fort in Charleston, S.C., on an island at the mouth of the city's harbor on the Atlantic Ocean. Built 1829–60 on a man-made island, it defended the city and was the first place fired upon (1861) by the Confederates in the Civil War. The fort was taken by the Confederates in two days and was not reoccupied by Union troops until the Confederate evacuation of Charleston in 1865. It was made a national monument in 1948.

sun The nearest star, lying at an average distance of 92.9 million mi (149.6 million km) from earth at the center of the *solar system. It has a diameter of 864,500 mi (1,392,000 km), a mass of 1.99×10^{30} kg, and rotates on its axis in a mean period of 25.38 days (the period lengthening as solar latitude increases). It is a typical yellow (G2) main-sequence star and is composed primarily (99%) of hydrogen and helium in the approximate ratio 3:1 by mass.

In its hot central core, about 250,000 mi (400,000 km) in diameter, energy is generated by nuclear fusion reactions. This energy is transported to the sun's surface, from where it is radiated into space, mainly as heat and light. The surface, called the *photosphere, is the boundary between the opaque outer (convective) zone of the sun's interior and its transparent atmosphere. The atmosphere comprises the *chromosphere and the inner and outer *corona. The corona extends many millions of kilometers into interplanetary space. There are regions of intense localized magnetic fields on the sun, extending from the photosphere through the chromosphere to the corona. A variety of phenomena occur in these active regions, including *sunspots, *solar prominences, and *solar flares. *See also* solar wind.

sun bear A *bear, *Helarctos malayanus*, of tropical forests of Asia, Sumatra, and Borneo. It is the smallest bear, (43–55 in [110–140 cm] long) and climbs well, hunting in tall trees for small vertebrates, fruit, and its favorite food, honey.

sunbird An arboreal bird belonging to a tropical family (*Nectariniidae*; 104 species) ranging from Africa to Australasia. Sunbirds are 3.5–6 in (9–15 cm) long and have a brilliant metallic plumage, slender down-curved bills, and long extensible tongues for feeding on nectar. Sunbirds are similar to New World hummingbirds but perch on flowers to feed rather than hovering in front of them.

sun bittern A Central American ground-dwelling bird, *Eurypyga helias*, that occurs in wet forests; 17 in (43 cm) long, it has a brown, yellow, black, and white spotted plumage and feeds on insects with its sharp bill. It is the only member of its family (*Eurypygidae*). Order: *Gruiformes* (cranes, rails, etc.).

Sunda Islands An Indonesian group of islands, the W part of the Malay Archipelago between the Indian Ocean and South China Sea. It consists of the **Greater Sunda Islands** including Sumatra, Java, Borneo, and Sulawesi and *Nusa Tenggara (formerly the Lesser Sunda Islands).

Sunday, Billy (William Ashley S.; 1862–1935) US revivalist and baseball player. He played professional baseball (1883–86), but then turned his attention to religion, becoming a Presbyterian in 1888. By 1903 he had become a minister and was soon well known for his fundamentalist revival meetings around the country.

Sunderland 54 55N 1 23W A port in NE England, at the mouth of the River Wear. Sunderland has exported coal from the Durham coalfield since the 14th century. Ship building and ship repairing are important industries; there is also engineering, glass, pottery, chemicals, and paper manufacture. Population (1981): 196,152.

sundew A perennial or annual *carnivorous plant of the genus *Drosera* (about 100 species), of temperate and tropical regions. Sundews have a basal rosette of leaves covered with sticky reddish gland-tipped hairs, used to trap insects. The cup-shaped flowers are usually borne in a group on a stalk 2.4–14 in (6–35 cm) long and are white, red, or purple. The fruit is a capsule. Family: *Droseraceae.*

sundial An instrument that indicates the time by the direction or length of the shadow cast by an indicator (gnomon) mounted on a calibrated hour scale. Sundials may be fixed (mounted perpendicularly or horizontally) or portable (in which case they incorporate a device for direction finding) and come in a wide range of shapes. Known from ancient Egypt, Greece, and Rome, sundials reached the peak of their popularity between about 1500 and 1800, being used as a check on the accuracy of mechanical *clocks, which eventually superseded them.

Sundsvall 62 22N 17 20E A port in E Sweden, on the Gulf of Bothnia. It is icebound in winter. Industries include timber processing and timber and wood pulp are the main exports. Population (1986 est): 93,000.

sunfish An omnivorous fish of the family *Molidae*, especially *Mola mola*, found in all tropical and temperate seas. It has a disk-shaped laterally flattened body, up to 10 ft (3 m) long, with the tail fin reduced to a wavy frill attached to the triangular dorsal and anal fins. Order: *Tetraodontiformes*.

The name is also applied to several carnivorous freshwater food and game fish of the North American family *Centrarchidae*. They have deep laterally flattened bodies, 1–32 in (2.5–80 cm) long, and a single long dorsal fin. Order: *Perciformes*.

sunflower A herbaceous plant of the genus *Helianthus*, native to North and South America but widely cultivated for its showy flowers. A popular annual sunflower is the giant *H. annuus*, about 10 ft (3 m) high with rough hairy leaves and yellow flower heads, up to 14 in (35 cm) in diameter. It is cultivated both for ornament and for its seeds, from which oil is obtained. Perennial sunflowers include *H. salicifolius* and *H. decapetalus*. Family: **Compositae*.

Sung. *See* Song.

Sungari River. *See* Songhua River.

sunn An annual herb, *Crotalaria juncea*, cultivated in India for its stem fibers—called sunn hemp or sann hemp. It grows to a height of 7–10 ft (2–3 m) and produces small yellow flowers that give rise to seed pods, at which stage the crop is cut. The fibers, comparable in strength to true *hemp, are used for netting, canvas, yarns, and in certain paper products. Family: **Leguminosae*.

Sunnites (*or* Sunni; Arabic *sunna*: custom) The name of the larger of the two main Muslim sects. In contrast to the *Shiite Muslims, the Sunnites accept the first three caliphs as Mohammed's legitimate successors. They are strictly orthodox in their obedience to the Koran and in the emphasis they place on following the deeds and utterances of the Prophet. They form the majority party in most Islamic countries except Iran.

Sunnyvale 37 23N 122 01W A city in W central California, SE of San Francisco. Settled in 1849, the aeronautic, aerospace, and electronic industries are now important to the economy. Other industries include chemicals and food processing. Population (1990): 117,229.

sun spider A large *arachnid (0.4–2 in [10–50 mm] long), also called sun scorpion, belonging to an order (*Solpugida* or *Solifugae*; 800 species) found in tropical and semitropical deserts. It has a hairy spiderlike body, usually golden in color, and a large powerful pair of pincers. Sun spiders are voracious carnivores, the larger species even killing small vertebrates.

sunspots Comparatively dark markings on the sun's *photosphere, typically a few thousand kilometers across with the central region being darkest and coolest. They tend to occur in groups. They are centers of intense localized magnetic fields, the majority forming and disappearing within two weeks. The number of sunspots seen in a year, and their mean solar latitude, varies in a cycle of about 11 years, known as the **sunspot cycle**.

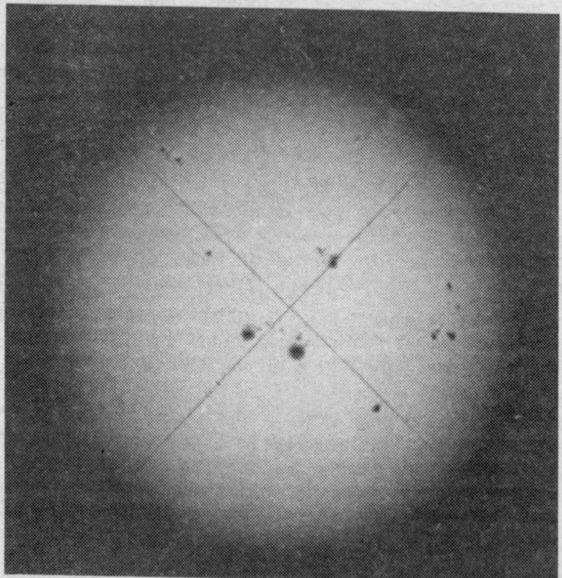

SUNSPOTS *The sun photographed using white light on Apr 9 1970.*

sunstroke A form of *heatstroke caused by overexposure to the sun. **Sunburn** is damage to the skin resulting from overexposure to the sun's rays. This may vary from slight reddening to large painful blisters: fair-skinned people are more susceptible to sunburn due to lack of the protective pigment melanin in the surface layers of the skin. The burn is treated with soothing creams.

Sun Yat-sen (*or* Sun Zhong Shan; 1866–1925) Chinese revolutionary. He qualified as a doctor but abandoned a medical career to pursue his political interests. After an abortive attempt to overthrow the Qing dynasty in 1895, he lived in exile and, while in Britain, was briefly imprisoned in the Chinese legation (1896). After establishing various revolutionary groups in Europe, he founded the Alliance Society in Japan (1905). Following the 1911 Chinese Revolution he returned to China and became president of the new republic but resigned almost immediately in favor of *Yuan Shi Kai. In 1913 Sun led an unsuccessful revolt against Yuan's dictatorial government and again left China. He returned after Yuan's death (1916) and in 1923 became president of a government based at Canton. Coming under Soviet influence he reorganized the *Guomindang (Nationalist People's party), cooperated with the communists, and elaborated his political thought, which was based on Three Principles of the People—nationalism, democracy, and social reform. He remains a hero of both the Nationalist and communist Chinese governments.

superconductivity A phenomenon in which the electrical resistance of certain metals (e.g. tin, zinc, and aluminum) vanishes when they are cooled to within a few degrees of *absolute zero. The temperature at which superconductivity occurs is called the transition temperature and varies for different metals. If a loop of a superconducting metal is placed in a weak magnetic field and cooled to below its transition temperature, a current will flow through the loop even when the field is removed. Known as the Meissner effect, this phenomenon is used to produce superconducting magnets.

supercooling The reduction in the temperature of a liquid below its freezing point without its solidification. The effect can only be achieved by slow and continuous cooling with pure liquids, since the presence of any solid matter would cause the liquid to solidify around it. A supercooled liquid is in a metastable state and any disturbance will cause solidification.

superego In *psychoanalysis, the part of the mind that acts as a moral conscience. It was believed by *Freud to result from the incorporation of the parent's instructions into a child's mind. *See also* ego; id.

superfluid A fluid that exhibits a very high thermal conductivity and virtually no friction at temperatures close to absolute zero. Such a fluid will flow up the sides and out of an open container. Liquid helium becomes a superfluid at 2.19 kelvins, called the lambda point.

supergiant The largest and most luminous type of star, bright enough to be visible in nearby galaxies. They are very rare. *Rigel, *Betelgeuse, and *Antares are examples.

superheated steam Dry steam that has been heated to a temperature above 212°F (100°C). It is widely used as a working medium for converting heat into mechanical energy, for which purpose it is more efficient than normal steam.

superheterodyne A system widely used in radio receivers; the incoming radio-frequency signal is combined with a locally generated carrier wave to give an intermediate frequency between radio- and audio-frequency (*see* modulation). The intermediate frequency is easier to amplify than radio-frequency, giving less noisy reception and better tuning.

Superior, Lake The largest of the Great Lakes in North America and one of the largest freshwater lakes in the world, situated between the US and Canada.

Its surrounding areas have valuable mineral resources and the lake is important for shipping (especially iron ore and grain). Area: 31,800 sq mi (82,362 sq km).

supernova A cataclysmic stellar explosion, seen as a sudden increase in a *star's brightness by a million times or more. It results from uncontrolled nuclear reactions in certain massive stars, late in their evolution. Most or all of the star's substance is blown off at high velocity, forming an expanding gas shell—the **supernova remnant**. If the star's core survives, it will most probably end up as a *neutron star or *black hole. *See also* Crab nebula.

superphosphates Highly active phosphorus-containing fertilizers. Single superphosphate is made by reacting sulfuric acid with insoluble calcium phosphate rock to form calcium sulfate and soluble calcium hydrogen phosphate $Ca(H_2PO_4)_2$. Often the process is carried out under pressure. The product also contains sulfates of impurities present in the calcium phosphate. Triple superphosphate is more concentrated, since phosphoric acid is used instead of sulfuric, thereby creating fewer by-products.

Suppiluliumas I King of the *Hittites (c. 1375–c. 1335 BC); founder of the Hittite empire. He subdued the Mitanni kingdom and conquered N Syria, displacing the Egyptians, then ruled by Akhenaton (*see also* Ankhesenamen). Suppiluliumas rebuilt the Hittite capital Hattusas (*see* Boğazköy).

supply and demand Two concepts fundamental to economics. Supply is the amount of a commodity that producers are willing and able to sell, while demand is that amount that consumers wish to and are able to buy. These amounts vary with price: as the price rises, producers wish to sell more, while consumers wish to buy less, and vice versa as the price goes down. There is one price (the equilibrium price) at which producers wish to sell the same amount as consumers wish to buy (i.e. the market clears). The **market forces** of supply and demand in a free economy thus control the market price. However, they are almost completely suppressed in communist economies and in *mixed economies they may have only a restricted effect, depending on the extent to which government policy influences supply, demand, or price.

suprematism An abstract Russian art movement founded (c. 1913) by the painter *Malevich. It was the first and one of the most austere geometrical styles of the 20th century. Although Malevich declared in 1919 that suprematism was over, it continued to be influential in the 1920s, particularly at the *Bauhaus (*see also* Kandinsky).

Supreme Court of the United States The highest judicial body in the US, consisting of a chief justice and eight associate justices, each of whom is appointed by the president for life. The Supreme Court, as one of the three autonomous branches of the federal government, is empowered to review the constitutionality of federal and state legislation with regard to individual rights and court procedures. The Supreme Court itself was authorized by Article III of the US *Constitution, but its organization and procedures were first established by the Judiciary Act of 1789. The nine-member composition of the court has remained constant since 1869. Although the Supreme Court's function in the early history of the United States was unclear, it became an important force for expansion of federal power during the term of Chief Justice John *Marshall (*see* Marbury v. Madison, Dartmouth College v. Woodward, and McCulloch v. Maryland). In the years before the Civil War, the court upheld the institution of slavery (*see* Dred Scott v. Sanford) and at the end of the 19th century, it upheld the practice of racial segregation (*see* Plessy v. Ferguson), but beginning in the 1950s it reversed its earlier position and became a protector of the civil rights of minority groups (*see* Brown v. Board of Education) and of defendants in criminal proceedings (*see* Gideon v. Wainwright and Miranda v. Arizona). Many of the liberal rulings of the court under Chief Justice Earl *Warren were later restricted by the justices of the more conservative court headed by Chief Justice Warren *Burger. Throughout its entire history, the Supreme Court was composed of male justices, but in 1981 Pres. Ronald Reagan broke that precedent by appointing Sandra Day *O'Connor to become the first woman justice on the Supreme Court.

Sur. *See* Tyre.

Surabaja 7 14S 112 45E A port in Indonesia, in E Java on the Mas estuary. It was bombed by the British in 1945 during the struggle for the Indonesian Republic. It is Indonesia's second largest city and chief naval base, with a naval college and university (1954). Its industries include ship building, oil refining, and rubber processing. Population (1980): 2,027,913.

Surakarta (*or* Solo) 7 32S 110 50E A city in Indonesia, in central Java on the Solo River. A cultural center noted for its shadow plays, it is the site of a sultan's palace (1745). Batiks, musical instruments, and gold objects are produced. Population (1980): 469,888.

Surat 21 10N 72 54E A city in India, in Gujarat on the Tapti River. It was the Mogul Empire's chief port (16th–17th centuries). The first British trading post was established there (1612) and it was the headquarters of the East India Company until 1687. It has textile industries. Population (1991): 1,496,943.

surface tension A force occurring on the surface of a liquid that makes it behave as if the surface has an elastic skin. It is caused by forces between the molecules of the liquid: only those at the surface experience forces from below, whereas those in the interior are acted on by intermolecular forces from all sides. Surface tension causes a meniscus to form, liquids to rise up capillary tubes, paper to absorb water, and droplets and bubbles to form. It is defined as the force acting tangentially to the surface on one side of a line of unit length (newtons per meter) or as the work required to produce unit increase in surface area (joules per square meter).

surfactant A substance that lowers the surface tension of a liquid, thus allowing easier penetration and spreading. For this reason they are often known as **wetting agents**. Surfactants active in water are usually organic substances, for example *alcohols, and *soaps, the molecules of which contain both a water-soluble and a water-repelling portion; it is the latter that forces the molecules to the surface. Surfactants are widely used in *detergents, emulsifiers, paints, adhesives, inks, etc.

surgeonfish A tropical marine fish, also called tang, belonging to the family *Acanthuridae* (about 100 species). Its deep laterally flattened body, up to about 20 in (50 cm) long, is often brightly colored, with a single long dorsal fin, and a sharp bladelike spine on each side of the tail. They feed mainly on algae. Order: *Perciformes*.

surgery The branch of medicine in which disorders and injuries are treated by operation, usually with the patient in a state of *anesthesia. Amputations and some elementary surgical operations have been performed since ancient times in Egypt, Greece, India, and China; the skills required were transmitted by Arab surgeons to Europe, where they were mostly practiced in monasteries. Bloodletting—regarded as an antidote for most ailments—was widely practiced.

The 19th century saw the foundation of modern surgery, with the introduction of anesthetics, *Lister's discovery of antisepsis, and a greater knowledge of anatomy and physiology. In the 20th century the advent of antibiotics has made surgery safe from infection, the use of blood transfusions, intravenous drips, and electrolyte control have overcome problems of shock, and better knowledge of anesthetics and relaxant drugs has made surgery a less hurried procedure. Moreover, specialization (e.g. gastrointestinal surgery, neurosurgery, ophthalmological surgery) and great ingenuity in the design of surgical instruments have made surgery a safe and usually successful procedure.

Recent advances include techniques in *transplantation surgery, operations on the exposed heart, the use of extreme cold to destroy tissues (cryosurgery), the use of *lasers and *ultrasonics, and the development of microsurgery, in which surgeons operate through a special microscope using miniaturized instruments. *See also* plastic surgery.

Suriname, Republic of (name until 1948: Dutch Guiana) A country on the N coast of South America, on the Atlantic Ocean. Much of the land is covered by tropical forest, with coastal plains rising to higher land in the interior. The majority of the population is of Indian and mixed descent, with minorities of African descent, East Indians, and others. *Economy*: based primarily on bauxite, the chief industry is aluminum processing, and bauxite, alumina, and aluminum comprise the main exports. Its great agricultural potential remains relatively underdeveloped, the rice industry being the only fully developed sector. The vast forests are largely unexploited. Fishing is important, especially for shrimps. Hydroelectricity is a valuable source of power. *History*: sighted by Columbus in 1498, the first permanent settlement was established by the English in 1650. It was ceded to the Netherlands in 1667. During the Revolutionary and Napoleonic Wars it was again (1799–1802, 1804–16) under British rule. In 1949 it gained a certain measure of self-government, subsequently becoming an autonomous part of the Netherlands (1954) and then an independent republic (1975). At independence some 40,000 Surinamers emigrated to the Netherlands, to the detriment of Suriname's economy. Following a coup in 1980, the National Military Council took power with Dr. Hendrick R. Chin A Sen as prime minister and later president. His government resigned in 1982. The National Military Council then announced a new administration and succeeded in maintaining power. Relations between Suriname and Netherlands were virtually suspended. Civilian government was restored in a 1987 constitution, and Ramsewak Shankar became president in 1988. He was ousted by the military in 1990. A special assembly elected Ronald Venetiaan to the presidency in 1991. A seven-year internal rebellion was ended by treaty in 1992. Official language: Dutch; English, Hindustani, and Javanese are widely spoken and the local vernacular, Surinamese, is used as a lingua franca. Official currency: Suriname guilder of 100 cents. Area: 63,020 sq mi (163,265 sq km). Population (1990): 408,000. Capital and main port: Paramaribo.

Surratt, Mary Eugenia (1820–65) US coconspirator in the assassination plot against Pres. Abraham *Lincoln. She owned a boarding house in Washington, D.C., where it is thought assassination plans, of which her son was a part, were discussed. Because of this association, she was tried and found guilty by a civil jury; she was hanged in 1865.

surrealism A European movement in art and literature of the 1920s and 1930s. Surrealism began as a literary movement, when its leader, the poet André *Breton, published the surrealist manifesto in Paris (1924). Unlike its predecessor, the *dada movement, surrealism was not anti-art. Instead it aimed, under the influence of *Freud, to embody in art and poetry the irrational forces of dreams and the subconscious mind. To achieve this, such new techniques as automatic drawing and writing were employed. These involved allowing the subconscious mind to guide the pencil or the thoughts to produce an unpremediated design or poem. The leading surrealists were the poets *Aragon and *Eluard and the painters *Ernst, *Miró, *Dali, *Magritte, *Delvaux, and *Tanguy.

Surrey A county in SE England, bordering on Greater London. It is mainly low lying with the North Downs running E–W across the middle of the county. Although it has developed primarily as a residential and recreational area, agriculture is important in the S. Industry is mainly concentrated in the NE. Area: 639 sq mi (1655 sq km). Population (1987): 1,000,000. Administrative center: Kingston-upon-Thames.

Surtsey 63 18N 20 37W An island in the N Atlantic Ocean off S Iceland. It was formed by an underwater volcanic eruption (1963). Many scientific studies have been made here, especially of the colonization of flora and fauna.

surveying The measurement of distances, levels, angles, etc., on, above, or below the earth's surface. It is necessary for the delineation of property lines (**boundary surveying**) and for planning the construction of almost any building or structure. **Plane surveying** is suitable for smaller areas as it neglects the earth's curvature, whereas **geodetic surveying** does not. Topographic surveys locate natural features and elevations for map making, dam planning, etc.

Surya In Hindu mythology, the sun-god. He appears as a major deity in the **Vedas* and remained prominent as patron of numerous Hindu royal dynasties. Like his Greek counterpart *Apollo, he is represented as a charioteer.

Susa (*or* Shushan) An ancient city in SW Iran. Occupied since the 4th millenium BC, it was a capital of *Elam, whose rulers made successful forays against *Ur and *Babylon during the 2nd millennium. Susa's heyday was as administrative capital of the *Achaemenian kings of Persia (521–331). It continued to be important under Seleucid, Parthian, and Sassanian rule.

Suslov, Mikhail (1902–82) Soviet politician. A Communist party member from 1921, Suslov rose in the party hierarchy during the 1930s and 1940s. He fought all deviation from Soviet policy, especially that of Yugoslavia in 1948. In 1964 he helped to oust *Khrushchev.

Susquehanna River A river in the E US. It rises in Otsego Lake in central New York State and flows mainly S through Pennsylvania before entering Chesapeake Bay. It caused serious flooding in 1972 to several cities, especially *Harrisburg. Length: 444 mi (715 km).

Sutherland, Graham Vivian (1903–80) British artist. After working primarily as an etcher and engraver he turned to painting in 1935, specializing in disturbing landscapes, usually magnifying insect and plant forms, and scenes of desolation. Also well known are his *Crucifixion* (1946), his tapestry for Coventry Cathedral, and his portraits, e.g. that of Somerset Maugham and his controversial portrait of Winston Churchill.

Sutherland, Joan (1926–) Australian operatic soprano. She established her reputation at Covent Garden in 1959 in the title role of Donizetti's *Lucia di Lammermoor*. She specializes in coloratura roles.

Sutlej River A river in India and Pakistan, the longest of the five rivers of the Punjab. Rising in SW Tibet, it flows mainly SW across the Punjab plain into Pakistan, where it joins the Chenab River. It is an important source of irrigation and hydroelectric power. Length: 850 mi (1368 km).

suttee An ancient Hindu custom of self-immolation of widows on their husbands' funeral pyres. It was officially abolished in India by the British in 1829.

Sutter, Johann Augustus (1803–80) US pioneer; born in Germany. He came to the US in 1834 and traveled westward, finally settling in California

(1839). There, he became a Mexican citizen and established Sutter's Fort. Gold, discovered on his land shortly before California became part of the US, precipitated the Gold Rush of 1848, and Sutter, unable legally to keep the squatters from his land, was financially ruined.

Sutton, Walter Stanborough (1877–1916) US geneticist, who linked observations of chromosome behavior during cell division with *Mendel's observations of inheritance of physical characteristics. Sutton postulated that chromosomes carried the units of inheritance (genes) and that their behavior during sex cell formation (meiosis) explained some of Mendel's findings.

Sutton Coldfield 52 34N 1 48W A city in England, in West Midlands, a mainly residential suburb of Birmingham. It contains Sutton Park, a large area of woodland, lakes, and heathland. Population (1981): 86,494.

Sutton Hoo The site of a Saxon ship burial near Woodbridge, in Suffolk (E England). Excavations in 1939 revealed the remnants of a 38-oar boat containing a magnificent treasure hoard: gilt bronze helmet, sword decorated with gold and garnets, royal scepter, silver dishes, drinking vessels, and jewelry. The mound is thought to be a cenotaph (as it contained no body) to King Raedwald (died c. 625 AD).

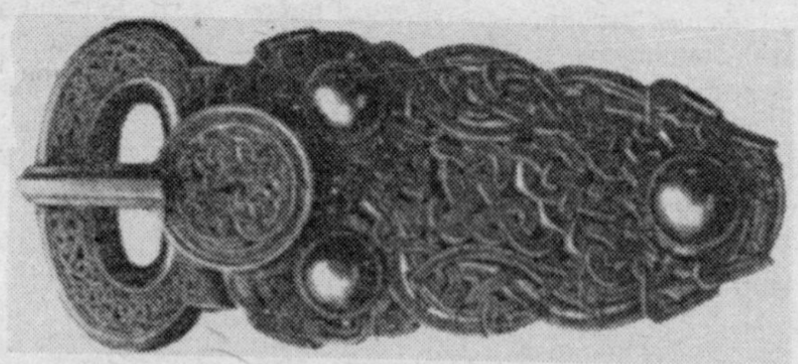

SUTTON HOO *A large inlaid gold buckle found in the burial ship.*

Suva 18 08S 178 25E The capital of Fiji, on the S coast of Viti Levu. Its industries include tourism and the production of coconut oil and soap. The University of the South Pacific was established there in 1968. Population (1986): 69,665.

Suvorov, Aleksandr Vasilievich, Count (1729–1800) Russian field marshal. Following outstanding victories against the French revolutionary armies in Italy (1799), the defeat of a Russian force at Zurich forced his withdrawal. The winter retreat, achieved against desperate odds, assured Suvorov's reputation as a brilliant tactician.

Suwanee River (*or* Swanee R.) A river in the SE US, flowing from the Okefenokee Swamp in SE Georgia across Florida to the Gulf of Mexico. It is the Swanee River of the well-known song by Stephen Foster. Length: 200 mi (400 km).

Suzhou (Su-chou *or* Soochow) 31 21N 120 40E A city in E China, in Jiangsu province on the Yangtze delta and the *Grand Canal. Famed for its many beautiful canals and gardens, it is a center of culture and handicrafts. Founded in about 484 BC, it prospered, especially between the 14th and 19th centuries, as a result of its silk industry. The chief industry is still textiles. Population (1990): 706,459.

Svalbard (*or* Spitsbergen) A Norwegian archipelago in the Arctic Ocean, the chief islands being Spitsbergen (formerly Vestspitsbergen), Edgeøya, Nordaustlandet, Barentsøya, and Prins Karls Forland. Following disputes over their sovereignty, they were granted to Norway in 1920. Mountainous and covered largely by icefields and glaciers their major importance is as a source of coal; other minerals include asbestos and copper. Area: 23,958 sq mi (62,050 sq km). Chief town: Longyearbyen.

Sverdlovsk (name until 1924: Ekaterinburg) 56 52N 60 35E A city in NW Russia. Nicholas II and his family were executed there in 1918. It is a major industrial and cultural center, with engineering, metallurgical, and chemical industries and many educational institutions. Population: (1987): 1,331,000.

Sverrir (*or* Sigurdsson; c. 1149–1202) King of Norway (1177–1202). He claimed the throne after being informed by his mother that he was the son of a former king, but did not defeat his predecessor, Magnus V (1156–84; reigned 1162–84), until 1184. His story is told in the Icelandic *Sverris Saga*.

Svevo, Italo (Ettore Schmitz; 1861–1928) Italian novelist. His first two novels, *A Life* (1892) and *As a Man Grows Older* (1898), were unsuccessful, but he was encouraged by James *Joyce, who taught him English in Trieste in 1907 and later publicized his work. His best-known novel is *Confessions of Zeno* (1923), a portrait of an introspective ineffectual hero.

Swabia (German name: Schwaben) A former region in SW Germany now divided between Germany, Switzerland, and France. Swabia became one of the leading German duchies in the Middle Ages, passing in 1079 to the *Hohenstaufen. When the dynasty died out in 1268 Swabia was divided among local noble families. A series of Swabian leagues culminated in that of 1488–1534, which foundered on religious differences during the Reformation. When Napoleon reconstructed European boundaries in 1807, Swabia was finally partitioned among neighboring states; its distinguishing dialect still survives.

Swahili (*or* Kiswahili) A Bantu language of East Africa and the lingua franca of Tanzania, Kenya, Zaïre, and Uganda. There are three main dialects but standard Swahili is based on the Zanzibari form known as Kiunguja. It has been much influenced by Arabic.

swallow A songbird belonging to a cosmopolitan family (*Hirundidae*; 78 species) of acrobatic fliers that catch insects on the wing. Swallows are 4–9 in (10–22 cm) long, with short necks, long pointed wings, short legs, and often forked tails. All temperate swallows migrate to hot climates for the winter. The barn swallow (*Hirundo rustica*) visits Europe and North America in summer and has a glossy blue-black upper plumage with a red forehead and throat, a blue breast band, and white underparts. *See also* martin.

swallowtail butterfly A *papilionid butterfly having long swallowlike tails on the hindwings. Many species are tropical and brightly colored, with the sexes often of different colors. The caterpillars feed on a variety of plants and possess scent organs behind the head, giving off a strong odor if the caterpillar is disturbed. □insect.

Swammerdam, Jan (1637–80) Dutch naturalist and microscopist, who first observed red blood cells. However, much of Swammerdam's work was concerned with collecting and studying insects, describing their anatomy and life histories, and classifying them into four groups, three of which are still embodied in modern classification systems. He discovered the Swammerdam valves in lymphatic vessels and established that muscles do not change in volume during contraction.

swamp An area of permanently water-saturated land, usually covered with such vegetation as reeds or mangroves. It is an intermediate stage between an entirely aquatic environment and a temporarily saturated marsh. Once drained, swamps produce fertile soils as a result of their high humus content.

swamp cypress A deciduous conifer, *Taxodium distichum*, also called bald cypress, native to swampy regions of the SE US and grown for its timber and as an ornamental. In waterlogged soils its roots produce domed "knees," which protrude above the water and probably help in respiration. Up to 150 ft (45 m) high, it has soft needles arranged in two rows and globular cones, 1 in (2.5 cm) across and brown when ripe. Family: *Taxodiaceae*.

swamp eel A slim eel-like bony fish of the order *Synbranchiformes*, unrelated to true eels and found in fresh and brackish tropical waters, 8–20 in (20–50 cm) long, they have no pectoral fins and the gills often have only one opening. Oxygen is sometimes absorbed through the throat or intestine. Swamp eels are used for food in Asia.

swan A large waterbird belonging to a genus (*Cygnus*; 7–8 species) occurring worldwide on fresh waters or sheltered coasts and estuaries; 40–63 in (100–160 cm) long, swans are usually white with black legs and have large feet, a long neck, and a powerful spatulate bill, which they use to feed on underwater plants. Immature swans have a mottled brown plumage until about two years old. *See also* black swan; mute swan; trumpeter. Family: *Anatidae* (ducks, geese, swans).

Swanscombe skull Fossil cranial remains of a *hominid, fragments of which were found at Swanscombe in Kent (England) in River Thames gravels (1935, 1936). It seems to be an early example of *Homo sapiens* dating from about 200,000 years ago. *See* Homo.

Swansea (Welsh name: Abertawe) 51 38N 3 57W A city and port in South Wales, on Swansea Bay. It is a major industrial center with tinplate manufacturing, chemicals, and oil refining. The main exports are coal and coke, steel rails, iron work, tinplate, and oil. Swansea University opened in 1920. Population (1981): 167,796.

swastika An ancient symbol of uncertain origin, generally held to signify prosperity and creativity. It is a cross, the four arms of which are deflected at right angles either clockwise or anticlockwise. It has been revered by Buddhists, Hindus, Celts, and North American Indians. The Nazis adopted the symbol, mistakenly believing it to be of pure Aryan origins.

Swatow. *See* Shantou.

Swazi A Bantu-speaking people who occupy Swaziland and adjacent areas of the E Transvaal (South Africa). They are an agricultural and pastoral people, traditionally ruled by a hereditary paramount chief together with his mother. Descent, inheritance, and group membership are patrilineal. Polygyny is practiced by senior men, the chief taking many wives who are dispersed in a number of royal villages throughout the territory. *Age-set organization was the basis of military service. Traditionally *ancestor worship, witchcraft, and magic were features of religious life.

Swaziland, Kingdom of A small country in SE Africa between South Africa and Mozambique. It consists of three distinct regions extending N–S: the Highveld in the W, the Middleveld in the center, and the Lowveld in the E (*see* veld). *Economy*: chiefly agricultural, the main food crop being maize. The chief cash crop is sugar; other crops include rice, citrus fruit, and cotton, and livestock raising is also important. Rich mineral resources include iron ore, asbestos, and coal, and hydroelectric plants provide irrigation as well as power. Exports include sugar, wood pulp, and asbestos. *History*: the *Swazi occupied the area in the late

18th century. It became a South African protectorate in 1894 and, in 1902, after the Boer War it came under British rule. It attained internal self-government in 1967 and became an independent kingdom within the British Commonwealth in 1968. In 1973, King Sobhuza II increased his personal power and, in the new constitution (1978), political parties were banned. With the death of Sobhuza II in 1982, a power struggle erupted within the royal family; Prince Bhekimpi Diamini emerged as head of state. In 1986, Crown Prince Makhosetive became King Mswati III. Subsequently controversy arose over South Africa's offer to turn over two black homelands to Swaziland. Conservative elements in Swaziland backed South Africa and cooperated with counterinsurgency efforts against the African National Congress, a guerrilla force that sought the overthrow of the South African government. Official languages: Siswati and English. Official currency: emalangeni of 100 lilangeni; South African currency is also legal tender. Area: 6705 sq mi (17,400 sq km). Population (1990): 779,000. Capital: Mbabane; Lomamba is the royal and projected legislative capital.

sweat (*or* perspiration) A watery fluid, consisting mainly of sodium chloride and urea in solution, that is secreted by the sweat glands in the □skin. Sweating is a means of excreting nitrogenous waste products, but it is also, and more importantly, a means of temperature regulation. Evaporation of sweat from the skin surface has a cooling effect; therefore in hot weather, or when the individual feels hot through exercise, more sweat is produced. Sweating is also increased by nervousness and nausea; it is decreased by colds.

sweating sickness An illness that devastated Renaissance Europe in several epidemics. It was characterized by copious sweating, high fever, pains in the extremities and over the heart, and breathlessness and was often fatal. It may have been a severe form of *influenza.

swede. *See* rutabaga.

Sweden, Kingdom of (Swedish name: Sverige) A country in N Europe occupying the E part of the Scandinavian peninsula. It borders on the Gulf of Bothnia and the Baltic Sea in the E and S and on the Kattegat and Skagerrak in the SW. Undulating land in the S rises to mountains in the N. There are numerous lakes and approximately half the country is forested. *Economy*: rich in mineral resources, notably iron ore, which forms the basis of the country's heavy industry (metalworking, steel, machinery, and chemicals) and is a major export. Other minerals include copper and zinc. Hydroelectric sources provide 70% of the power. The large forests support important pulp and paper industries as well as ship building. There is a thriving fishing industry. Agricultural activities are concentrated in the S, the principal crops being barley, wheat, oats, and potatoes, although there is some livestock raising in the N. *History*: the area was inhabited from early times by German tribes, the Swedes in the N and the Goths in the S, and its people participated in the exploits of the Vikings. Christianity was introduced in the 9th century but not established until the 12th century. Finland was acquired in the 13th century and the 14th century witnessed the Kalmar Union of Sweden with Denmark and Norway. Independence was achieved in 1523 under Gustavus I Vasa, during whose reign Lutheranism was introduced, and in the 17th century, under Gustavus Adolphus, Sweden emerged from the *Thirty Years' War as a major European power, a position undermined by the Great *Northern War (1700–21). In 1809, during the Napoleonic Wars, Finland was surrendered to Russia. In 1814 Norway was ceded to Sweden, the two countries remaining united until 1905, and in 1818, with the extinction of the *Vasa dynasty, a Frenchman, *Bernadotte, became Charles XIV John. Sweden remained neutral in both world wars, and for four decades (1932–76) was governed by the Social Democrats, during which time a highly developed welfare state was developed. On the accession of Carl XVI Gustaf in 1975 a new constitution considerably reduced the power of the monarchy. In 1976 a center-right government led by Thorbjörn Fälldin came to power. This resigned in 1978 but Fälldin was returned as prime minister in 1979. The Social Democrats led by Olof Palme were returned to power in the 1982 elections. The country was shocked in 1986 by the assassination of Prime Minister Palme, who was succeeded by Ingvar Carlsson. He resigned in 1991 after parliamentary elections weakened his party's hold on the majority. Moderate party leader Carl Bildt became the first non-Social Democrat in 60 years and the first conservative prime minister in 63 years. Official language: Swedish. Official currency: krona of 100 oere. Area: 158,830 sq mi (411,479 sq km). Population (1990 est): 8,407,000. Capital and main port: Stockholm.

Swedenborg, Emanuel (1688–1772) Swedish scientist, mystic, and philosopher. He did pioneering scientific work in such fields as magnetic theory and crystallography but later became more concerned to show by scientific and logical analysis that the universe was of spiritual origin. After 1743 his ideas became more mystically orientated in accordance with the visions that he claimed to have had. His work includes *Arcana Coelestia* (1756), *The New Jerusalem and Its Heavenly Doctrine* (1758), and *Divine Love and Wisdom* (1763). The sect calling itself the New Jerusalem Church was founded by his followers in London in 1787.

Swedish A language belonging to the *Scandinavian branch of the North *Germanic group. It is the official language of Sweden and is spoken by a minority of the population of Finland, where it is also officially recognized. The standard literary form is based mainly on the dialect of Stockholm known as Svea.

sweet briar A stiffly branched prickly fragrant *rose, *Rosa rubiginosa* (or *R. eglanteria*), also called eglantine. Found in scrub and chalk grassland across the N hemisphere, it grows to a height of 7 ft (2 m) and has bright pink flowers.

sweet gale A widely distributed shrub, *Myrica gale*, also called bog myrtle, that grows to a height of 24–100 in (60–250 cm) in bogs and wet heaths. It produces reddish-brown catkins and the leaves yield an aromatic resin used in medicines. Family: *Myricaceae*.

sweet gum A tree, *Liquidambar styraciflua*, native to E North America. Up to 150 ft (45 m) high, it has triangular-lobed leaves, small greenish flowers, and spiky fruits and yields a useful timber (satin walnut). The oriental sweet gum (*L. orientalis*), of SW Asia, is the chief source of *storax, a fragrant balsam. Family: *Hamamelidaceae*.

sweet pea An annual climbing herb, *Lathyrus odoratus*, native to Sicily and widely cultivated as a garden ornamental. The scented flower consists of a large petal (the standard) with two lateral wing petals and a front keel petal. Many color varieties have been developed, including shades of red, purple, blue, white, and yellow. The fruit is a hairy pod, about 2 in (5 cm) long. Family: **Leguminosae*.

sweet potato An annual herb, *Ipomoea batatas*, native to tropical America and widely cultivated for its starchy edible tubers (swollen roots), which are reddish-brown with white or orange flesh. The trailing stems bear pinkish flowers and, after a growing season of 4–5 months, the tubers are lifted and cooked like potatoes or yams. Family: *Convolvulaceae*.

sweetsop A small tree, *Annona squamosa*, also called sugar apple, native to tropical America and cultivated for its yellowish-green edible fruits. The yellow flesh is soft and sweet and makes a tasty dessert. Family: *Annonaceae*.

sweet william A usually biennial herb, *Dianthus barbatus*, native to S Europe and widely cultivated as a garden ornamental. Growing to a height of 12–27.5 in (30–70 cm), sweet williams produce dense flower heads, colored red or pink in the wild but of various shades and patterns in cultivated varieties. Family: *Caryophyllaceae*.

Sweyn I Forkbeard (d. 1014) King of Denmark (c. 986–1014). After conquering Norway in 1000, Sweyn's regular raids on SE England to avenge Ethelred's massacre of Danes in 1002 culminated in an invasion in the course of which he died. He was the father of *Canute II.

swift A bird belonging to a widely distributed family (*Apodidae*; 75 species); 3.5–9 in (9–23 cm) long, swifts have gray or brown plumage with white markings; a wide slightly curved bill, and forked tail. With scimitar-shaped wings and a high-speed flight that may reach nearly 70 mph (110 kph), they spend much of their time flying, capturing insects and even mating and sleeping on the wing. Order: *Apodiformes* (swifts, hummingbirds, etc.).

Swift and Company v. United States (1905) US Supreme Court decision that upheld the *Sherman Anti-Trust Act. Meat-packing companies, accused of creating a monopoly by price fixing and restraining sales, claimed exemption from antitrust laws because these practices occurred within one state, not interstate. The Court ruled that the implications reached far outside the boundaries of one state, and, therefore, laws regulating interstate commerce applied.

Swift, Jonathan (1667–1745) Anglo-Irish clergyman, poet, and satirist. Born in Dublin, he became an Anglican priest in 1695. In England he met Hester Johnson (1681–1728), the "Stella" of his letters recounting his life in London and later collected as *Journal to Stella* (1710–13). He was also close to Esther Vanhomrigh (1690–1723), whom he called "Vanessa" in his writings. While in England, he wrote the satire *A Tale of a Tub* (1704). He became the leading Tory political journalist and was appointed dean of St Patrick's, Dublin, in 1713. After the accession of George I in 1714, he returned to Dublin, where he wrote his satirical masterpiece, *Gulliver's Travels* (1726), the story of an imaginary voyage.

swiftlet A small *swift belonging to a genus (*Collocalia*; 15–20 species) occurring in SE Asia and Australia; 3.5–6 in (9–15 cm) long, swiftlets use echolocation to navigate in the caves where they nest; their nests, made chiefly of saliva, are the main ingredient of bird's nest soup.

swift moth A moth belonging to the widely distributed family *Hepialidae* (about 300 species), also called ghost moth. The adults lack a proboscis and are unable to feed. The caterpillars feed underground on roots and the pupae are soft-skinned and active, moving to the surface before the adults emerge.

swimming Moving through water by means of leg and arm strokes, popular for recreation and sport. Major competitive events, held in pools 55 yd (50 m) long, include freestyle races (the crawl—invented in Australia—is invariably used) over 100, 200, 400, 800, and 1500 m and the 4 × 100 m and 4 × 200 m relay; breaststroke, butterfly, and backstroke races over 100 and 200 m; and medley races over 200 and 400 m and 4 × 100 m relay. The most popular marathon swim is across the English Channel (first swum in 1875).

Swinburne, Algernon Charles (1837–1909) British poet. His poetry, especially in the first volume of *Poems and Ballads* (1866), is characterized by sensuous flowing rhythms and imagery. He supported republican movements in Europe and rebelled against conventional British morality. His alcoholism led to the collapse of his health, and from 1879 he was cared for by his friend, the critic Theodore Watts-Dunton (1832–1914).

Swindon 51 34N 1 47W A city in S England, in Wiltshire. It developed around the workshops of the former Great Western Railroad and has a railroad museum. Population (1981): 91,136.

swine fever An infectious virus disease of pigs also known as hog cholera. In young pigs the disease is usually acute, with fever, loss of appetite, lethargy, diarrhea, and distressed breathing, resulting in death. In older pigs the symptoms are less noticeable. Animals are treated with antibiotics to combat secondary infection.

swing A style of *jazz popular in the 1930s. The original jazz band was expanded to include the saxophone and additional cornets and trombones, making an average swing band of 15 players. Colorful orchestrations replaced the improvisational qualities of early jazz, and the swing bands of Benny Goodman, Duke Ellington, and Glenn Miller functioned chiefly as dance bands.

switch grass A perennial pasture *grass, *Panicum virgatum*, which is a major component of the North American prairie flora. It forms clumps, 40–80 in (1–2 m) tall, and is sometimes used to control erosion because of its penetrating underground stems.

Swithin, St (d. 862) English churchman. A counselor to Kings Egbert and Ethelwulf, he was appointed bishop of Winchester in 852. His tomb in Winchester Cathedral has become a famous shrine and according to legend the weather conditions on his feast day, July 15, continue for 40 days.

Switzerland, Confederation of (French name: Suisse; German name: Schweiz; Italian name: Svizzera) A small landlocked country in central Europe. Undulating land in the N rises to the Jura Mountains in the W and the high peaks of the Alps in the S, reaching heights of over 14,500 ft (4500 m). The Rhine River and Lake Constance form most of the N and E boundaries, while in the S the Rhône River flows through Lake Geneva to the French border. The majority of the population is German, with large French and Italian minorities; there is a very small Romansch population. *Economy*: although lacking in mineral wealth, Switzerland owes much of its prosperity to its terrain and central European position. The latter has led to its development as a center for trade, banking, and insurance, while the magnificent scenery has long been a major tourist attraction. The fast-flowing rivers of the Alps provide abundant hydroelectric power and heavy industries, such as engineering and chemicals, have been developed as well as the smaller traditional industries (watches and clocks, precision instruments, and jewelry). Agricultural products include dairy goods, grains, and fruit and vegetables, and there is an important wine industry. The principal exports are machinery, watches, chemicals, and textiles. *History*: its Celtic inhabitants (the Helvetii) were conquered by the Romans in the 1st century BC and the region was overrun by German tribes in the 5th century AD, becoming part of the Holy Roman Empire in the 10th century. In 1291 Uri, Schwyz, and Nidwalden formed the Everlasting League, which is traditionally regarded as the origin of the Swiss Federation. By 1499 the Federation had achieved virtual independence of the Empire and in the 16th century became an important center of the Reformation, notably under Zwingli in Zürich. In 1648, at the conclusion of the Thirty Years' War, its independence was formally recognized by the European powers. The French conquered Switzerland in 1798, establishing the Helvetian Republic, but after Napoleon's fall (1815) the Congress of Vienna guaranteed Swiss neutrality. Religious conflict led to war between Protestant and Roman Catholic cantons and a modified constitution (1848) by which Switzerland became a unified federal state. It maintained its neutrality through both world wars and has become the headquarters of many international organizations. Switzerland's postwar prosperity has been assisted by migrant workers (*see* migration, human), the repatriation of whom was rejected in a referendum in 1975. Another controversial issue was the enfranchisement of women, which was finally achieved in 1971. Switzerland is governed by a federal council composed of seven councillors, elected for four years, from whom a president and vice president are elected yearly. In the 1980s Switzerland, long a bastion for banking secrecy, began to allow suspect Swiss bank accounts to be opened to foreign investigators. Official languages: French, German, Italian, and Romansch. Official currency: Swiss franc of 100 centimes (*or* Rappen). Area: 15,941 sq mi (41,288 sq km). Population (1990 est): 6,628,000. Capital: Bern.

sword A weapon consisting of a cutting or stabbing blade on a short handle, used in hand-to-hand fighting. Of uncertain origin, the sword evolved in the Bronze Age. The Roman soldier's principal weapon was a short, two-edged, iron-bladed sword (*gladius*). In the Middle Ages heavier and longer swords, some needing to be wielded with two hands, developed in response to heavier armor. The advent of gunpowder forced foot soldiers gradually to abandon swords, but cavalry units until the 20th century fought with long, often curved blades. *See also* fencing.

swordfish A food and game fish, *Xiphias gladius*, related to tuna and found in all tropical and temperate seas. It has an elongated body, up to 15 ft (4.6 m) long, a triangular front dorsal fin, no pelvic fins, and an elongated swordlike snout used to slash at shoaling fish on which it feeds. It is the only member of its family (*Xiphiidae*).

swordtail A tropical freshwater fish of the genus *Xiphophorus*, especially *X. helleri.* It has an elongated body, up to 5 in (13 cm) long, and males have a long swordlike extension of the lower lobe of the tail fin. Swordtails are naturally green with a red strip on each side, but have been bred in many colors for aquariums. Family: *Poeciliidae*; order: *Atheriniformes.*

Sybaris 39 39N 16 20E A Greek settlement founded about 700 BC near present-day Terranova di Sibari in S Italy. Territorial expansion and a monopoly of Etruscan trade brought prosperity and Sybarites were famous for their luxurious lives (hence the word sybaritic, meaning pleasure seeking). In 510 and again in 457 Sybaris was destroyed by its neighbor Croton. Rebuilt a third time, its inhabitants were subsequently exiled by the Athenians.

sycamore A large *maple tree, *Acer pseudoplatanus*, native to central and S Europe and widely grown elsewhere. Up to 100 ft (30 m) tall, it has five-lobed leaves and produces clusters of winged □fruits. The wood is used for violin cases, carvings, and furniture.

Sydney 33 55S 151 10E The oldest and largest city in Australia, the capital of New South Wales, situated on *Port Jackson inlet. It is essentially a commercial, cultural, and financial center dependent on its port for its prosperity. The N site of Port Jackson is predominantly residential, industry being located to the S. The two shores are connected by Sydney Harbor Bridge (1932), the second largest single-span bridge in the world. Industry is diverse and includes ship building, chemicals, and the manufacture of consumer goods; Botany Bay is developing as the main industrial area. The chief exports are wheat and wool. A cultural center, Sydney possesses three universities, including Sydney University (1850), and the world-famous Sydney Opera House (opened 1973), designed by Jøern Utzon as the result of an international competition in 1955. There are abundant sports facilities, including many nearby beaches. *History*: a penal settlement (Sydney Cove) was established by Capt. Arthur Phillip at Port Jackson (in 1788). Under the governorship of Lachlan Macquarie (1810–21), aided by a convict-architect,

Francis Greenway, it developed into a thriving town and grew rapidly between 1850 and 1890. Area: 670 sq mi (1735 sq km). Population (1991 est): 3,698,500.

Sydney 46 10N 60 10W A city and port in SE Canada, in Nova Scotia on Cape Breton Island. Founded in 1785, it is located on a major coalfield and has an important steel industry. Population (1986): 29,750.

SYDNEY *As seen from the northern approaches to the Sydney Harbor Bridge. Behind the bridge rise the tall blocks of the city center and on the left are the sail-like roofs of Sydney Opera House.*

syenite A range of coarse-grained intrusive rocks (*see* igneous rocks) consisting mainly of alkali feldspar or feldspathoids, together with hornblende and biotite.

Syktyvkar 61 42N 50 45E A city in NW Russia and the capital of the Komi associate republic. Founded in the 16th century, it became a place of exile for criminals and political prisoners. Notable industries are timber and paper and pulp manufacturing. Population (1991 est): 224,000.

syllabaries Writing systems in which each symbol represents a syllable in the language rather than a concept (*compare* ideographic writing systems). The only major language using a syllabary today is Japanese. However, the North *Semitic alphabet, from which all the world's major alphabets are derived, almost certainly developed out of a syllabary, in which the symbols came to represent speech sounds rather than concepts as in ideography.

syllogism A form of deductive argument, rules for the validity of which were developed by *Aristotle. Each syllogism must be composed of three propositions—two premises and a conclusion—and one of its forms may thus be schematically represented: "All As are Bs. All Cs are As. Therefore all Cs are Bs." Since the conclusion that all Cs are Bs "follows" from the premises, one cannot without self-contradiction assert the premises and deny the conclusion, and this is true of all forms of valid syllogism.

Sylvester II (Gerbert of Aurillac; c. 940–1003) Pope (999–1033), who was also a mathematician and astronomer. He attempted to reform abuses and organized the Churches of Poland and Hungary. His reputation as a scholar (his learning was popularly credited to have been acquired by magic) survived his pontificate.

symbiosis Any close relationship between individuals of two different species of organisms. The term can therefore include parasitism (*see* parasite), *commensalism, and *inquilinism but is often restricted to—and used synonymously with—**mutualism**, in which both partners (symbionts) benefit from the association. An example of such a symbiotic relationship is provided by a sea anemone (*Adamsia paliata*), which lives attached to the snail shell inhabited by the hermit crab (*Eupagurus prideauxii*). The anemone protects and camouflages the crab, from which it receives food and transport in return.

symbolists A group of French poets in the late 19th century whose poetry, which they regarded as a means of transcending reality, was determined by their belief in the power of words and images to evoke responses in the subconscious mind. They included *Mallarmé, *Verlaine, and *Rimbaud, and acknowledged the influence of *Baudelaire. They were precursors of the surrealist movement and had a profound influence on poets in Russia and many other countries.

Symons, Arthur (William) (1865–1945) British poet and critic. He coedited the literary journal *Savoy* (1896) with Aubrey Beardsley and published several volumes of lyrical poetry, the best of which he selected and published in *Poems* (2 vols, 1902). A disciple of Walter *Pater, his critical work included the influential study *The Symbolist Movement in Literature* (1899).

symphonic poem (*or* tone poem) A one-movement orchestral composition based on a literary, dramatic, or pictorial theme. The symphonic poem was invented by *Liszt, who composed a series of such works, the most famous of which is *Les Préludes* (1854), after Lamartine's poem *Méditations Poétiques*. Smetana, Richard Strauss, Tchaikovsky, Sibelius, Respighi, and Elgar, among others, composed notable works in this genre.

symphony An orchestral composition, usually in four movements. The classical symphony evolved in the mid-18th century and was perfected by Haydn and Mozart: the fast first movement was generally in *sonata form, the second was slow and expressive, the third a *minuet and trio, and the fourth fast. Beethoven extended the formal and emotional range of the symphony, introducing a chorus and soloists in the last movement of his ninth symphony. In the 19th century Schubert, Schumann, Mendelssohn, Brahms, Dvořák, and Tchaikovsky all wrote symphonies broadly in this tradition. In the hands of such composers as Bruckner and Mahler the symphony underwent further enlargement: Mahler's eighth symphony (1907) requires a thousand performers. Sibelius developed a concentrated approach to symphonic writing: his seventh symphony (1924) is in one movement. Nielsen, Shostakovich, Vaughan Williams, and others have all developed the symphony in differing ways.

synagogue A Jewish place of worship. The synagogue probably originated during the *Babylonian exile as a substitute for the Temple at Jerusalem. In antiquity it was a public meeting place, devoted mainly to the reading and exposition of the *Torah. It is now primarily a house of prayer, but often has a communal center attached. The principal piece of furniture is the cupboard (Ark) containing the Torah scrolls. A synagogue service requires a quorum (*minyan*) of 10 adult males. US Reform Judaism prefers the term "temple."

synapse The meeting point between one nerve cell and another (*see* neuron). The nerve impulse, as it arrives at the end of one nerve process, causes a chemical neurotransmitter (e.g. *acetylcholine or noradrenaline) to be released. This reaches receptors on the opposite neuron and produces a new nerve impulse.

synchrocyclotron A type of *cyclotron in which the frequency of the accelerating electric field can be varied to compensate for the relativistic increase in the mass of the accelerated particles. This enables energies of up to 500 MeV to be obtained.

synchrotron A particle *accelerator, similar to the *cyclotron, in which protons or electrons are accelerated in a circular path by an alternating electric field. The frequency of the field is synchronized with the energy of the particles to counteract their relativistic increase in the mass. Proton energies of several hundred GeV have been attained in these devices. *See also* bevatron.

synchrotron radiation Electromagnetic radiation emitted in certain directions by a charged particle when the presence of a magnetic field confines its motion to a circle. The particle has to be moving at speeds comparable to that of light for a noticeable amount of radiation to be emitted. Therefore a high magnetic field is needed. Such fields are used in *synchrotrons, a type of particle *accelerator. The emission of radio-frequency radiation also occurs from interstellar gas clouds in radio galaxies and, by analogy, is also known as synchrotron radiation.

syncline A trough-shaped fold or downfold in folded rock strata, the strata dipping toward a central axis (*compare* anticline). The youngest rocks occur in the core unless very complex deformation has occurred. Where the strata dip inward from all directions the resulting feature is called a structural basin.

syndicalism A type of *socialism, advocated by *Sorel, under which the workers, not the state, would take over the productive resources of industry. Syndicalists were widely influential in Europe from the late 19th century until World War I. They worked through industrial action, rather than political or parliamentary means, to substitute for the state a federation of functional economic units called syndicats.

Synge, John Millington (1871–1909) Anglo-Irish dramatist. Most of his plays, the realism and poetic intensity of which contributed greatly to the *Irish Literary Renaissance, were inspired by his experience of life in an isolated Irish community, recorded in *The Aran Islands* (1907). His best-known play, *The Playboy of the Western World* (1907), caused riots at its first performance at the Abbey Theatre, Dublin.

synodic period The average time taken by a planet or satellite to return to the same point in its orbit, relative to the sun, as seen from earth. It is therefore the interval between *oppositions or between identical *phases.

synovitis Inflammation of the synovium—the membrane lining the joints. This usually results from mild injuries to joints, such as those affecting athletes early in the season, and causes pain and swelling.

syntax. *See* grammar.

synthesizer A device that can reproduce the sounds of conventional instruments electronically or produce a variety of artificial tones. Electronic oscillators produce a range of signals, which after amplification and appropriate filtering are converted to sound waves, of which some have the characteristic resonances of musical instruments, some are pure tones, and some are arbitrary combinations of sounds. Individual circuits can be plugged in and out by the player, enabling a wide range of sounds to be produced. The Moog synthesizer, invented by Robert Moog (1934–   ) in 1965, can play one note at a time and is controlled by a keyboard. More recent **polyphonic synthesizers** can be programmed to produce any number of different tones simultaneously.

synthetism A style of painting developed by *Gauguin and Émile Bernard (1868–1941) in Brittany in 1888. The visual arts' counterpart to the symbolist literary movement, synthetism sought to express an idea or emotion through formal correspondences of line and color. It was also known as cloisonnisme, since its use of rich unmodulated color contained within thick black contours resembled *cloisonné enamelware, as well as Japanese prints. Synthetism greatly influenced the art of the *Nabis.

syphilis A venereal disease caused by the *spirochete bacterium *Treponema pallidum*, which in nearly all cases is transmitted during sexual intercourse. The effects of the disease occur in three stages. In primary syphilis chancres (hard ulcers) appear after about 25 days at the site of infection (usually the genitals). The chancre disappears after about eight weeks, but weeks or months later the rash of secondary syphilis occurs. Arthritis, meningitis, and hepatitis may also occur at this stage. Without treatment the tertiary stage of syphilis may appear up to 30 years later and give rise to a variety of symptoms, including large tumorlike masses (gummas) in many organs, heart disease, blindness, and madness and paralysis (general paralysis of the insane). The disease can be passed on to an unborn child by an infected mother (congenital syphilis). Syphilis can be treated with penicillin. The *Wasserman test is one of many blood tests available for diagnosing the disease.

Syracuse (Italian name: Siracusa) 37 04N 15 18E A seaport in Italy, in SE Sicily on the Ionian Sea. Founded by Greeks from Corinth in 734 BC, it became an important cultural center in the 5th century. The Greek poet Theocritus and the Greek mathematician and scientist Archimedes were born there. In 212 BC Syracuse fell to the Romans after a three-year siege. There are many ancient remains, including a Greek temple, a Roman amphitheater, and a fortress built by Dionysius I. Today Syracuse is a processing center for agricultural produce, with some light industry. Population (1991 est): 125,444.

Syracuse 43 03N 76 10W A city in N central New York. Founded in 1788, it had a thriving salt-making industry until after the Civil War. In 1819 the Erie Canal was opened and the railroads followed, attracting many industries. Today its many manufactures include aircraft parts, typewriters, and chemicals. Syracuse University was established in 1849. Population (1990): 163,860.

Syr Darya River (ancient name: Jaxartes) A river in Kyrgyzstan, Uzbekistan, and Kazakhstan, rising in the Tian Shan and flowing mainly W to the Aral Sea. It is the longest river in Central Asia. Length: 1800 mi (2900 km).

Syria (official name: Syrian Arab Republic) A country in the Middle East, bordering on the Mediterranean Sea. In the W the Ghab depression (an extension of the *Great Rift Valley) runs N–S, separated from the coast by a mountain range. To the E of this is plateau of steppe and desert with some mountains. The main fertile areas, in which the population is concentrated, are the coastal strip and the basin of the Euphrates River (*see* Fertile Crescent). Nomads live in the center and E; ethnic minorities include Kurds (in the NE), Turks, Armenians, Assyrians, Circassians, and Jews. The population is predominantly Muslim (mainly Sunnites with some Shiites). *Economy*: largely agricultural; cotton and grain are the main crops and livestock are kept. Natural resources include oil, natural gas, phosphates, and salt. Industries, mainly developed since the 1940s, include food processing, oil refining, and the manufacture of textiles, clothing, cement, and chemicals. Syria has a planned socialist economy; much of its industry is nationalized, and land has been redistributed in favor of the peasants (1958, 1963, and 1966). *History*: before the 20th century Syria, together with Palestine, extended over the area that is now Lebanon, Israel, Jordan, W Iraq, and N Saudi Arabia. In ancient times the *Amorites settled there and later *Phoenicia flourished. It was frequently conquered; Islam was introduced by conquering Arabs (c. 640 AD). Under Turkish control from the 11th century, it was the site of battles with the Crusaders. From 1517 until World War I it was part of the Ottoman Empire. In 1920 it became part of a French mandate, from which Lebanon was separated in 1926. Demands for Syrian independence were finally satisfied in 1946. Since then Syria's history has been marked by economic growth, political instability with many coups, and militant participation in the Arab-Israeli Wars. It united briefly with Egypt in the United Arab Republic (1958–61) but withdrew because of Egyptian domination. In 1971 Syria, Libya, and Egypt united loosely in the Federation of Arab Republics but disagreement with Egypt developed over its attitude toward Israel. Syria intervened in the civil war in Lebanon (1975–76), at first as a mediator but then supporting the Christians. It remained in occupation of the eastern part of the country, from which after 1982 it aided Muslim factions opposed to the national government of Christian leader Amin Gemayel as well as to Israeli occupation forces in southern Lebanon. Syria's connection with international terrorist groups led to criticism in the world community, including the UK's severing of relations in 1986. After Iraq's annexation of Kuwait in 1990, Syria observed the embargo on trade with Iraq and contributed a large number of troops to the UN coalition forces that were victorious over Iraq in the Persian Gulf War. In the early 1990s, Syria moved to become more active in Arab affairs and to improve relations with the US. President: Hafiz al-Assad. Official language: Arabic. Official currency: Syrian pound of 100 piastres. Area: 72,772 sq mi (185,680 sq km). Population (1990 est): 12,471,000. Capital: Damascus.

Syriac A *Semitic language based on the dialect of *Aramaic spoken in Edessa (now Urfa, SE Turkey). It became an important literary and liturgical language in which many scriptures, biblical commentaries, hymns, etc., were written during the 3rd to the 7th centuries AD when Edessa was an important Christian center.

syringa. *See* lilac; mock orange.

syrinx The vocal organ of birds, located at the base of the windpipe. Air from the lungs vibrates membranes within a resonating chamber. Muscular tension alters pitch, and the two halves of the syrinx can produce different notes simultaneously.

Syros (Modern Greek name: Síros) A Greek island in the S Aegean Sea, in the Cyclades. The chief town, Hermopolis, is the capital of the Cyclades. Area: 33 sq mi (85 sq km).

systole. *See* blood pressure; heart.

Szczecin (German name: Stettin) 53 25N 14 32E A city in the extreme NW of Poland, on the Oder River 40 mi (65 km) upstream from the Baltic Sea. It is a major port, the chief export being coal. Ship building is the principal industry; others include engineering, chemicals, and the manufacture of textiles. *History*: it became a member of the Hanseatic League in 1360. Seized by the Swedes (1648) it passed to Prussia in 1720, remaining under German control until being ceded to Poland (1945). It suffered severe damage during World War II. Population (1992 est): 414,000.

Szechwan. *See* Sichuan.

Szeged 46 15N 20 09E A city in S Hungary, on the Tisza River. Replanned with concentric and radiating streets after a flood in 1879, it has a university (1872) and considerable industry. Population (1991 est): 176,000.

Székesfehérvár 47 11N 18 22E A city in W central Hungary. It was the capital of the Hungarian kingdom from the 10th until the 16th century. It was almost totally destroyed in World War II. Population (1991 est): 109,000.

Szell, George (1897–1970) Hungarian conductor. He studied in Vienna, conducted in various German opera houses, and came to the US in 1942. In 1946 he became permanent conductor of the Cleveland Orchestra, a post he held until his death.

Szent-Györgyi, Albert (von Nagyrapolt) (1893–1986) US biochemist, born in Hungary. He identified the role of ascorbic acid in living cells and later showed it to be *vitamin C. Szent-Györgyi determined certain organic compounds involved in the breakdown of carbohydrates by cells to produce energy—a prelude to *Krebs's major discoveries in this field. He also found that the proteins actin and myosin, working in conjunction with ATP, formed the basis of the contractile apparatus of muscles. Szent-Györgyi was awarded a Nobel Prize (1937).

Szilard, Leo (1898–1964) US physicist, born in Hungary, who in 1934, while working in England, conceived the idea of a self-sustaining nuclear chain reaction. Szilard emigrated to the US in 1937 and when he heard of *Hahn and *Meitner's work on the fission of uranium, recognized its significance in terms of nuclear weapons. He joined *Teller in persuading Einstein to write to Roosevelt to warn him of the possibility that Germany might make an atom bomb first. During World War II he actually worked on the atom bomb, but later regretted its development and pressed for the abolition of all nuclear weapons.

Szymanowski, Karol (1882–1937) Polish composer. He studied at the Warsaw conservatory, where in 1926 he became director. The influences on his music include Chopin, Liszt, Scriabin, Debussy, and Polish folk music. His works include three symphonies, a *Symphonie Concertante* (for piano and orchestra; 1931–32) two violin concertos, the ballet *Harnasie* (1926), the opera *King Roger* (1920–24), and *Mythes* (for violin and piano; 1915).

T

Tabari, Muhammad ibn Jarir al- (838–923 AD) Arab historian. His works include an important commentary on the Koran and the *Annals*, a history of the world from the Creation to the year 915 AD.

tabasco A hot red pepper or sauce made from the entire fruits of a variety of the South American plant **Capsicum frutescens* and used to flavor soups, stews, curries, etc. Family: *Solanaceae.*

tabernacle 1. The portable sanctuary or "tent of meeting" used by the Israelites in the wilderness (Exodus 25–31, 33, 35–40). **2.** The English name of the *sukkah*, a hut made of greenery, used by Jews during the autumn festival of Tabernacles (*sukkot*). For seven days it is customary to live, or at least eat, in the *sukkah.*

Table Bay 33 50S 18 25E An inlet of the Atlantic Ocean, on the coast of SW Africa. The Dutch settled there in 1652, founding Cape Town on the S shore. Length: about 6 mi (10 km).

table tennis (*or* Ping-Pong) An indoor game for two or four players. It is played on a table 9 ft (2.74 m) long and 5 ft (1.52 m) wide, divided across its width by a net 6 in (15.25 cm) high and along its length by a line separating right-hand from left-hand half courts for doubles play. The players hit a resilient small hollow plastic ball with a rubber-faced wooden paddle. A point is scored when the opponent fails to return the ball after it has bounced once. Each player serves five consecutive points and the winner of a game is the first to reach 21 points with at least a two-point lead.

taboo A ritual prohibition relating to things that are considered either sacred, powerful, and dangerous (*see also* totemism) or unclean and polluting. The term is derived from Polynesian *tapu*, forbidden, and may apply to things, animals, plants, people, places, words and names, or actions. Customs of this kind are widespread in all societies, but actual practices vary greatly. Certain things may be taboo for all people in a society (as eating pork is for Jews). Other things are taboo for only certain categories of persons (*see* incest). Some things are taboo for particular people at particular times (e.g. in many societies menstruating women are subject to restrictions as to what they may touch).

Tabora 5 02S 32 50E A city in W central Tanzania. It was an important center for trade in ivory and slaves; today trade remains significant and includes groundnuts and sunflower seeds. Population (1988): 214,000.

Tabriz 38 05N 46 18E A city in NW Iran, close to the Azerbajani and Turkish borders. It has several times suffered earthquakes. The most notable buildings are the Blue Mosque (15th century) and the citadel, and Tabriz is famous for its carpets; it is connected by rail to Tehran and Azerbaijan and has an airport. Tabriz University was opened in 1949. Population (1986): 971,482.

tachometer An instrument for measuring the speed of rotation of a shaft, such as a revolution counter in a car. Centrifugal tachometers measure the force experienced by rotating masses. Others are electrical or magnetic, measuring electrical current or force generated by a small generator in the instrument.

tachyon A hypothetical particle that travels faster than the speed of light. Such a particle would have either an imaginary rest mass or an imaginary energy and no such particle has ever been detected.

Tacitus, Cornelius (c. 55–c. 120 AD) Roman historian. After holding various provincial administrative posts he established his reputation as a public orator in Rome and became consul in 97 AD; in 112–13 he was governor of Asia. In 98 he wrote two historical monographs, *Germania* and *Agricola*, the latter an account of his father-in-law's career. His major works, the *Histories* and the *Annals*, survey Roman history during the periods 69–96 AD and 14–68 AD and are noted for their terse and vivid style and acute understanding of the men and issues involved. Although claiming impartiality, Tacitus appears to concentrate on the evils of imperial government.

Tacoma 47 16N 122 30W A city in Washington, on Puget Sound. Founded in 1868, it grew as the terminus of the North Pacific Railroad (1873). The University of Puget Sound was established there in 1888. An important port, its main industry is timber; other industries include meat packing, railroad workshops, and foundries. Tacoma is the gateway to several national parks. Population (1990): 176,664.

tadpole The aquatic larva of frogs and toads. The newly hatched tadpole feeds on vegetation but later becomes carnivorous. The external gills of the young tadpole are gradually replaced by internal gills, and after about 10 weeks the limbs start to appear, the tail degenerates, the lungs develop, and the circulatory system changes to enable the adult to lead a terrestrial life. Metamorphosis is complete after about three months, depending on the external temperature and available food.

tadpole shrimp A freshwater crustacean belonging to an order (*Notostraca*) that occurs in North America and the Arctic. Up to 1.2 in (30 mm) long, it has a shieldlike carapace, short antennae, 35–70 pairs of appendages, and two long tail filaments. Subclass: **Branchiopoda*.

Tadzhiks. *See* Tajiks.

Taegu 35 52N 128 36E A city in SE South Korea, the capital of North Kyongsang province. An old cultural center, it is the site of a university (1946). It has an important textile industry. Population (1990): 2,228,834.

Taejon 36 20N 127 26E A city in SE South Korea, capital of South Chungchong province. It is an agricultural and industrial center, with a university (1952). Some 70% of the city was destroyed during the Korean War (1950–53). Population (1990): 1,062,084.

Taft, William Howard (1857–1930) US statesman and jurist; 27th president of the US (1909–13). Taft first came to national prominence as US solicitor general during the administration of Pres. Benjamin *Harrison (1890–92) and as a federal judge (1892–1900). After the *Spanish-American War, he served as governor of the Philippines (1901–04) and was named secretary of war in the cabinet of Pres. Theodore *Roosevelt. With Roosevelt's decision not to seek reelection, Taft received the Republican nomination in 1908, and defeated the Democratic candidate, William Jennings *Bryan. As president, Taft supported vigorous enforcement of the *Sherman Anti-Trust Act, but his high tariff policies aroused considerable opposition within his own party. Although he was renominated in 1912, he was defeated in the general election by Woodrow *Wilson.

After a brief retirement from public life, Taft was appointed by Pres. Warren G. *Harding in 1921 to become chief justice of the US Supreme Court and became the only individual in American history ever to hold both the presidency and the chief justiceship. Taft's tenure on the court was characterized by a conservative judicial philosophy, restricting the power of labor unions and overturning federal legislation against child labor. His son, **Robert Alphonso Taft**

(1889–1953), served as US senator from Ohio (1938–53) and became one of the leaders of the Republican party. Although he was an unsuccessful candidate for the Republican presidential nomination in 1940, 1944, 1948, and 1952, he secured the passage of several important legislative proposals, including the *Taft-Hartley Act of 1947.

Taft-Hartley Act (*or* Labor-Management Relations Act; 1947) US law, sponsored by Sen. Robert A. Taft and Republican Fred A. Hartley, aimed at correcting union and employer abuses. It further amended the Wagner Act (1935) and reorganized and enlarged the *National Labor Relations Board. Closed shops were banned and union shops were allowed only by employee vote. It also required unions to limit political activity, reveal certain aspects of financial standing, and sign non-Communist affidavits. The government was granted permission to invoke an 80-day injunction in cases of strikes thought to endanger national safety.

Tagalog A people of Luzon and Mindanao islands in the Philippines who speak an *Austronesian language. Although less numerous than the speakers of the related language of Cebuano, they tend to dominate in the economic, professional, and political spheres. Tagalog is the basis of the national language and is spoken by the population of the capital, Manila. The rural Tagalog are mainly rice farmers.

Taganrog 47 14N 38 55E A port in SW Russia, on the Gulf of Taganrog in the Sea of Azov. Its port serves the coal mines of the Donets Basin and industries include steelmaking. The playwright Chekhov was born there. Population (1991 est): 293,600.

Tagore, Rabindranath (1861–1941) Indian poet, philosopher, and teacher. Knighted in 1915, he resigned the honor in 1919 as a protest against the Amritsar massacre. He wrote poetry, drama, and fiction in the Bengali language and was also a celebrated artist and musician. In 1901 he founded a school near Calcutta, which later became an international university. He advocated cultural links between the East and the West and won the Nobel Prize in literature in 1913 after the publication in English of *Gitanjali* (1912), a volume of spiritual poetry.

Tagus River (Portuguese name: Tejo; Spanish name: Tajo) A river in SW Europe. Rising in E central Spain, it flows NW and then SW across the arid areas of Spain and Portugal to the Atlantic Ocean at Lisbon. Length: 626 mi (1007 km).

Tahiti The largest of the Society Islands in the S central Pacific Ocean, in French Polynesia. Mountainous and famous for its beauty, it was *Gauguin's home for two years (1891–93). Settled by Polynesians in the 14th century, it was first visited by Europeans in 1767. It became French in 1842. Tourism is important, and copra, sugarcane, vanilla, and coffee are exported. Area: 388 sq mi (1005 sq km). Population (1988 est): 115,800. Chief town: Papeete.

tahr A wild goat belonging to the genus *Hemitragus* (3 species), inhabiting forested mountain slopes of S Asia; 24–40 in (60–100 cm) high at the shoulder, the large Himalayan tahr (*H. jemlahicus*) and the smaller Nilgiri tahr (*H. hylocrius*) have long coarse shaggy brownish hair; the Arabian tahr (*H. jayakari*) is slender and sandy-colored.

Tai Peoples of SE Asia and China who speak a group of related languages probably belonging to the *Sino-Tibetan family. They are traditionally rice cultivators dwelling in villages with elected headmen. The nuclear family is the basic social unit and women have high status. They are mainly Theravada Buddhists, the monks having considerable influence and authority. Major groupings are the Thai or Siamese, the Lao, Shan, and Lu. *See also* Austro-Asiatic languages.

Taibei. *See* Taipei.

T'ai-chung. *See* Taizhong.

taiga The coniferous forests, composed chiefly of spruces, pines, and firs, in the N hemisphere in subpolar latitudes. It extends from Norway across Sweden, Finland, and Russia (including Siberia), in Eurasia. The coniferous forests of North America, extending across Canada and Alaska, are also known as taiga.

Taika (Japanese: great change; 645–50 AD) The period associated with the first major upheaval in Japanese history. Influenced by the Tang dynasty of China, Japanese leaders introduced a Chinese-style system of government, including land nationalization and the establishment of a centralized bureaucracy. Their program was not completed, however, until the erection of a permanent capital at Nara in 710.

taille An income and property tax in France before the Revolution. Originally levied for royal expenses and paid in lieu of military service, the taille was a major source of grievance since clergy and nobility were exempt and commoners alone paid the tax. It was abolished in 1789.

tailorbird A S Asian *warbler belonging to the genus *Orthotomus* (9 species), named for its habit of sewing the edges of a large leaf together with plant fibers or gossamer to form a bag in which the nest is built.

Taimyr Peninsula (*or* Taymyr Peninsula) A promontory in N central Russia, between the Kara Sea and the Laptev Sea with Cape *Chelyuskin at its extremity.

Tainan 23 01N 120 14E A city in SW Taiwan, the island's third largest. It is the island's former capital (1683–1891). The National University was established in 1971. An agricultural and fish market, it has varied industries and handicrafts. Population (1991 est): 683,000.

Taine, Hippolyte Adolphe (1828–93) French writer and critic. In contrast to the prevailing *romanticism, Taine was intensely logical and positivist in his approach. In works such as the *Philosophy of Art* (1865–69), his analysis is conducted in scientific, mathematical, physiological, or environmental terms.

taipan A small-headed *cobra, *Oxyuranus scutellatus*, that occurs in NE Australia and New Guinea. Up to 11 ft (3.3 m) long, it has a ridged brown back and a yellow belly. The venom of the taipan contains a blood-clotting agent that is fatal within a few minutes.

Taipei (*or* Taibei) 25 00N 121 32E The capital of Taiwan, in the N of the island. Founded in the 18th century, it was under Japanese occupation (1895–1945) and became the seat of the Nationalist government (*see* Guomindang) in 1949. It is an important industrial center, especially for textiles, food processing, and machinery. The National University was founded in 1928. Population (1992 est): 2,717,000.

Taiping Rebellion (1851–64) A peasant rebellion in China that seriously undermined the Qing dynasty. In 1851 a Hakka peasant, *Hong Xiu Quan, claiming he was the brother of Christ come to save his people from their Qing rulers, proclaimed himself "Heavenly King of the Taiping (Heavenly Peace) Kingdom." He soon won converts among the southern peasantry and anti-Qing secret societies. The rebels marched N, capturing Nanjing in 1853 and declaring it their Heavenly Capital. They then marched on Peking but imperial forces, and cold weather, drove them back. The rebellion, which devasted 17 provinces, was weakened by internal division and finally crushed. When Nanjing fell, Hong and his followers committed mass suicide.

Taira An important Japanese military clan of imperial descent. After gaining many vassals in the provinces, the Taira became involved in politics in the capital, Kyoto, in the 12th century and under the leadership of Taira Kiyomori (1118–81) came to dominate the imperial government. Shortly before Kiyomori's death, Taira power was challenged by the leaders of a rival clan, the Minamoto (*see* Minamoto Yoritomo), and destroyed in the Gempei War (1180–85).

Taiwan (Republic of China) An island off the SE coast of mainland China. Together with several nearby islands, including the Penghu Islands and the islands of *Jinmen and *Mazu, it comprises the Republic of China. Taiwan Island is largely mountainous, apart from narrow plains along the W coast, and two-thirds of the land is under forest. The people are predominantly Chinese, but there is friction between the island Chinese, who make up the overwhelming majority of the population, and those who came from the mainland. *Economy*: in recent years the balance of the economy has shifted from agriculture to industry, a trend that began under the Japanese and has continued under the *Guomindang with US economic aid. Iron and steel are important and the large volume of exports also includes television and radio sets, plastic goods, chemicals, textiles, sugar, and vegetables. As well as coal, gold, and other minerals, small quantities of oil and natural gas have been found, although timber remains the main natural resource. Agriculture is still important, the chief crops being sugarcane, rice, and sweet potatoes. Fishing has increased in recent years, particularly since the introduction of fish farming. *History*: the island, named Formosa ("beautiful") by the Portuguese, who discovered it in 1590, was ceded by China to Japan in 1897. It surrendered to Gen. *Chiang Kai-shek in 1945 and after the defeat of his Nationalist (Guomindang) government by the Chinese communists he fled there in 1949. Following threats by the People's Republic of China the US undertook in 1955 to protect Taiwan from outside attacks. However, Taiwan's importance in international affairs has diminished, as the People's Republic has gained increasing recognition by the major powers: in 1971 it lost its seat at the UN to the People's Republic and in 1979 the US, on establishing diplomatic relations with mainland China, severed those with Taiwan. Chiang Kai-shek died in 1975 and power was held by his son, Gen. Jiang Jing Guo (Chiang Ching-kuo) until his death in 1988. Under his successors, relations with the People's Republic improved, and in 1993 a cooperation pact was signed. Official language: Mandarin Chinese. Official currency: new Taiwan dollar of 100 cents. Area: 13,892 sq mi (35,981 sq km). Population (1992 est): 20,725,000. Capital: Taipei. Main port: Kaohsiung.

Taiyuan 37 50N 112 30E A city in NE China, the capital of Shanxi province. An ancient fortified city, it is a center of technology, coal mining, and heavy industry. Population (1991 est): 1,534,000.

Taizé A Protestant religious community based in Taizé, a village in the SE of France. Founded in 1940 by Roger Schutz (1915–), its members pursue a life of celibacy, obedience, and community of goods in the ways of traditional monasticism and it is also an ecumenical center for young people interested in furthering Christian unity.

Tajikistan, Republic of (*or* Tadzhikistan) A republic in central Asia, a constituent republic of the Soviet Union known as Tadzhikistan until 1991. It is largely mountainous. Some 53% of the population are *Tadzhiks. The economy is primarily agricultural, although there are growing mining, engineering, and other industries. Health resorts have grown up around its many mineral springs.

Area: 55,240 sq mi (143,100 sq km). Population (1992 est): 5,565,000. Capital: Dushanbe.

Tajiks (*or* Tadzhiks) An Iranian people of Afghanistan and central Asia. They are an agricultural people using irrigation to grow cereal crops and fruit trees. Trade has also been important traditionally because of their position on the caravan routes between China, India, and Persia. They speak a form of Persian and are Muslims.

Taj Mahal The mausoleum in Agra (N India) built (1631–53) for Mumtaz-i-Mahal, wife of the Mogul emperor *Shah Jahan, who is also buried there. Set in formal gardens, the Taj Mahal is built mainly of white marble, delicately carved and inlaid with precious stones. Its graceful and symmetrical design reflects Persian influence. *See also* Mogul architecture.

TAJ MAHAL *Over 20,000 workmen were employed in the building of the mausoleum (1631–53), which was constructed from pure white Makrana marble.*

takahe A rare flightless New Zealand bird, *Notornis mantelli*, thought to be extinct but rediscovered on South Island in 1948; 24 in (60 cm) tall, it has a bright blue-and-green plumage and a heavy red conical bill surmounted by a red frontal shield. Takahes feed on seeds. Family: *Rallidae* (rails).

Takao. *See* Gaoxiong.

Takoradi. *See* Sekondi-Takoradi.

talapoin The smallest *guenon monkey, *Cercopithecus talapoin*, of central West Africa, also called pygmy guenon. With head and body only 12 in (30 cm) long, it has slightly webbed fingers and inhabits swampy forests. It has olive-green fur and conspicuously swollen genitals.

talc A white or pale-green mineral consisting of hydrated magnesium silicate, $Mg_3(Si_4O_{10})(OH)_2$, with a layered structure. It is soft (hardness 1 on *Mohs' scale) and greasy to the touch. Soapstone (steatite) is a rock consisting almost wholly of talc. Talc is formed by the hydrothermal alteration of basic and ultrabasic igneous rocks and by the low-grade thermal metamorphism of siliceous dolomites. Besides its use as talcum powder, it is also used as a mineral filler in many manufacturing processes, as a soft abrasive, and as a lubricant.

Talca 35 28S 71 40W A city in central Chile. The site of the declaration of Chile's independence (1815), it was rebuilt following an earthquake in 1928.

Talca serves a rich wine-producing area and has a large match industry. Population (1991 est): 183,000.

Talcahuano 36 40S 73 10W A major port in S Chile, on Concepción Bay. It serves as an outlet for Concepción and is Chile's chief naval base. Population (1991 est): 251,000.

Ta-lien. *See* Lüda.

Taliesin (6th century AD) Welsh poet. He is mentioned in the 9th-century *Historia Britonum* of Nennius. The poems attributed to him in the manuscript *Book of Taliesin* (c. 1275) include odes eulogizing the Welsh king Urien Rheged and lamenting the death of his son Owain.

talipot palm A *palm tree, *Corypha umbraculifera*, cultivated in India, Sri Lanka, and Myanmar (Burma). Its trunk, up to 85.5 ft (26 m) high, bears fan-shaped leaves with a diameter of up to 16 ft (5 m). Trees may be 80 years old before flowering, after which they die. The pyramid-shaped flower cluster, more than 23 ft (7 m) tall, is the largest in the plant kingdom. The hard seeds are used for buttons and ornaments and the leaves for matting, fans, and thatching.

Tallahassee 30 26N 84 19W The capital city of Florida. It is the site of Florida State University (1857) and an agricultural and mechanical university (1887). A trade center for timber, cotton, and livestock, industries include metal and concrete. Population (1990): 124,773.

Talleyrand (Charles Maurice de Talleyrand-Périgord; 1754–1838) French politician and diplomat. He took holy orders in 1775 but was excommunicated by the pope for the part he played in the reform of the church during the *French Revolution. He was foreign minister from 1797 until 1807, when he quarreled with Napoleon, and again under the restored Louis XVIII. He represented France at the *Congress of Vienna and ended his career as ambassador to Great Britain (1830–34).

Tallien, Jean Lambert (1767–1820) French politician in the *French Revolution. He helped overthrow Robespierre in 1774 and under the *Directory was a member of the Council of Five Hundred. He subsequently served in Napoleon's Egyptian campaign.

Tallinn (German name: Reval) 59 22N 24 48E A port city and the capital of Estonia on Tallinn Bay in the Gulf of Finland. Its varied industries include ship building and it possesses many educational institutions and historic buildings. *History*: it occupies the site of an ancient settlement and was ruled by Denmark and then Sweden before being captured (1710) by Peter the Great. A member of the Hanseatic League, it was a prominent trading center in the Middle Ages. It was independent Estonia's capital (1918–40) and, following annexation by the Soviet Union, was occupied by the Germans in World War II. Population (1991 est): 482,000.

Talmud Two of the most important works of Jewish religious literature: the Babylonian and the Palestinian (or Jerusalem) Talmud. The Babylonian Talmud is more than three times as long as the Palestinian and enjoys greater authority. Both Talmuds have the same form: they are written in a mixture of Hebrew and Aramaic and are presented as a commentary (*gemara*) on the *Mishnah. They contain records of rabbinic discussions on a wide range of subjects but concentrating especially on *halakhah. The rabbis mentioned in the Talmuds are called *Amoraim* (as opposed to *Tannaim*, the rabbis of the Mishnah, and *Savoraim*, later rabbis thought to have edited the Babylonian Talmud). The Palestinian *Amoraim* flourished in the 3rd and 4th centuries AD; the Babylonian *Amoraim* continued to about 500.

talus (*or* scree) The accumulation of weathered debris at the foot of a cliff that has originated from erosion of the rock face above.

Tamale 9 26N 0 49W A city in N Ghana. It is an educational center and has a trade in cotton and groundnuts. Population (1988 est): 151,000.

tamandua An insect-eating mammal, *Tamandua tetradactyla*, of Central and South American forests, also called lesser *anteater. Almost 40 in (1 m) long including the long prehensile tail, it is pale in color and has a shorter snout than the giant anteater. It feeds on termites using its long sticky tongue. Family: *Myrmecophagidae*; order: *Edentata*.

tamarin A South American monkey found in open woodland and forests, closely related to *marmosets. Tamarins are 15.5–35 in (39–88 cm) long including the tail (8–16.5 in; 20–42 cm), have tusklike lower canine teeth, and feed on fruit, insects, eggs, etc. Chief genera: *Leontocebus* (21 species), *Leontideus* (3 species); family: *Callithricidae*.

tamarind An evergreen tree, *Tamarindus indica*, probably native to tropical Africa and cultivated in tropical regions for its fruit. It grows to a height of 80 ft (24 m) and bears clusters of yellow flowers. The fruit is a plump pod containing seeds and a bittersweet pulp, which is used in chutneys, curries, and medicines. Family: **Leguminosae*.

tamarisk A tree or shrub belonging to the genus *Tamarix* (90 species), native to W and S Europe, central Asia, and India. Tamarisks have small scalelike leaves and produce feathery clusters of small pink flowers. Their deep roots enable them to grow on arid salt flats and sand dunes and they have been widely planted to stabilize sand dunes. *T. mannifera* of the Middle East and central Asia exudes a sweet white edible substance (manna) when the stems are punctured by certain insects. The false tamarisks (genus *Myricaria*; 10 species), native to temperate Eurasia, are similar to the true tamarisks. Family: *Tamaricaceae*.

tamarou (*or* tamarau) A rare hoofed mammal, *Anoa mindorensis*, of lowland forests of the Philippines. A little larger than the closely related *anoa, it is similarly dark brown or black with short horns and it feeds at night on sugarcane and water plants.

Tamatave (*or* Toamasina) 18 10S 49 23E The chief port of Madagascar, on the Indian Ocean. It was destroyed by hurricane in 1927. Since rebuilt, it is the country's major commercial center and industries include rum distilling. Population (1990 est): 145,500.

Tambov 52 44N 41 28E A city in W Russia. It is an important engineering center. Population (1987): 305,000.

Tamerlane. *See* Timur.

Tamil A *Dravidian language of S India and Sri Lanka. It is the official language of the state of Tamil Nadu. There are a number of regional dialects as well as those associated with different caste groups, such as Brahmins and non-Brahmins. It is written in a script known as Vattelluttu and there are marked differences between the written and spoken forms. Tamil society is highly stratified into caste groups and based on descent in the male line. They are mainly Hindu, and devotional (*bhakti*) cults are prevalent.

Tamil Nadu (name until 1968: Madras) A state in SE India, at the tip of the peninsula. From the Western *Ghats it slopes E over lower plateaus and the Eastern Ghats to the Bay of Bengal. Important crops include rice, cotton, and coffee. One of India's more urbanized states, it produces cotton textiles, machinery, and electrical and leather goods. Tamil literature, music, and dance continue to thrive. *History*: flourishing Hindu dynasties extended Tamil influence into medieval SE Asia until Muslims conquered Tamil Nadu (1565). British power was established in the 17th century. The present state was formed in 1956. Area: 50,318 sq mi (130,357 sq km). Population (1991): 55,638,318. Capital: Madras.

Tammany Hall The Democratic party organization in New York City, which became notorious for its political corruption. It maintained power by the use of bribes and patronage. Among its most notorious "bosses" was William M. *Tweed. Its power was largely curtailed by the reforming mayor *La Guardia and disintegrated during the administration (1966–73) of John V(liet) Lindsay.

Tammuz A Mesopotamian fertility god identified with the Greek *Adonis. Originally a pastoral god, he became an agricultural god of Assyria. The annual seasonal cycle was symbolized in the myth of his descent to the underworld, from whence he was recovered by the goddess *Ishtar.

Tampa 28 10N 82 20W A city and port in Florida, on Tampa Bay. It is a major resort and phosphate-mining center. Manufactures include cigars, cement, and fertilizers. Two universities are situated there. Population (1990): 280,015.

Tampere (Swedish name: Tammerfors) 61 32N 23 45E The second largest city in Finland. It has a 20th-century cathedral and a university (1925). It is the country's main industrial center, being well provided with hydroelectric power from the Tammerkoski Rapids. Its manufactures include railroad rolling stock, textiles, wood pulp, paper, and footwear. Population (1992 est): 174,266.

Tampico 22 18N 97 52W A port and winter resort in SE Mexico, on the Río Panuco. Oil refining is the chief industry. Population (1980): 267,000.

tam-tam. *See* gong.

Tana, Lake (*or* Lake Tsana) 12 00N 37 20E A lake in NW Ethiopia. Its surface is 6004 ft (1830 m) above sea level and it is the source of the Blue Nile River. Area: about 1200 sq mi (3100 sq km).

tanager A brightly colored songbird belonging to a family (*Thraupidae*; 222 species) occurring in tropical and subtropical America. Tanagers are 4–8 in (10–20 cm) long, plumpish, with a short neck and a conical bill. They live mainly in forests and feed on fruit, nectar, and insects.

Tanagra figurines In Greek art, molded terra-cotta statuettes of about 300 BC found at Tanagra (Boeotia). These charming and technically excellent figures represent everyday subjects, usually women in quiet poses.

Tananarive. *See* Antananarivo.

Tancred (c. 1078–1112) Norman Crusader, prominent at the siege of Antioch and the conquest of Jerusalem (1099; *see* Crusades), who was regent of Antioch (1101–03, 1104–12) for Bohemond I. He is portrayed in *Tasso's *Gerusalemme liberata* (1575).

Taney, Roger Brooke (1777–1864) US lawyer; chief justice of the Supreme Court (1836–64). After serving in various state positions in Maryland, including attorney general (1827–31), he became US attorney general in 1831. His appointments as secretary of the treasury (1833) and associate justice on the Supreme Court (1835) were never confirmed by the Senate. In 1836 when Pres. Andrew Jackson appointed him chief justice of the Supreme Court, a change in Senate membership allowed confirmation, and he succeeded John *Marshall. He presided over the court during the **Dred Scott* v. *Sanford* decision.

Tang (*or* T'ang; 618–906 AD) A Chinese dynasty that established an empire extending over much of central Asia and Korea. In Tang times foreign trade was encouraged and many Chinese scientific ideas, such as gunpowder, which was invented under the Tang for fireworks, spread to the West. Arts, especially poetry, flourished, Neo-Confucianism was revived, printing was invented (the world's first known book, the Buddhist *Diamond sutra*, was printed in 868), and paper money was used for the first time. In 751 Arab forces recaptured Turkestan and the Tang empire began to disintegrate. Disastrous revolts and invasions decimated the population and two great rebellions finally led to the collapse of the dynasty and the division of China into many kingdoms.

Tanga 5 07S 39 05E A port in Tanzania, in NE Zanzibar. It became an important port under German colonial rule but has since declined in importance. Population (1988): 187,634.

Tanganyika. *See* Tanzania, United Republic of.

Tanganyika, Lake A lake in E central Africa, in Zaïre, Burundi, Tanzania, and Zambia. Discovered for Europeans by Burton and Speke in 1858, it is drained intermittently to the W by the Lukuga River. Area: about 12,750 sq mi (33,000 sq km).

Tange Kenzo (1913–) Japanese architect. The most famous modern Japanese architect, Tange combines the influence of *Le Corbusier with traditional Japanese architecture. He has built many civic buildings in Japan, notably the Kurashiki city hall (1960). Other designs include the National Gymnasium (1961–64) for the 1964 Tokyo Olympics and St Mary's Cathedral (1962–64) in Tokyo. As a town planner he has produced programs for Tokyo (1960) and Skopje, Yugoslavia (1965).

tangent A straight line that touches a curve at only one point, known as the point of contact. A tangent plane is one that touches a curved surface at one point. *See also* trigonometry; calculus.

tangerine The fruit of a tree, **Citrus reticulata*, also called mandarin, native to SE Asia and cultivated in the S US and the Mediterranean region. The orange fruit, which peels easily and readily splits into segments, is usually eaten fresh. Many varieties have been developed, including the satsuma and clementine. The temple orange is a hybrid between the *orange and the tangerine.

Tangier (*or* Tangiers) 35 48N 5 45W A port in N Morocco, on a bay on the Strait of Gibraltar. An important Roman town, it was held successively by many powers until it was established as an international zone in 1923. During World War II it was under Spanish occupation (1940–45) and its international status was abolished on Moroccan independence (1956). It has a university (1971). Its industries include cigarette and textile manufacture, fishing, and market gardening, and it is also a tourist center. Population (1982): 266,346.

tango **1.** A Spanish flamenco dance. **2.** A ballroom dance in $\frac{2}{4}$ time, first performed in a fast form in the 1880s in the poor quarters of Buenos Aires. In the 1920s it spread to the US and Europe, where it developed melancholic musical rhythms and a stylized elegance.

Tangshan 39 37N 118 05E A city in NE China, in Hebei province. A center of heavy industry, its coal mines were under British control until 1952. China's first railroad began there (1882). Population (1990): 1,044,194.

Tanguy, Yves (1900–55) French surrealist painter. Entirely self-taught, in 1927 he began to paint bizarre forms, partly organic and partly mechanical, which he situated in barren landscapes. He continued to explore this unique vision after emigrating to the US in 1939.

Tanizaki Jun-ichiro (1886–1965) Japanese novelist. His first short stories of the early 1900s were a brilliant success. Their sensuous and grotesque themes are reminiscent of Edgar Allan Poe's work. In the 1930s, while updating *The Tale of Genji* by *Murasaki, he became strongly influenced by early Japanese literature. Such later novels as *The Makioka Sisters* (1943–48) show appreciation for the traditional Japanese way of life.

Tanjore. *See* Thanjavur.

tank An armor-plated military vehicle, self-propelled on caterpillar tracks and typically armed with a *gun (usually turret-mounted) and machine guns. Tanks are classified as main battle tanks (MBTs), for independent operation, and light tanks, for reconnaissance and other specialized uses. First used in World War I during the Somme offensive in France in September 1916, their true value became evident at Cambrai in November 1917. In World War II the Germans initially achieved great success by using their Panzer divisions as an independent force rather than as infantry support or cavalry replacement. Tank battles across Europe and N Africa replaced the static trench warfare of World War I. They were also important in the Korean War but played a more limited role in the Vietnam War, where the jungle terrain hindered their effectiveness. In the Arab-Israeli War of 1973 guided missiles caused heavy Israeli tank losses. Modern tank development has concentrated on improving weapons, armor, and computer-aided navigation and fire control. *See also* armored car.

tanker A seagoing vessel equipped with a large cargo tank for transporting liquids, especially oil. The forerunner of the modern tanker, the *Gluckauf* (2307 tons) was built in 1885; modern **supertankers** with a carrying capacity of 75,000 tons were developed after World War II in response to the increased world demand for oil. Ultra-Large Crude Carriers (ULCCs) have deadweights of up to nearly half a million tons. Size is not always an advantage, however, as such vessels can only enter certain ports, cannot negotiate the Suez Canal, and can cause ecological disasters if they are wrecked and spill their enormous cargoes into the sea.

Tannenburg, Battles of **1.** (July 5, 1410) The battle in which Polish and Lithuanian troops defeated the *Teutonic Knights, whose drive into E Europe was thereby arrested. **2.** (Aug 26–30, 1914) The battle early in World War I in which Germany defeated Russia, thus thwarting the Russian invasion of Prussia. Some 100,000 Russians were captured.

Tannhäuser (c. 1200–c. 1270) German poet. A Minnesinger, several of whose lyrics survive, he traveled widely, serving in various courts. Wagner's opera is based on the legend of his seduction by Venus, his life of sensuality at her court, and his pilgrimage to seek papal forgiveness.

tannin (*or* tannic acid) One of a group of phenol derivatives present in the bark, leaves, fruits, and galls of many plants. Tannins are used as mordants for many dyes, in tanning leather, and in making ink.

tansy A perennial herb, *Tanacetum* (or *Chrysanthemum*) *vulgare*, native to temperate Eurasia. Growing to a height of 12–40 in (30–100 cm), it has flat-topped clusters of yellow flowers and was formerly cultivated for its aromatic leaves, used for cooking and medicinal purposes. Family: *Compositae*.

Tanta 30 48N 31 00E A city in Egypt, on the Nile Delta. It is noted for its fairs and Muslim festivals and is an important commercial center with cotton and tobacco industries. Population (1986 est): 373,500.

tantalum (Ta) A very hard gray dense metallic element, discovered in 1802 by A. K. Ekeberg (1767–1813). It is similar to niobium (Nb) and is difficult to separate from it. Tantalum occurs naturally in the ore columbite ($Fe(Nb,Ta)_2O_6$). It is resistant to chemical attack and is used in alloys, for example in surgical materials for implantation in the body and in incandescent filaments. The oxide (Ta_2O_5) is used in special glass, with high refractive index, for camera lenses. At

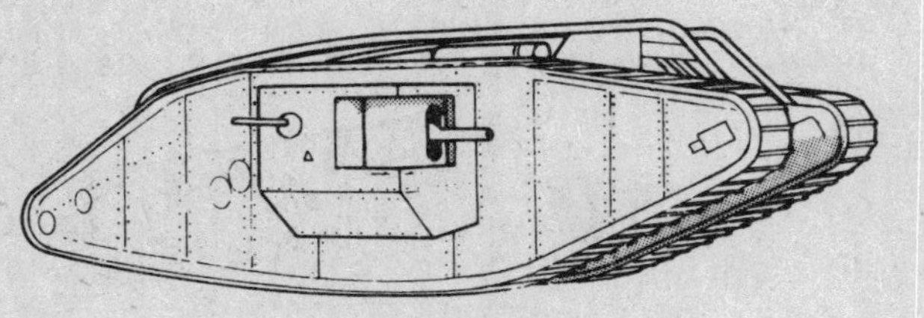

Mark IV British *Tanks were first successfully used during World War I in the battle of Cambrai in November 1917. They were designed to be able to cross trenches.*

German Pz III *At the beginning of World War II the German Panzer divisions were based on Pz III tanks, armed with a 50-mm gun and having a maximum speed of 30 mph (48 kph).*

Soviet T-34 *The Nazi invasion of the Soviet Union (1941) met resistance from the T-34, then probably the best design in the world. It had a 76.2-mm gun and a top speed of 32 mph (51 kph).*

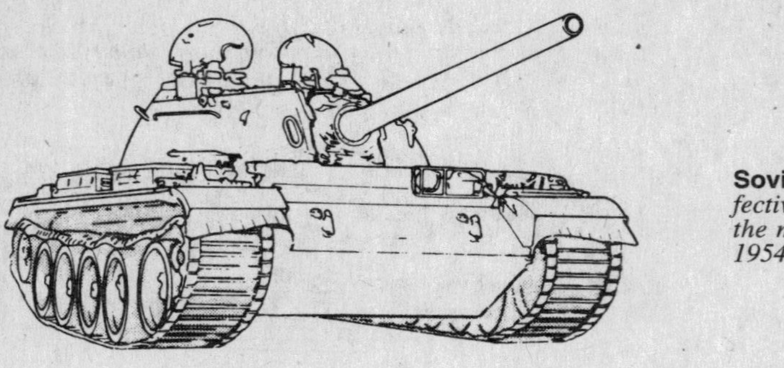

Soviet T-54 *This main battle tank, with its 100-mm gun, effective use of armor, and road speed of 34 mph (54 kph) was the most advanced tank in the world when it appeared in 1954.*

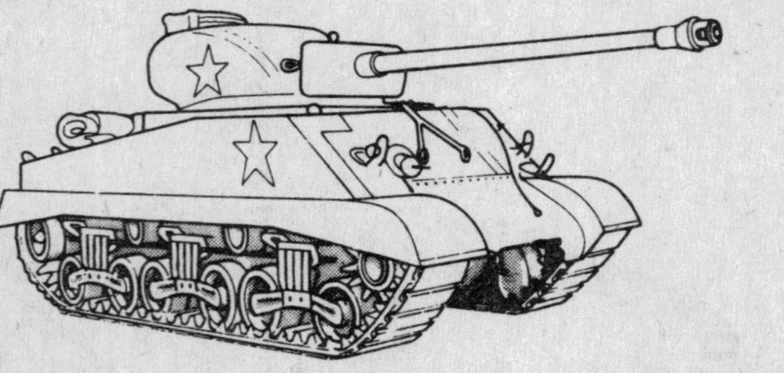

US M-4 *A US design used extensively in World War II was the M-4, known as the "General Sherman." Introduced in 1942, it had a 75-mm gun and a top speed of 24 mph (38 kph).*

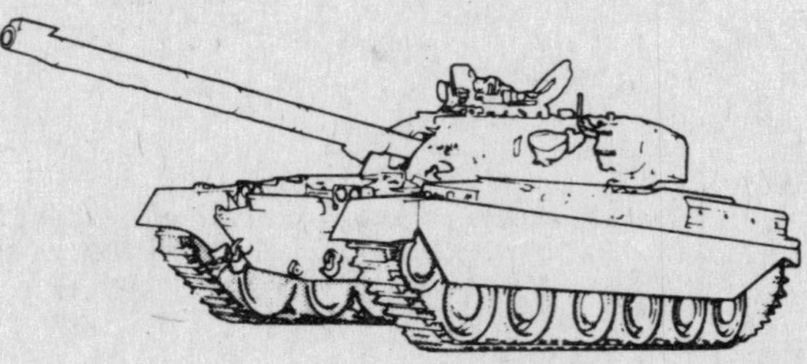

British Chieftain *Introduced in 1966, this main battle tank is heavily armed with a high-velocity 120-mm gun and has a top speed of 25 mph (40 kph).*

no 73; at wt 180.948; mp 5430°F (2996°C); bp 10,007 ± 180°F (5425 ± 100°C).

Tantalus A legendary Greek king of Lydia, son of Zeus and Pluto and father of *Niobe and *Pelops. In Hades he was punished for certain offenses against the gods by being made to stand within reach of water and fruits that moved away whenever he tried to drink or eat.

Tantras A group of Sanskrit religious texts written in India in the 5th century AD. The contents are miscellaneous but they form the basis of esoteric systems of meditation in both Hinduism and Buddhism. In the **Tantric yoga** of Hinduism, two principles are postulated: Shiva and Shakti, male and female, mind and creative energy, situated in the head and at the base of the spine, respectively. The object of tantric practices is to arouse the female element, which can be focused in various centers of the body, and ultimately to unite it with the male principle. **Tantric Buddhism** involves an elaborate system of meditation by means of mudras (gestures), mantras (symbolic sounds; *see* Om), and mandalas (diagrams). The imagery of sexual union is the distinctive feature of both systems, which are unusual in emphasizing the fulfillment of bodily desires rather than the ascetic practices that are more typical of Hinduism and Buddhism.

Tanzania, United Republic of A country in East Africa, on the Indian Ocean. It consists of a mainland area (formerly the republic of Tanganyika) and the islands of *Zanzibar and *Pemba, as well as some smaller islands. On the mainland its boundaries are formed partly by Lakes Victoria, Tanganyika, and Malawi. The land rises from the coast through plateaus to mountains, especially in the N, with Mount Kilimanjaro at 19,520 ft (5950 m). The majority of the population is African, mainly of Bantu origin. *Economy*: chiefly agricultural, especially subsistence farming. In mainland Tanzania the chief crops are cotton, corn, and cassava. Sisal, once important, is now in decline and there are plans for diversification of crops as well as development in forestry and livestock. Zanzibar (with Pemba) is the world's largest producer of cloves, with coconuts as the second cash crop. Food crops include rice, bananas, and cassava. Minerals extracted in Tanzania include diamonds, gold, tin, and salt; coal and iron have been found, as well as offshore gas. Hydroelectricity is a valuable source of power. The main exports are coffee, cloves, cotton, and diamonds. Tourism is important with Tanzania's many game parks and beaches. *History*: important prehistoric remains have been found by the *Leakey family. The area was visited by the Arabs in the Middle Ages and by the Portuguese in the 16th century. Tanganyika was occupied by the Germans in the 1880s, becoming a German protectorate in 1891. After World War I it was under British rule, first under League of Nations mandate and then as a UN trust territory. It gained independence in 1961 and in 1962 became a republic within the British Commonwealth with Dr. Julius K. Nyerere as its first president. In 1964 Tanganyika and Zanzibar joined to form the United Republic of Tanganyika and Zanzibar, now known as Tanzania. In 1977 the official political parties of the two countries merged to form the Revolutionary party. In the Arusha Declaration (1967) Nyerere launched a policy of decentralization, which involved the division of rural areas into cooperative communities (Ujamaas). Tanzania was instrumental in the overthrow in Uganda of *Amin. Relations with Zambia were close, particularly from the opening of the Chinese-built Tanzam Railway (1975). Nyerere's great socialist experiment, espousing social and economic self-reliance, appeared to be faltering in the wake of the acute economic hardships of the early 1980s. His charismatic personality continued to anchor the political processes of the country until his retirement in 1985. He was replaced by Ali Hassan Mwinyi. Nyerere retired as chairman of the ruling party in 1990. Mwinyi instituted economic and political reforms in the early 1990s. Official languages: Swahili and English. Official currency, since 1966: Tanzanian shilling of 100 cents. Area: 364,900 sq mi (945,087 sq km). Population (1990 est): 26,070,000. Capital: Dodoma. Main port: Dar es Salaam.

Taoism Emerging in the 6th century BC, Taoism is one of the two great native Chinese religio-philosophical systems (the other is *Confucianism) and a major influence in the development of Chinese culture. The goal of Taoism as a philosophy, as expressed in the *Tao Te Ching* of *Lao-zi, the *Chuang Tzu*, and the *Lieh Tzu*, is profound, joyful, mystical, and practical harmony with the universe. In politics and livelihood, the Taoist seeks the effective path of least resistance and of inconspicuousness. All extreme positions revert to their opposites. All is in flux except Tao (the Way) itself. *Yin* (the feminine) balances *yang* (the masculine). Meditation, spontaneity, and simplicity are stressed. *Te* (virtue) and *Ch'i* (energy) represent the power of effortless action accessible to the Taoist. As a religion Taoism emphasizes the alchemical relations between macrocosm and microcosm, seeking a formula for immortality by breath control, diet, exercises, sexual continence, or chemical elixirs. A priesthood, a huge hierarchical pantheon of gods, and a multitude of sacred texts and rituals associated with various sects arose. Later monasticism developed. Since the Chinese Cultural Revolution (1966–68) religious Taoism survives mainly in Taiwan. Western interest has been aroused by philosophical Taoism, especially by the *I Ching*, an oracular work that claims to demonstrate purpose in chance events.

tape recorder A device for recording and playing back sound stored on magnetic tape. In recording, the sound is converted to an electrical signal by a *microphone and then amplified before being fed to an electromagnet in the recording head. The varying field of the magnet leaves a pattern of magnetization in the iron (or sometimes chromium) oxide coating of the tape as it passes through the machine. To play back, the magnetized tape induces a current in a coil as it passes the reproducing head. The coil current is then amplified and fed to loudspeakers. Tape recorders provide a compact and portable means of recording sounds of all kinds; the tapes are usually wound into *cassettes or cartridges which can be purchased prerecorded with music, etc., or clean for recording upon.

tapestry A decorative or pictorial woven textile, used as a wall hanging, furniture cover, etc. Tapestry weaving has been practiced since antiquity but it only flourished in Europe from the 14th century, the major centers of production being Arras, Tournai, and Brussels in Flanders, and Beauvais and the *Gobelins factory in France. Medieval tapestries, often of floral and leaf patterns, were used as portable draft screens; others showing religious scenes were made for churches. From the 16th century painters, notably *Raphael and *Boucher, were commissioned to design tapestries. In the 19th century machine-made tapestries were introduced.

tapeworm A parasitic hermaphrodite *flatworm of the class *Cestoda* (about 3000 species). Tapeworms range from 0.75 in to 50 ft (20 mm to 15 m) in length and anchor themselves inside the intestine of their host by means of hooks and suckers on the head. They have no gut or sense organs, the body consisting of a chain of progressively large segments through which food is absorbed. The terminal segments—full of eggs—are regularly shed, passing out of the host's body to infect a secondary host, where larvae invade muscle tissue. Species infecting man include the beef tapeworm (*Taenia saginata*) and the pork tapeworm (*T. solium*).

tapioca. *See* cassava.

tapir A shy nocturnal hoofed mammal belonging to the genus *Tapirus* (4 species). The largest species is the black-and-white Malayan tapir (*T. indicus*), reaching about 40 in (1 m) at the shoulder and weighing up to 770 lb (350 kg). The remaining species of Central and South America are brown. All have a sparse covering of hairs and a large head with a short fleshy snout. Young tapirs are marked with white spots and stripes. Tapirs inhabit forests near water, feeding on leaves and shoots. Family: *Tapiridae*; order: **Perissodactyla*.

tar A thick black semisolid substance of organic origin, especially coal tar obtained when coal is heated to over 1834°F (1000°C) in the absence of air (2.2 lb [1 kg] of coal yielding about 1.8 oz [50 g] of tar). Tar can be used as it is, e.g. for the production of roofing felt, or can be distilled to produce a wide range of organic chemicals including benzene, naphthalene, and anthracene and their derivatives. The substance remaining is called pitch.

Tara 53 34N 6 35W A village in the Republic of Ireland, in Co Meath. The Hill of Tara was the ancient religious and political center of Ireland and where the early Irish Kings lived and were crowned. The original coronation stone is reputed to have been taken to Scone, Scotland.

Taranto 40 28N 17 15E A seaport in Italy, in Apulia on the Gulf of Taranto. Founded by the Greeks in the 8th century BC, it has an 11th-century cathedral. It is an important naval base, with shipyards. Its large iron- and steelworks were established in 1965. Population (1991 est): 244,033.

tarantula A large dark hairy spider (up to 3 in [75 mm] long) of the family *Theraphosidae*, found in tropical America. Many tarantulas live on trees or in burrows in the soil, feeding mainly at night on insects and occasionally frogs, toads, mice, and small birds. Their poisonous bite is painful but not fatal to man.

The name was originally given to a *wolf spider (*Lycosa tarentula*) of Taranto (Italy). In the Middle Ages it was believed that the poisonous effects of the bite of this spider could be eliminated by dancing (the dance came to be known as the tarantella).

Tarbell, Ida (Minerva) (1857–1944) US muckraking journalist and writer. An editor (1894–1906) of *McClure's Magazine*, she exposed unfair practices in the oil industry through articles that were consolidated in *A History of the Standard Oil Company* (1904). From 1906 she coedited *American Magazine*, a publication she helped to establish. Other works included *Life of Abraham Lincoln* (1900), *The Tariff in Our Times* (1911), *The Business of Being a Woman* (1913), and *The Nationalizing of Business, 1878–1898* (1936).

Tarbes 43 14N 0 05E A city in SW France, the capital of the Hautes-Pyrénées department. A Huguenot stronghold (16th–17th centuries), it has a 13th-century cathedral and trades in horses and agricultural produce. Population (1975): 57,765.

Tardigrada A phylum of tiny invertebrate animals (about 350 species), known as water bears, sometimes regarded as a class of arthropods. About 0.04 in (1 mm) long, they are almost transparent, with four pairs of short legs ending in claws. Tardigrades are found in terrestrial, freshwater, and marine habitats, feeding on the sap of mosses and other plants.

tare One of several annual herbs of the genus *Vicia* (which also includes *vetches) that grow as weeds on cultivated land throughout the world. Tares have slender trailing stems, up to 24 in (60 cm) long, and branches with paired leaflets and terminal climbing tendrils. The tiny white or bluish flowers give rise to seedpods. Family: **Leguminosae*.

targum (Aramaic: translation) An Aramaic translation of part of the Bible. There are several targumim, notably those of Onkelos (of the Torah) and Pseudo-Jonathan (of the Prophets). They were produced in Palestine and Babylonia in the Talmudic and Gaonic periods, and include a great deal of *Midrash.

Tariff of 1828 (*or* Tariff of Abominations) US law that levied high taxes on wool, hemp, and other raw materials, as well as on finished goods. Passed for political reasons, parts of the bill were revised by the Tariff of 1832.

Tariff of 1832 US legislation that revised the Tariff of 1828. It removed a tariff on raw wool and flax imports and increased the duty on finished woolen goods. It was nullified in 1833.

tariffs A surcharge imposed by a government on imported goods. Several arguments are used to justify tariffs. The "infant industry" argument is that tariffs are needed to protect a domestic industry while it becomes established. Other arguments include the need to protect employment in domestic industries, the need to provide a counter to "dumping" (foreign industries selling goods at a lower price abroad than at home), and the benefit of the revenue that will accrue from tariffs. The secretariat of the *General Agreement on Tariffs and Trade serves as a center for negotiating tariff agreements. *See also* customs unions.

Tarim Basin A great depression in NW China, covering the area between the *Tian Shan in the N and the *Kunlun Mountains in the S. Drained by the Dalimu (*or* Tarim) River, it consists of the Takelamagan (*or* Takla Makan) Desert with the salt lake of *Lop Nor in the E, where nuclear tests have been held. Although there are oasis towns, the region is largely undeveloped. Area: about 350,000 sq mi (906,500 sq km).

Tarkington, (Newton) Booth (1869–1946) US novelist. His first novel, *The Gentleman from Indiana*, was published in 1899. Subsequent novels, *The Magnificent Ambersons* (1918) and *Alice Adams* (1921), were awarded Pulitzer Prizes, and he is well known for his classic teenage novels, *Penrod* (1914) and *Seventeen* (1916).

taro A perennial herbaceous plant, *Colocasia esculenta*, also known as eddo, dasheen, and elephant's ear, native to tropical Asia and widely cultivated in tropical and subtropical areas for its edible tubers. The tubers, which are large, starchy, and spherical, contain more protein than potatoes and are eaten cooked as vegetables or made into puddings or bread. Family: *Araceae*.

tarot A pack of 78 cards used primarily in fortune-telling, although they are also the forerunners of modern *playing cards, and games are still played with them. They originated in 14th-century Italy, although their symbolism probably draws on a far older tradition. The original pack is now known as the Greater Arcana; this consists of 22 cards (believed to correspond to the letters of the Hebrew alphabet), 21 numbered cards representing natural elements, vices, and virtues and a "Fool" (the original joker). During the 14th century these were combined with 56 number cards of the Asian kind then also beginning to be used. Now known as the Lesser Arcana, these 56 are in 4 suits: cups, swords, money, and clubs or rods, representing clergy, nobility, merchants, and peasants. Each suit consists of number cards from 1 to 10 and four court cards: king, queen, knave, and knight.

tarpan A Eurasian wild horse, *Equus caballus*, that became extinct in the early 20th century. It was small and dun-colored with a long flowing mane. Attempts have been made to reconstitute the tarpan by crossing various modern breeds that are thought to be related to it.

TAROT *The Wheel of Fortune, the 10th card of the Greater Arcana, from a pack of French tarot cards.*

Tarpeia In Roman legend, a Roman commander's daughter who offered to betray Rome to the attacking Sabines in return for what they wore on their left arms, meaning their golden bracelets. When the Sabines overran the citadel, they literally obeyed her wish by crushing her to death with their shields.

tarpon A marine game fish belonging to the family *Elopidae*. It has a slender body covered by large thick silvery scales. The Atlantic tarpon, *Tarpon* (or *Megalops*) *atlanticus*, reaches up to 7 ft (2 m) in length and occurs inshore in warm waters. Order: *Elopiformes*.

Tarquin the Proud (Tarquinius Superbus) The last king of Rome, who ruled, according to Roman tradition, from 534 to 510 BC. Tarquin is probably a historical figure but many myths evolved to account for the nickname Superbus; he was expelled from Rome and brought monarchy into permanent disrepute there.

tarragon A perennial herb, *Artemisia dracunculus*, native to central Asia and widely cultivated. It grows to a height of about 24 in (60 cm) and has slender leaves and flowers, which are often dried and used in salads, sauces, pickles, etc. It also yields an essential oil used in cooking and perfumery. Family: *Compositae*.

Tarragona (Latin name: Tarraco) 41 07N 1 15E A port in NE Spain, in Catalonia on the Mediterranean Sea. It was a major Roman port and has many

Roman ruins, including an aqueduct; it also possesses a cathedral (12th–13th centuries). An agricultural center, it also has a petrochemicals industry. Population (1991 est): 110,000.

Tarrasa 41 38N 2 00E A city in NE Spain, in Catalonia. An important industrial center, it is famous for its woolen textiles; other industries include glass and fertilizers. Population (1991 est): 154,000.

tarsier A small nocturnal *prosimian primate belonging to the genus *Tarsius* (3 species), of Sumatra, Borneo, Celebes, and the Philippines; 9–17 in (22–43 cm) long including the naked tail (5–11 in; 13–27 cm), tarsiers have enormous eyes, large hairless ears, and gripping pads at the end of their digits. They are mainly arboreal, using both hands to seize small insects and lizards. Family: *Tarsiidae*. □mammal.

Tarsus 36 52N 34 52E A city in central S Turkey, near Adana. The first known settlement there was Neolithic; it was Assyrian for many centuries and an important town in the Roman and Byzantine Empires. St Paul was born there. Population (1990): 187,508.

tartan. *See* Highland dress.

tartaric acid ($C_4H_6O_6$) A white crystalline powder with an acid taste; it is a constituent of *baking powder.

Tartarus In Greek religion, the place of punishment and perpetual torment in the underworld. The *Titans were imprisoned there after their defeat by the gods.

Tartu (German and Swedish name: Dorpat) 58 20N 26 44E A city in SE Estonia. Although an industrial center, it is best known for its university founded (1632) by Gustavus II Adolphus of Sweden, Tartu being held successively by Sweden, Poland, and Russia, to which it was ceded in 1704. Population (1991 est): 115,300.

Tasaday A people of the rain forests of Mindanao in the Philippines having an extremely rudimentary culture based on food gathering using simple stone and wooden tools. They are cave dwellers who wear leaves for clothing and only became known to the outside world in 1971.

Tashkent 41 16N 69 13E The capital city of Uzbekistan. It is the oldest and largest city of central Asia, being a major communications, industrial, and cultural center. Textiles (based on cotton from the surrounding oasis), food- and tobacco-processing, and chemical industries are important. *History*: dating from at least the 1st century BC, it fell successively to the Arabs (7th century) and the Turks (12th century), becoming a great commercial center under Timur. It was captured by Russia in 1865. Tashkent was severely damaged by earthquake in 1966. Population (1991 est): 2,113,300.

Tasman, Abel Janszoon (c. 1603–c. 1659) Dutch navigator. Commissioned in 1642 by van *Dieman to explore the S Pacific, Tasman sighted present-day Tasmania (which he named Van Dieman's Land, after his patron), New Zealand, and in 1643 Tonga and Fiji. In 1644 he sailed along the N coast of Australia, thus proving it continuous.

Tasmania An island and the smallest state of Australia, separated from the SE corner of the mainland by Bass Strait. Discovered by Abel *Tasman in 1642, it was called Van Dieman's Land until 1856. It is the most mountainous of the Australian states and is dominated by the Central Plateau. Agriculture is important with mixed and dairy farming, sheep rearing, and the cultivation of apples and hops. More than 40% of the island is covered by forest and the export of wood chips to Japan is a significant industry. Large mineral deposits include tin, iron ore, zinc, lead, and copper; King Island, off the NW coast, is Australia's main producer of tungsten. Area: 26,383 sq mi (68,332 sq km). Population (1992 est): 470,900. Capital: Hobart.

Tasmanian devil A carnivorous marsupial, *Sarcophilus harrisi*, formerly found on the Australian mainland but now restricted to Tasmania. About 40 in (1 m) long, it is black with a large head and wide jaws containing doglike teeth. Strong and heavily built, it feeds on wallabies, birds, and lizards and fights ferociously when cornered. Family: *Dasyuridae* (dasyures).

Tasmanian wolf. *See* thylacine.

Tasman Sea A section of the SW Pacific Ocean, lying between SE Australia and Tasmania on the W and New Zealand on the E. Area: about 900,000 sq mi (2,300,000 sq km).

Tass. *See* news agency.

Tassili-n-Ajjer A sandstone massif in the central Sahara containing numerous caves decorated with rock paintings of people and animals (c. 8000–c. 100 BC). Depictions of hippopotamuses and vast herds of cattle indicate a far damper climate than at present.

Tasso, Torquato (1544–95) Italian poet. After studying law at Padua and publishing his epic *Rinaldo* (1562) he joined the court of the Este family at Ferrara, where he wrote the pastoral drama *Aminta* (1573) and his major work, the romantic epic *Gerusalemme liberata* (1575). For the rest of his life he suffered from mental instability but continued to write lyrics, religious poems, philosophical dialogues, and a tragedy, *Re Torrismondo* (1587).

taste. *See* tongue.

Tatar Autonomous Republic (*or* Tataria) An administrative division in W central Russia. The *Tatars, who comprise some 50% of the population, were conquered by Ivan the Terrible in the 16th century. The region became an autonomous republic in 1920. The region is the country's main producer of oil and natural gas and also has deposits of coal and other minerals. There are highly developed engineering, oil, and chemical industries, and the timber, textile, and food industries are now also expanding. Agricultural products include fodder crops and cereals. Area: 26,250 sq mi (68,000 sq km). Population (1991 est): 3,679,400. Capital: Kazan.

Tatars A people, mainly living in the Tatar Autonomous Republic of Russia, who belong to the NW division of the Turkic-speaking peoples. They traditionally lived by farming and herding. There are many Tatar dialects, one of which, Kazan Tatar, is a literary language that goes back to the 13th century. The Tatars are descended from peoples associated with the various states of the Mongol empire and the name was often used to refer to all the nomadic Turkic and Mongol peoples of the steppes. Their society was traditionally a stratified one divided into noble and commoner groups ruled by khans. They are mainly Muslim. *See also* Golden Horde.

Tate, Allen (1899–1979) US poet and critic. He was one of the founders of the Fugitives, a group of agrarian poets at Vanderbilt University. The Civil War is the main subject of his novel *The Fathers* (1938) and his best-known poem "Ode to the Confederate Dead" (1926). He published a great deal of criticism, including *On the Limits of Poetry* (1948), and his verse is collected in *Collected Poems* (1978).

Tate, Nahum (1652–1715) British poet. Born in Dublin, he is best remembered for his version of Shakespeare's *King Lear*, which omitted the Fool and ended happily with Cordelia marrying Edgar. He was coauthor of the second part of Dryden's *Absalom and Achitophel* (1681). He became Britain's poet laureate in 1692.

Tate Gallery An art gallery in London, England, housing paintings of the British school and modern foreign paintings and sculpture. It was built in 1897 with the financial support of Sir Henry Tate (1819–99), who had donated his collection of British paintings to the nation in 1890. Highlights are its Pre-Raphaelite works and the paintings by *Turner.

Tati, Jacques (J. Tatischeff; 1908–82) French film actor and director. He was a music-hall performer before he turned to films. He wrote, directed, and acted in a number of popular award-winning comedies, such as *Jour de Fête* (1947), *Monsieur Hulot's Holiday* (1952), *Mon Oncle* (1958), and *Playtime* (1968), the humor of which is achieved by imaginative visual gags and Tati's talent for pantomime.

Tatra Mountains Two mountain ranges in central E Europe: the **High Tatras** (Polish name: Tatry Wysokie; Czech name: Vysoké Tatry), which extend 55 mi (90 km) E–W along the Polish-Slovak border and constitute the highest area of the *Carpathian Mountains, and, to the S, the **Low Tatras** (Czech name: Nizké Tatry), which run parallel for some 95 mi (150 km) and rise to 6703 ft (2043 m).

Tatum, Art(hur) (1910–56) US jazz pianist, who began playing as a child when he was already blind. A well-known soloist in the 1930s, he formed his own trio in 1943. His superb technique and advanced sense of harmony earned him a high reputation among both jazz and classical musicians.

Tatum, Edward Lawrie (1909–75) US geneticist, who (working with G. W. *Beadle on mutant strains of bread mold) provided evidence that specific genes determine the structure of specified enzymes. In 1946, Tatum and J. *Lederberg discovered the phenomenon of genetic recombination in certain bacteria. Tatum shared a Nobel Prize (1958) with Beadle and Lederberg.

tau particle An elementary particle with a very short lifetime (5×10^{-12} second) and a mass about 3500 times that of the *electron. It is classified as a lepton (*see* particle physics). It reacts by the *weak interaction.

Taupo, Lake (*or* Taupomoana) The largest lake in New Zealand. It lies on the volcanic plateau of central North Island and is drained by the Waikato River. Area: 238 sq mi (616 sq km).

Taurus (Latin: bull) A large constellation in the N sky near Orion, lying on the *zodiac between Gemini and Aries. The brightest star is *Aldebaran. The constellation contains the *Hyades and *Pleiades star clusters and the *Crab nebula with its associated pulsar.

Taurus Mountains A mountain range in S Turkey. It extends 348 mi (560 km) parallel to the Mediterranean coast and rises to 12,251 ft (3734 m) at Ala Dağ, or to 12,848 ft (3916 m) at Erciyas Dağı if the Anti-Taurus range (an extension to the NE) is included.

tautology A statement that is always true and therefore gives no information. For example, "It is either raining or it is not raining."

tautomerism. *See* isomers.

Tawney, R(ichard) H(enry) (1880–1962) British economic historian. Influenced by the theories of Max *Weber, Tawney wrote on capitalism, his most famous book being *Religion and the Rise of Capitalism* (1926). A professor at London University (1931–49), he was a formative influence on the British Labour Party.

tawny owl A common *owl, *Strix aluco*, occurring in Europe and SE Asia; 15 in (38 cm) long, it has short rounded wings, dark brown eyes, a mottled brown plumage, and lacks ear tufts.

taxation The means by which a government raises funds to finance its spending and, to some extent, by which it regulates the economy (*see* fiscal policy) or achieves its social and political aims (e.g. the equal distribution of wealth). Direct taxes are paid by individuals (e.g. *income tax, *capital-gains tax), or companies through corporation taxes directly to the tax authorities; indirect taxes are levied on goods and services (e.g. sales taxes). In most cases taxation is levied when funds change hands. Progressive taxation, in which those with higher incomes or greater wealth pay more in proportion than those with lower incomes or less wealth, is a means of achieving social or political objectives. *See also* customs and excise duties.

tax haven (*or* tax shelter) A country or area that has low taxes and can therefore offer advantages to foreign individuals or companies that pay high taxes in their own countries. Individuals have to take up residence in these countries, giving up their domiciliary rights in their own countries; companies can open offices and subsidiary companies in the haven countries, through which they can conduct part of their business.

taxi. *See* cab.

taxidermy The art of making lifelike zoological models of creatures by preserving their skins and mounting them on suitable dummies. Taxidermy dates from the 17th century but improved technology and the use of plastic body forms have resulted in greater degrees of realism.

Taxila The site of an *Achaemenian and Greek city near Rawalpindi (N Pakistan). Occupied from the 5th century BC, it was a famous center of learning. Excavations revealed a blend of Greek and Buddhist elements, typical of the *Gandhara culture. The *Huns destroyed Taxila in 460 AD.

taxis The movement of a living organism or cell in response to an external stimulus: the movement is either toward or away from the stimulus, i.e. a positive or negative taxis. Taxes are specified according to the type of stimulus. For example, **chemotaxis** is the respond to a change in the concentration of a chemical. Many insects, for example, respond chemotactically to the scents emitted by the opposite sex. **Phototaxis** is the response to light: cockroaches are negatively phototactic. *Compare* tropism.

taxonomy The study of the classification and nomenclature of organisms. The principles of taxonomy were established in the 18th century by the work of *Linnaeus (*see also* binomial nomenclature). As far as possible, organisms are arranged into a hierarchy of groups (called taxa) based on degrees of relationship (*see* phylogeny). When knowledge of the evolution of a group is lacking, taxonomy is based on structural and other similarities. The basic unit of classification is the *species. Related species are grouped into genera, which are arranged into orders and then classes. Related classes are regarded as belonging to the same *phylum. The two main methods used in determining taxonomic positions are classical taxonomy, which is based on morphological and biochemical data, and numerical taxonomy, in which mathematical and statistical methods are used to assess similarities and differences.

Tay River The longest river in Scotland, rising in the Grampian Mountains and flowing generally NE through Loch Tay before flowing SE to enter the North Sea through the Firth of Tay. Length: 120 mi (193 km).

Taylor, A(lan) J(ohn) P(ercivale) (1906–90) British historian, who specializes in modern European political history. Among his many books is *The Origins of the Second World War* (1961).

Taylor, Brook (1685–1737) English mathematician, best known for the Taylor series in calculus. He also made contributions to the mathematics of perspective. Taylor, educated at Cambridge, was secretary of the Royal Society between 1714 and 1719.

Taylor, Elizabeth (1932–) US film actress, born in England. She began her career as a child star, notably in *National Velvet* (1944). Her other films include *Giant* (1956), *Butterfield 8* (1961), *Who's Afraid of Virginia Woolf* (1966), in which she costarred with Richard *Burton, to whom she was twice married, and *The Blue Bird* (1976).

Taylor, Frederick Winslow (1856–1915) US engineer, who pioneered the techniques of scientific management. In 1881, while working for the Midvale Steel Company, he introduced time and motion study as a means of increasing efficiency, incurring considerable resentment from those affected by it. He later became a management consultant to many firms.

Taylor, Zachary (1784–1850) US general and statesman; 12th president of the US (1849–50). His military career began in the *War of 1812. Taylor later participated in the *Black Hawk and *Seminole wars and served as commander of the Department of Florida (1838–40). During the *Mexican War, Taylor gained national acclaim and his nickname "Old Rough and Ready" for his important victories at Monterrey and at the Battle of *Buena Vista. Receiving the presidential nomination of the Whig party in 1848, Taylor defeated the Democratic candidate, Lewis Cass, in the general election. However, Zachary Taylor served as president for less than two years, dying in office in 1850.

Tbilisi (Russian name: Tiflis) 41 43N 44 48E A city in and capital of Georgia, on the Kura River. A major industrial center, engineering and the manufacture of textiles, wine, and food are the principal economic activities; Tbilisi also has a lively cultural life. *History*: founded in the mid-5th century, it fell successively to the Persians, Byzantines, Arabs, Mongols, Turks, and finally, the Russians (1801). Its name was changed to the Georgian Tbilisi in 1936. Population (1991 est): 1,279,000.

Tchaikovsky, Peter Ilich (1840–93) Russian composer. He studied under Anton Rubinstein in St Petersburg and became professor at the Moscow conservatory in 1866. After the success of his first piano concerto, Tchaikovsky was offered financial support from Nadezhda von Meck (1831–94), a wealthy widow, whom he never met. In 1877 Tchaikovsky made a disastrous marriage and began to suffer from depression, although many of his works were extremely successful. He died of cholera, from drinking unboiled water, in 1893. Among his compositions are six symphonies, including the *Pathétique* (1893), three piano concertos (one unfinished), a violin concerto, string quartets, the opera *Eugene Onegin* (1877–78), and the ballets *Swan Lake* (1876–77) and *The Nutcracker* (1891–92).

tea The dried leaves and shoots of the evergreen shrub or tree *Camellia sinensis*, which yield a beverage when infused with water. Native to parts of India and China, the tea plant has three major varieties—China, Assam, and Cambodia—and numerous hybrids, ranging from 9–60 ft (2.75–18 m) in height. The shoots and young leaves are picked by hand and left to wilt before being lightly rolled and dried. Before drying, the leaves may be allowed to ferment, producing either black tea, or if only partially fermented, oolong tea. Leaves that are not fermented produce green tea. The major tea exporters are India and Sri Lanka;

most of China's production goes for home consumption. Tea is also produced in SE Asia and parts of Africa and South America. Tea is sold in the form of chopped leaves—loose or contained in small porous paper bags (tea bags)—or as a soluble powdered extract (instant tea). Its stimulating effect is due to the caffeine content (about 3.5%); flavor depends on the presence of volatile oils, and tannins are responsible for its color. Family: *Theaceae*.

Tea Act. *See* Boston Tea Party.

tea ceremony. *See* cha-no-yu.

Teach, Edward (d. 1718) British pirate, nicknamed Blackbeard, who molested shipping in the Atlantic from his headquarters in North Carolina. In 1718 he was killed by a punitive force sent from Virginia.

teak A tropical □tree, *Tectonia grandis*, native to SE Asia and cultivated for its timber. Growing to a height of 150 ft (45 m) in its natural state, it has small white flowers and fleshy fruits. The aromatic golden-yellow heartwood becomes brown with darker mottling when seasoned and is very hard and durable, being used for furniture, door and window frames, construction purposes, etc. Myanmar (Burma) is the major teak exporter. Family: *Verbenaceae*.

teal A small *dabbling duck, *Anas crecca*, of the N hemisphere, nesting on marshes and wintering on mudflats and estuaries; 14 in (35 cm) long, it feeds on water plants and aquatic invertebrates. Drakes are grey and have a chestnut head with a cream-edged green eye stripe and a white wing stripe; females are mottled brown and both sexes have a green-and-black wing patch.

Teapot Dome Scandal (1921–24) US political scandal during the administration of Pres. Warren G. *Harding that involved the illegal leasing of government oil reserve lands. Secretary of the Interior Albert B. Fall leased navy oil reserve lands at Elk Hills, Calif., and Teapot Dome, Wyo., to private businessmen Harry F. Sinclair and Edward Doheny, in exchange for payments totaling $409,000. Secretary Fall was prosecuted and convicted of bribery charges; Sinclair and Doheny were acquitted of conspiracy charges. The reputation of the entire Harding administration was clouded by the affair.

tear gas (*or* lachrymator) A substance, generally an atomized liquid rather than a gas, that is used to control unruly crowds. Tear gas causes acute eye irritation with temporary blindness and copious flow of tears. Side effects of tear gas may include lasting damage to the eyes and nasal and lung tissues and dermatitis. Chloroacetophenone (Mace) is the best-known example. *See also* chemical warfare.

Teasdale, Sara (1884–1933) US poet. Using simple, traditional lyric forms, she wrote the collections *Helen of Troy and Other Poems* (1911) and *Rivers to the Sea* (1915) before being awarded a Pulitzer Prize for *Love Songs* (1917). Other works include *Flame and Shadow* (1920), *Rainbow Gold* (1922), *Dark of the Moon* (1926), and *Strange Victory* (1933), which was published after her suicide.

teasel A biennial herb, *Dipsacus fullonum*, native to Europe, W Asia, and N Africa. The prickly stems grow to a height of 7 ft (2 m) and bear conical heads of blue, purple, or white flowers with stiff hooked bracts. Fuller's teasel (*D. fullonum sativus*) was formerly cultivated for its flower heads, which were used to tease fabrics and raise a nap. Family: *Dipsacaceae*.

technetium (Tc) A silvery-gray radioactive element that was the first to be produced artificially. It does not occur naturally on earth but has been observed spectroscopically in a number of stars, where it is being continuously formed by nuclear reactions. It is chemically similar to rhenium and the compound $KTcO_4$

is a remarkable corrosion inhibitor in steels. At no 43; at wt (99); mp 4045°F (2227°C); bp 8369°F (4627°C).

tectonics The study of the major structural features of the earth's crust and the processes by which they are constructed. Thus a feature described as tectonic is formed by deformational movements of the earth's crust or by volcanic action rather than by geomorphological processes. A tectonic map shows structural features, usually over large areas. The most modern interpretation of global tectonics is the theory of *plate tectonics.

Tecumseh (c. 1768–1813) American Shawnee Indian chief, who led an Indian confederacy against the advance of white settlement in the NW. After his tribe was surprised at the battle of Tippecanoe (1811) he swore eternal war on the settlers. The conviction among frontiersmen that the British in Canada were helping Tecumseh led to a demand among the so-called War Hawks in Congress for war with Britain, the *War of 1812, in which Tecumseh was killed.

Tees River A river in N England. Rising in the Pennines in Cumbria, it flows mainly E into the Teesmouth estuary at Middlesbrough to join the North Sea. Length: 70 mi (113 km).

teeth Hard structures in the mouth, embedded in the jaws, used for biting and chewing food. The human adult (permanent) dentition consists of 32 teeth, including incisors (8), canines (4), premolars (8), and molars (12). Young children have a milk (deciduous) dentition of 20 teeth (incisors, canines, and molars), which are replaced by the permanent teeth between the ages of 6 and 12. The third molar (wisdom tooth) on each side of both jaws does not normally appear until the age of about 20 (sometimes later). The crown of a tooth consists of very dense hard enamel (largely *apatite) overlying the yellow bonelike dentine, which is slightly spongy and very sensitive to touch, temperature, and pain. The pulp at the center contains blood vessels and nerve fibers.

Tegucigalpa 14 20N 87 12W The capital of Honduras, situated in the center of the country in a high valley. Population (1989 est): 608,100.

Tehran (*or* Teheran) 35 40N 51 26E The capital of Iran, in the N center of the country at the foot of the Elburz Mountains. Most of its buildings are modern. Tehran is the commercial, industrial, administrative, and cultural center of the country, with six universities (oldest 1934). It became the capital in 1788 and has been greatly enlarged this century. Fierce rioting there preceded the overthrow (1979) of the shah of Iran. Population (1986): 6,042,584.

Tehran Conference (1943) The conference in World War II attended by Pres. Franklin D. Roosevelt (US), Stalin (Soviet Union), and Churchill (UK). Its chief purpose was to coordinate Allied strategy in W and E Europe.

Tehuantepec, Isthmus of An isthmus in S Mexico, between the Gulf of Campeche and the Gulf of Tehuantepec.

Teilhard de Chardin, Pierre (1881–1955) French Jesuit theologian and paleontologist. In his books *The Phenomenon of Man* (1955) and *Le Milieu divin* (1957), he maintained that the universe and mankind are in constant evolution toward a perfect state.

Tejo River. *See* Tagus River.

tektites Small glassy objects which are apparently composed of rapidly cooled molten material probably from meteorites.

Telanaipura. *See* Jambi.

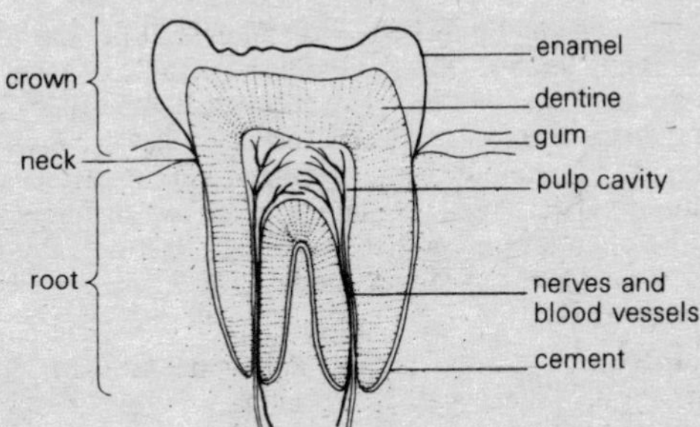

molar tooth *The root of the tooth is anchored into the socket by a bonelike substance, cement.*

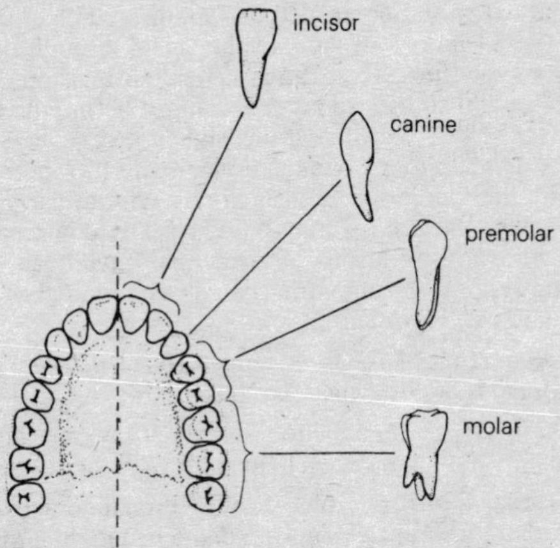

teeth in the adult upper jaw *The incisors and canines are used principally for biting; the premolars and molars are for grinding and chewing. The lower jaw contains the same number and type of teeth.*

TEETH

Tel Aviv-Yafo 32 05N 34 46E A city in central Israel, on the Mediterranean coast. Most of the buildings in the city are modern structures, but some old streets have been restored. It is the largest city in Israel, and the country's commercial, industrial, and cultural center. Israel's stock exchange is there, and there are two universities (1953 and 1974). The city's port is at Ashdod, to the S. Population (1990 est): 321,700.

telecommunications The transfer of information by any electromagnetic means, such as wire or radio waves. It includes telephones, telegraphy, *radio, *television, etc. Generally, a telecommunications system consists of a transmitter, a transmission channel, and a receiver. The input to the transmitter is usually coded in some way and then fed to a modulator, in which it is combined with a carrier signal (*see* modulation).

The transmission channel may be a wire, an optical fiber, or radio waves within a specified frequency range (the bandwidth). A single channel may carry several signals if a *multiplexer is used. The receiver demodulates the signal and decodes it, converting it into the desired form of output, which may be sound, an electrical signal to a computer, a teleprinter printout, etc. Distortion may occur in the transmission because the signal has taken two different paths (shadowing) or because the channel may not respond equally to all the frequencies being transmitted. Noise (spurious signals) may arise at any stage of the transmission and reception process.

The **telephone**, which was invented by Alexander Graham Bell in 1875, carries speech in the form of electrical signals along a wire. A carbon *microphone in the mouthpiece produces an electrical signal that passes through a network of exchanges and relays to the receiving earpiece, where it is converted back into sound by a small diaphragm *loudspeaker. Telephone connections are now normally made automatically, first going through a local exchange and then, for long-distance calls, through the trunk network. All the switching operations are activated by the caller and controlled and monitored electronically. Telephone connections exist to almost all parts of the world through undersea cables and *communications satellites. **Telegraphy** is the transmission of written or printed messages by electrical signals and was developed before the telephone, in 1837, by Samuel F. B. *Morse. Now telegrams and *telex messages are carried along the same wires as telephone conversations, using different frequency ranges. Radiotelegraphy uses radio waves instead of a wire to carry the message. Like long-distance telephone links it may be relayed by communications satellites. Optical fibers transmitting beams of laser light have been developed and can carry considerably more information than an electric cable of the same thickness. *See also* teletext; viewdata.

telekinesis Apparent change in or movement of material objects, caused by mental effort alone. It is also called psychokinesis (PK).

Telemachus In Greek legend, the son of *Odysseus and *Penelope. He searched for his lost father and then helped him kill the suitors of Penelope.

Telemann, Georg Philipp (1681–1767) German composer, born in Magdeburg. While studying law at Leipzig University he taught himself to play various instruments and to compose. His output was very large and included operas, oratorios, church music, and much chamber music.

teleology The philosophical study of ends, goals, and the ultimate good. It has application in both ethics (*see* utilitarianism) and *metaphysics.

teleost Any *bony fish belonging to the infraclass *Teleostei* (over 20,000 species), which includes nearly all the important food and game fish and many aquarium fish. Teleosts have a symmetrically divided (homocercal) tail fin and an air-filled swim bladder, which is emptied or filled to regulate buoyancy and to give great maneuverability. They are solitary or shoaling fish and most lay eggs on rocks or plants, or freely in the water, although some bear live young. Males or sometimes the females may guard the young.

telepathy. *See* extrasensory perception.

telephone. *See* telecommunications.

telephoto lens A camera lens that gives a bigger image than a normal lens without moving the camera closer to the subject or extending the camera. It consists of two groups of lenses. The front unit converges the light rays and the rear unit partially corrects this. The light reaching the film appears to converge from a point some distance in front of the camera. Telephoto lenses tend to result in a slightly flattened perspective in the final picture.

telescope An optical instrument that produces a magnified image of distant objects. It is used on land and as a major research tool in astronomy. The first **reflecting telescope** was produced by *Newton in 1668. In the reflecting telescope the light from an object is collected by a concave, usually paraboloid, mirror of long focal length. This primary mirror reflects the light into a secondary optical system, which in turn reflects it into a short-focus eyepiece. The eyepiece lenses produce a magnified image that can be viewed by eye, photographed, or otherwise analyzed. Depending on the secondary optics, reflectors are called **Gregorian, Newtonian, Cassegrain,** or **coudé telescopes.**

The **refracting telescope** was invented in 1608 by *Lippershey in Holland and developed by *Galileo as an astronomical instrument a year later. The light in the refracting telescope falls on a converging long-focus objective lens. The resulting image is then magnified by the short-focus eyepiece to produce the final image. An example is the **Keplerian telescope,** which was the first major improvement on Galileo's original design. Refractors are also used as terrestrial telescopes, usually containing an additional lens or a prism to cause the inverted image to be seen erect.

A telescope's light-gathering power depends on the area of the primary mirror or the objective lens. Since large mirrors are easier to fashion and mount than large lenses, the major astronomical telescopes are reflectors. In addition, unlike the objective in refractors, the reflector's mirror suffers no chromatic *aberration and its spherical aberration and coma are minimal. The world's largest optical telescope has a 20 ft (6 m) reflector. *See also* Schmidt telescope; radio telescope.

Telesio, Bernardino (1509–88) Italian humanist. His philosophy was influenced by the ancient Greeks and was strongly empirical and opposed to *Aristotelianism. He founded a scientific society (1566) to propagate his approach and among those he influenced were *Campanella and Giordano *Bruno.

teletext An information service in which pages of text are transmitted together with normal television broadcasts for display on a modified domestic television set. The system utilizes two of the unused lines between picture frames. All the stored information, which may be weather reports, news flashes, sports results, etc., is sent out continuously in the blanking period of the television signals. The required pages are selected for display by keyboard, and the user may have to wait a few minutes for them to come up on the screen if the cycle is a long one containing a large number of transmissions.

television (TV) The broadcasting of pictures and sound by *radio waves or electric cable. Television was invented by John Logie Baird in 1926. At a TV studio or outside-broadcast unit, a television *camera converts the picture into an electrical signal. In the US the picture consists of 525 lines made by an electron beam scanning the screen of a *cathode-ray tube, 30 such pictures being formed every second. In most of Europe 625 lines and 25 frames per second are used. A brightness signal and a synchronization signal (to form the lines and frames of the picture) make up the picture signal, which is used to modulate (*see* modulation) a VHF or UHF carrier wave and is broadcast with the modulated sound carrier wave (which has a slightly different frequency). In color TV, a color signal has to be added to the picture signal.

The aerial of the TV receiver detects the broadcast radio waves and the picture and sound signals are separated within the receiver. The picture signal is demodulated, and the resulting current is used to control the electron beam in a cathode-ray tube so that the picture is reconstructed, the scanning being sufficiently fast to give the impression of a continuous moving picture.

TELESCOPE

refractors

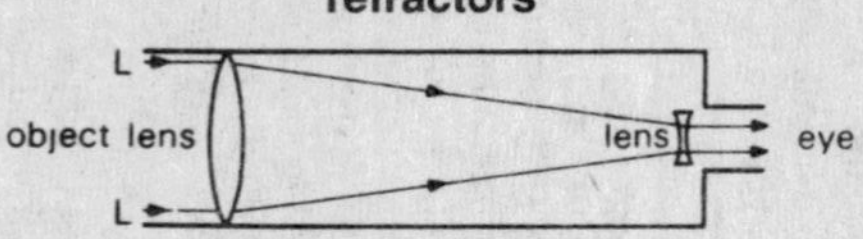

Galilean *The simplest practical form of refracting telescope was developed by Galileo in about 1609 from Lippershey's invention.*

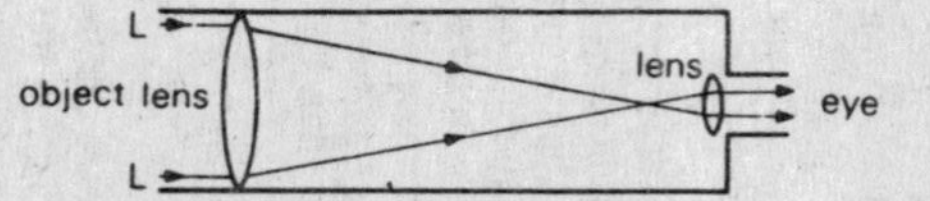

Keplerian *Kepler's arrangement produces an inverted image but was much used for astronomical observations in which the inversion did not matter.*

reflectors

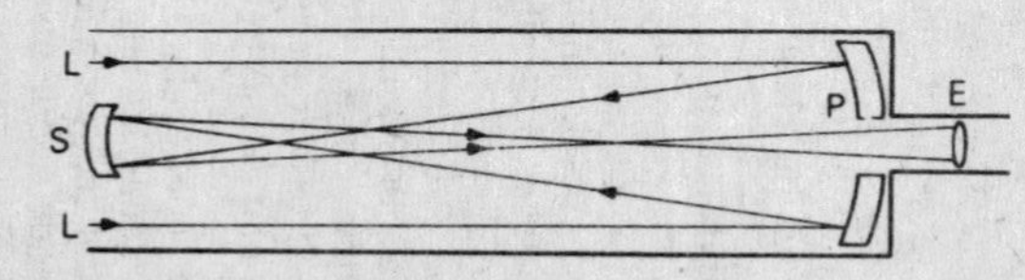

Gregorian *James Gregory proposed this design in 1663 but it has had little general application.*

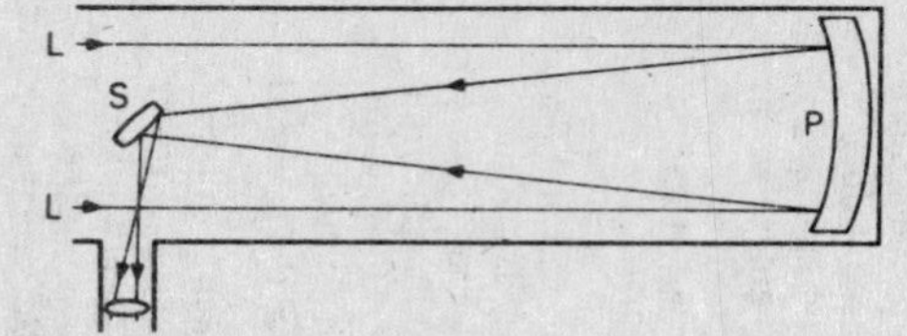

Newtonian *In Newton's 1671 design the secondary mirror is placed at an angle of 45° to the axis of the beam.*

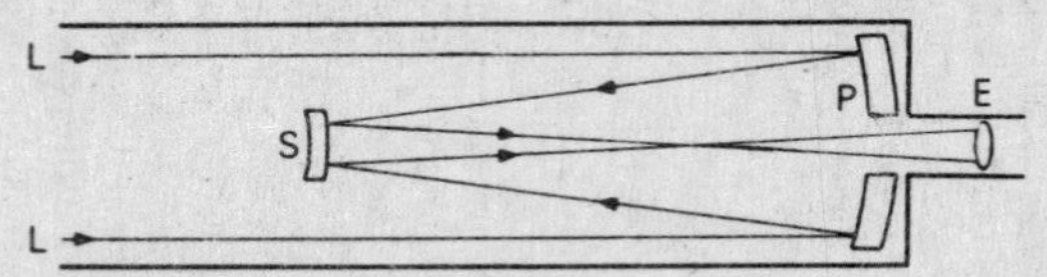

Cassegrain *Widely used, this form was invented by the obscure French astronomer N. Cassegrain in 1672.*

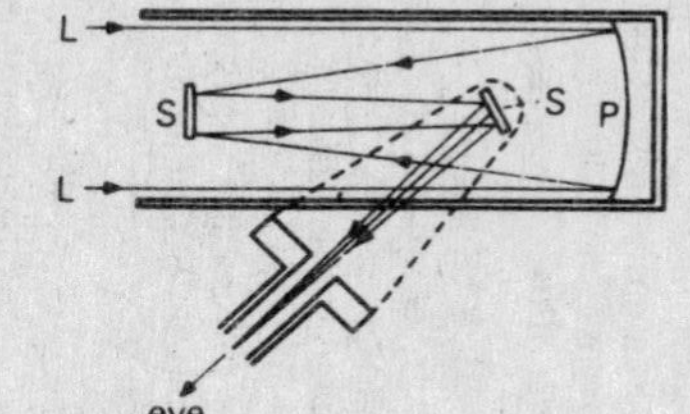

coudé (French: angled) *This arrangement is valuable in larger telescopes as it increases their focal length.*

L = *light rays* P = *primary mirror*
E = *eyepiece* S = *secondary mirror*

In a **color television** camera light from the scene to be televised is filtered into three primary color components: red, green, and blue. Light of each color goes to a separate image tube. There are three systems in use for encoding color picture information for transmission: the US system, also used in Canada, Mexico, and Japan; the PAL (phase alteration line) system used in most W European countries; and SECAM (système électronique couleur avec mémoire), used in France, E Europe, and some other countries. All of these combine color and intensity information with sound and synchronization in a similar way to black-and-white television. The color television receiver splits the signal into red, green, and blue components and applies these to three separate electron guns. The beam from each gun activates a set of phosphor dots of that color on the screen, thus reconstructing the red, green, and blue components of the picture.

telex A telegraphy system that used telephone lines to transmit printed messages from one terminal (the teleprinter) to another. The message was typed onto a keyboard transmitter, which converted the characters into a coded electrical signal for transmission. A printing receiver (combined with the transmitter) carried out the reverse process, typing out messages as they arrived. Telex messages were directed through the telephone lines by the subscribers' numbers, each subscriber also being identified by his call sign. The system was extensively used by commercial and other organizations, because it cost less than a telephone call and provided both parties with a written copy of the messages. To increase the speed of transmission most teleprinters were equipped with a paper-tape punch to prerecord messages. Telexes have today been largely replaced by facsimile machines.

Tell, William A Swiss national hero who is first mentioned in a 15th-century chronicle and who, in Schiller's play *Wilhelm Tell* (1804), embodies the Swiss struggle for independence from the Austrian Hapsburgs. After refusing to do homage as required by Gessler, the Austrian governor, Tell was ordered to shoot an apple from his son's head with a crossbow at 80 paces. He passed this test and later killed Gessler.

Tell el-Amarna The site of Akhetaten, the capital founded (c. 1375 BC) by the heretic Egyptian pharaoh *Akhenaten. It was to have been the center of Akhenaten's new religion but was abandoned shortly after his death (c. 1360). Amarna is associated with a naturalistic art style and a diplomatic correspondence (the *Amarna Tablets) showing the decline of Egyptian prestige in W Asia.

Teller, Edward (1908–) US physicist, born in Hungary. After studying in Germany he left in 1933, going first to London and then to Washington, D.C. He worked on the fission bomb during World War II and subsequently on the fusion bomb, making a significant contribution to its development. He is sometimes known as "the father of the H-bomb." Teller's unfavorable evidence in the Robert *Oppenheimer security-clearance hearing lost him some respect among scientists.

tellurium (Te) A silvery-white semiconductor of the sulfur group, discovered by Müller von Reichenstein in 1782. The hydride (H_2Te) is volatile and toxic, with a powerful smell of bad eggs. Bismuth telluride (BiTe) is used as an effective thermoelectric cooler. The metal is used in some special alloys and in some semiconducting devices. At no 52; at wt 127.60; mp 842 ± 0.5°F (449.5 ± 0.3°C); bp 1814 ± 5°F (989 ± 3°C).

Telstar. *See* communications satellite.

Telukbetung 5 28S 105 16E A port in Indonesia, in S Sumatra on the Sunda Strait. It was devastated by the eruption of *Krakatoa in 1883. Exports include rubber, coffee, and cinchona. Population (1980): 284,275.

2502

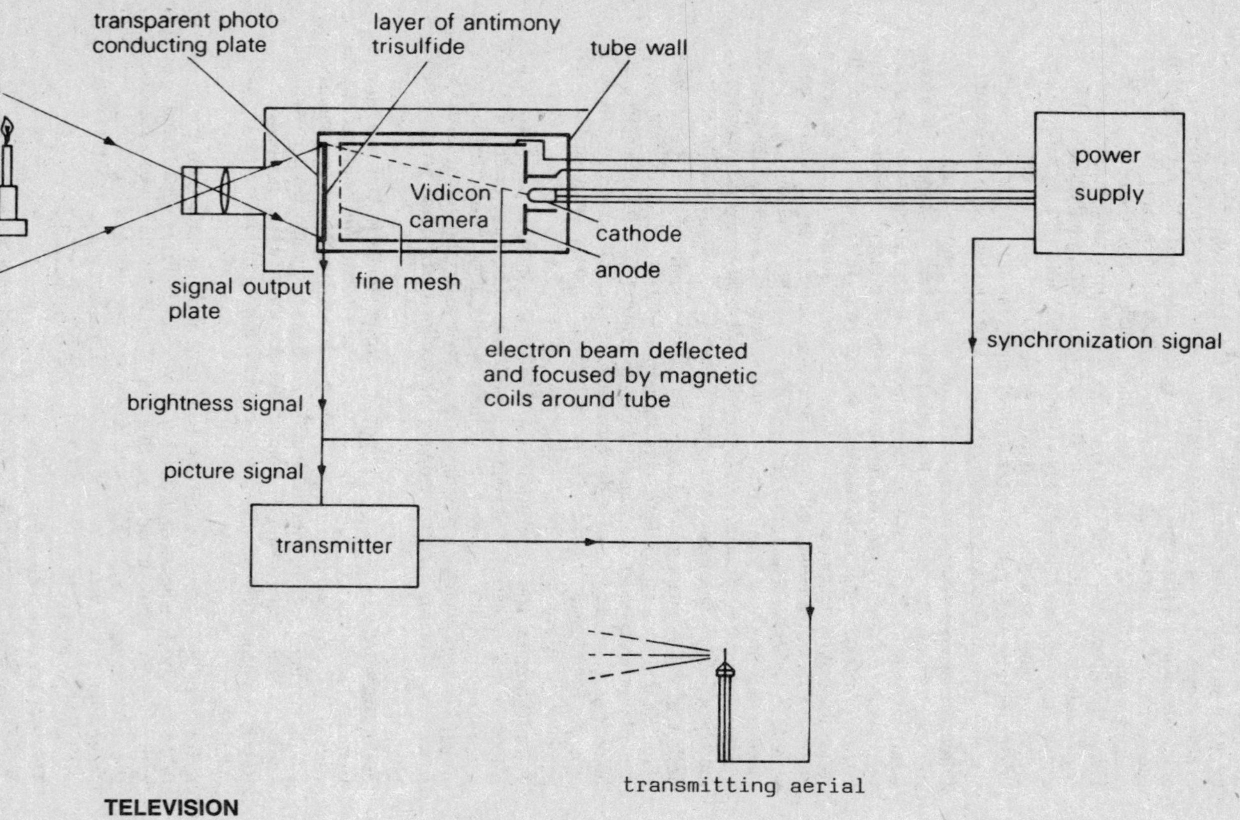

TELEVISION

TELEVISION

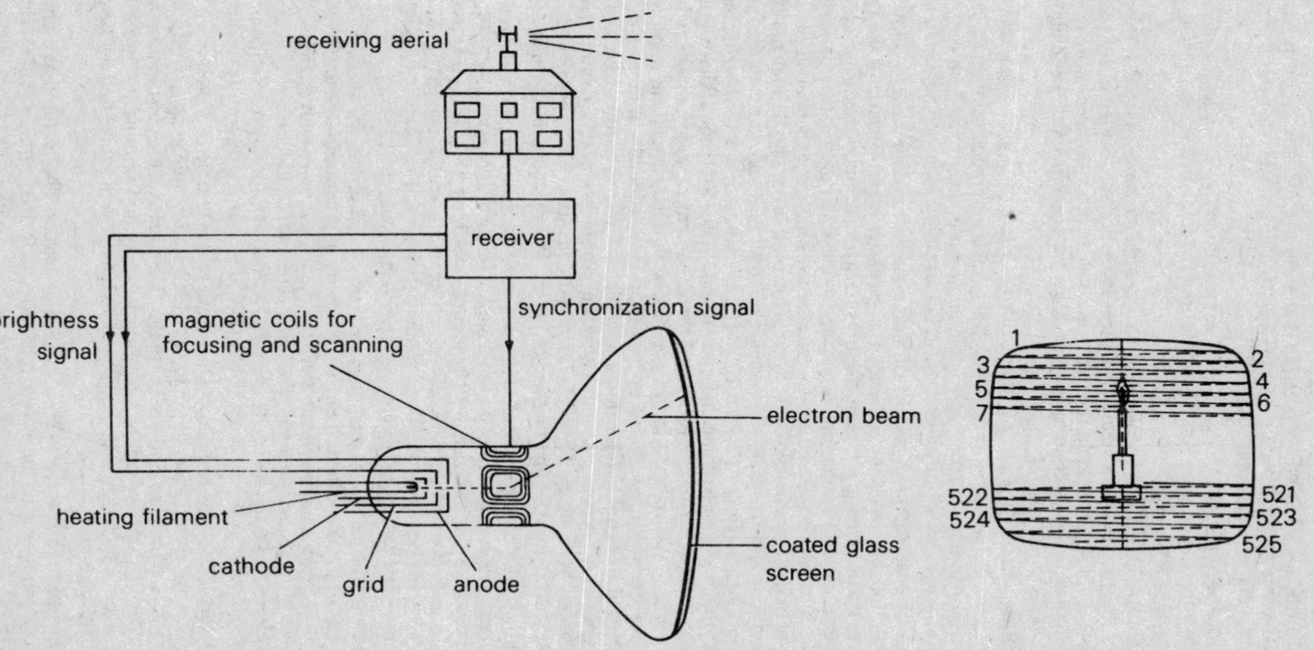
receiving aerial
receiver
synchronization signal
brightness signal
magnetic coils for focusing and scanning
electron beam
heating filament
cathode
grid
anode
coated glass screen
1
2
3
4
5
6
7
521
522
523
524
525

Tema 5 41N 0 00E A port in Ghana, on the Atlantic coast. It has Africa's largest man-made harbor (opened 1962). Industries include oil refining, chemicals, and fishing. Population (1988 est): 110,000.

Tempe, Vale of (Modern Greek name: Témbi) A valley in N Greece, leading down to the Aegean Sea SE of Mount Olympus. In ancient times it was dedicated to the god Apollo.

Tempe 33 25N 111 56W A city in S central Arizona, on the Salt River, just SE of Phoenix. Arizona State University (1885) is there. Settled in 1871 as a mill, it is a popular retirement, health, and tourist resort because of its dry climate. Clothing, steel, and electronic products are manufactured. Population (1990): 141,865.

tempera A method of painting, using ground pigment and a water-soluble gelatinous base, usually egg yolk. It was a very common medium for murals and easel paintings until it was supplanted by oils during the 15th century. It has lately been revived by German and US artists for its strong pure colors.

temperament The method of tuning the notes of the scale to allow music in all *tonalities to sound in tune. The necessity arises because of the way scales are constructed in Western music; systems of temperament sharpen or flatten certain notes in order to compensate for the slight discrepancy that arises in the interval between C and the C seven octaves higher. This interval should be (on the basis of seven octaves) $2^7 = 128$. However, in passing through the cycle of 12 keys, each using as its fundamental the fifth of its predecessor, the interval between Cs becomes $(^3/_2)^{12} = 129.75$. This difference, known as the comma of Pythagoras, can be compensated in several ways. From the 16th to the early 18th centuries the system of **meantone temperament** prevailed, in which the interval of a fifth was reduced to $\sqrt[4]{5} = 1.495$; with this arrangement music written in tonalities with few sharps or flats sounded acceptably in tune. This was succeeded by **equal temperament**, in which the interval between each of 12 semitones of the octave is exactly equal; the advantages of this system were demonstrated by Bach in *The Well-Tempered Clavier* (1722, 1744), a collection of keyboard preludes and fugues in all keys. This system prevails today.

temperance movement The promotion of abstinence from, or at least moderation in, the consumption of alcohol. The earliest organized temperance societies were the 19th century US groups, which by 1833 had 6000 local groups (*see also* Prohibition). The Ulster Temperance Society, founded in 1829, was the first European society. The movement then spread to Scandinavia, where societies were established in Norway (1836) and Sweden (1837).

temperature A physical quantity that is a measure of the average *kinetic energy of the constituent particles of a body. It determines the direction in which *heat flows when two bodies are in contact, the body with the higher temperature losing heat to that with the lower. The temperature of a body is measured in kelvins, degrees Celsius, or degrees Fahrenheit either by a *thermometer, if the temperature is below about 933°F (500°C), or, if above, by a *pyrometer.

Templars (Poor Knights of Christ and of the Temple of Solomon) A religious order of knighthood founded (c. 1120) in Jerusalem by a group of French knights. The Templars were, with the *Hospitallers, the most important military order of the *Crusades. Accused of heresy and immorality by Philip IV of France, who feared their power, the Templars were suppressed by the papacy in 1312 with great cruelty.

Temple, Shirley (1928–) US film actress. She featured as a child star in many films during the 1930s, including *Little Miss Marker* (1934), *Bright Eyes* (1934), *Heidi* (1937), and *Rebecca of Sunnybrook Farm* (1938). She won a special Academy Award in 1934. During the 1960s she went into politics and was appointed a delegate to the UN (1969). In 1974 she served as US chief of protocol. She was also US ambassador to Ghana in 1974 under her married name, Shirley Temple Black.

Temple of Jerusalem The ancient center of Jewish religious life. The first Temple was built by King Solomon (c. 950 BC) and destroyed by Nebuchadnezzar in 586 BC. The second Temple was built in the later 6th century BC, restored by the *Maccabees and later by Herod the Great, and destroyed by the Romans in 70 AD. The Temple was a place of pilgrimage and worship. It was a magnificent building, richly furnished and decorated, and set in a fortified enclosure. The worship, which included animal sacrifices, was directed by priests, assisted by *Levites, who also provided the music. An attempt was made to rebuild the Temple under the Roman emperor Julian (362 AD) but it was abandoned and the site is now a Muslim holy place. *See also* high priest; Holy of Holies; Wailing Wall.

temples In ancient Greece and Rome, the sanctuaries of the gods. The first Greek temples were built of timber or brick but by the 6th century BC stone and marble were being used. They were rectangular buildings surrounded by a colonnade, with an inner sanctum containing the altar and a sculpture of the deity to whom they were dedicated. The best known is the *Parthenon.

Roman temples were raised on pedestals and usually had solid walls and a deep central *portico. The Maison Carrée at Nîmes, France (1st century BC), and the domed *Pantheon in Rome are famous surviving examples.

Temuco 38 45S 72 40W A city in S Chile and the gateway to Chile's lake district. It serves an area producing chiefly cereals, apples, and timber. Population (1991 est): 249,000.

tench An elongated food and game fish, *Tinca tinca*, that is related to *carp and occurs in European fresh waters. Its slimy body, 7–18 in (18–45 cm) long, is greenish or blackish above with lighter undersides. It lives in quiet waters that are rich in vegetation, feeding on small animals and plants.

Ten Commandments The *covenant, also called the Decalogue, delivered by Jehovah to Moses on two stone tablets at Mount Sinai (Exodus 20.1–17; Deuteronomy 5.6–21). According to Exodus, Moses broke the original tablets when he descended from Mount Sinai and discovered the idolatry of the Israelites; they were replaced by two others, which were kept in the *Ark of the Covenant. Jews, Roman Catholics, and Protestants are not agreed as to the exact numbering of the commandments. The New Testament insists that unlike many other Old Testament laws they are binding on all mankind.

tendon A strong fibrous cord that joins a muscle to a bone. The tendon fibers merge with the muscle fibers and extend to the fibrous tissue lining the bone, serving to concentrate the pull of the muscle on a small part of the bone.

Tenerife 28 15N 16 35W A Spanish island in the Atlantic Ocean, the largest of the Canary Islands. Its Pico de Teide mountain is, at 12,172 ft (3710 m), the highest in Spain. Early fruit and vegetables, such as bananas and tomatoes, are produced and the island is popular for vacations. Area: 780 sq mi (2020 sq km). Population (1986): 759,388. Chief town: Santa Cruz de Tenerife.

Teng Hsiao-p'ing. *See* Deng Xiao Ping.

Teniers the Younger, David (1610–90) Flemish painter. Known chiefly for his peasant scenes, he also made historically valuable copies of the paintings in the collection of Archduke Leopold Wilhelm, whose court painter he became in

Brussels in 1651. His father **David Teniers the Elder** (1582–1649) was a painter of religious subjects.

Ten Lost Tribes of Israel The Hebrew tribes that rebelled against *Solomon's successor, Rehoboam, and formed a separate kingdom. This kingdom, which they called Israel, lay to the N of the territory occupied by the two remaining tribes of *Judah and of *Benjamin, which together constituted the southern kingdom of Judah. In 722 BC the northern kingdom was conquered by the Assyrians, many of its inhabitants deported, and their ethnic identity lost.

Tennessee A S central state bordered by Kentucky and Virginia (N); North Carolina (E); Georgia, Alabama, and Mississippi (S); and the Mississippi River (W), beyond which lie Arkansas and Missouri. Geographically, the state can be divided into east, middle, and west Tennessee. In the E there is an upland region of thickly wooded mountains and in middle Tennessee, in the loop of the Tennessee River, an area of upland plateau and rolling hills gives way in the W to an area of lowland plains and swamps situated between the Tennessee and Mississippi rivers. An agriculturally poor state, its major crops are tobacco, soybeans, and cotton. Beef and dairy products are also important. Manufacturing is being encouraged especially by the Tennessee Valley Authority (*see* Tennessee River) and the leading industries produce chemicals, food products, electrical and nonelectrical machinery, and textiles. The state is an important hardwood producer in the S. It is the US's largest producer of zinc and the extraction of stone is a major source of revenue. Memphis, on the Mississippi River, is the largest and commercially the most important city; the state capital of Nashville has long associations with country music. *History*: the area was first explored by the Spanish in the 16th century. Thinly settled before the American Revolution, it attracted easterners hungry for land after the war. North Carolina had claims to the region and the unrecognized state of Franklin was organized before Tennessee became a territory (1790) and a state (1796). Although Tennessee joined the Confederacy in the Civil War, Union sentiment was strong in the nonslaveholding eastern parts of the state. Because of its strategic importance on the border of the Union and on the Mississippi, many key Civil War battles were fought there. Industrial development began in the late 19th century. Martin Luther *King, Jr. was assassinated in Memphis in 1968. Area: 42,244 sq mi (109,411 sq km). Population (1990): 4,877,185. Capital: Nashville.

Tennessee River A river in SE US. It follows a U-shaped course from E Tennessee, flowing through NE Alabama before returning across Tennessee to join the Ohio River as its main tributary at Paducah, Ky. **The Tennessee Valley Authority,** created in 1933, constructed a series of dams along the river to control floods and arrest soil erosion as well as to generate electricity. Length: 652 mi (1049 km).

Tennessee Walking Horse A breed of □horse developed in Tennessee and used by plantation owners for its characteristic running walk, which gives a smooth ride. It is solidly built with a thick neck and full mane and tail. The coat may be black, brown, bay, chestnut, or roan. Height: 15½–16 hands 5 ft 2 in–5 ft 4 in (1.57 m–1.63 m).

tennis (*or* lawn tennis) A game for two or four players using rackets to hit a cloth-covered rubber ball on a grass or composition (hard) court. It originated in England in the mid-19th century and was highly popular by 1877, when the first Wimbledon championships were staged. A match lasts a maximum of five sets for men and three for women and the minimum number of games per set is six. A lead of two games is needed to win a set. However, if the score reaches six games each a tiebreaker is played. The scoring system derives from real or court tennis and a minimum of four points is needed for a game: 15, 30, 40, and game;

a lead of two points is also needed to win a game. A score of 40 on both sides is called "deuce"; the side that wins the next point then has the "advantage," which can either be clinched to win the game with a further point or nullified by the opposing side winning a point, in which case the score returns to deuce. Players take turns to serve for a game. A player is allowed two attempts to serve into the service court diagonally opposite, alternating courts between points. To win points players must return the ball over the net either before it bounces (volley) or after the first bounce, trying to position it so that their opponents cannot return it. The game is immensely popular at all levels of play, from beginners to professionals.

Tennis Court Oath (1789) The oath taken by the Third Estate of the *States-General of France at the start of the French Revolution. After declaring itself a National Assembly, the Third Estate was excluded from its meeting place at Versailles. Adjourning to a nearby tennis court, the Assembly defiantly swore not to disband until the French kingdom had a written constitution.

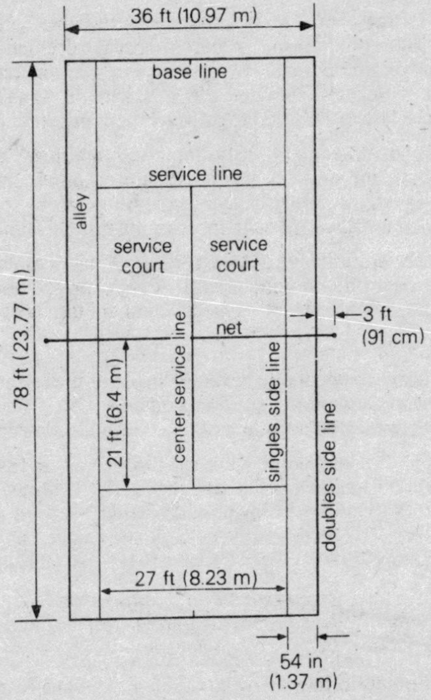

TENNIS *The dimensions of the court. For singles games the posts holding the net are moved to inside the doubles sidelines. The net is 3 ft (91.4 cm) high at the center.*

Tennyson, Alfred, Lord (1809–92) British poet. He published two volumes in 1830 and 1832, but he gained general acclaim only with his 1842 volume, which included "Morte d'Arthur." In 1850 he married, became Britain's poet laureate, and published *In Memoriam*, a sequence of elegaic lyrics mourning the death of his close friend Arthur Hallam (1811–33). Now established as the national poet of the Victorian age, he reinforced his popularity with *Idylls of the King* (1859) and other poems.

tenor A high adult male singing voice. The word comes from the Latin *tenere*, to hold; in Renaissance polyphonic music the tenor part held the melody on which the music was based. Range: C on the bass stave to C two octaves above.

tenrec An insect-eating mammal belonging to the family *Tenrecidae* (30 species), found only in Madagascar and the Comoro Islands. Tenrecs measure 2–16 in (5–40 cm), some with long tails and some tailless, and generally have a brownish coat of bristly hairs or spines. Most tenrecs live in burrows and are nocturnal, feeding mainly on small invertebrates with some plant material. They are prolific breeders, producing litters of over 20. Order: **Insectivora*.

tensile strength The ability of a material to withstand a "pulling" stress (**tensile stress**). It is usually measured by taking a bar of the material and stretching it to destruction. The ultimate tensile strength is the maximum load divided by the bar's cross-sectional area and is measured in newtons per square meter.

Tenure of Office Act (1867) US law that restricted presidential powers. Because Pres. Andrew *Johnson wished to oust government officials who favored harsh Reconstruction policies, Congress passed a law that prohibited presidential removal of Senate-appointed officials without Senate approval. Johnson's defiance of the law in 1868 led to impeachment proceedings.

Tenzing Norgay (c. 1914–86) Sherpa mountaineer, who, with Sir Edmund *Hillary, was the first man to reach the summit of Mount Everest (1953), after working as a porter in 19 Himalayan expeditions from 1935. He later became a director at the Himalayan Mountaineering Institute, Darjeeling.

Teotihuacán An ancient city in central Mexico. Between 300 and 650 AD Teotihuacán controlled a wide area. It was destroyed about 750. The pyramid temples of the sun, moon, and *Quetzalcóatl are the most impressive remains.

tepee. *See* wigwam.

tequila A Mexican alcoholic beverage made of the fermented juice of an agave plant, water and, sometimes, sulfuric acid and yeast. The spirit is distilled twice in potstills, then may be aged in casks. It is produced near the town of Tequila.

terbium (Tb) A *lanthanide element, discovered in 1843 by C. G. Mosander (1797–1858) and named for the village Ytterby in Sweden. It is obtained from monazite ($CePO_4$), and the brown oxide (Tb_2O_3) is used as a phosphor in color-television tubes. The metal is silvery-gray and can be cut with a knife. At no 65; at wt 158.92; mp 2473°F (1356°C): bp 5511°F (3041°C).

terebinth A small tree, *Pistacia terebinthus*, native to the Mediterranean region. It has small flowers producing purple fruit and was formerly an important source of turpentine. Family: *Pistaciaceae.*

Terence (Publius Terentius Afer; c. 185–c. 159 BC) Roman dramatist. Born in Carthage, he was taken to Rome as a slave by a senator who educated and later freed him. His six plays were all adapted from Greek New Comedy writers, especially Menander. He achieved popular success only with *The Eunuch* (161 BC), his style being more refined and sophisticated than that of his rival *Plautus. His work influenced several 17th- and 18th-century European writers.

Teresa, Mother (1910–) Yugoslav nun, who founded the Order of the Missionaries of Charity in Calcutta in 1948. Her nuns work throughout the world helping lepers, cripples, and the aged and dying. She received the first Pope John XXIII Peace Prize (1971) and the 1979 Nobel Peace Prize.

Teresa of Ávila, St (1515–82) Spanish Carmelite nun and mystic, who dedicated her life to reforming the Carmelite order. Of noble birth, she joined the Carmelites at Ávila in 1533 and in 1555 experienced a spiritual awakening followed by several visions. To restore the original Carmelite rule she founded the Convent of St Joseph in Ávila in 1562 and later other religious houses with the help of St *John of the Cross. The mystical side of her life is described in her books, notably *Life* (1562–65), *The Way of Perfection* (after 1565), and *The Interior Castle* (1577), which are regarded as classics of mysticism.

Teresina 5 09S 42 46W A city in NE Brazil, the capital of Piauí state on the Rio Parnaíba. It is a commercial center; exports include cattle, hides, cotton, rice, and manioc. Its university was founded in 1968. Population (1980): 339,264.

Terman, Lewis Madison (1877–1956) US psychologist, who published the first widely used intelligence test in the US. Developed at Stanford University, his Stanford–Binet test was scored on an *intelligence quotient (IQ) rating based on both chronological and mental ages. In 1921 Terman established a long-term study of gifted children and he also estimated the IQs of famous people, rating Goethe at 210 and Darwin at 165.

terminal velocity The maximum velocity attained by a body falling through a fluid. It occurs when the drag balances the gravitational force on the body: until the terminal velocity is reached the falling body accelerates; thereafter the velocity remains constant. According to *Stokes' law the terminal velocity of a sphere (radius r) falling through a fluid with a coefficient of viscosity η is $2\phi r^2 g/9\eta$, where ϕ is the difference between the body and fluid densities and g is the acceleration of free fall.

termite A social □insect, also called white ant (although unrelated to the ants), belonging to the mainly tropical order *Isoptera* (2000 species). Termite colonies nest in tunnels and galleries in wood, soil, or earth mounds (termitaria). There are three major castes: winged reproductives, workers, and soldiers. The reproductives swarm to found new colonies, a single pair (king and queen) producing huge numbers of offspring. The workers construct galleries, feed the colony, and care for the young, while the soldiers are concerned with defense. Termites eat cellulose and are very destructive when they invade houses and attack wood products.

tern A seabird belonging to a subfamily (*Sterninae*; 35–40 species) occurring around coasts and inland waters worldwide and often called sea swallow or noddy; 8–22 in (20–55 cm) long, terns have long wings, short legs, usually a forked tail, and their plumage is white, black-and-white, or almost totally black. They feed on fish and crustaceans and often migrate long distances (*see* Arctic tern). Family: *Laridae* (gulls and terns).

Terni 42 34N 12 39E A city in Italy, in Umbria on the Nera River. Industries include the manufacture of iron and steel, machinery, firearms, soap, and textiles. It is reputed to be the birthplace of Tacitus. Population (1991 est): 109,809.

terpenes Naturally occurring hydrocarbons found in the essential oils of plants. Typically they are volatile compounds with pleasant odors and are widely used in flavoring foods and in perfumes. Their molecules are made up of isoprene units (C_5H_8). *Rubber is an example of a polyterpene.

terra-cotta (Italian: baked earth) A fired clay, usually reddish in color, used to make sculpture, tiles, bricks, containers, etc. It is principally associated with sculpture. Terra-cotta figurines, often painted, were very common in ancient Greece and Rome, a famous Greek type being the *Tanagra figurines. The art was revived during the *Renaissance, when the *Della Robbia family in Florence specialized in enameled terra-cotta Madonnas. Later sculptors in terracotta include the Frenchman *Clodion.

terrapin A small edible turtle belonging to the family *Emydidae*, occurring chiefly in the New World. The diamondback terrapin (*Malaclemys terrapin*), which occurs in coastal waters and salt marshes of North America, has diamond-shaped patterns on its dark carapace and is yellow with black speckles underneath. It is one of several terrapins regarded as a table delicacy and often reared for this purpose. □reptile.

terrarium A transparent receptacle for land plants, used for propagation, decoration, or scientific study. The plants grow in a bottom layer usually consisting of sand or pebbles mixed with some charcoal and covered by topsoil.

Terre Adélie (*or* Adélie Land) The only French territory in Antarctica, in the French Southern and Antarctic Territories on the coast of the Indian Ocean between longitudes 136°E and 142°E. It is the site of a French research station.

terrier One of about 20 breeds of □dog characterized by their small compact sturdy build and traditionally used for hunting vermin and rousing foxes and badgers from cover. The Scottish breeds, such as the *cairn terrier, *Scottish terrier, *Skye terrier, and *West Highland white terrier, tend to be smaller and longer haired than other terriers, which are descended from the ancient black-and-tan hunting terrier and other breeds.

territory In ecology, a defined area defended by an animal against intrusion by another animal, usually of the same species. Territories can either reduce competition for food or serve to protect mates and young from interference. They vary in size according to their function, the fitness of the defending animal, and the population density of the species.

Terry, Dame Ellen (Alice) (1847–1928) British actress. A member of a large and talented family of actors, from 1878 to 1898 she acted with Sir Henry *Irving, achieving particular success in the major Shakespearean roles. She later managed the Imperial Theatre, toured extensively, and gave lectures on Shakespeare. Her correspondence with G. B. *Shaw was published in 1931.

Tertiary period The first geological period of the Cenozoic era, following the Cretaceous period and preceding the Quaternary (which is sometimes considered a continuation of the Tertiary). It lasted from about 65 to 1.8 million years ago and contains the Paleocene, Eocene, Oligocene, Miocene, and Pliocene epochs, in ascending order. Most of the rocks of the period were laid down in shallow water. Modern invertebrates and mammals evolved and became increasingly abundant; the modern angiosperms became the dominant plants. The Alpine period of mountain formation extended through the period and reached its peak in the Miocene. The climate began to deteriorate in the Oligocene, finally leading to the Ice Age of the Pleistocene.

Tertullian(us), Quintus Septimius Florens (c. 160–225 AD) African Father of the Church, born in Carthage. Educated in law, he was converted to Christianity by 197 and became a leading Christian apologist. He strongly defended the Montanists (*see* Montanism), whom he joined in 213. His writings, which include *Apologeticum*, *Ad nationes*, and *De praescriptione haereticorum*, were the first major Christian works in Latin.

terza rima A verse form consisting of a series of three-line stanzas the second lines of which rhyme with the first and third lines of the preceding stanza (aba/cac/dcd/ede/. . .). It originated in Italy and was used by *Dante in the *Divine Comedy*. It was introduced into England by Sir Thomas *Wyatt in the 16th century. *See also* rhyme.

tesla (T) The *SI unit of magnetic flux density equal to one weber per square meter. Named for Nikola *Tesla.

Tesla, Nikola (1856–1943) US electrical engineer, born in Croatia, who recognized the advantages of distributing electricity as alternating current, rather than direct current, and did much to make this feasible. He fought a long and bitter battle with Thomas *Edison over this principle. The unit of magnetic flux density (*see* tesla) is named for him.

Test Acts In England, the acts stipulating that public office holders must take Holy Communion in the Church of England (1673) and excluding all Roman Catholics except the duke of York (later James II) from Parliament (1678). They were not formally repealed until the mid-19th century.

testes The organ of male animals in which *sperm is produced. In men there is a pair of testes, or testicles, which produce both sperm and sex hormones (*see* androgen). Before birth the testicles descend into the scrotum—a sac of skin outside the abdominal cavity—since sperms require a temperature lower than that of the body to mature. The sperms complete their development in a convoluted tube (epididymis) outside the testis. At ejaculation the sperms pass through a duct (the vas deferens) to the urethra and out through the penis.

testosterone A steroid hormone—the most important of the *androgens. First isolated from bull testes in 1935, testosterone is now manufactured for medical uses, including the treatment of certain forms of sterility in men.

test-tube baby A baby produced by fertilizing the mother's egg cell with sperm from the father in a test tube: the fertilized egg is then implanted surgically into the mother's womb and allowed to come to term in the normal way. It is a means of overcoming sterility in a woman due to blocked Fallopian tubes or any similar defect. The technique was developed in Britain, and the first test-tube baby was born in 1978. Since that time test-tube babies have been born in many countries.

tetanus A serious disease caused by the bacterium *Clostridium tetani* entering wounds and producing a powerful toxin (poison) that irritates the nerves supplying muscles. The organism is particularly prevalent in soil contaminated with animal droppings. After an incubation period of 7–10 days, stiffness, spasm, and rigidity of the muscles affects the jaw (hence the popular name—lockjaw) and spreads to other muscles. In severe cases the whole body is seized with spasms and the patient may die from asphyxia. The disease is treated with tetanus antitoxin and penicillin; it can be prevented by completing a full course of antitetanus immunization.

Teton Range A mountain range in W Idaho and E Wyoming, S of Yellowstone National Park. Grand Teton, the highest point, rises at 13,766 ft (4196 m). Much of the range, especially in the S, is included in Grand Teton National Park (1929).

tetra One of several small brightly colored freshwater fish of the family *Characidae* (*see* characin), found in South America and Africa and popular for aquaria. Well-known species include black tetra (*Gymnocorymbus ternetzi*), glowlight tetra (*Hemigrammus erythrozonus*), neon tetra (*Hyphessobrycon innesi*), and silver tetra (*Ctenobrycon spilurus*).

tetracyclines A group of *antibiotics derived from *Streptomyces* bacteria. Tetracyclines are active against a large number of different bacteria (i.e. they are broad-spectrum antibiotics) and are frequently the first choice of antibiotic for infections in which the causative organism has not been identified. Tetracyclines, which are taken by mouth, may cause the side effects of diarrhea, nausea, and discoloration of growing teeth and bones.

tetraethyl lead ($Pb(C_2H_5)_4$) A colorless poisonous oily liquid. It is made by treating lead-sodium alloys with chloroethane and was long added to gasoline to prevent *knocking in internal-combustion engines.

Tetrazzini, Luisa (1871–1940) Italian coloratura soprano. Born in Florence, she attended the Liceo Musicale there with her sister Eva, making her debut as Inez in Meyerbeer's opera *L'Africaine* in 1895. She toured the US, Russia, Mexico, and Europe with great success.

Tetuán 35 34N 5 22W A city in N Morocco. Its port, on the Mediterranean coast, handles livestock and agricultural produce. The city produces textiles and light manufactured products. Population (1982): 365,000.

Tetzel, Johann (c. 1465–1519) German Dominican friar, a famous preacher of *indulgences. His attempt to sell indulgences, which had been authorized to raise funds for the renovation of St Peter's in Rome, provoked Luther's publication of the 95 theses and a famous debate between the two men.

Teutonic Knights (Knights of the Teutonic Order) A religious order of knighthood founded (c. 1190) at Acre. In 1211 they moved from Palestine to E Europe, where they campaigned against pagan peoples, notably the Prussians, whom they had conquered by the end of the 13th century. They colonized Prussia and established their headquarters at Marienburg in 1309. They also gained control over much of the E Baltic region, as well as parts of Germany. During the 15th century they were repeatedly defeated by the Poles, of whose king the order's grand master became a vassal. At the Reformation the order was dissolved except for one branch, which survived in Germany until its abolition by Napoleon (1809).

Texas The second largest state and the third most populous, situated in the SW and bordered by Oklahoma (N), Arkansas and Louisiana (E), the Gulf of Mexico and Mexico (S), and New Mexico (W). It consists of four main physical regions: the West Gulf Coastal Plain in the SE covering more than two-fifths of the state; the Central Lowland; the Great Plains, which extend mainly W from the Central Lowland into New Mexico; and the Trans-Pecos or mountainous area in the W. The Rio Grande forms the border with Mexico and is the chief river. The chief producer of minerals since 1935, it leads the nation in the production of oil and natural gas; it is also a major producer of sulfur. Oil-related industries dominate the manufacturing sector, the most important being the chemical industry, especially along the Gulf Coast. There is also an important space center at Houston and Dallas is a major commercial and industrial center. Texas is a major agricultural region and has more farmed land than any other US state. It produces a variety of crops, especially cotton, sorghum grains, rice, and peanuts, and it is a leading livestock producer. *History*: explored by the Spanish in the 16th century and colonized by them in the 17th as part of Mexico, it was entered in large numbers by US settlers, led by Stephen F. *Austin, after Mexico became independent in 1821. In 1836 the Texans set up a provisional government in opposition to the Mexican dictatorship of Antonio López de Santa Anna and following the heroic defense of the *Alamo, the revolutionary army under Sam Houston finally defeated Mexican forces in April of the same year. A republic was established and Texas remained independent for almost a decade until annexation by the US was agreed upon and Texas became a state. It was a supporter of the Confederate cause during the US Civil War. Sustained growth for the state began in 1901 when the famous Spindletop oil discovery was made. Oil and gas soon replaced livestock in importance, and the economy is now supported by a variety of high technology and defense industries. Changes in the course of the Rio Grande, which forms part of the border between Texas and Mexico, has led to several border disputes between the US and Mexico and in 1970 the two countries agreed on plans to prevent any further substantial changes in the river's course. From the 1970s through the early 1990s, the influx of illegal Mexican immigrants into Texas strained the state's social services and relations with Mexico. Area: 267,338 sq mi (692,402 sq km). Population (1990): 16,986,510. Capital: Austin.

Texas Rangers US law enforcers. Begun by Stephen F. *Austin in 1823 to protect the frontier in Mexican Texas, it became an official law enforcement agency of Texas in 1836. They fought bravely in the *Mexican War, and by 1881 the Rangers had ended Indian hostilities in Texas. Since 1935 a part of the Texas Department of Public Safety, the Rangers work with other state law enforcement agencies.

Texas v. White (1869) US Supreme Court decision that affirmed the indissolubility of the US and the illegality of state secession. Government bonds, paid to Texas in 1850, came due in 1864. When the Civil War broke out, Texas seceded from the Union and sold the bonds to George White. After the war Texas, under reconstructive government, sued White for return of the bonds. The court ruled that states cannot secede from the Union and, therefore, the bonds had been sold illegally.

textiles Fabrics made from natural or synthetic *fibers. Textiles can either be made directly from these fibers, as in felt and bonded fabrics, or be woven or knitted from yarn spun from the fibers. Braiding, netting, and lace making are less common ways of producing textiles from yarn. The fibers used include animal fibers, such as *wool, hair, and *silk; vegetable fibers, such as *cotton, *flax, and *hemp; and synthetic fibers, such as rayon, nylon, and acrylic. Wool and hair were used in prehistoric times; *linen, derived from flax, was also an early discovery, which only began to decline in use when cotton textiles, mass produced by the new industrial machines, became available cheaply. The invention of synthetic fibers and their combination with natural fibers has enormously increased the textile industry's range. *See also* spinning; weaving.

Tezcatlipoca The Aztec god of the night sky, identified with the constellation Ursa Major and associated with witchcraft and evil. He was a creator-god and had many different functions. He was usually portrayed with an obsidian mirror as a foot.

Thackeray, William Makepeace (1811–63) British novelist. He was educated at Cambridge University and became a professional journalist. After publishing several early novels in magazines under pseudonyms, he won fame and financial success with *Vanity Fair* (1847–48), which he followed with the semi-autobiographical *The History of Pendennis* (1848–50) and the historical novel *Henry Esmond* (1852).

Thailand, Kingdom of (name until 1939: Siam) A country in SE Asia, on the Gulf of Thailand. Fertile plains and hills in the S rise to mountains in the N. The main river is the Chao Phraya and the Mekong forms part of the E boundary. Most of the population is Thai, with Chinese and Malay minorities. *Economy*: the chief food crop is rice, which is also the main export. Production is being increased by irrigation projects, such as the Chao Phraya Dam. Forests cover 60% of the land, producing especially teak and rubber in the N. Rich and varied mineral resources include tin, manganese, antimony, and zinc. Industry is based mainly on textiles and cement. Tourism is important. *History*: there are indications of human settlement from very early times, and by the 6th century AD the Thais had reached the area from the N. They conquered the Mons to the S and in succeeding centuries gained power and influence in the region, being involved in frequent struggles with the Burmese and Khmers. In the 19th century they lost some territory to the French and the British but remained independent. In 1932 the long-standing absolute monarchy was replaced by a constitutional monarchy; civil and military governments have since alternated, accompanied by political upheavals and violence. The country was occupied by the Japanese in World War II. After a 1976 military coup, the country for the most part was under the control of the military. Prem Tinsulanonda came to power in 1980 and was reelected in 1983 and 1986. Elections in 1988 brought Chatichai Choonhavan to the prime ministership. A military coup in 1991 replaced Chatichai's allegedly corrupt government with a civilian interim government. One month after March 1992 elections, Gen. Suchinda Kraprayoon was selected to fill the prime minister's office. His appointment sparked demonstrations protesting the halt of democratic reforms, and by late spring he had been replaced by a civilian. Although relations with Vietnam deteriorated to a state of war in 1980 over Thailand's accepting refugees from Vietnam, relations between the two countries were somewhat improved by the early 1990s. Repatriation of Cambodian refugees in Thailand began in 1992. Head of state: King Bjumibol Adulyadej. Official language: Thai. Official religion: Hinayana Buddhism. Official currency: baht of 100 satang. Area: 198,250 sq mi (514,000 sq km). Population (1990 est): 54,890,000. Capital and main port: Bangkok.

Thais (4th century BC) Greek courtesan, who accompanied *Alexander the Great's army during its invasion of Persia. According to tradition, she instigated the burning of the palace of Xerxes in Persepolis in 331 BC.

thalassemia A form of *anemia caused by an inherited abnormality of the hemoglobin molecule (the pigment of red blood cells). The disease is seen most commonly around the Mediterranean but can also affect any people of Mediterranean origin. Patients inheriting the abnormality from both parents suffer from the major form of the disease, which requires repeated blood transfusions; such patients rarely live to adulthood. Those inheriting the disease from one parent are often free of symptoms.

Thales (c. 624–547 BC) The first of the Greek speculative scientists, born at *Miletus. He used the data from Babylonian astronomers to predict the solar eclipse of May 28, 585 BC, advised on stellar navigation, and introduced Egyptian methods of land measurement into Greece. He held that all things derive from water and set the *pre-Socratics on their quest for the basic substance of the universe.

Thalia In Greek religion, one of the nine *Muses, the patron of comedy. She was the mother, by Apollo, of the *Corybantes.

thalidomide A sedative drug that was found to cause severe developmental defects in the fetus when taken during pregnancy. The most common thalidomide-induced abnormality is phocomelia, in which the feet and hands develop normally without corresponding growth of the bones of the arms and legs. Some 8000–10,000 afflicted children were born to mothers who took the drug, primarily in European countries, before the effects were discovered in 1961. The drug was never used clinically in the US.

thallium (Tl) A metallic element, discovered spectroscopically by Sir William Crookes in 1861 and named for the Greek *thallos*, a green shoot, because of its bright-green spectral line. The metal is soft and malleable and reacts easily to form numerous salts. The sulfate (Tl_2SO_4) is widely used as a rat poison as it is tasteless and odorless. It occurs naturally in sulfide ores of lead and zinc and in iron pyrites (FeS_2). At no 81; at wt 204.37; mp 578.8°F (303.5°C); bp 2657 ± 18°F (1457 ± 10°C).

Thallophyta In some plant classification systems, a subkingdom containing all those plants that lack true stems, leaves, and roots, i.e. the algae, fungi, and lichens. The plant body is a thallus and lacks the vascular (conducting) tissue of higher plants.

Thames River The longest river in England. Rising in the Cotswold Hills near Cirencester, it flows mainly ESE through Oxford, Reading, and London to enter the North Sea at the Nore. It is tidal as far as Teddington, and Tilbury can dock the largest oceangoing vessels. It is economically the most important river is the UK, with vast amounts of cargo passing through the Port of *London. Length: 210 mi (338 km).

Thanksgiving Day A US national holiday, celebrated on the fourth Thursday in November. Thanksgiving Day was originally observed by the Pilgrim Fathers, who in 1621 celebrated their first harvest in North America. It became a national holiday in 1863. Americans traditionally eat roast turkey and pumpkin pie on Thanksgiving Day. It is also celebrated in Canada, on the second Monday in October.

Thant, U (1909–74) Burmese diplomat; secretary general of the UN (1962–72), elected after serving as acting secretary general following the death in office of his predecessor Dag Hammarskjöld. U Thant helped to resolve the US-Soviet crisis over the Soviet installation of missile bases in Cuba.

Thapsus, Battle of (46 BC) The battle in which Julius Caesar crushed *Pompey's supporters in North Africa. The battle was part of Caesar's campaign to retain control of Rome after defeating Pompey at Pharsalus.

Thar Desert (*or* Great Indian Desert) A large arid area lying along the central 500 mi (800 km) of the India-Pakistan border, mostly in India. Area: about 96,500 sq mi (250,000 sq km).

Tharpe, Twyla (1941–) US choreographer and dancer. She danced for the Paul Taylor Dance Company (1963–65) and began choreographing her own pieces for the group. By 1965 she had formed her own company. Her early works were performed on bare stages, outside or in gyms, without scenery and music, and with basic costumes. She based her movements on various dance styles, including jazz and tap, as well as ballet, and became known for her "pop" ballets. Her works include *Eight Jelly Rolls* (1971), *The Raggedy Dances* (1972), *Deuce Coupe* (1973), *Push Comes to Shove* (1976), and *Baker's Dozen* (1979).

Thásos A Greek island in the N Aegean Sea. Much archeological excavation has been done there and zinc is mined. Area: 154 sq mi (399 sq km).

Thatcher, Margaret (Hilda) (1925–) British stateswoman; Conservative prime minister (1979–1990). After working as a research chemist and then a barrister, she entered Parliament in 1959 and was appointed minister of pensions and national insurance in 1961. In 1969 she became opposition spokesman on education and was secretary of state for education and science from 1970 to 1974. In 1975 she succeeded Edward Heath as Conservative leader and in 1979 became the first female prime minister of the UK. She instituted cuts in government spending and faced a worsening economy. In 1982 she gained great popularity when she successfully used Britain's military forces to retain control of the Falkland Islands. Her government continued following a landslide victory in 1983 and reelection in 1987, but she was forced to resign in 1990 amid dissension in her cabinet over several issues, especially a national poll tax.

theater of cruelty A term derived from the theories of Antonin *Artaud, who believed that drama was essentially a ceremony, the ritual function of which was to destroy the superficial restraints of civilized life and liberate repressed emotions from the subconscious. *Les Cenci* (1935), his chief experimental production, was a failure, but his theories influenced many later writers and directors, including Jean-Louis *Barrault, *Camus, and *Genet.

MARGARET THATCHER *After the Conservatives won the general election (1979) she became prime minister.*

theater of the absurd A term ("the absurd" being borrowed from the existentialist philosophy of Albert *Camus) popularized in the 1960s to describe certain plays in which the human condition is presented as absurd. It was applied to the plays of Eugene *Ionesco, Samuel *Beckett, Arthur *Adamov, and others, which were characterized by lack of logical form and which use comic effects in developing pessimistic philosophical themes. The influence of Alfred *Jarry and the surrealists is discernible in the works of some of these playwrights.

theaters and stages The design of buildings specifically for the staging of plays has been governed by the shifting religious and social significance of the drama and the type of illusion or effect intended by different sorts of play. Ancient Greek theaters adjoined such religious centers as *Athens, *Epidaurus, and *Delphi. The secularized theaters that were a feature of most Roman towns were particularly adapted to the production of *Roman comedy. Christian drama evolved from the liturgy but in late medieval Europe moved outside the churches as the craft guilds assumed responsibility for productions of *miracle plays. Renaissance court theaters mainly imitated Roman models, while the open-air Elizabethan theater represented a more popular tradition. During the 17th century elaboration of stage machinery (*see* masque), demands for illusionism, and the development of *opera and *ballet stimulated the spread of the proscenium arch stage design, which was virtually universal until the 20th century. The modern drama's tendency toward abstraction and evocation of mood, going hand-in-hand with nonrealistic scenery and stage lighting, have fostered renewed interest in theater-in-the-round (seats around a central acting arena) and the potential of the Elizabethan apron stage.

Thebes An ancient city in Upper Egypt and capital of all Egypt (c. 1570–c. 1085 BC). Thebes's power was linked with the supremacy of its god *Amon in the Egyptian pantheon. With its associated sites of *Karnak, *Luxor, and the *Valley of the Kings, Thebes testifies to the splendor of ancient Egyptian civilization.

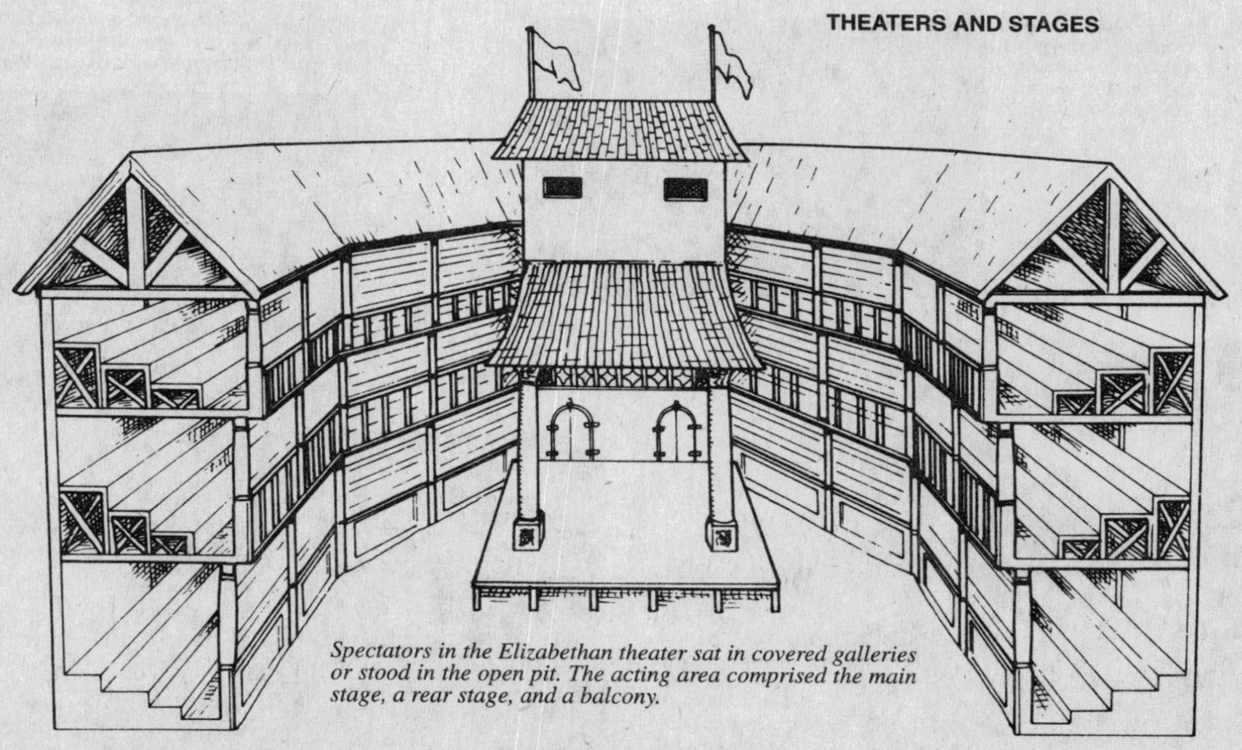

Spectators in the Elizabethan theater sat in covered galleries or stood in the open pit. The acting area comprised the main stage, a rear stage, and a balcony.

THEATERS AND STAGES

The Theater of Dionysus at Athens during the Hellenistic period. The chorus stood in the front semicircular area (orchestra). Behind them were musicians, while the speaking actors performed in front of the screen.

Medieval miracle and mystery plays were performed on large wagons in public places. Different wagons were used for different scenes.

The proscenium arch allowed the audience to view a scene as if through a window. The depth and width of the stage made possible the use of elaborately realistic scenery and lighting.

The theater-in-the-round design recalls a primary feature of Elizabethan theater—close contact between actors and audience.

Thebes 88 19N 23 19E A city in Boeotia, in central Greece. It was founded in Mycenaean times and its legendary history was a favorite theme in Greek drama. Predominant among its Boeotian neighbors, Thebes lost influence by supporting the Persians in 480 BC. Expedient alliances subsequently increased its power and Thebes briefly became the leading Greek state after defeating the Spartans at Leuctra (371). Opposition to Macedonian expansionism led to destruction (336). Although refounded, it never regained significance. Population (1971 est): 15,899.

thegn A person in Anglo-Saxon England who held land from his lord in return for service. The status of thegn (meaning one who serves) was hereditary. The king's thegns had military and administrative duties and also attended the *witan (king's council). Their importance declined in the early 11th century, and the thegns died out after the Norman conquest.

theism The belief in a personal God as creator and preserver of the universe, who reveals himself by supernatural means to his creatures. Apparently coined (1678) by *Cudworth as an opposite to *atheism, theism has been refined in meaning to exclude both *pantheism and *deism. It is central to Christian, Judaic, and Islamic thought.

Themis The Greek goddess of justice and wisdom, often portrayed carrying a pair of scales. She was a Titan, the daughter of Uranus and Gaea and the second wife of Zeus. As the wife of the Titan Iapetus, she was also the mother of *Prometheus.

Themistocles (c. 528–462 BC) Athenian statesman, who built Athens' naval power. Themistocles persuaded Athens to expand its navy (483) and to transfer its port from Phaleron to the more defensible Piraeus. These policies, and his leadership at the battle of *Salamis, saved Greece from Persia (480) (*see* Greek-Persian Wars). Themistocles argued successfully for the fortification of Athens, despite Spartan opposition, but his opponents caused him to be ostracized in about 471. Themistocles subsequently fled to Asia, where he died.

Thénard, Louis-Jacques (1777–1867) French chemist, who in 1808 was the first to isolate the element *boron in collaboration with *Gay-Lussac. He also discovered hydrogen peroxide in 1813 and produced a pigment known as Thénard's blue, which is stable at high temperatures and so can be used in porcelain.

Theocritus (c. 310–250 BC) Greek poet. Born in Sicily, he worked for part of his life on the island of Cos and at Alexandria. His surviving poems, the *Idylls*, include six poems cast in the dramatic form of dialogues or contests between countrymen. These poems on Sicilian rural life are unsurpassed examples of the pastoral, a form which Theocritus originated and which influenced many later works, such as Milton's *Lycidas*.

theodolite An instrument used in *surveying to measure horizontal and vertical angles. It consists of a telescope, with crosshairs in the eyepiece for focusing on the target, that can swivel on horizontal and vertical axes, which pass through two circular scales. It has a spirit level to indicate when the instrument is horizontal and is mounted on a tripod with adjustable legs.

Theodora (c. 500–48 AD) Byzantine empress (527–48); the wife of *Justinian I. Theodora was the daughter of a circus bearkeeper and had been an actress before she married Justinian in 525 and became one of the most influential women in the history of the Eastern Roman Empire. Justinian consulted her on all affairs of state and his reign achieved little of consequence after her death. She was noted for her early championship of the rights of women.

Theodorakis, Mikis (1925–) Greek composer, who led a revival of Greek folk music in the 1960s and has incorporated elements of it into his compositions, which include music for the film *Zorba the Greek* (1964). He has also been politically active in Greece.

Theodore I Lascaris (c. 1175–1222) The founder of the Byzantine empire at Nicaea after Constantinople fell to the Crusaders (1204). In 1214, following a period of warfare, Theodore and the Latins determined the borders between Constantinople and Nicaea.

Theodoric the Great (c. 445–526) King of the Ostrogoths (471–526), who ruled Italy (493–526). He defeated *Odoacer in 493 and established an Ostrogothic kingdom with its capital at Ravenna, ensuring peace by religious toleration and marriage alliances with the other barbarian kingdoms. However, territorial expansion brought conflict with the Frankish king *Clovis and his death left Italy leaderless and ripe for Byzantine annexation.

Theodosius (I) the Great (347–95 AD) Roman emperor in the East (379–94) and sole emperor (394–95). Theodosius allowed the Visigoths independence on Roman territory by a treaty in 382 and they undertook to supplement the Roman army. A devout and orthodox Christian, he imposed Christianity on the Empire in 391, closing pagan temples and forbidding sacrifices.

Theodosius II (401–50 AD) Eastern Roman emperor (408–50). He was strongly influenced by his sister, his wife, and a series of advisers. He sponsored the compilation of the **Theodosian Code** (438), a collection of laws that had been issued since 312.

theology Literally, the study of *God. Each of the higher religions has its own theology. Christian theology includes within its scope the nature of God, his relationship with the universe, his providence regarding man, and the teachings of the Church. Different traditions exist within the Roman Catholic, Orthodox, and Protestant communions, but typical subdivisions of theology are dogmatic, historical, and pastoral theology. Until the emergence of Renaissance *humanism, theology was accounted the highest science (*see* scholasticism) but in the 19th and 20th centuries its findings came under hostile scrutiny from physicists, philosophers, anthropologists, and others.

Theophilus (d. 842 AD) Byzantine emperor (829–42). He was a man of great learning and, despite frequent attacks by the Muslims, stimulated a resurgence of cultural activity. He was the last emperor to uphold *iconoclasm.

Theophrastus (c. 370–286 BC) Greek philosopher and scientist. He studied under *Plato and became *Aristotle's closest friend, succeeding him as head of the *Lyceum. He established botany as a science and lectured and wrote on a vast number of subjects.

theorbo A large double-necked *lute having two sets of strings. One set could be stopped against a fingerboard, the other plucked as open strings.

theosophy Speculation tending toward a mystical understanding of the divine. The term originated in *Neoplatonism but is now mainly applied to the blend of Hindu and Neoplatonic doctrines propounded by the Theosophical Society, which was founded by Helena *Blavatsky in 1875. *Compare* anthroposophy.

Thera (*or* Santoríni; Modern Greek name: Thíra) A Greek island in the Aegean Sea, the southernmost of the Cyclades group. The present island is the E side of a volcano the catastrophic explosion of which (c. 1450 BC) precipitated the decline of *Minoan civilization on Crete, 70 mi (110 km) to the S (*see also* Atlantis). In 1966 a well-preserved Minoan town was found on Thera itself. Area: 29 sq mi (75 sq km).

therapsid An extinct reptile belonging to the order *Therapsida*, which lived during the Permian and Triassic periods (280–200 million years ago). Therapsids were the ancestors of the mammals and had a number of mammal-like features: the limbs were positioned under the body to carry it well off the ground; the skull was deep with a fairly large braincase; and the teeth were specialized for different functions. There were both carnivorous and herbivorous forms.

Theravada The old conservative school of *Buddhism, also called Hinayana (Pali: lesser vehicle) by its detractors. Prevalent in Myanmar (Burma), Cambodia, Laos, Sri Lanka, and Thailand, it emphasizes the ideal of the *arhat*—one who, as a monk, achieves enlightenment by his own efforts. In Theravada, the *Buddha is revered but not the Bodhisattvas, and only the oldest works, the Pali canon, are considered orthodox.

Thérèse, St (Marie Françoise Thérèse Martin; 1873–97) French *Carmelite nun, known as the Little Flower of Jesus. She entered the Carmelite convent at Lisieux when only 15 and died there 9 years later of tuberculosis. Her fame rests on her spiritual autobiography, *Histoire d'une âme* (1898), showing that spiritual perfection could be attained through childlike humbleness and goodness. She was canonized in 1925. Feast day: Oct 3.

thermae Ancient Roman public baths. They reached their height of architectural sophistication under the Empire, being equipped with libraries and other amenities for relaxation. The best surviving examples include the baths of Titus (81 AD) and Caracalla (217).

thermal reactor A nuclear reactor (*see* nuclear energy) in which natural or enriched uranium is used with a moderator, in most cases to generate heat for a *power station. The moderator slows down the neutrons emitted during the fission of uranium 235, so that their velocities are comparable to the velocities of gas molecules ("thermal" velocities).

In a thermal reactor, fuel rods made of uranium metal or oxide are surrounded by a moderator (together forming the reactor core), the heat of the reaction being removed by a coolant. After leaving the core, the coolant passes to a heat exchanger in which steam is raised. The rate of reaction is controlled by a series of control rods, which can move in and out of the core: the rods contain a neutron-absorbing element, such as boron or cadmium.

The first nuclear reactor was built by *Fermi in 1942, using natural uranium, a graphite moderator, and a water coolant. British thermal reactors use a gas coolant (usually carbon dioxide) and later types use an enriched fuel. American designs use a liquid as both moderator and coolant. Using ordinary water in a pressurized-water reactor or a boiling-water reactor, enriched fuel is needed; using heavy water, natural uranium can be used. *Compare* fast reactor.

Thermidorian Reaction. *See* French Revolution.

thermionic valve A device consisting of a sealed glass or metal tube, either evacuated or containing gas at low pressure, into which two or more electrodes are inserted. One heated electrode, the cathode, emits electrons, which are attracted to the positively charged anode, forming an electric current. This current flows in one direction only and can be controlled by the voltage applied at one or more other electrodes (called grids). The **diode valve** was invented in 1904 by Sir John Ambrose Fleming. It has two electrodes and functions as a simple *rectifier. The **triode valve** with one grid was invented in 1910 by Lee De Forest; it was the first to function as an amplifier. The weak signal fed to the grid produces a stronger signal in the anode circuit. Diode and triode valves made possible the development of radio transmitters and receivers, although now *semiconductor diodes and *transistors have largely replaced them. The gas-filled **thyratron** functions as a switch by using a positive grid voltage pulse to initiate a continuing discharge of electrons from the cathode to the anode. It is used in switching and counting circuits, but, like most thermionic valves, has been superseded by its semiconductor equivalent, the *thyristor.

thermistor A *semiconductor device with an electrical resistance that decreases sharply as temperature increases. It is used in temperature-control circuits and can be calibrated for use as a thermometer.

thermite A mixture of powdered aluminum and iron oxide. When ignited, aluminum oxide and iron are produced. The reaction is highly exothermic, yielding molten iron at a temperature of over 3636°F (2000°C). It is used in welding steel and in incendiary bombs.

thermocline A layer within the oceans between about 325 ft (100 m) and 650 ft (200 m) below the surface, in which there is a marked increase in temperature with depth. Above and for some distance below it, there is little vertical temperature gradient.

thermocouple A type of thermometer consisting of an electric circuit formed by two dissimilar metals joined at each end. One junction is exposed to the temperature to be measured, a voltage being generated between it and the other (reference) junction as a result of the temperature difference between them (*see* thermoelectric effects). The output is usually displayed on a *galvanometer. Copper-constantan junctions are used up to 933°F (500°C) and platinum-rhodium alloy up to 2735°F (1500°C). A **thermopile** consists of several thermocouples connected in series to increase the voltage output for a particular temperature difference.

thermodynamics The study of *heat and its relationship with other forms of energy. Thermodynamics is primarily a statistical subject, thermodynamic quantities, such as *temperature and *entropy, being dependent on the statistical behavior of the particles that comprise a system. There are three fundamental laws of thermodynamics. The first law states that the energy of a closed system remains constant during any process. This law is a restatement of the law of *conservation of mass and energy. The second law states that heat cannot flow from a cold body to a hot body without the expenditure of external work. Another way of stating this law is to say that the entropy of a closed system can never decrease. If the entropy change is zero then the process is said to be reversible. The third law states that as the thermodynamic temperature of a system approaches *absolute zero, its entropy approaches zero.

Thermodynamics has proved most valuable in studying *heat engines and chemical reactions, but it also has wider implications in other statistical sciences. *See* heat death of the universe.

thermoelectric effects The effects of changes of temperature on electric circuits or devices. The **Seebeck effect**, named for Johann Seebeck (1770–1831), provides the basis for the *thermocouple; it occurs when a circuit has two junctions between dissimilar metals. If the junctions are maintained at different temperatures, a voltage is generated between them. The **Peltier effect**, named after Jean Peltier (1785–1845), is the converse of this. One junction heats up and the other cools down when a steady current flows through such a circuit. In the **Thomson** (*or* Kelvin) **effect**, named for Lord *Kelvin, a temperature gradient along a single metal conductor causes a current to flow through it.

thermoluminescence *Luminescence caused by heating a substance and thus liberating electrons trapped in its crystal defects. The phenomenon is used as a dating technique, especially for pottery. The number of trapped electrons is assumed to be related to the quantity of *ionizing radiation to which the specimen has been exposed since firing (as the crystal defects are caused by ionizing radiation). Thus, by measuring the amount of light emitted on heating, an estimate of the age of the pottery can be made by assuming that the amount of ionizing radiation to which it has been exposed is related to its age.

thermometer An instrument used for measuring temperature. Thermometers make use of some property of a substance that varies uniformly with temperature, most commonly the expansion of a liquid, such as mercury or alcohol colored with dye. A clinical thermometer is a typical mercury-in-glass thermometer; it has a constriction in the stem above the bulb so that the mercury stays at its maximum reading until "shaken down". More accurate thermometers use the expansion of a gas, which is much greater than that of a liquid. Other thermometers include the resistance thermometer, which depends on the variation in the resistance of a wire (usually platinum); the bimetallic strip in which the unequal expansion of two metals welded together to form a strip causes a pointer to move round a dial; and the thermistor, in which the change in conductivity of a semiconductor is used as a measure of temperature. High temperatures are measured by a *pyrometer.

thermonuclear reactor A reactor in which a fusion reaction (*see* nuclear energy) takes place with the controlled release of energy. After over 30 years of research in several countries, it is now generally accepted that a working thermonuclear reactor is unlikely to be in commission before the next century.

A typical fusion reaction is the combination of deuterium and tritium to form helium ($^{2}_{1}H + ^{3}_{1}H = ^{4}_{2}He + n + 17.6$ MeV). To overcome the *electromagnetic interaction between nuclei a temperature of about 72 million °F (40 million °C) is needed. Containing the *plasma (as the high-temperature ionized gas is called) is the problem to be solved. In magnetic containment a high current passed through the plasma creates a *magnetic bottle that keeps the plasma away from the containing walls. To produce useful energy at this temperature, the product of the plasma density and the containment time must exceed 10^{14} particle seconds per cm^3. Russian toroidal Tokamak devices have so far only achieved a figure of 10^{12}; moreover the problems of magnetic instabilities have not yet been solved. Other possible devices include a pellet of fuel exposed to pulses from *laser beams. The virtually inexhaustible supply of thermonuclear fuel (hydrogen and its isotopes) makes the fusion reactor an extremely attractive goal.

thermopile. *See* thermocouple.

Thermopylae, Battle of (480 BC) The battle in which the Greeks under the Spartan king *Leonidas attempted for three days to hold the pass of Thermopylae in E central Greece against the Persians. After the main Greek force had retreated the Spartans and Thespians, surrounded and outnumbered, fought to the death. Their heroic stand inspired continued Greek resistance to Persia (*see* Greek-Persian Wars).

Theseus A legendary Greek hero, son of Aegeus, king of Athens, or of Poseidon. He freed the Athenians from their annual tribute to *Minos by killing the *Minotaur of Crete with the help of *Ariadne, who escaped with him. He extended the rule of Athens over various Attic communities and was the subject of many legends. He was father of *Hippolytus by Hippolyte, queen of the Amazons, and he married *Phaedra, sister of Ariadne.

Thespiae An ancient city of Boeotia at the foot of Mount Helicon, the Muses' traditional home. *Praxiteles' famous Statue of Eros was at Thespiae. Thespians were the only Boeotians to resist the Persian invasion (*see* Greek-Persian Wars) and fought alongside the Spartans at *Thermopylae (480 BC). It retained its importance under the Romans.

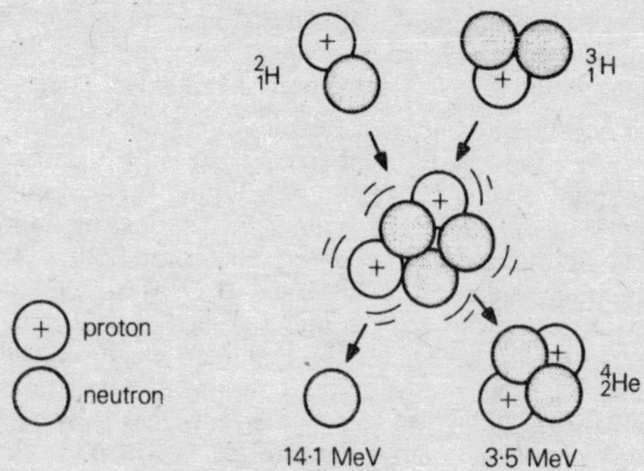

deuterium-tritium fusion reaction

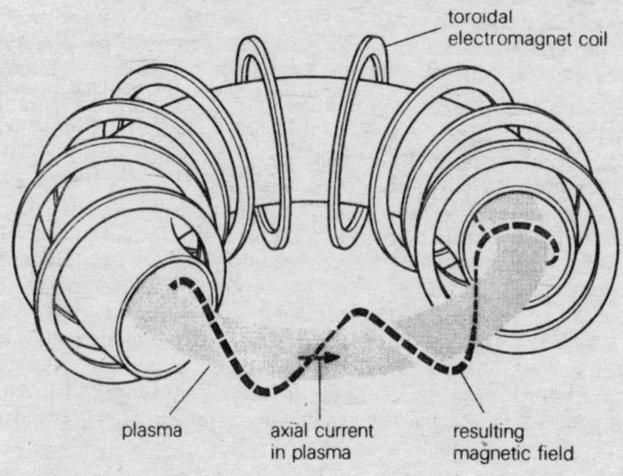

fusion reactor experiment

THERMONUCLEAR REACTOR *The combination of deuterium ($^2{}_1H$) and tritium ($^3{}_1H$) in a fusion reaction that forms helium. This is being attempted using a toroidal electromagnet to contain plasma consisting of deuterium and tritium nuclei.*

Thespis (6th century BC) Semilegendary Greek poet. He won a prize for tragedy at Athens in about 534 BC. Traditionally held to be the inventor of tragedy, he was said to have introduced a single actor in dramatic performances that had hitherto been exclusively choral. He was also believed to have introduced the wearing of linen masks.

Thessalonians, Epistles of Paul to the Two New Testament books written by Paul to new converts in Thessalonica in about 51 AD. They are therefore among the earliest books of the New Testament. The first letter is filled with reminiscences, thanksgiving, and instruction but gives special prominence to the second coming of Christ. The second letter is a sequel, warning against the neglect of everyday duties caused by an overenthusiastic expectation of the second coming.

Thessaloníki (English name: Salonika) 40 38N 22 58E The second largest port in Greece, in Macedonia on the Gulf of Salonika. Founded in 315 BC as Thessalonica, it became the capital of Macedonia. It was captured by the Turks (1430) and remained in the Ottoman Empire until ceded to Greece (1913). During World War I it was a base for Allied operations. Notable Byzantine architecture includes the Panaghia Chalkeon (1028). Its university was founded in 1925. The port handles about one-third of Greek exports, including chrome, manganese, and agricultural produce. Industries include the manufacture of textiles and food processing. Population (1981): 402,443.

Thessaly (Modern Greek name: Thessalía) A region of E central Greece, bordering on the Aegean Sea. In the 4th century BC it was briefly a strong and united state before falling to Philip of Macedon. Freed from Macedonian rule by Rome in 196 BC, it was incorporated in the Roman province of Macedonia in 148 BC. It subsequently formed part of the Byzantine Empire, falling to Turkey in the late 14th century AD. It was annexed by Greece in 1881.

Thetis In Greek mythology, one of the *nereids. She was courted by Zeus and Poseidon, but after hearing that she was fated to bear a son greater than its father they married her to the mortal Peleus, to whom she bore *Achilles.

thiamine. *See* vitamin B complex.

thiazine An organic compound that has a molecular structure containing a ring of four carbon atoms and two sulfur atoms. Thiazine derivatives are used in such drugs as tranquilizers, antihistamines, and antibiotics, as well as in various dyes.

thiazole (C_3H_3NS) An organic compound that has a molecular structure containing a ring of three carbon atoms, one sulfur atom, and one nitrogen atom. Thiazole derivatives occur in thiamine (vitamin B_1), penicillin, and in numerous synthetic drugs, dyes, and chemicals.

Thibaud, Jacques (1880–1953) French violinist. He studied at the Paris conservatory and after a period playing at the Café Rouge in Paris he made his concert debut in 1898. In 1905 he formed a trio with Cortot and Casals. He was killed in an airplane crash.

thickhead An insectivorous songbird belonging to a family (*Pachycephalidae*; 35 species) occurring in mangrove swamps, scrub, and open forests in S Asia and Australasia. Thickheads are 6–7 in (15–18 cm) long and have large heavy heads and a loud whistling song. Male birds of the chief genus, *Pachycephalus*, are typically yellow and green with black, white, or brown markings.

Thiers, Louis Adolphe (1797–1877) French statesman and historian; the first president of the Third Republic (1870–73). He served Louis Philippe in various ministerial posts and was a critic of Napoleon III, after whose fall during the Franco-Prussian War Thiers became president. He negotiated peace with Prussia and his economic policies facilitated France's economic recovery. He was responsible for the suppression of the Commune of Paris (1871). His publications include *Histoire de la Révolution française* (10 vols, 1823–27).

Thimphu (*or* Thimbu) 27 29N 89 40E The capital of Bhutan since 1962, situated in the foothills of the E Himalayas. Population (1987 est): 15,000.

Thíra. *See* Thera.

Third Reich (1933–45) The Nazi regime in Germany. The name refers to the Nazi ambition to revive the medieval Holy Roman Empire (the first Reich) and the German Empire (the second Reich; 1871–1918). The Third Reich succeeded the Weimar Republic and ended with Germany's defeat in World War II.

third stream A name for a type of music created by the fusion of jazz and classical music. The word was coined by the composer Gunther Schuller, who encouraged classically trained jazz musicians, such as Charlie Mingus and John Coltrane, and composers interested in jazz, such as Milton Babbitt, to work together.

Third World. *See* developing countries.

Thirteen Colonies The 13 North American colonies that became the United States of America in 1776 (*see* American Revolution). They were Connecticut, Delaware, Georgia, Maryland, Massachusetts, New Hampshire, New Jersey, New York, North Carolina, Pennsylvania, Rhode Island, South Carolina, and Virginia.

thirty-eighth parallel The latitude of 38°N that approximates to the border between North and South Korea. It was the line, agreed at the *Yalta Conference at the end of World War II, N of which Soviet troops accepted the Japanese surrender and S of which US troops did so. Hostility between the Soviet-dominated North Korea and the US-dominated South Korea led to the *Korean War, after which the thirty-eighth parallel was confirmed as the demarcation line.

Thirty-Nine Articles (1563) The doctrine, together with the book of *Common Prayer, of the *Church of England. The articles do not represent a creed; rather they deal with specific points that were matters of controversy and give in broad terms the Anglican position with regard to these points, especially as distinguished from the Roman Catholic, Calvinist, or Anabaptist views. The clergy of the Church of England promise not to teach beliefs that contradict them. Other Anglican churches, such as the Protestant Episcopal Church in the US, have adopted many of the articles.

Thirty Years' War (1618–48) The conflict between rival dynastic and religious interests in the Holy Roman Empire that escalated into a major European war. It was caused by the revolt of Protestants in Bohemia against the Counter-Reformation policies of the imperial government at Prague. Although imperial forces defeated the Bohemians in 1620, the revolt spread, with the German Protestants under *Mansfeld receiving sporadic support from the English, Dutch, and Danes. With the Edict of Restitution (1629) Emperor Ferdinand II, helped by the armies of *Wallenstein and *Tilly, dispossessed many German Protestants, who were only saved by the intervention in 1630 of Sweden under *Gustavus II Adolphus. In 1635 France, hoping to contain the power of Spain and the Empire, entered the conflict. The war ended with the Peace of *Westphalia (1648), although the Franco-Spanish conflict continued until 1659 (*see* Pyrenees, Treaty of the). The war caused serious economic and demographic reverses in Germany.

Thisbe. *See* Pyramus and Thisbe.

thistle A prickly leaved herb belonging to one of several genera of the family **Compositae*, especially *Carduus* (120 species), *Cirsium* (120 species), *Carlinus* (20 species), and *Onopordum* (20 species), distributed throughout the N hemisphere. Thistles characteristically have heads of small purple flowers and spiny stems. The perennial creeping thistle (*Cirsium arvense*) grows to a height of 40 in (1 m) and is a persistent weed, having spreading roots that give rise to new plants. *See also* globe thistle; sow thistle.

Thistlewood, Arthur. *See* Cato Street Conspiracy.

Thomas, Clarence (1948–) US jurist, Supreme Court associate justice (1991–). Born in Georgia, he graduated from Yale Law School, and after service as an assistant attorney general in Missouri (1974–77) and as a Senate aide (1977–81), he became chairman (1982–90) of the Equal Employment Opportunity Commission until appointed (1990) a federal appeals court judge by President Bush. Thomas became the second African American on the court only after highly publicized confirmation hearings that included charges of sexual harassment against a female associate. His early decisions indicated that he would be a conservative justice.

Thomas, Dylan (1914–53) Welsh poet. Born in Swansea, Wales, he moved to London after the publication of *18 Poems* in 1934 and worked for the BBC. *Deaths and Entrances* (1946) contains many of his best-known poems. In 1949 he returned to Wales, where he wrote his popular radio play *Under Milk Wood* (1954). Alcoholism precipitated his death, while on a US tour.

DYLAN THOMAS

Thomas, Norman (Mattoon) (1884–1968) US socialist leader, reformer, and author. He founded the National Civil Liberties Bureau in 1917 and joined the Socialist party in 1918. His early pacifism and his concern for civil liberties led to leadership of the Socialist party from 1926 and its nomination for president six times—from 1928 to 1948. His works include *The Conscientious Objector in America* (1923), *Socialism of Our Time* (1929), *Socialist's Faith* (1951), and *Socialism Reexamined* (1963).

Thomas, St In the New Testament, one of the 12 Apostles. He is known as "Doubting Thomas" because he refused to believe in the Resurrection until he had seen and touched Christ. Feast day: Dec 21.

Thomas à Kempis (Thomas Hemmerken; c. 1380–1471) German spiritual writer and monk. He spent most of his life writing and teaching novices at the Augustinian convent of Agnietenberg near Zwolle (Netherlands). His fame rests on his devotional treatise, *The Imitation of Christ*, although his authorship has been doubted by some scholars.

Thomson, Sir Joseph John (1856–1940) British physicist, who discovered the *electron. Thomson studied *cathode rays, the nature of which was then unknown and in 1897 he succeeded in deflecting cathode rays by an electric field, thus showing that they consisted of negatively charged particles. He also measured the ratio of their charge to mass and, using the known figure for the minimum charge on an ion, deduced that electrons were about 2000 times lighter than the hydrogen atom. Thomson thought that atoms consist of electrons embedded in a positively charged sphere, a concept that was superseded by *Rutherford's model. For his discovery of the electron, Thomson was awarded the Nobel Prize in 1906. His son **Sir George Paget Thomson** (1892–1975), also a physicist, discovered the effect of electron diffraction (1927). He shared the 1937 Nobel Prize with Clinton Davisson (1881–1958), who had independently discovered the same effect.

Thomson, Virgil (1896–1989) US composer, music critic, and conductor. He studied composition with Nadia Boulanger in Paris. His compositions include two operas with libretti by Gertrude Stein: *Four Saints in Three Acts* (1928) and *The Mother of Us All* (1947). He composed a variety of other vocal and instrumental music, including music for the film *Louisiana Story* (1948). His writings include *The Art of Judging Music* (1948) and *American Music Since 1910* (1971).

Thomson, William. *See* Kelvin, William Thomson, 1st baron.

Thomson effect (*or* Kelvin effect). *See* thermoelectric effects.

Thonburi 13 43N 100 27E A city in central Thailand, part of Bangkok Metropolis on the Chao Phraya River. It is noted for the Wat Arun temple. Industries include rice and timber milling. Population (1989 est): 227,000.

Thor The Teutonic god of thunder, in some legends the son of *Odin. He presided over the home and controlled the weather and crops; he was also worshiped as a god of war. Armed with a magic hammer, similar to a boomerang, and a belt, which increased his strength, he battled frequently against giants and monsters. His name survives in *Thursday*. □Ragnarök.

thorax In mammals (including man), the region of the body between the *diaphragm and the neck, which contains the lungs and heart and their associated vessels. The skeleton of the thorax is formed by the breastbone at the front, the spine at the back, and the ribs at the sides. In arthropods the thorax is the part of the body between the head and abdomen.

Thoreau, Henry David (1817–62) US naturalist and writer. His early work appeared in the *Dial* and also included *A Week on the Concord and Merrimack Rivers* (1849). Thoreau is best known for his Walden experiment (1845–46) during which he lived as a recluse in the woods of Walden near his native Concord, Mass. He developed a great love and knowledge of animals, which was more intuitive than scientific. *Walden* was published in 1854. Influenced by *Emerson and *Hawthorne, Thoreau also wrote poems and essays, many about his beloved homeland. His best-known essay, "Civil Disobedience," grew out of his opposition to the Mexican War. *See also* transcendentalists.

thorium (Th) A naturally occurring radioactive metal. It is possible that thorium-fueled nuclear reactors may be developed in the future, since it is more abundant than uranium and does not produce plutonium 239 in appreciable quantities (*see* uranium). Thorium oxide (ThO_2) has one of the highest known melting points (5972°F; 3300°C), which led to its use in gas mantles, as it glows white when heated. At no 90; at wt 232.038; mp 3185°F (1750°C); bp 6878°F (3800°C).

thorium series One of three naturally occurring series of radioactive decays. The thorium series is headed by thorium 232, which undergoes a series of alpha and beta decays ending with the stable isotope lead 208. *See also* actinium series; uranium series.

HENRY DAVID THOREAU *Writer whose observations on life and his surroundings were recorded in* Walden.

thorn apple An annual herb, *Datura stramonium*, also called jimsonweed, occurring in N temperate and subtropical regions. Growing to a height of 40 in (1 m), it has white trumpet-shaped flowers producing a fruit with a spiny capsule that splits to release the black seeds. All parts of the plant are very poisonous, containing the alkaloids hyoscyamine, hyoscine, and scopolamine. Family: **Solanaceae.*

thornbill A drab-colored Australian bird belonging to one of three genera, especially *Acanthiza*, and occurring in trees and thickets. The yellow-tailed thornbill (*A. chrysorrhoea*) builds a very long oval nest with several nest chambers, the upper being used to rear young and the lower providing accommodation for the male. Family: *Muscicapidae* (*see* flycatcher).

Thorndike, Dame Sybil (1882–1976) British actress. She acted many Shakespearean roles at the Old Vic between 1914 and 1918 and played the title role in the first production of G. B. Shaw's *St Joan* in 1924. She also acted in several films.

Thornhill, Sir James (1675–1734) English *baroque decorative painter. One of the first native-born English painters with any pretensions to an international reputation, Thornhill is best remembered for his decoration of the Painted Hall at Greenwich Hospital (1704), the interior of the dome of *St Paul's Cathedral (1707), and the hall at Blenheim Palace. He was the teacher and father-in-law of *Hogarth.

Thoroughbred A breed of □horse descended from three Arab stallions brought to England between 1689 and 1728. Thoroughbreds have a refined streamlined build and a sensitive temperament and are noted for speed and stamina, being used worldwide for racing and as bloodstock to improve other breeds. They may be any solid color. Height: 15–17 hands (5 ft/1.5 m–5 ft 9 in/ 1.73 m).

Thorpe, Jim (James Francis T.; 1888–1953) US athlete. Of Indian descent, he was an all-American football player (1911, 1912) while attending the Carlisle Indian School. He won gold medals for the decathlon and the pentathlon in the Olympic games (1912), but was forced to return the medals because he had played baseball semiprofessionally. (They were returned to his descendants in 1973.) Named the greatest athlete of the first half of the 20th century, he played professional baseball (1913–19) and professional football (1915–26) and headed the American Professional Football Association in 1920.

Thorvaldsen, Bertel (*or* B. Thorwaldsen; 1768–1844) Danish sculptor. His highly successful career began in Rome, where he worked from 1797 until his return to Copenhagen in 1838. Reviving the tradition of ancient Greek sculpture in his mythological and religious statues, he became one of the leading figures in *neoclassicism. Many of his works are in the Thorvaldsen Museum, Copenhagen.

Thoth The Egyptian god of learning, the scribe and arbiter of the gods, usually portrayed with the head of an ibis. He was the inventor of writing, arithmetic, and geometry and the keeper of various magic formulae. *See also* Hermes Trismegistos.

Thousand, Expedition of the (1860) The expedition of about a thousand volunteers, led by Giuseppe *Garibaldi, which embarked from Genoa and, after landing in Sicily, overthrew the Kingdom of the Two Sicilies, enabling S Italy to be united with the N. *See also* Risorgimento.

Thousand Islands A group of about 1700 small islands and islets in North America, in the St Lawrence River. They are chiefly in Ontario (Canada) with a few in New York state and are a popular resort area.

Thrace The Balkan region bordered by the Black Sea, the Aegean, Macedonia, and the Danube River. From the 8th century BC Greek cities colonized the coasts, while the independent inland tribes were an easy target for invaders—the Persians in about 516 BC and then Philip II of Macedon in the mid-4th century. After Alexander the Great's death (323) it passed to his general Lysimachus (c. 355–c. 281 BC) and then to Macedonia before coming under the influence of Rome in 168 BC; it became a Roman province in 46 AD. Famous for its horses and horsemen, and for ecstatic religious rituals, Thrace was traditionally the birthplace of the mysteries and orgiastic rites associated with the worship of Dionysus. It is now divided between Turkey, Greece, and Bulgaria.

Thrale, Hester Lynch. *See* Piozzi, Hester Lynch.

threadfin A fish, also called threadfish, belonging to the family *Polynemidae* (about 24 species), that is found along warm seashores. It has a silvery elongated body, usually 12–24 in (30–60 cm) long, two dorsal fins, and four to seven long threadlike pectoral fin rays. Order: *Perciformes*.

threadworm. *See* pinworm.

Three Mile Island An island in the Susquehanna River in SE Pennsylvania, just S of Harrisburg. The nuclear power plant located there was the focus of attention in 1979 when one of its reactors experienced a breakdown in its emergency core cooling system. Although widespread dissemination of radioactive material never occurred, the incident precipitated far-reaching investigations of the proper design, maintenance, and operation of nuclear reactors.

Three Rivers. *See* Trois-Rivières.

Three Wise Men. *See* Magi.

thresher shark A *shark of the family *Alopiidae* (5 species), found usually in offshore waters of tropical and temperate seas. About 20 ft (6 m) long, it has a long scythelike extension of the upper tail lobe, which it uses to thrash the water while circling its prey (squid and schooling fish), forcing them into tighter groups, which it then attacks. □fish.

thrift A perennial herb, *Armeria maritima*, also called sea pink, native to mountains, salt marshes, and sandy coastal regions of N Europe. The flower stem, up to 12 in (30 cm) high, rises from a basal tuft of long narrow grasslike leaves and bears a cluster of rose-pink or white flowers. The Jersey thrift (*A. arenaria*) is taller with a denser tuft of broader leaves and grows on sand dunes in central and S Europe. Family: *Plumbaginaceae*.

thrips A minute insect, also called thunder fly, belonging to the order *Thysanoptera* (about 3000 species). Thrips have dark slender bodies, 0.01–0.2 in (0.5–5 mm) long, and usually two pairs of narrow fringed wings. Many species suck the juices of flowering plants, often causing serious damage and spreading plant diseases. Others eat fungi, decaying organic material, mites, and small insects. In some species there are no males and the larvae develop from unfertilized eggs (*see* parthenogenesis).

thrombosis The formation of a blood clot inside a blood vessel, which often obstructs the flow of blood. Thrombosis is more likely to occur if the blood vessel is damaged, if the blood flow is very slow, or if the blood is in a condition in which it is more likely to clot. The commonest site of thrombosis is in the veins of the legs. This is particularly likely to occur if a person is bedridden for a long time and it is often accompanied by inflammation of the vein (*see* phlebitis). The clot may become detached and carried to the lungs, causing pulmonary *embolism. The patient is treated with *anticoagulants.

Thrombosis can also occur in the arteries supplying the heart (coronary thrombosis), causing a heart attack (*see* myocardial infarction), or the brain, causing *stroke.

thrush (bird) A songbird belonging to a family (*Turdidae*; 300 species) found throughout the world but predominantly in Old World regions. Thrushes are slender billed, 5–12 in (13–30 cm) long, and usually brown—often with speckling or patches of red, yellow, or blue. They may be terrestrial or arboreal, feeding chiefly on insects and fruit and often having melodious songs. Northern species are migratory. *See also* blackbird; fieldfare; mistle thrush; redwing; ring ouzel; song thrush.

thrush (disease). *See* candidiasis.

Thucydides (c. 460–c. 400 BC) Greek historian. He served as an Athenian general in the Peloponnesian War but was banished in 424 BC for allowing the Spartan general Brasidas to capture the colony of Amphipolis. He remained in exile until 404 BC. His eight-volume *History of the Peloponnesian War*, written in a plain narrative style, is notable for its political, moral, and psychological analysis of the issues and leaders involved.

Thugs (Sanskrit word: *sthaga*, deceiver) A Hindu sect, members of which worked in small gangs, murdering (usually by strangulation), robbing, and burying travelers in India. They worshiped Kali, the Hindu goddess of death, and observed strict rules, employing a private language among themselves. They were suppressed in the 1830s.

Thuja. *See* arborvitae.

Thule **1.** A far northern land first described in the 4th century BC by *Pytheas. It is tentatively identified with Norway or Iceland. **2.** An Eskimo culture of the Arctic region, dating from between about 500 and 1300 AD.

thulium (Tm) The least abundant of the *lanthanide elements, discovered in 1879 by P. T. Cleve (1840–1905). It forms the oxide Tm_2O_3. Radioactive ^{169}Tm is used in portable X-ray generators. At no 69; at wt 168.934; mp 2816°F (1545°C); bp 3540°F (1947°C).

Thunder Bay 48 20N 89 23W A city and port in E Canada, in Ontario on Lake Superior. Settled after 1800, it consists of Fort William and Port Arthur, which amalgamated in 1970. A major wheat-exporting port, Thunder Bay is also a transportation hub and mining center. Pulp and paper, timber, aircraft, buses, and ship building are economically important. Lakehead University (1965) is situated there. Population (1991): 113,746.

thunderstorm A storm of rain, hail, or snow, accompanied by thunder and *lightning. A lightning flash is an electrical discharge causing sudden heating and expansion of air as the flash passes through the atmosphere, resulting in the sound of thunder. Although both occur simultaneously, thunder is heard later than lightning is seen, as light travels faster than sound. An approximate measure of distance from a storm is 1 mi (1.6 km) for every 5 seconds between flash and thunder.

Thurber, James (1894–1961) US humorous writer and cartoonist. An early and continuing contributor to the *New Yorker*, he satirized intellectual fashions and domestic habits with irony and sophistication. His essays and stories are collected in *The Thurber Carnival* (1945) and other volumes.

Thuringia A historic region of central Germany, N of Bavaria and W of Saxony. Dominated by the Thuringian forests and strategically positioned, Thuringia became a buffer state against invaders from the E. Frequently partitioned during the Middle Ages, it passed to the Wettin family in 1265.

Thurmond, (James) Strom (1902–) US politician; senator (1954–). A Democrat, he was governor of South Carolina (1947–51) and ran for president (1948) as the States' Rights Democrat (Dixiecrat) candidate. He switched to the Republican party in 1964. He became president pro tempore of the Senate (1981) and chairman of the Judiciary Committee (1981) and was elected to a seventh term in the Senate in 1990.

Thursday Island 10 37S 142 10E An Australian island in Torres Strait, off the N coast of Queensland. Pearl fishing is the main industry. Area: 1.5 sq mi (4 sq km). Chief town: Port Kennedy.

Thutmose I King of Egypt (c. 1512–c. 1504 BC) of the 18th dynasty. He conquered Nubia beyond the Fourth Nile Cataract and Syria as far as the Euphrates River. He enlarged and embellished the temple of Amon at *Karnak.

Thutmose II King of Egypt (c. 1525–c. 1512 BC) of the 18th dynasty, the son of *Thutmose I and the brother and husband of *Hatshepsut. He crushed a rebellion in Nubia before dying young.

Thutmose III (d. 1450 BC) King of Egypt (c. 1504–1450 BC) of the 18th dynasty, who ruled Egypt at its most powerful and prosperous. In his first year of independent rule, after the death of his half-sister *Hatshepsut (1468), he defeated Syrian rebels at Megiddo and in later campaigns advanced beyond the Euphrates River. He organized and supervised the country's complicated administration and was an outstanding athlete and big-game hunter. A patron of art and architecture, he collected foreign plants, birds, and beasts on campaign. His mummy is to be seen in Cairo.

Thutmose IV King of Egypt (1425–17 BC) of the 18th dynasty. He cultivated the alliance of Babylonia and the Mitanni kingdom against the Hittites and built extensively at *Karnak.

thylacine The largest carnivorous *marsupial, *Thylacinus cynocephalus*, also called Tasmanian wolf or tiger. About 5 ft (1.5 m) long, it resembles a dog with dark stripes across its gray-brown back. Its teeth—adapted for eating meat—include pointed canines and shearing premolars. The dingo has exterminated thylacines on the Australian mainland, but a few may have survived in Tasmania. Family: *Dasyuridae*.

thyme A small shrub belonging to the genus *Thymus* (about 50 species), native to temperate Eurasia. Garden thyme (*T. vulgaris*) is cultivated for its fragrant leaves and small mauve flowers, which are dried and used as a culinary herb. An oil extract is used in perfumes and medicines. The common wild thyme (*T. drucei*) has a branching creeping stem up to 3 in (7.5 cm) long and clusters of rose-purple flowers. Family: **Labiatae*.

thymus An organ situated at the base of the neck, above the heart. The thymus is well developed at birth and grows until puberty, after which it shrinks and ceases to function. During infancy the thymus produces lymphocytes (a type of white blood cell) that form the *antibodies associated with allergic responses and the rejection of transplanted tissues and organs. *See also* immunity.

thyratron. *See* thermionic valve.

thyristor A solid-state electronic device, also called a semiconductor or silicon-controlled rectifier; it consists of four layers of *semiconductor forming three p-n junctions. It acts as a switch, blocking the current through two terminals until it has been turned on by a pulse applied to the third terminal. This pulse can be initiated by light or a temperature change. Thyristors are used in a wide range of power-switching and control-circuit applications. They can pass currents ranging from milliamperes to several hundred amperes and for many purposes have replaced the thyratron (*see* thermionic valve).

thyroid gland An *endocrine gland situated at the base of the neck, in front and on either side of the windpipe. It secretes two hormones, the most important of which is thyroxine, which controls the basal metabolism of the body; thyroxine secretion is regulated by thyroid-stimulating hormone, released from the *pituitary gland. Because thyroxine production requires iodine, deficiency of iodine causes the thyroid to enlarge in an attempt to produce adequate amounts of the hormone (*see* goiter). *See also* cretinism; hyperthyroidism; myxedema.

Tiananmen Square Public square in Beijing (Peking), China. Prodemocracy demonstrations, mainly by students, were held on the square in 1986–87; further protests against the Communist government two years later involved factory workers, union officials, and professionals. In June 1989, the government declared martial law and violently dispersed the demonstrators. Deaths in the initial crackdown exceeded 500. Mass arrests of dissidents followed; some were executed. International protests were launched against these human rights violations and many Western nations, including the US, imposed economic sanctions on China.

Tianjin (T'ien-ching *or* Tientsin) 39 08N 117 12E An administratively autonomous port in NE China, the third largest city in the country, on the *Grand Canal. A prosperous city for centuries, it was the scene of much friction between Chinese and Europeans in the late 19th century. It is the site of two universities. Industries include chemicals, machinery, and textiles. Population (1990): 8,785,402.

Tian Shan (*or* Tien Shan) A mountain system of central Asia. It extends about 1500 mi (2500 km) NE from the *Pamir Mountains in Tajikistan, through NW China to the Mongolian border, reaching 24,406 ft (7439 m) at Pobeda Peak.

Tibaldi, Pellegrino (1527–96) Italian architect and painter, a leading exponent of *mannerism. Paintings by him survive in Rome and Bologna. In Spain (1587–96), at the invitation of Philip II, he oversaw the construction and decoration of the *Escorial.

Tiber River (Italian name: Tevere; Latin name: Tiberis) A river in central Italy, rising in the Apennines of Tuscany and flowing mainly S through Rome to the Tyrrhenian Sea near Ostia. Length: 252 mi (405 km).

Tiberias 32 48N 35 32E A city in N Israel, on the W shore of the Sea of Galilee. Founded by Herod Antipas in about 20 AD and named for the Roman Emperor Tiberius, it became the center of Jewry in Palestine after the Roman destruction of Jerusalem. It is now a resort. Population: 23,900.

Tiberias, Sea of. *See* Galilee, Sea of.

Tiberius (42 BC–37 AD) Roman emperor (14–37 AD). Tiberius, who was *Livia Drusilla's son by her first husband, was recognized by his stepfather, Emperor Augustus, as his successor in 4 AD. As emperor his policies were unambitious though sound but he faced the Senate's hostility, family intrigue, and military rebellion. Tiberius's reign saw a series of treason prosecutions before his retirement to Capri in 26 AD, where he gained a reputation for depravity.

Tibesti Mountains A mountain range in N Africa, in the central Sahara. It lies chiefly in NW Chad but extends NE into Libya and rises to 11,204 ft (3415 m) at Emi Koussi, the highest peak in the Sahara.

Tibet (Chinese name: Xizang Autonomous Region) An administrative region in W China, bordering on India, Nepal, Bhutan, and Myanmar (Burma). It consists of a high plateau and is surrounded by mountains, including the Himalayas and the Kunlun Mountains. Most agriculture and the country's cities are in the river valleys, while nomads herd such animals as yaks on the plateau. The area is rich in minerals, not mined until the 1950s because of religious proscription. Tibet is famous for its Buddhist-inspired art and its handicrafts. *History*: Buddhism, introduced in the 7th century AD, has exerted a profound influence on Tibetan history. The lamas (priests) of *Tibetan Buddhism attained political power in the 13th century, when Kublai Khan gave the government of his conquests in E Tibet to the Sa-skya lama. Subsequent disunity was brought to an end in 1642, when the fifth *Dalai Lama became ruler of all Tibet. In 1720 the Chinese Qing dynasty established control over Tibet that lasted until the Qing's overthrow in 1911. Independence was declared, but in 1950 Tibet again fell to the Chinese. An uprising in 1959 was brutally suppressed and the Dalai Lama, together with thousands of refugees, fled. Tibet was subsequently subjected to greater Chinese influence and control. Area: 471,660 sq mi (1,221,601 sq km). Population (1990): 2,196,010. Capital: Lhasa.

Tibetan Buddhism (*or* Lamaism) A form of Mahayana Buddhism as practiced in Tibet and Mongolia. Introduced into Tibet in the 7th century AD, it is characterized by a complex symbolic literature and monastic discipline, with surviving features of *Bon shamanism. Buddhist elements are explored in their esoteric significance, hence the array of deities, *mandalas, etc. The *guru is of prime importance; some are held to be reincarnations of previous lamas. Until the Chinese invasion of Tibet in 1959, the *Dalai Lama was both temporal and spiritual head of the state. *See also* Panchen Lama.

tibia. *See* leg.

Tibullus, Albius (c. 55–c. 19 BC) Roman poet. He lived quietly on his estate near Rome and was a friend of Horace and Ovid. His elegaic poetry, noted for its smooth and rhythmical style, is mostly addressed to his patron, M. Valerius Messalla. Two books of his poems were published during his lifetime and were known as "Delia" and "Nemesis" after the pseudonyms of the women who were the subjects of the poems.

Ticino River A river in Switzerland and Italy. It flows mainly S from the Leopontine Alps to the Po River near Pavia in Italy. Length: 154 mi (248 km).

tick A parasitic *arachnid of the worldwide suborder *Metastigmata* (850 species), which sucks the blood of birds and mammals and may transmit such diseases as *typhus and relapsing fever. Its round unsegmented body, up to 1.2 in (30 mm) long, bears eight bristly legs and may be covered by a dorsal shield. After feeding for a certain time, the adults drop off the host and lay eggs on the ground. The larvae attach themselves to a suitable victim, feed, then drop off and molt into nymphs, which repeat the procedure. Order: *Acarina* (or *Acari*). *Compare* mite.

tides The regular rising and falling of seawater level resulting from the gravitational attraction between the earth, sun, and moon. Variations in their relative positions produce variations in tidal range (*see* spring tide; neap tide). Most parts of the world experience semidiurnal tides (occurring twice per tidal day—24 hours 5 minutes). Tidal currents are periodic horizontal flows of water resulting from the rise and fall of the tide. Near the coast they are usually perpendicular to it and reversing, but in the ocean they flow in a rotary manner around a series of nodal points; water level remains approximately constant at these points, tidal range increasing concentrically outward, and high water rotates about them.

Tieck, (Johann) Ludwig (1773–1853) German writer. Associated with *Novalis, the *Schlegels, and other romantic writers centered in Jena, Tieck was highly versatile, writing romantic and realistic tales, novels, and plays, translating, and publishing a collection of medieval lyrics. His works include the romantic fairytale, *Der blonde Eckbert* (1797) and the satirical comedy, *Der gestiefette Kater* (1797).

Tientsin. *See* Tianjin.

Tiepolo, Giovanni Battista (1696–1770) Venetian *rococo painter, who was one of the greatest decorators of the 18th century. Influenced by *Veronese, his early somber style evolved into the exuberance of his first major frescoes, for the Archbishop's Palace at Udine (1725–29). These were followed by decorations for many N Italian palaces and churches. Abroad he decorated the Residenz Palace, Würzburg, built by the rococo architect *Neumann, with historical and allegorical subjects (1750–53), and the Royal Palace in Madrid (1762–66). One of his assistants and imitators was his son **Giovanni Domenico Tiepolo** (1727–1804), best known for his paintings of clowns and acrobats.

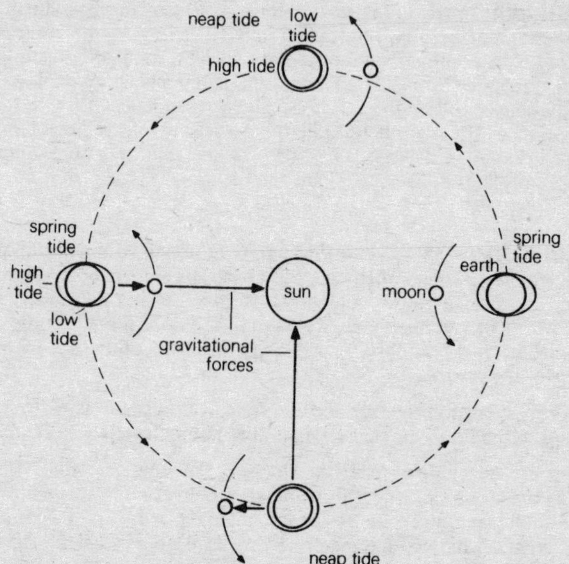

TIDES *The force of gravity between the earth and the moon pulls the waters of the seas towards the moon, creating high tides once a day. The second daily high tide occurs because the moon pulls the earth itself away from the water on the far side from the moon. Exceptionally high spring tides occur twice monthly when the gravitational force of the moon is in line with that of the sun. The lower neap tides occur when these two forces are at right angles.*

Tierra del Fuego An archipelago separated from the mainland of S South America by the Strait of Magellan. The W and S belong to Chile, the E to Argentina. Sheep farming and oil production are the principal economic activities. Chief towns: Punta Arenas (Chile); Ushuaia (Argentina).

Tiflis. *See* Tbilisi.

tiger A large *cat, *Panthera tigris*. Tigers are usually about 10 ft (3 m) long, but the race of Siberian tigers can reach 13 ft (4 m). Tigers evolved in Siberia and have spread south to most of Asia; they shed their coat seasonally and shelter from hot sun during the day. They hunt at night, stalking their prey (mainly antelope). A fully grown tiger will eat up to 55 lb (25 kg) of meat at one feeding.

tiger beetle A long-legged beetle, with pointed mandibles, belonging to a family (*Cicindelidae*; 2000 species) occurring mainly in the tropics and subtropics. Tiger beetles range from 0.24–2.75 in (6–70 mm) in length; although most are black or brown some are brilliantly colored. Both adults and larvae are predatory—the adults hunt for their prey while the larvae wait at the entrance to their burrows.

tigerfish Any fish that resembles a tiger, especially members of the genus *Hydrocynus*, family *Characidae* (*see* characin), found in fresh waters of Africa and South America. They have horizontally striped elongated bodies, reaching 40 in (1 m) in length, and feed voraciously on other fish. Tigerfish of the family *Ther-*

aponidae (order *Perciformes*) occur in Indo-Pacific marine and fresh waters and include the three-striped tigerfish (*Therapon jarbua*), also called saltwater zebra fish.

tiger moth A moth belonging to the family *Arctiidae*, occurring in Eurasia, N Africa, and North America. The adults have a stout body and are brightly colored, often orange and black. The hairy larvae, commonly called woolly bears, incorporate their hairs into the cocoon and are seldom destructive, eating various wild plants.

tiger shark A large *requiem shark, *Galeocerdo cuvieri*, that lives mainly in tropical seas. It has a grayish-brown body, up to about 18 ft (5.5 m) long, patterned with vertical bars and a lighter underside. It is a voracious omnivore and eats virtually anything, including mammals, birds, fish, invertebrates, refuse, and man.

Tiglath-pileser I King of Assyria (c. 1120–1074 BC), who greatly extended Assyrian territory, reaching the Mediterranean coast in the W. He patronized art and architecture and collected one of the oldest surviving libraries.

Tiglath-pileser III King of Assyria (c. 745–727 BC). Probably a usurper, he restored Assyrian military power in Babylonia, Syria, and against Urartu in the N. He also improved the efficiency of Assyrian administration, appointing provincial governors.

tigon A sterile hybrid cat, resulting from the mating of a lion and a tiger, also called a liger. This can only happen in captivity, because lions and tigers naturally inhabit different continents.

Tigre. *See* Amhara.

Tigris River A river in SW Asia, rising in SE Turkey and flowing SE through Diyarbakir, along the Turkish-Syrian border, and into Iraq; 118 mi (190 km) from the Persian Gulf it joins the Euphrates River to form the Shatt al-Arab. Length: 1150 mi (1850 km).

Tihwa. *See* Ürümqi.

Tijuana 39 29N 117 10W A city in NW Mexico, on the US border. It is the main entry point to Mexico from California and is a popular tourist resort. Population (1980): 429,500.

Tikal An ancient *Maya city in N Guatemala. After about 300 AD it grew into the largest Mayan ceremonial center, with imposing pyramid temples. It was mysteriously abandoned about 900.

Tilak, Bal Gangadhar (*or* Lokamanya; 1856–1920) Indian nationalist leader. Joining the *Indian National Congress (1885) he changed its policy to one of resistance to British rule, advocating Indian independence. He was the first leader to propose the adoption of Hindi as the national language.

Tilburg 51 34N 5 05E A city in the S Netherlands, in South Brabant province. A major industrial center, it produces textiles. Population (1991 est): 158,846.

Tilden, Samuel Jones (1814–86) US political leader, lawyer, and reformer. A member of the New York bar from 1841 and a successful businessman, he allied himself with the *barnburners and *Free-Soil party in the 1840s and then joined the Democratic party. As New York state Democratic Committee chairman (1866–74), he was instrumental in breaking the Tweed ring (*see* Tweed, William Marcy). He was governor of New York (1874–76) and was the Democratic presidential nominee in 1876. He won the popular vote in the election, but the electoral college, in a contested vote, elected Rutherford B. *Hayes.

till (*or* boulder clay) The unstratified material that ranges from clay to angular stones and boulders, deposited by glaciers and ice sheets. Its form depends on the rock from which it originated. Large areas of N Europe are covered by till remaining from the Ice Age.

Tillich, Paul (Johannes) (1886–1965) US Protestant theologian of German birth. A Lutheran pastor and later a professor at several German universities, he moved to the US in 1933, when Hitler came to power. He lectured in New York and at Harvard and Chicago Universities. In *Systematic Theology* (3 vols, 1950–63) he attempted to demonstrate Christianity's relevance to contemporary life.

Tilly, Johan Tserclaes, Graf von (1559–1632) Bavarian general, who commanded the Catholic League in the *Thirty Years' War. He won the battle of the White Mountain (1620) and went on to gain control of NW Germany. He defeated the Swedes at Lutter (1626) and, in command of imperial forces, as well as the League's, razed Magdeburg (1631), gaining a reputation for brutality. He was killed in action after being defeated (1631) by the Swedes at Breitenfeld.

Tilsit. *See* Sovetsk.

Tilsit, Treaties of (1807) The two treaties that France signed at Tilsit (now Sovetsk, Russia) with Russia and Prussia respectively after Napoleon's defeat of the Prussians at *Jena and Auerstädt and the Russians at *Friedland. Russia became an ally of France and Prussia, its territory considerably reduced, was occupied by French troops. Both Russia and Prussia joined the *Continental System of blockade against British trade.

timber Sawed wood used for purposes other than fuel. Timber is divided into hardwoods (derived from broad-leaved trees) and softwoods (derived from conifers). The bulk of the world's softwoods are derived from Russia, Canada, and US, and Scandinavia. Hardwoods, which take longer to grow, are not confined to one specific climate zone. Uses for timber include furniture manufacture (usually hardwoods), building construction, and paper manufacture (largely softwoods).

timber wolf A large shaggy-coated *wolf of North America, also called the gray wolf. A Texas variety with a tawny coat is called the red wolf.

timbre A quality in the sound of a musical instrument, voice, etc., that distinguishes it from others. Thus a violin and a clarinet sound different even when they are playing the same note. The difference arises because each type of instrument produces different overtones in different strengths when a note is played. The production of overtones is controlled by the way the note is produced (plucking, blowing, etc.) and by the characteristics of the individual instrument.

Timbuktu (French name: Tombouctou) 16 49N 2 59W A town in E central Mali, on the Niger River. It was an important center on the trans-Saharan caravan route and an Islamic cultural center (1400–1600). It declined after its conquest by Morocco (1591). Population (1976): 20,500.

time A concept that measures the duration of events and the periods that separate them. It is a fundamental parameter of all changes, measuring the rates at which they occur; it provides a scale of measurement enabling events that have occurred to be distinguished from those that are occurring and those that will occur. It appears, intuitively, to be flowing at a constant rate in one direction only, for all observers. According to Einstein's theory of *relativity, however, this is not the case. The rate at which time passes (as measured by a clock) is not the same for observers in different frames of reference that are moving at a constant velocity with respect to each other. Thus, according to the *time-dilation effect, if two observers are moving at a constant velocity relative to each other it appears to each that the other's time processes are slowed down. This means that events that appear to be simultaneous to observers in the same frame of reference would not be simultaneous to observers in different frames of reference. In order to pinpoint an event in the universe, its position in a four-dimensional space-time continuum must be specified. This continuum consists of three space dimensions and one of time.

Historically, the measurement of time on earth has been based on astronomical observations—the time taken for the earth to revolve on its axis (the day) or for it to complete its orbit round the sun (the year). However, in modern science the basis of time measurement is the *second, which is defined in terms of the frequency of the radiation emitted in a specified transition of an isotope of cesium (*see* cesium clock).

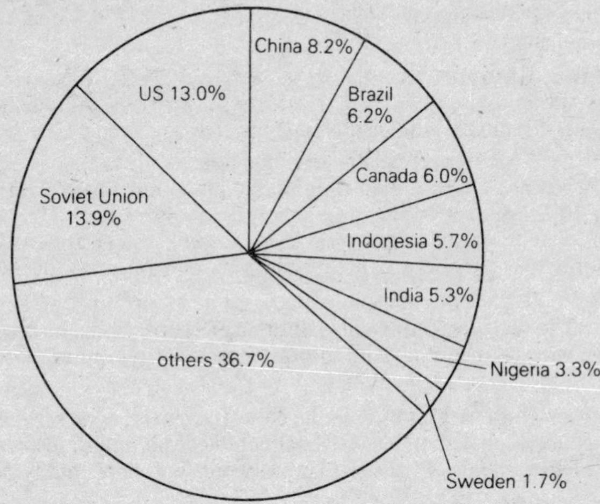

TIMBER *World production of timber, both hardwoods and softwoods.*

time and motion study A study of a machine and its operator in a factory, measuring the time taken to complete each action and the sequence of the operator's movements. The study is then used to recommend methods of speeding up the operation and reducing the effort involved in order to utilize labor as economically as possible.

time dilation An effect predicted by Einstein's special theory of *relativity. If two observers, A and B, are moving at a velocity v relative to each other, it will appear to A that B's clock will show that *time is running more slowly; thus a time t measured on A's clock will be $t(1-v^2/c^2)^{1/2}$ on B's clock, where c is the velocity of light. The effect has been observed in some particles moving at high velocities, which appear to have an anomalously long lifetime.

Time of Troubles A period of political confusion in Russian history following the death of Boris *Godunov (1605). Godunov was succeeded by a Polish-supported pretender, the so-called False Dimitrii, who claimed to be the son (murdered in 1591, perhaps by Godunov) of Tsar Ivan the Terrible. The False

Dimitrii was assassinated in 1606 by Muscovite nobles, who raised Vasilii Shuiski (1552–1612) to the throne. His rule was threatened by a second False Dimitrii, who established a rival court at Tushino in 1608. Shuiski was deposed and the second False Dimitrii was murdered in 1610, following a successful Polish invasion of Russia. A third False Dimitrii asserted his claim during 1611–12 but a successful rebellion against the Poles brought *Michael Romanov to the throne in 1613 and the end of the Time of Troubles.

Timişoara (Hungarian name: Temesvár) 45 45N 21 15E A city in W Romania near the Yugoslav border. It is a commercial and cultural center with a university (1945) and has two cathedrals. Population (1992): 334,278.

Timor An Indonesian island, the largest of the *Nusa Tenggara group. Mountainous and dry, it is largely undeveloped. Crops include coffee, coconut, and sandalwood. *History*: in 1859 it was divided between Portugal and Holland. West (Dutch) Timor was included in independent Indonesia (1949). East Timor, scheduled for independence from Portugal in 1978, erupted in civil war in 1975 and was annexed by Indonesia (1976). Area: 11,883 sq mi (39,775 sq km). Chief cities: Kupang and Dili.

Timoshenko, Semyon Konstantinovich (1895–1970) Soviet marshal, who rebuilt the army after the initial defeats in the *Russo-Finnish War. He commanded at *Stalingrad in World War II but failed to stem a German advance (1942–43) and was reassigned to the staff.

timothy A perennial *grass, *Phleum pratense*, also called herd's grass or cat's tail, native to Europe. It forms large clumps, 20–40 in (0.5–1 m) tall, with swollen bulblike bases and dense cylindrical flower clusters. It is widely cultivated as a hay and pasture grass, especially as part of a mixture with other grasses.

Timothy, St In the New Testament, a disciple of *Paul, whom he accompanied on many missions. According to tradition he was martyred in Ephesus. Feast day: Feb 6.

The Epistles of Paul to Timothy, in the New Testament, consist of advice and directions concerning Timothy's personal conduct and public responsibilities. The second letter contains Paul's last known words before his martyrdom under Nero.

timpani (*or* kettledrums) Tuned percussion instruments consisting of a large copper bowl or "kettle" with parchment or plastic stretched across the top. The pitch can be altered by means either of metal keys around the circumference or a pedal mechanism. The sound also depends on the type of sticks used and where they strike the head; a glissando can be obtained by use of the pedals. □musical instruments.

Timur (*or* Tamerlane; c. 1336–1405) Mongol conqueror, a descendant of Genghis Khan. After winning control of Turkestan in central Asia, Timur left his capital Samarkand to conquer the world. Ruthlessly sweeping through Mongolia, Persia, Turkey, Russia, and India, leaving death and destruction behind him, he sought conquest rather than a permanent empire. Paradoxically, he spared and encouraged all kinds of artists.

tin (Sn) A silvery-white metal known to the ancients. Its principal ore is the oxide cassiterite (SnO_2), often found in alluvial concentrations. The element exists as at least two allotropes—the gray alpha-tin, and beta-tin, which is the common form above 13.2°C. At low temperature beta-tin slowly changes into alpha-tin causing **tin plague**. It is obtained by reduction with coal in a reverberatory furnace. In addition to the oxide, compounds include tin chloride ($SnCl_2$), which is used as a reducing agent and in the dyeing industry. The major use of tin is in *tinplate. It alloys with copper to form *bronzes and with niobium to give a superconducting composition, which is used in electromagnets. Some organic compounds of tin are toxic. At no 50; at wt 118.69; mp 160.69°F (231.89°C); bp 4122°F (2270°C).

tinamou A solitary ground-dwelling bird belonging to a family (*Tinamidae*; 50 species) occurring in Central and South America; 9–15 in (23–38 cm) long, tinamous are well camouflaged with a mottled gray or brown plumage. They have small wings and a very short tail and are poor fliers. They feed on seeds, fruit, and insects and are the only members of the order *Tinamiformes*.

Tinbergen, Jan (1903–) Dutch economist. Tinbergen was adviser to the League of Nations from 1936 to 1938. He was corecipient with Ragnar *Frisch of the first Nobel Prize in economics (1969).

Tinbergen, Niko(laas) (1907–88) Dutch zoologist and pioneer ethologist. Like Konrad *Lorenz, Tinbergen concentrated on studying the behavior of animals in their natural surroundings. Tinbergen, with Lorenz, was responsible for tracing the evolutionary development of social behavior patterns, such as courtship displays. His works include *The Herring Gull's World* (1953), *Social Behavior in Animals* (1953), and *Animal Behavior* (1965). Tinbergen shared a Nobel Prize (1973) with Lorenz and von *Frisch.

tineid moth A moth of the widespread family *Tineidae*. The adults are usually small with a golden or silvery sheen and frequently do not feed. The caterpillars feed on a variety of plant and animal matter; especially well known are those of the *clothes moth.

tinplate A mild *steel sheet coated with a very thin film of tin, usually deposited by *electrolysis. Tinplate combines the strength and rigidity of steel with the attractive appearance and corrosion resistance of tin. It began to be used in the 19th century for cans in which to preserve food, still its widest use, although it was used for decorative purposes in the 13th century.

Tintoretto (Jacopo Robusti; 1518–94) Venetian painter, whose nickname, meaning "little dyes," derived from his father's profession of silk dyeing. His three paintings of the *Miracles of St Mark* (1562–66) for the Confraternity of S Marco were followed by his series of the life of Christ (1564–87; Scuola di S Rocco) and his paintings for the Doge's Palace, including the enormous *Paradise*. He combines Michelangelo's figure style and Titian's rich color with dramatic movement and perspectives. As a portraitist, he was particularly adept at painting old men, for example *Bearded Man with Fur* (Kunsthistorisches Museum, Vienna).

Tippecanoe, Battle of (1811) US–Indian conflict in NW Indiana, on the Tippecanoe River near Lafayette. *Shawnee Indians led by *Tecumseh's brother, the Prophet, and US forces under William Henry *Harrison fought over US settlement on Indian lands in Indiana Territory. The victory for Harrison and his troops greatly enhanced Harrison's reputation. Losses were heavy for both sides.

Tipperary (Irish name: Contae Tiobraid Árann) A county in the S Republic of Ireland, in Munster. Mountainous in parts, it contains part of the Golden Vale (one of the most fertile areas in Ireland) in the SW. Predominantly agricultural, dairy farming is especially important. Industries are mainly related to processing agricultural produce. Area: 1643 sq mi (4255 sq km). Population (1986): 136,600. County town: Clonmel.

Tippett, Sir Michael (1905–) British composer. He has written four operas: *The Midsummer Marriage* (1947–52), *King Priam* (1958–61), *The Knot*

Garden (1966–70), and *The Ice Break* (1977), acting as his own librettist. His other works include four symphonies, four string quartets, three piano sonatas, a concerto for double string orchestra (1939), the oratorio *A Child of Our Time* (1940), the cantata *The Vision of St Augustine* (1965), and choral music *The Mask of Time* (1982). In 1983 he was appointed president of the London College of Music.

Tipu Sahib (1749–99) Sultan of Mysore (1782–99); the son of *Hyder Ali. A good administrator in his own state, he was an opponent of British power in India and entered into a tentative alliance with the French. Defeated by *Cornwallis in 1792, he continued his opposition and was killed by the British while defending his capital Seringapatam.

Tirana (Albanian name: Tiranë) 41 20N 19 49E The capital of Albania, situated on a fertile plain in the center of the country. Founded in the 17th century by a Turkish general, it became the capital in 1920. There has been considerable industrial expansion since World War II. The university was founded in 1957. Population (1990 est): 243,000.

Tiresias In Greek legend, a blind Theban seer who lived for seven generations. For part of his life he was transformed into a woman, after coming upon a pair of snakes and killing the female. *Oedipus learned from him of his own patricide and incest and *Odysseus consulted him in the underworld, where he retained his prophetic powers. According to one of various legends, he was struck blind by Hera after supporting Zeus's opinion in an argument, namely that love was more enjoyable for women than men. In compensation Zeus granted him longevity and the gift of prophecy.

Tirich Mir, Mount 36 18N 71 55E A mountain in NW Pakistan, the highest in the Hindu Kush. Height: 25,236 ft (7692 m).

Tirol (*or* Tyrol) A mountainous federal state in W Austria, bordering on Germany and Italy. It is alpine in character, having an international reputation for winter sports, especially at Kitzbühel, and tourism is important throughout the year. The chief occupations are agriculture and forestry, with some mining and manufacturing industries. Area: 4883 sq mi (12,648 sq km). Population (1991): 630,358. Capital: Innsbruck.

Tirpitz, Alfred von (1849–1930) German admiral, who as secretary of state for the navy (1897–1916) rebuilt the German fleet to rival Britain's naval supremacy. His advocacy of intensive submarine warfare in World War I was opposed by the chancellor, Bethmann-Hollweg, and Tirpitz resigned.

Tirso de Molina (Gabriel Téllez; c. 1584–1648) Spanish dramatist, a literary disciple of Lope de *Vega, who wrote over 300 comedies and historical and religious plays. His tragedy *El Burlador de Sevilla* (1635) is the earliest recorded literary portrayal of *Don Juan.

Tirthankara In Jainism, one who has attained spiritual liberation from rebirth and serves as a guide for others. Every eon is said to produce 24 Tirthankaras, each associated with a particular symbol and color. *Mahavira is the last of the present series.

Tiryns A *Mycenaean citadel near Mycenae (S Greece). First excavated (1884–85) by *Schliemann, Tiryns was occupied from Neolithic times. The Bronze Age Mycenaean palace, first built in the early 14th century BC and sacked about 1200 BC, possessed frescoes showing *Minoan influence and massive defensive walls, much of which still stand.

tissue In anatomy, a group of cells specialized to perform a particular function. The cells may be of the same type (e.g. the muscle cells of muscles) or of different types (as in connective tissue). Combinations of tissues make up organs. The study of tissues is *histology.

TIROL *The winter sports resort of Seefeld, NW of Innsbruck.*

Tisza River (Slavonic and Romanian name: Tisa) A river in S central Europe. Rising in W Ukraine, it flows generally W and S across the Hungarian Plain to join the Danube River below Novi Sad in Yugoslavia. It is a source of irrigation and power, especially in NE Hungary. Length: 610 mi (980 km).

tit A small acrobatic songbird (also called titmouse) belonging to a family (*Paridae*; 65 species) occurring in North America, Eurasia, and Africa. Tits are versatile birds and frequent woodlands and gardens, feeding chiefly on insects. They are 2.8–8 in (7–20 cm) long. The best-known species is the tufted titmouse, about 6 in (15 cm) long, which is white underneath and gray above, topped by a prominent crest. *See also* blue tit; coal tit; crested tit; great tit; long-tailed tit.

Titanic A luxury British passenger ship that on Apr 14–15, 1912, struck an iceberg near Newfoundland on its maiden voyage and sank causing the loss of 1513 lives. Because of its special design it was thought to be unsinkable and carried enough lifeboats for only half the passengers. As a result of the disaster, safety rules for ships at sea were drawn up by the International Convention for Safety of Life at Sea (1913) and the International Ice Patrol was established.

titanium (Ti) A relatively light strong transition metal discovered in 1791 by W. Gregor (1761–1817). It occurs in nature in the minerals rutile (TiO_2), ilmenite ($FeTiO_3$), sphene ($CaTiO_3$), and in some iron ores. Rutile and ilmenite beach sands are mined as a source of titanium. The dioxide (TiO_2) is widely used as a constituent of white paint as it has excellent opacity. The metal is as strong as steel but 45% lighter (relative density 4.54) and 60% heavier than aluminum but twice as strong. It is therefore used in alloys for missiles and high-speed aircraft. At no 22; at wt 47.90; mp 3023°F (1660°C); bp 5955°F (3287°C).

titanothere An extinct North American mammal, related to horses and rhinoceroses, that lived between 45 and 20 million years ago. Later Oligocene forms were 15 ft (4.5 m) long and 8 ft (2.8 m) high at the shoulder. They fed on soft vegetation and became extinct possibly because their simple teeth were unable to cope with a change in the vegetation.

Titans In Greek mythology, 12 primeval gods and goddesses, the children of Uranus (Heaven) and Gaea (Earth). They were Oceanus, Coeus, Crius, Hyperion, Iapetus, Cronus, Thea, Rhea, Themis, Mnemosyne, Phoebe, and Tethys. They were overthrown by Zeus and the Olympian deities.

tithes The 10th part of an income allotted to religious purposes. Originating in the offering of the "first fruits" as a divine sacrifice, tithes were decreed by Mosaic law, which demanded payment in kind from all agricultural produce. Christian ecclesiastical law also enjoined tithes to maintain churches and clergy. Gradually exemptions were made, money payments replaced payments in kind, and as organized religion declined the tithe laws were repealed. Tithes are still voluntarily paid by individual believers.

titi A small monkey belonging to the genus *Callicebus* (8 species), of the Amazonian jungle. Titis are 20–45 in (50–115 cm) long including the tail (10–22 in [25–55 cm]) and live in treetops in family groups. They have soft thick fur, often brightly colored. Family: *Cebidae*.

Titian (Tiziano Vecellio; c. 1488–1576) Venetian painter of the High Renaissance, born in Pieve di Cadore, in the Dolomites. His earliest influences were Giovanni Bellini, his teacher, and Giorgione, with whom he collaborated on frescoes for the façade of the German Exchange (1508). In his *Assumption of the Virgin* (Sta Maria dei Frari) his more monumental style links him with such Florentine painters as Raphael. His greatest works for the Hapsburgs, who patronized him from 1530 onward, were the equestrian portrait of Emperor Charles V at Mühlberg (1548; Prado) and *Philip II* (1550–51; Prado). He painted Pope Paul III twice, in Bologna (1543) and in Rome with his grandsons (1546). Both portraits are in Naples. His mythological works include *Bacchus and Ariadne* (National Gallery, London). His last religious paintings, such as the *Pietà* (Accademia, Venice), seem to be inspired by a new emotional intensity.

Titicaca, Lake A lake in South America, between Peru and Bolivia, in the Andes. At an altitude of 12,497 ft (3809 m) it is the world's highest lake navigable to large vessels. It is fed by 25 rivers but possesses only one outlet, the Desaguadero River. Area: 3141 sq mi (8135 sq km). Depth: 1214 ft (370 m).

titmouse. *See* tit.

Tito (Josip Broz; 1892–1980) Yugoslav statesman; president 1953–80. Tito was captured by the Russians in World War I and subsequently fought with the Red Army in the Russian civil war. He returned to Yugoslavia in 1920, joined the Communist party, and was briefly imprisoned (1928–29); in 1937 he became secretary general of the party. In World War II he led the partisans in resistance to the German occupation, becoming a marshal in 1943, when he also gained Allied recognition, previously given to the *Chetniks. He became Yugoslavia's postwar leader and introduced the policy of decentralization to workers' councils that distinguished Yugoslav socialism. Following Yugoslavia's expulsion (1948) from the *Cominform, Tito successfully maintained his country's independence from Soviet interference, pursuing a foreign policy of nonalignment.

Titograd (name until 1948: Podgorica) 42 28N 19 17E A city in S Yugoslavia, the capital of Montenegro. It was renamed in honor of Marshal Tito on being rebuilt following extensive damage during World War II. Its university was established in 1973. Population (1981): 132,300.

Titus (Flavius Vespasianus) (39–81 AD) Roman emperor (79–81). He fought with his father Vespasian in Judea and ended the Jewish revolt (70) by capturing Jerusalem. Proclaimed emperor after Vespasian's death, Titus proved a popular ruler; when Vesuvius erupted (79), he aided the victims generously. At his death he was called "darling of the human race" and deified.

TITO *The Yugoslav leader (right) discusses strategy with Britain's General Alexander in Belgrade (February 1945).*

Titus, St In the New Testament, a disciple and assistant of Paul. He organized the collection of alms for poor Christians in Judea and replaced Timothy as Paul's commissioner at Corinth. Feast day: Feb 6. In the **Epistle of Paul to Titus**, written between 60 and 64 AD, Paul tells Titus how to organize and superintend the new churches of Crete.

Tivoli 41 58N 12 48E A city in central Italy, in Lazio. A summer resort in Roman times, it possesses the remains of Hadrian's villa and the Renaissance Villa d'Este, with its terraced water gardens. Paper and wine are produced. Population (1981): 52,000.

Tiw. *See* Tyr.

Tjirebon (*or* Cheribon) 6 46S 108 33E A port in Indonesia, in N Java on the Java Sea. The **Tjirebon Agreement** of Indonesian independence was signed there (1946) by the Dutch. It is an agricultural and manufacturing center. Population (1980): 223,776.

Tlaloc An Aztec rain god, equivalent in status with the sun and war god *Huitzilopochtli. He possessed both creative and destructive powers and children were ritually sacrificed to him.

Tlaxcala (*or* Tlaxcala de Xicohténcatl) 19 20N 98 12W A city in Mexico, on the central plateau. One of the oldest cities in Mexico, it is the site of the Church of San Francisco, which was founded by *Cortés (1521) and is the oldest in the Americas. Population: 21,424.

Tlemcen (Latin name: Pomaria) 34 55N 1 20W A city in NW Algeria, near the Moroccan border. It became an important Islamic religious center in the

Middle Ages, flourishing until the 16th century; many old buildings remain, notably the 12th-century Great Mosque. Industries include leatherwork and carpets; blankets and olive oil are exported. Population (1987): 126,882.

Tlingit A North American Indian people of the NW Pacific coast in SE Alaska. There were 14 tribes divided into independent matrilineal clans, each headed by a chief. They lived by salmon fishing and hunting, built wooden houses, and practiced the *potlatch at the death of a chief. Their language belongs to the *Na-Dené group.

TNT (trinitrotoluene; $C_6H_2(NO_2)_3CH_3$) A highly explosive pale yellow crystalline solid. It is prepared from toluene treated with concentrated sulfuric and nitric acids and is used in shells, bombs, etc., as well as in commercial blasting explosives.

toad A tailless amphibian belonging to a widely distributed order (*Anura*; about 2600 species). Toads usually move on land by leaping, having long hind legs and short forelegs; they swim by means of partially webbed feet. They have a long sticky tongue, attached at the front of their mouth, that can extend very rapidly to capture flying insects. Some species use the throat as a resonating chamber to amplify their mating calls. *See also* clawed frog; midwife toad; natterjack; tree frog; spadefoot toad.

toadfish A bottom-dwelling carnivorous *bony fish of the order *Batachoidiformes* (about 45 species), found mainly in tropical and subtropical seas. It has a heavy brownish body, up to 12 in (30 cm) long, a broad flat head, and a wide mouth. It makes grunting or croaking sounds resembling a toad. *See also* midshipman.

toadflax An annual or perennial herb belonging to the genus *Linaria* (about 150 species), especially *L. vulgaris*, found in the Mediterranean area, temperate Eurasia, and North America. It grows to a height of 12–30 in (30–80 cm) and has an elongated terminal cluster of yellow snapdragon-like flowers (*see* Antirrhinum). Purple toadflax (*L. purpurea*) is cultivated in gardens. Family: *Scrophulariaceae*.

toadstool. *See* mushroom.

tobacco A plant belonging to the genus *Nicotiana*, especially *N. tabacum* and *N. rustica*, which are cultivated for their leaves, used to make *cigarettes, *cigars, *snuff, etc. Commercial tobacco plants grow to a height of 3–10 ft (1–3 m) and bear pink, white, or greenish flowers. After harvesting, their large sticky leaves are slowly dried in the sun, hot air, or smoke for up to two months and then fermented for another four to six weeks. The main growing regions are the US, China, and India, with additional production in E Europe, South America, SE Asia, and S Africa.

Tobacco contains about 2–4% nicotine, which produces its stimulant and addictive properties. However, it is the tar content that is responsible for the diseases caused by smoking and chewing tobacco. Family: *Solanaceae*.

Tobago Island. *See* Trinidad and Tobago, Republic of.

Tobata. *See* Kitakyushu.

Tobey, Mark (1890–1976) US painter. He is known for paintings in which colored forms are overlaid by white brush strokes. He adopted this so-called "white writing" technique after he visited Japan and China (1934), where he was influenced by Oriental calligraphy. His work in this style developed from representational treatments to more abstract paintings in his later years.

tobogganing The recreation and sport of sliding down snow or ice on a toboggan, a low platform on steel runners, of which there are two competitive types:

the luge, for one or two riders lying almost flat on their backs, and the skeleton or Cresta (named for the Cresta Run at St Moritz, Switzerland), for one rider lying prone. Like *bobsledding, both were developed at St Moritz and other Swiss resorts in the late 19th century. In races competitors slide, one vehicle at a time, down a narrow icy chute some 1094 yd (1000 m) long with high banked turns, reaching speeds of over 80 mph (130 kph) and steering only by shifts of weight and by touching down with either foot.

Tobruk A port in NE Libya, on the Mediterranean coast. During World War II it was the scene of heavy fighting and changed hands five times before being finally recaptured by the British in 1942. Population (1984): 94,000.

Toby jug An English pottery jug in the shape of a seated middle-aged man in 18th-century dress, holding a tankard and pipe. Toby jugs, first made in the 1760s, depict various characters, e.g. Squire Toby and Sailor Toby. Production of Toby jugs still continues.

Tocharian An extinct *Indo-European language of the Tarim Basin region of Chinese Turkistan. It is mainly known from Buddhist scriptures written between about 500 and 1000 AD in the N Indian Brahmi script. Its relationship to the other Indo-European languages is highly debatable.

Tocqueville, Alexis de (1805–59) French political scientist, historian, and politician. After visiting the US (1831–32) Tocqueville wrote *Démocratie en Amerique*, a study of US democracy that also dealt with the constitutions of France and Europe. Tocqueville argued that the French Revolution had not achieved a break with the past, since an egalitarian society required greater centralization and thus sacrificed liberty. Elected to the Chamber of Deputies in 1839, he became vice president of the Constituent Assembly and briefly minister of foreign affairs in 1849. After Louis Napoleon's coup de'état he retired to write *L'Ancien Régime et la révolution* (1856).

Todd, Alexander Robertus, Baron (1907–) British biochemist, who helped determine the molecular basis of genetics through his work on nucleic acids (DNA and RNA). In 1949 Todd synthesized ADP and *ATP, substances vital to energy utilization by living cells. He received a Nobel Prize (1957).

toga The outer garment worn by the ancient Romans, originally by both sexes and all classes but finally only by male patricians on formal occasions. It consisted of a semicircular piece of cloth draped intricately around the body; color and markings were prescribed according to status.

Toghril Beg (c. 990–1063) Sultan of Turkey (1055–63), who founded the Seljuq dynasty. His conquests in central Asia culminated in the conquest of Baghdad (1055). An uprising forced his expulsion in 1058 but by 1060 he had suppressed it.

Togliatti (name until 1964: Stavropol) 53 32N 49 24E A city in Russia, on the Volga River. It was renamed in honor of the Italian communist leader Palmiro Togliatti. Industries include ship repairing, engineering, and food processing. Population (1987): 627,000.

Togliatti, Palmiro (1893–1964) Italian politician, the leader of the Italian Communist party (1926–64). In exile from 1926 to 1944, after Mussolini's fall he became a minister (1944) and then vice premier (1945). He was the author of *Italian Road to Socialism* and his ideas greatly influenced communism in Italy and were also influential in the Soviet Union.

Togo, Republic of (French name: République Togolaise) A small narrow country in West Africa, on the Gulf of Guinea between Ghana and Benin.

Coastal swamps rise to higher land in the interior. The majority of the population is African, mainly Ewe in the S. *Economy*: chiefly agricultural, food crops consist mainly of cassava, maize, and rice and cash crops include cocoa, coffee, and cotton. Forests produce not only timber but oil palms and dyewoods. There are rich deposits of phosphates, which, with cocoa and coffee, are the main export. Bauxite was found in the 1950s and there is some, as yet unexploited, limestone and iron ore. Industry is being developed, concentrating mainly on food processing, but there is also a large cement plant and a new oil refinery. *History*: settled by the Ewe in the 12th and 13th centuries, the area was raided for slaves from the 17th to 19th centuries. From 1884 to 1914 Togoland was a German protectorate and after World War I it was divided between France and the UK, first (1922) under League of Nations mandate and then (1946) as a UN trustee territory. The French territory became an autonomous republic within the French Union in 1956 and gained full independence in 1960. (The British part joined Ghana in 1957.) The president was killed in a coup in 1963 and a further coup in 1967 brought Lt. Col. (later Gen.) Etienne Gnassingbe Eyadéma to power. Under a new constitution, he was reelected in 1979 and 1986. A national conference on democracy formed an interim government in 1991; Eyadéma remained president but most of his powers were transferred to a succession of interim governments. Official language: French. Official currency: CFA (Communauté financière africaine) franc of 100 centimes. Area: 21,616 sq mi (56,000 sq km). Population (1990 est): 3,566,000. Capital and main port: Lomé.

Togo Heihachiro (1847–1934) Japanese admiral. His destruction of the Russian fleet in the battle of Tsushima Strait in May 1905, ensured Japan's victory in the *Russo-Japanese War (1904–05).

Tojo Hideki (1884–1948) Japanese general, who was war minister (1940–44) and also prime minister (1941–44) during World War II. After Japan's defeat he was executed as a war criminal.

Tokaj (*or* Tokay) 48 08N 21 23E A small town in NE Hungary, at the confluence of the Bodrog and Tisza rivers. It has given its name to the famous wine produced in the area.

tokay. *See* gecko.

Tokelau Islands A group of three coral atolls in the SW Pacific Ocean, an overseas territory of New Zealand. Chief exports are copra and woven goods. Area: 4 sq mi (10 sq km).

Tokugawa The military family that controlled Japan from 1603 to 1867. *Tokugawa Ieyasu secured the title of *shogun (military overlord) from the emperor in 1603 and established his capital at Edo (Tokyo). Ieyasu's immediate successors were responsible for isolating Japan from the outside world, a policy that established domestic peace but ultimately led to political stagnation and technological backwardness. After Japan's reopening under Western pressure in the 1850s the reluctance of the family to abandon its monopoly of power brought about the overthrow of the last shogun, Tokugawa Keiki (1827–1913; ruled 1867–68).

Tokugawa Ieyasu (1542–1616) Japanese *shogun (military overlord), who completed the reestablishment of central authority in feudal Japan. A vassal of both Oda Nobunaga and Hideyoshi, he steadily increased his domain and in 1600 was able to defeat his rivals in the decisive battle of Sekigahara. In 1603, having confiscated much enemy territory, he acquired from the emperor the title of shogun. He passed this to his son in 1605 but continued to supervise the *Tokugawa administration.

Tokyo 35 40N 139 45E The capital of Japan, in E central *Honshu on Tokyo Bay (an inlet of the Pacific). Administratively joined to its port Yokohama and to the industrial center of Kawasaki, Greater Tokyo is the world's largest city. It has over 100 universities, including the University of Tokyo (1877). *History*: site of human settlements from very early times, the village of Edo was founded in the 12th century, growing in importance as a city by the 17th century. As Tokyo, it replaced Kyoto as imperial capital in 1868. It was badly damaged by an earthquake in 1923 and by bombing during World War II, since which its industrial growth has been spectacular. Industrial development has not been without problems, however, and Tokyo now suffers from serious atmospheric pollution as well as traffic congestion. Population (1991): 8,154,404.

TOKYO *Ginza, one of the city's main shopping streets.*

Toledo 41 40N 83 35W A city in Ohio, at the mouth of the Maumee River on Lake Erie. The development of the coalfields and the discovery of oil and gas in the late 19th century stimulated its growth and today it is a major Great Lakes port, shipping oil, coal, and farm products. Industrial activities include ship building and oil refining. Population (1990): 332,943.

Toledo 39 52N 4 02W A city in central Spain, in New Castile on the Tagus River. It was formerly the capital of Spain. It has a magnificent cathedral (13th–17th centuries). Famous for its swords and knives, it produces metalwork engraved in the Moorish tradition. Population (1989 est): 60,000.

Tolkien, J(ohn) R(onald) R(euel) (1892–1973) British scholar and writer. He was professor of Anglo-Saxon (1925–45) and of English language and literature (1945–49) at Oxford University. His trilogy *The Lord of the Rings* (1954–55), in which he created a richly detailed fantasy world, became an international best-seller. Related works include *The Hobbit* (1937) and *The Silmarillion* (1977). Previously unpublished works were issued after his death.

Toller, Ernst (1893–1939) German playwright and poet. After being wounded in World War I, he became committed to revolutionary politics and in 1919 was imprisoned for five years for his activities. His reputation was established soon after his release by experimental expressionist plays, such as *Die Wandlung* (1919) and *Masse Mensch* (1920). Driven into exile in 1932, he committed suicide in New York.

Tolpuddle Martyrs Six English union members from Tolpuddle, Dorset. They were unfairly charged with administering unlawful oaths and transported to Australia. They were pardoned in 1836. The Tolpuddle Martyrs are regarded as among the founders of English labor unionism.

Tolstoy, Leo (Nikolaevich), Count (1828–1910) Russian writer and moralist. After active service in the Crimean War, he traveled in Europe and then returned to his family estate of Yasnaya Polyana, where he devoted much energy to the education of his peasants. Following his marriage in 1862, he wrote two novels, *War and Peace* (1865–69), concerning the Napoleonic War, and *Anna Karenina* (1875–77), both acknowledged masterpieces of Russian literature. Around 1879 he underwent a spiritual crisis from which he emerged with a faith in an extreme form of Christian anarchism. He worked and dressed as a peasant, became a vegetarian, espoused total pacifism, repudiated his former literary works, and divided his property among the members of his family. His numerous moral tracts and stories gained him an international discipleship, but his family relationships suffered. He died at 82 of pneumonia a few days after secretly leaving his home in order to live in solitude. Tolstoy was one of the most prolific of writers, his literary work filling 45 volumes. His other works include the story "The Death of Ivan Ilyich" (1884–86) and the novel *Resurrection* (1899).

Toltecs An Indian people who dominated much of central Mexico between the 10th and 12th centuries AD. Their language, *Nahuatl, was also spoken by the Aztecs. A militaristic people, they sacked the city of *Teotihuacán (c. 750) and eventually fused the many small states of the area into an empire. They introduced the cult of *Quetzalcoatl and were accomplished temple builders. The *Aztecs destroyed their capital of *Tula in the mid-12th century.

Toluca (*or* Toluca de Lerdo) 19 20N 99 40W A city in central Mexico. The center of a stock-raising area, its industries include the processing of agricultural products. Population (1980 est): 357,100.

toluene ($C_6H_5CH_3$) A colorless flammable liquid obtained by catalytic reforming of *oil. It is used in aviation fuels, as a solvent, and to produce *phenol and *TNT.

tolu tree A tree, *Myroxylon balsamum*, native to South America. Growing to a height of over 65 ft (20 m), it has whitish flowers and yields a *balsam from its trunk, used in cough mixtures and perfumery. Family: **Leguminosae.*

tomato An annual plant, *Lycopersicon esculentum*, native to South America and widely cultivated for its fleshy red □fruit. In warm temperate regions, tomatoes are grown in fields and are low branching and spreading plants; the hothouse tomatoes of cooler regions are often trained to grow a single erect fruiting stem. The clusters of yellow flowers produce rounded or pear-shaped fruits, 0.8–4 in (2–10 cm) in diameter, which are eaten fresh or canned and made into purée, pickles, etc. Family: **Solanaceae.*

Tombstone 31 44N 110 04W A town in Arizona. Scene of a silver rush from 1877, it is famous for the gunfight (1881) that took place at the OK Corral between the Clanton gang and Wyatt Earp, his brother Virgil, and Doc Holliday. Population (1991): 506,600.

Tomsk 56 30N 85 05E A port in central Russia, on the Tom River. Industries include engineering and it has several educational institutions, including a university (1888). Population (1991 est): 506,600.

Tom Thumb (Charles Stratton; 1838–83) US midget, who was publicly exhibited by the circus impresario P. T. *Barnum. He grew to a height of only 40 in. In 1863 he married another midget, Lavinia Warren (1841–1919).

ton A short ton is a unit of weight equal to 2000 lb (907 kg). A long ton is equal to 2240 lb or 1016 kilograms. The metric ton (or **tonne**) is equal to 1000 kilograms.

tonality The presence of a tonal center or *key in a musical composition. Musical compositions from at least the early 17th century to about 1900 are in distinct keys. These are based on individual scales, in which certain notes (the tonic and dominant degrees) form tonal centers to which the music periodically returns. Once such a center has been established, the music can modulate into other keys and return to the home key (or underlying tonality). Music in which tonal centers are deliberately avoided exhibits *atonality; this is characteristic of some music written after 1900. *See also* serialism.

Tone, (Theobald) Wolfe (1763–98) Irish nationalist, who was inspired by the French Revolution to work for an independent Irish republic. In 1791 he founded the Society of United Irishmen and unsuccessfully sought French aid for a revolt against British rule. He was captured and sentenced to death, but committed suicide before the sentence could be carried out.

tone poem. *See* symphonic poem.

Tonga, Kingdom of (*or* Friendly Islands) A country in the SW Pacific Ocean, E of Fiji. It consists of 169 small islands (36 of them permanently inhabited); the E islands are low lying, while those to the W are hilly and volcanic. *Economy*: chiefly agricultural, the main products and exports are copra and bananas. Oil has been discovered recently, and tourism is becoming increasingly important. *History*: under King Taufa'ahau Tupou (George I; 1797–1893) in the 19th century, the civil war between rival dynasties was ended and the islands converted to Christianity. The country became a British protectorate in 1900, and in 1970 became an independent state within the British Commonwealth. Head of State: King Taufa'ahau Tupou IV. Official languages: Tongan and English. Official currency: pa'anga of 100 seniti. Area: 270 sq mi (700 sq km). Population (1988): 95,000. Capital and main port: Nuku'alofa.

tongue A muscular organ situated in the floor of the mouth. The root of the tongue is attached by muscles to the U-shaped hyoid bone in the neck. The tongue is the main organ of taste: its surface is covered by minute projections (giving it a rough appearance) around which the taste buds are grouped, detecting sweet, sour, salt, and bitter tastes. It also manipulates food during chewing and swallowing and plays an important role in the articulation of speech. Furring of the tongue is a symptom of fever; a smooth and sore tongue is seen in some forms of anemia.

Tong Zhi (*or* T'ung-chih; 1856–75)) The title of Cai-chun (*or* Tsai-ch'un), Chinese emperor (1862–75); the son of *Zi Xi, who acted as regent until he was 17. The Tong Zhi Restoration (his title means Union for Order) aimed to repair the upheaval of the *Taiping Rebellion but was thwarted by the corrupt court, which dominated the young emperor.

tonic sol-fa. *See* solmization.

tonka bean The seed of the tonka tree, *Coumarouna odorata*, native to N South America. Coumarin, a fragrant edible extract of the black almond-shaped seeds, has been used as a flavoring in perfumes and in snuff. Family: **Leguminosae*.

Tonkin (*or* Tongking) A region in N Vietnam, long ruled from Hanoi. The Chinese, who had occupied it in 111 BC, were driven out in 939 AD, and from then until 1802 it was an independent state. Following the dissolution of the Vietnamese empire it became a French protectorate (1884). In 1949 it became part of independent Vietnam.

Tonkin, Gulf of (Chinese name: Beibu Gulf) An inlet of the South China Sea between China, N Vietnam, and Hainan Island.

Tonle Sap A lake in W central Cambodia. For most of the year it is drained by the River Tonle Sap into the Mekong, but in the monsoon season the swollen Mekong reverses the flow, and the lake roughly quadruples in depth and area to about 3850 sq mi (10,000 sq km). There is carp fishing.

tonsillitis Inflammation of the *tonsils due to infection of the upper respiratory tract. Symptoms include fever, a sore throat, and difficulty in swallowing. If the tonsils become chronically infected, causing recurrent sore throats, they can be surgically removed.

tonsils Patches of tissue situated on each side at the back of the mouth and below the tongue that produce lymphocytes: a type of white blood cell that protects the body against infection. Inflammation of the tonsils may be caused by a variety of infections (*see also* tonsillitis).

tontine A financial scheme to provide life *annuities to a group of subscribers; when a member dies his share is divided among the others until the last survivor enjoys the whole income. The idea of an Italian banker (Lorenzo Tonti) in 1653, it was popular in the 18th century.

Toowoomba 27 34S 151 54E A city in Australia, in SE Queensland. It is a commercial center for an agricultural region specializing in sheep and dairy farming. It is the site of the Perseverance Creek Water Supply Scheme. Population (1986): 73,400.

topaz A mineral consisting of a hydrous fluosilicate of aluminum, $Al_2SiO_4(OH,F)_2$. It occurs in acidic igneous rocks, in pegmatites and veins. It is usually colorless or yellow, and when cut and polished it is used as a gemstone. The finest specimens come mainly from the Urals, Brazil, and Ceylon. All yellow gemstones were formerly known as topaz. Birthstone for November.

tope A slender *requiem shark, *Galeorhinus galeus*, that is up to 7 ft (2 m) long with a dark-gray body and a white belly. It lives in shallow tropical and temperate seas and feeds on bottom-dwelling fish and invertebrates.

Topeka 39 02N 95 41W The capital city of Kansas, on the Kansas River. An agricultural trading and processing center, Topeka is famous as a center for psychiatric research and is the site of the Menninger Clinic. Population (1990): 119,883.

top minnow. *See* killifish.

topology The branch of *geometry concerned with the properties of an object that do not change under *homeomorphisms, i.e. when the object is bent, stretched, or shrunk but not torn or deformed so that several points on it are fused. The hole in a doughnut is such a property; for example if a rubber doughnut is distorted to the shape of a cup the hole is still there in the handle. Topology is often called rubber-sheet geometry because rubber objects can be suitably distorted. It was formerly called analysis situs. One application is in networks (e.g. an electricity-distribution network) in which the topological properties depend on the so-called Euler characteristic (named for Leonhard *Euler) $V - E + F$, where V is the number of vertices in the network, E the number of edges, and F the number of areas enclosed by the edges.